1st Workshop on NLP for Languages Using Arabic Script (AbjadNLP 2025)

Abu Dhabi, United Arab Emirates
19 January 2025

ISBN: 979-8-3313-1359-3

Printed from e-media with permission by:

Curran Associates, Inc.
57 Morehouse Lane
Red Hook, NY 12571

CURRAN ASSOCIATES INC. proceedings.com

Some format issues inherent in the e-media version may also appear in this print version.

Printed with permission by Curran Associates, Inc. (2026)

Association for Computational Linguistics
209 N. Eighth Street
Stroudsburg, Pennsylvania 18360

Phone: 1-570-476-8006
Fax: 1-570-476-0860

acl@aclweb.org

Additional copies of this publication are available from:

Curran Associates, Inc.
57 Morehouse Lane
Red Hook, NY 12571 USA
Phone: 845-758-0400
Fax: 845-758-2633
Email: curran@proceedings.com
Web: www.proceedings.com

The 31st International Conference on Computational Linguistics

AbjadNLP

The 1st Workshop on NLP for Languages Using Arabic Script

Editors

Mo El-Haj   Amal Haddad   Cynthia Amol

Sina Ahmadi   Hugh Paterson III

Ignatius Ezeani   Saad Ezzini   Paul Rayson

Proceedings of the Workshop

January 19, 2025

https://wp.lancs.ac.uk/abjad

Order copies of this and other ACL proceedings from:

Association for Computational Linguistics (ACL)
209 N. Eighth Street
Stroudsburg, PA 18360
USA
Tel: +1-570-476-8006
Fax: +1-570-476-0860
acl@aclweb.org

Preface

It is my pleasure to welcome you to the inaugural edition of the AbjadNLP Workshop, an event dedicated to advancing research and applications for languages that use the Arabic script in Natural Language Processing (NLP). This workshop serves as a vital platform to unite researchers and practitioners addressing the linguistic, cultural, and computational challenges inherent to these languages, fostering innovative solutions for low-resource and historically underrepresented languages.

We received 27 submissions, of which 16 papers were accepted, resulting in an acceptance rate of approximately 59%. This strong start underscores the growing recognition of the significance of Arabic-script languages within the NLP community.

The submissions to this workshop showcased remarkable diversity, reflecting the linguistic and cultural richness of languages that utilise the Arabic script. Contributions span a variety of languages, including Wolofal, a form of Ajami script used for the Wolof language in West Africa; Persian, which, despite its long tradition of NLP research, continues to face challenges related to limited resources in stylistic and dialectal variations; and Turkish, focusing on the integration of Arabic-origin words into the Turkish language and its linguistic evolution. Additionally, research on Perso-Arabic scripts, used in languages such as Persian, Urdu, Pashto, and others, underscores the flexibility and adaptability of the Arabic script across diverse linguistic families and regions.

The workshop also includes studies on Arabic, exploring fundamental challenges and methodologies that can inform research on other low-resource Abjad and Ajami languages. Collectively, these contributions highlight the breadth of research addressing both resource-rich and low-resource languages, advancing our understanding of the unique computational challenges posed by Arabic-script languages.

I am deeply grateful to our co-organisers, reviewers, and authors for their invaluable contributions to this workshop. Their dedication and expertise have ensured the high quality of this year's programme, and their work paves the way for future innovations in this field.

This workshop represents a significant step towards building a vibrant and collaborative community dedicated to Arabic-script languages in NLP. We look forward to inspiring presentations, engaging discussions, and continued growth in the coming years.

Thank you for joining us, and I hope you find this workshop as inspiring as we do.

Mo El-Haj
Chair Organiser
AbjadNLP Workshop

Organizing Committee

Mo El-Haj
Hugh Paterson III
Saad Ezzini
Ignatius Ezeani
Mahum Hayat Khan
Muhammad Sharjeel
Sina Ahmadi
Cynthia Amol
Amal Haddad Haddad
Jaleh Delfani
Ruslan Mitkov
Paul Rayson

Table of Contents

Conference Program

Sunday, January 19, 2025

9:00–9:05 Welcome and Opening Remarks

09:05–09:25 *The Best of Both Worlds: Exploring Wolofal in the Context of NLP*
Ngoc Tan Le, Ali Mijiyawa, Abdoulahat Leye and Fatiha Sadat

09:25–09:45 *MultiProp Framework: Ensemble Models for Enhanced Cross-Lingual Propaganda Detection in Social Media and News using Data Augmentation, Text Segmentation, and Meta-Learning*
Farizeh Aldabbas, Shaina Ashraf, Rafet Sifa and Lucie Flek

09:45–10:05 *Towards Unified Processing of Perso-Arabic Scripts for ASR*
Srihari Bandarupalli, Bhavana Akkiraju, Sri Charan Devarakonda, Harinie Sivaramasethu, Vamshiraghusimha Narasinga and Anil Vuppala

10:05–10:25 *In-Depth Analysis of Arabic-Origin Words in the Turkish Morpholex*
Mounes Zaval, Abdullah İhsanoğlu, Asım Ersoy and Olcay Taner Yıldız

Coffee Break

11:00–11:20 *DadmaTools V2: an Adapter-Based Natural Language Processing Toolkit for the Persian Language*
sadegh jafari, Farhan Farsi, Navid Ebrahimi, Mohamad Bagher Sajadi and Sauleh Eetemadi

11:20–11:40 *Developing an Informal-Formal Persian Corpus: Highlighting the Differences between Two Writing Styles*
Vahide Tajalli, Mehrnoush Shamsfard and Fateme Kalantari

11:40–12:00 *Boosting Sentiment Analysis in Persian through a GAN-Based Synthetic Data Augmentation Method*
Masoumeh Mohammadi, Mohammad Ruhul Amin and Shadi Tavakoli

12:00–12:20 *Psychological Health Chatbot, Detecting and Assisting Patients in their Path to Recovery*
sadegh jafari, Mohammad Erfan Zare, Amireza Vishte, Mirzae Melike, Zahra Amiri, Sima Mohammadparast and Sauleh Eetemadi

Lunch Break

13:20–13:40 *A Derivational ChainBank for Modern Standard Arabic*
Reham Marzouk, sondos krouna and Nizar Habash

13:40–14:00 *Sentiment Analysis of Arabic Tweets Using Large Language Models*
Pankaj Dadure, Ananya Dixit, Kunal Tewatia, Nandini Paliwal and Anshika Malla

14:00–14:20 *Evaluating Large Language Models on Health-Related Claims Across Arabic Dialects*
Abdulsalam obaid Alharbi, Abdullah Alsuhaibani, Abdulrahman Abdullah Alalawi, Usman Naseem, Shoaib Jameel, salil kanhere and Imran Razzak

14:20–14:40 *Can LLMs Verify Arabic Claims? Evaluating the Arabic Fact-Checking Abilities of Multilingual LLMs*
Ayushman Gupta, Aryan Singhal, Thomas Law, Veekshith Rao, Evan Duan and Ryan Luo Li

14:40–15:00 *Can LLMs Translate Cultural Nuance in Dialects? A Case Study on Lebanese Arabic*
silvana yakhni and Ali Chehab

15:00–15:20 *Automated Generation of Arabic Verb Conjugations with Multilingual Urdu Translation: An NLP Approach*
Haq Nawaz, Manal Elobaid, Ali Al-Laith and Saif Ullah

Coffee Break

16:00–16:20 *Evaluation of Large Language Models on Arabic Punctuation Prediction*
Asma Ali Al Wazrah, Afrah Altamimi, Hawra Aljasim, Waad Alshammari, Rawan Al-Matham, Omar Elnashar, Mohamed Amin and Abdulrahman AlOsaimy

16:20–16:40 *Evaluating RAG Pipelines for Arabic Lexical Information Retrieval: A Comparative Study of Embedding and Generation Models*
Raghad Al-Rasheed, Abdullah Al Muaddi, Hawra Aljasim, Rawan Al-Matham, Muneera Alhoshan, Asma Al Wazrah and Abdulrahman AlOsaimy

16:40–16:45 *Closing Remarks and Wrap-Up*
Dr Mo El-Haj

The Best of Both Worlds: Exploring Wolofal in the Context of NLP

Ngoc Tan Le[1], **Ali Mijiyawa**[1], **Abdoulahat Leye**[1], **Alla Lo**[2], **Elhadji M. Nguer**[3], **Fatiha Sadat**[1]

[1]Université du Québec à Montréal-Canada, [2]Université Numérique Cheikh Hamidou KANE-Sénégal, [3]Université Gaston Berger - Saint-Louis-Sénégal

leye.abdoulahat@courrier.uqam.ca, mijiyawa.ali@courrier.uqam.ca, alla.lo@university.sn, elhadjimamadou.nguer@unchk.edu.sn,
Correspondence: le.ngoc_tan@uqam.ca, sadat.fatiha@uqam.ca

Abstract

This paper examines the three writing systems used for the Wolof language: the Latin script, the Ajami script (Wolofal), and the Garay script. Although the Latin alphabet is now the official standard for writing Wolof in Senegal, Garay and Ajami still play an important cultural and religious role, especially the latter. This article focuses specifically on Ajami, a system based on the Arabic script, and describes its history, its use, and its modern writings. We also analyze the challenges and prospects of these systems from the perspective of language preservation.

1 Introduction

African languages represent a unique linguistic and cultural diversity, and many use alternative scripts to the Latin alphabet, such as Ajami, a script derived from Arabic. The use of Ajami for African languages, including Wolof or Hausa - the rich African cultural heritage of the Hausa community (Gee, 2005), is of particular importance because of its role in the transmission of religious, cultural, and educational knowledge (Sane, 2010).

Hausa, one of Africa's most widely spoken languages, has a rich linguistic heritage that extends beyond its contemporary use of the Latin script. Historically, Hausa has also been written in the Ajami script, a modified form of Arabic adapted to represent Hausa's unique phonological system (Inuwa-Dutse, 2023; Adamu, 2023). The origins of Hausa Ajami can be traced to the introduction of Islam in the region during the 14th century, which brought Arabic literacy to the Hausa-speaking communities (Philips, 2004). Over time, this script was adapted to accommodate sounds specific to Hausa, enabling scholars and communities to document their language and culture while maintaining ties to Islamic traditions.

Ajami served as a vital tool for education, religious scholarship, and administrative purposes across Wolof-speaking or Hausa-speaking regions. Despite its historical prominence, the use of Ajami has faced challenges, including regional orthographic variations and a lack of standardization (Bondarev, 2019; Library, 2020). Today, with the advent of natural language processing (NLP), Hausa Ajami presents an opportunity for linguistic innovation (Abdullahi, 2022). By leveraging its structural similarities to Arabic, researchers aim to enhance digital applications such as machine translation, text recognition, and language modeling, ensuring that this culturally significant script remains relevant in modern technological contexts. However, the lack of resources and suitable tools hinders the development of NLP for Ajami texts.

This article aims to analyze the writing systems of the Wolof language, particularly the Ajami script, its cultural and religious importance, and recent progress. This document discusses Ajami in Wolof, from a Natural Language Processing (NLP) perspective, examining the specific challenges of analyzing this writing system and assessing recent research and developments.

2 Linguistic Context and Writing Forms of Wolof

Wolof, the lingua franca of Senegal and the mother tongue of many speakers, has a long tradition of writing in Ajami (Cissé and Sadat, 2003). This adaptation of the Arabic, Wolof, alphabet allows the sound of local languages to be represented, but it also includes specific morphological and phonological adaptations (Ngom, 2004).

Wolof is a language spoken in Senegal (over 80% of the Senegalese population), the Gambia, and Mauritania (Cissé and Sadat, 2024). It belongs to the Atlantic branch of the Niger-Congo languages (Ngom, 2000). Historically, there are three writing systems for transcribing Wolof. The Latin alphabet based on modern school characters,

Processings of the 1st Workshop on NLP for Languages Using Arabic Script (AbjadNLP), pages 1–6
January 19, 2025.

the Ajami script or Wolofal (Ngom, 2016) based on the Arabic alphabet and widely used in religious circles, and the Garay transcription system invented in 1961 by Assane Faye and inspired by African linguistic characteristics (Everson, 2016). The use of the Latin alphabet is now dominant in educational systems and administrative documents, but it remains largely reserved for the schooled population.

The Garay script, an Indigenous and minority writing systems according to the Atlas of Endangered Alphabets[1], was invented by Assane Faye of Senegāl in 1961, for writing the Wolof language (James, 2012). It runs right-to-left like Arabic, and some of the shapes are reminiscent of Arabic (James, 2012). The Garay script takes into account the phonetic characteristics of Wolof and aims to offer a transcription system used mainly in artistic and community contexts.

Finally, Ajami is a legacy of the Islamization of West Africa and remains at the heart of the religious and cultural practices of the Wolof people educated in Quranic schools (Ngom and Kurfi, 2017).

The Ajami script has been used historically to disseminate religious, poetic, and educational writings, but its modern usage is limited compared to the Latin alphabet, which today dominates publishing and education. However, the research, in terms of NLP applied to Ajami texts remains limited (Vydrin, 2014) or even non-existent, largely due to the challenges of data collection and digitization (Ngom et al., 2023).

Few studies have focused on automatic text processing in Ajami. The NLP literature on Wolof is growing, but it mainly focuses on the Latin script. Some research projects, notably in Senegal, have started to digitize and annotate corpora in Ajami, but the data remains limited. The absence of standardized linguistic resources, such as lexi cons, grammars and parallel corpora, constitutes a major obstacle to the advancement of NLP for Wolof in Ajami.

3 Linguistic features

Wolof has distinctive linguistic features that differentiate it from neighboring languages. Here are some key elements of its linguistic structure:

[1]https://www.endangeredalphabets.net/

3.1 Phonology

The Wolof language is characterized by simple consonants and vowels, but it also includes nasal sounds and consonants borrowed from other languages. It does not distinguish tones (as in some African languages) but uses a particular prosody (Souag, 2010).

3.2 Morphology

Wolof is an agglutinative language, which means that words are often formed by combining several morphemes. Personal pronouns, for example, can be modified according to the grammatical situation and social context. Unlike French, Wolof does not have grammatical genders (masculine/feminine) (McLaughlin, 2017).

3.3 Syntax

The basic syntactic structure of Wolof is Subject-Verb-Object (SVO), as in French. However, the word order can vary depending on the desired stress or accentuation (Torrence, 2013). The structure of Wolof sentences reflects a simple grammar, but its rich vocabulary allows for great expressiveness (Dione, 2021).

3.4 Vocabulary

Wolof has incorporated several lexical borrowings from French, Arabic and neighboring languages, such as Tarifiyt Berber, a variant of Amazigh language (Thiam, 2020) due to colonial, religious and commercial influences. For example, terms related to Islam and trade are often borrowed from Arabic.

4 Analysis of the Three Writing Systems

4.1 Latin alphabet

Since its standardization in the 1970s, the Latin alphabet has become the official writing system of the Wolof language, particularly in legal, educational, and administrative documents (Diagne, 2018). For examples:
• Bët (eye) / Bëtt (to pierce)
• Dég (thorn) / Dégg (to hear)

Its presence in digital resources, notably the translation of websites and software into Wolof, along with a significantly reduced illiteracy rate, contributes to its increasing use by new generations. It is written from left to right like French, English, etc. However, the Latin script remains unfamiliar to most of the rural population, who rather use Ajami in their daily communications(Ngom, 2020).

4.2 Garay alphabet

The Garay script, which was designed by Assane Faye in 1961, is a transcription system adapted to the African phonetic characteristics of Wolof (Pandey, 2011). Garay, in the Figure 1, is written from right to left and includes special features such as nasalized letters and variations of uppercase and lowercase letters (Everson, 2016). Although Garay represents a significant innovation for the Wolof language, its usage remains limited due to a lack of institutional support and relative complexity.

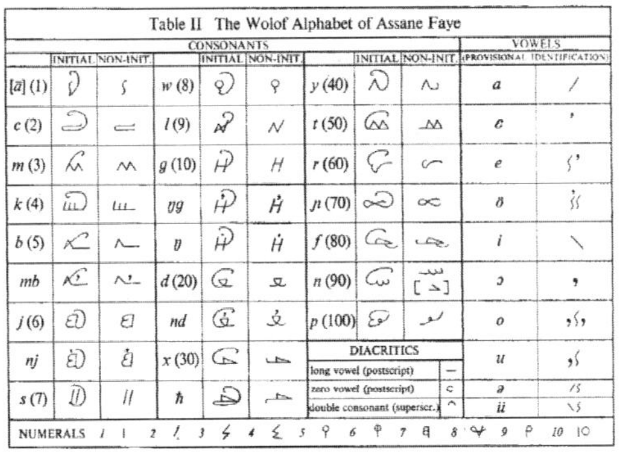

Figure 1: Script of Assane Faye's alphabet for the Wolof (Everson, 2016)

4.3 Ajami alphabet (Wolofal)

The history of the Ajami script, or Wolofal, in the Figure 2, dates back to the introduction of Arabic writing in West Africa through Quranic schools called "daara" since the earliest contacts between the local population and Arab-Muslim culture in the 8th and 9th centuries CE (Cissé, 2010). In Senegal, Ajami is used by speakers who have learned to read and write Arabic but do not necessarily know French or the Latin alphabet (Ngom, 2016).

5 Challenges of NLP about Ajami for Wolof

5.1 Linguistic Complexity and Lack of Standardization

Ajami for Wolof presents dialectal and stylistic variations, complicating normalization and automatic recognition (Gauthier et al., 2016). Each writer may have preferences in the use of certain letters or diacritics to transcribe specific sounds of Wolof that have no direct equivalent in Arabic.

5.2 Lack of Corpus and Language Models

NLP relies heavily on large annotated corpora, which are nonexistent for Wolof in Ajami. To address the lack of annotated corpora for Ajami beyond manual efforts, we propose two approaches such as community-driven methods and transfer learning from Arabic.

First, the community-driven approach involves developing a methodology for crowdsourcing annotations. Second, transfer learning from Arabic offers a technological solution to augment Ajami NLP capabilities. Pretrained Arabic language models can serve as a foundation and be adapted to Ajami-specific applications. This involves fine-tuning these models on Ajami text corpora to enhance their understanding of the script and its unique linguistic features. Additionally, domain adaptation techniques can be applied to bridge the structural and linguistic differences between Arabic and Ajami, ensuring the transfer is both efficient and effective.

Furthermore, current optical character recognition (OCR) systems for Arabic scripts are not easily adaptable to Ajami due to typographical divergences and specific diacritics (Nguer et al., 2020). OCR technologies are essential for digitizing ancient handwritten texts in Ajami (Mangeot and Sadat, 2014). Recent research in deep learning has shown progress for other languages using non-Latin scripts, but adjustments are needed to account for the particularities of Ajami (Mbaye and Diallo, 2023).

6 NLP advances and developping techniques for Wolof in Ajami

6.1 Transliteration models

To overcome the barrier between users of the Latin script and users of the Ajami script, several efforts have been launched to develop transliteration tools for this digraphy of the language. The Latin2Ajami algorithm (Fall et al., 2016) is an automatic transliteration tool that allows converting text written in Latin Wolof into Ajami script. The Latin2Ajami algorithm was used to evaluate a cutting-edge transliteration solution, which addresses the digraphy (the use of multiple writing systems for one language). Let's take one example, of transliteration with Latin2Ajami, of the word "sañ-sañ", which means "right" or "freedom" in Wolof:

- Writing in Latin alphabet: sañ-sañ

• Transliteration in Ajami: سانسان

The algorithm performs this conversion by using a phonetic correspondence between the graphemes of the Latin alphabet and the characters of Ajami, independently of the pronunciation. The operation is reversible and therefore depends on the target writing system, but not on the language (Fall et al., 2016).

The scalability of the Latin2Ajami tool when working with larger datasets or addressing dialectal differences in Wolof involves several considerations such as data quality and diversity. To handle dialectal differences, this tool could face the phonetic variations, and the ambiguity in grapheme mapping due to the rich morphology of Wolof language. We suggest a plausible solution which consists of incorporating dialectal data into the training set and developing region-specific transliteration rules or a dialect-adaptive mode or hybrid systems.

6.2 Deep learning models

Some researchers are exploring deep learning models to train OCR systems for Ajami, using transfer learning approaches from models pre-trained on standard Arabic texts. Techniques such as convolutional neural networks (CNNs) and recurrent networks (RNNs) can be useful, but require specific data for Wolof in Ajami (Ignat et al., 2022; Cissé and Sadat, 2024).

6.3 Annotated Corpus Development

Manual annotation of existing Ajami texts is an essential step for the development of NLP models. Crowdsourcing, with native speakers and linguistic experts, can accelerate this process, especially for the transcription and translation of Ajami texts into Latinized Wolof or other working languages (Couty et al., 1968; Diagne, 2023).

6.4 Perspectives for Multilingual Models

Integrating multilingual models, such as BERT (Devlin, 2018) or XLM-R (Conneau, 2019), could provide an interesting solution by learning shared representations between different scripts. This may pave the way for models capable of processing both Ajami and Latinized Wolof, facilitating translation and information retrieval tasks (Dione et al., 2022; Cissé and Sadat, 2024).

7 The social and cultural role of Wolof

Wolof plays a central role in Senegalese culture and reflects the history, values and beliefs of the people. Indeed, it is often the language of orality and tradition, conveying tales, proverbs and popular poems. Music, particularly mbalax (a Senegalese musical genre) and rap, is widely performed in Wolof and conveys social messages (Couty et al., 1968; Ngom, 2000).

In daily life, Wolof allows for social and linguistic cohesion between populations of different ethnic groups in Senegal. Its use in the media and in politics reinforces its importance in public spaces, thus contributing to the diffusion of Wolof culture beyond national borders (Cissé, 2010).

8 Preservation and contemporary challenges

Wolof faces several challenges in the context of globalization and the dominance of European languages such as French. The lack of written documentation and teaching materials is a barrier to the structured teaching of this language, especially for future generations (Hashimi, 2020).

However, efforts are being made for its preservation and standardization. Cultural and linguistic organizations in Senegal are working to create educational programs in Wolof, while the media and social networks contribute to its visibility and valorization. These initiatives aim to strengthen the use of Wolof not only in homes, but also in formal education and administration (Sinatti, 2014).

9 Conclusion and Perspectives

This paper presents a first study on the three writing systems used for Wolof. Ajami remains an important cultural medium for Senegalese Muslim communities, while Latin and Garay contribute to diversifying options for linguistic preservation, even though nowadays the Latin script is the most used due to public schools that have reduced illiteracy rates, enabling the majority of the Senegalese population to read and write the Wolof language.

The Wolof language, rich in culture and history, remains a pillar of Senegalese and West African identity. It plays a fundamental role in society, both as a language of communication and as an expression of cultural identity. Although faced with contemporary challenges, Wolof benefits from initiatives aimed at preserving and promoting this language. Recognition of its heritage value and support for its teaching could ensure its sustainability for future generations.

References

Aminu Aliyu Abdullahi. 2022. Deep neural networks for the recognition of hausa ajami script. *Nigerian Journal of Computing, Engineering and Technology (NIJOCET)*, 1(2):106–111.

Abdalla Uba Adamu. 2023. The gutenberg principle: Hausa digital alàrammà and ajamīzation of knowledge.

Dmitry Bondarev. 2019. Standardisation et variantes régionales de l'ajami haoussa. *Transliteration Studies*, 5:45–67.

Momar Cissé. 2010. Parole chantée et communication sociale chez les wolof du sénégal.

Thierno Ibrahima Cissé and Fatiha Sadat. 2024. Advancing language diversity and inclusion: Towards a neural network-based spell checker and correction for wolof. In *Proceedings of the Fifth Workshop on Resources for African Indigenous Languages@ LREC-COLING 2024*, pages 140–151.

Thierno Ibrahima Cissé and Fatiha Sadat. 2003. Automatic spell checker and correction for underrepresented spoken languages: Case study on wolof.

Thierno Ibrahima Cissé and Fatiha Sadat. 2024. Advancing language diversity and inclusion: Towards a neural network-based spell checker and correction for wolof.

A Conneau. 2019. Unsupervised cross-lingual representation learning at scale. *arXiv preprint arXiv:1911.02116*.

Philippe Couty, Jean Copans, and BK Dia. 1968. Contes wolof du baol. *Paris, ORSTOM*, page 1967.

Jacob Devlin. 2018. Bert: Pre-training of deep bidirectional transformers for language understanding. *arXiv preprint arXiv:1810.04805*.

Abibatou Diagne. 2018. *La terminologie wolof dans une perspective de traduction et de combinatoire lexicale restreinte*. Ph.D. thesis, Université de Lyon.

Abibatou Diagne. 2023. Constitution et usage de corpus pour langues terminologiquement peu documentées. *Littérature, Langues et Linguistique*, (14).

Cheikh M Bamba Dione. 2021. Multilingual dependency parsing for low-resource african languages: Case studies on bambara, wolof, and yoruba. In *Proceedings of the 17th International Conference on Parsing Technologies and the IWPT 2021 Shared Task on Parsing into Enhanced Universal Dependencies (IWPT 2021)*, pages 84–92.

Cheikh M Bamba Dione, Alla Lo, Elhadji Mamadou Nguer, and Sileye Ba. 2022. Low-resource neural machine translation: Benchmarking state-of-the-art transformer for wolof<-> french. In *Proceedings of the Thirteenth Language Resources and Evaluation Conference*, pages 6654–6661.

Michael Everson. 2016. Proposal for encoding the garay script in the smp of the ucs.

El hadji M. Fall, El hadji Mamadou NGUER, Sokhna Bao Diop, Mouhamadou KHOULE, Mathieu MANGEOT, and Mame T. CISSE. 2016. Digraphie des langues ouest africaines: Latin2ajami: un algorithme de translittération automatique. In *Atelier Traitement Automatique des Langues Africaines TALAf 2016, conférence JEP-TALN-RECITAL 2016*.

Elodie Gauthier, Laurent Besacier, and Sylvie Voisin. 2016. Speed perturbation and vowel duration modeling for asr in hausa and wolof languages. In *Interspeech 2016*.

Quintin Gee. 2005. Review of script displays of african languages by current software. *New review of hypermedia and multimedia*, 11(2):247–255.

AO Hashimi. 2020. Ajami tradition in non-islamic society: The roles of ajami-arabic scripts in keeping records and documentation. *NIU Journal of Humanities*, 5(2):373–379.

Oana Ignat, Jean Maillard, Vishrav Chaudhary, and Francisco Guzmán. 2022. Ocr improves machine translation for low-resource languages. *arXiv preprint arXiv:2202.13274*.

Isa Inuwa-Dutse. 2023. The first large scale collection of diverse hausa language datasets. *Proceedings of AfricaNLP workshop at ICLR2023*.

Ian James. 2012. Garay script for wolof.

British Library. 2020. *Hausa and Ajami Manuscripts: A Historical Perspective*. British Library Publishing, London.

Mathieu Mangeot and Fatiha Sadat. 2014. Actes de l'atelier sur le traitement automatique des langues africaines talaf 2014.

Derguene Mbaye and Moussa Diallo. 2023. Beqi: Revitalize the senegalese wolof language with a robust spelling corrector. *arXiv preprint arXiv:2305.08518*.

Fiona McLaughlin. 2017. Ajami writing practices in atlantic-speaking africa. *The Atlantic Languages*, pages 1–30.

Fallou Ngom. 2000. Sociolinguistic motivations of lexical borrowings in senegal.

Fallou Ngom. 2004. Ethnic identity and linguistic hybridization in senegal.

Fallou Ngom. 2016. *Muslims beyond the Arab world: The odyssey of ajami and the Muridiyya*. Oxford University Press.

Fallou Ngom. 2020. Ajami scripts in the senegalese speech community. *Journal of Arabic and Islamic Studies*.

Fallou Ngom and Mustapha H. Kurfi. 2017. *Ajamization of Islam in Africa*, volume 8. Islamic Africa.

Fallou Ngom, Daivi Rodima-Taylor, and David Robinson. 2023. ajamī literacies of africa: The hausa, fula, mandinka, and wolof traditions. *Islamic Africa*, 14(2):119–143.

Elhadji Mamadou Nguer, Alla Lo, Cheikh M Bamba Dione, Sileye O Ba, and Moussa Lo. 2020. Sencorpus: A french-wolof parallel corpus. In *Proceedings of the Twelfth Language Resources and Evaluation Conference*, pages 2803–2811.

Anshuman Pandey. 2011. Introducing the wolof alphabet of assane faye.

John Edward Philips. 2004. Hausa in the twentieth century: An overview. *Sudanic Africa*, 15:55–84.

Sokhna Sane. 2010. Decolonization and questions of language: The case of senegal. *HAGAR Studies in Culture, Polity and Identities*, 9(2):181–87.

Giulia Sinatti. 2014. 11 masculinities and intersectionality in migration: transnational wolof migrants negotiating manhood and gendered family roles. *Migration, gender and social justice: Perspectives on human insecurity*, pages 215–226.

Lameen Souag. 2010. Ajami in west africa. *Afrikanistik online*, 2010.

Alioune Badara Thiam. 2020. Typology of linguistic borrowing in the wolof language. pages 145–159.

Harold Torrence. 2013. The clause structure of wolof.

Valentin Vydrin. 2014. Ajami script for the mande languages valentin vydrin.

Appendix

Ajami Alphabet (Wolofal)

Phonetic Sounds	Arabic Orthography	Wolofal Orthography
1. [ʔ], [a:]	ا	ا
2. [b]	ب	ب
3. [t]	ت	ت
4. [θ]	ث	X
5. [dʒ], [ɟ]	ج	ج
6. [ħ]	ح	ح
7. [x]	خ	خ
8. [d]	د	د
9. [ð]	ذ	X
10. [r]	ر	ر
11. [z]	ز	X
12. [s]	س	س
13. [ʃ]	ش	X
14. [sˤ]	ص	X
15. [dˤ]	ط	X
16. [tˤ]	ط	X
17. [zˤ]	ظ	X
18. [ʕ]	ع	X
19. [ɣ]	غ	X
20. [f]	ف، ڢ	ف، ڢ
21. [q]	ق، ڧ	ق، ڧ
22. [k]	ک	ک
23. [l]	ل	ل
24. [m]	م	م
25. [n]	ن	ن
26. [h]	ه	ه
27. [w], [u:]	و	و
28. [j], [i:]	ي	ي
29. [ʔ]	ء	ء[4]

Figure 2: Arabic orthography, Wolofal orthography and their corresponding IPA symbols (Ngom, 2016)

MultiProp Framework: Ensemble Models for Enhanced Cross-Lingual Propaganda Detection in Social Media and News using Data Augmentation, Text Segmentation, and Meta-Learning

Farizeh Aldabbas[*,†], **Shaina Ashraf** [*,†], **Rafet Sifa** [*,‡], **Lucie Flek**[*,†]

[*]University of Bonn, [†]Conversational AI and Social Analytics (CAISA) Lab, [‡]Fraunhofer IAIS
fi.db.73@gmail.com, sashraf@bit.uni-bonn.de
Rafet.Sifa@iais.fraunhofer.de, flek@bit.uni-bonn.de

Abstract

Propaganda, a pervasive tool for influencing public opinion, demands robust automated detection systems, particularly for under-resourced languages. Current efforts largely focus on well-resourced languages like English, leaving significant gaps in languages such as Arabic. This research addresses these gaps by introducing MultiProp Framework, a cross-lingual meta-learning framework designed to enhance propaganda detection across multiple languages, including Arabic, German, Italian, French and English. We constructed a multilingual dataset using data translation techniques, beginning with Arabic data from PTC and WANLP shared tasks, and expanded it with translations into German Italian and French, further enriched by the SemEval23 dataset. Our proposed framework encompasses three distinct models: MultiProp-Baseline, which combines ensembles of pre-trained models such as GPT-2, mBART, and XLM-RoBERTa; MultiProp-ML, designed to handle languages with minimal or no training data by utilizing advanced meta-learning techniques; and MultiProp-Chunk, which overcomes the challenges of processing longer texts that exceed the token limits of pre-trained models. Together, they deliver superior performance compared to state-of-the-art methods, representing a significant advancement in the field of cross-lingual propaganda detection.

1 Introduction

Propaganda detection in text has gained significant attention, driven by the need to identify biased or misleading content across various platforms. While progress has been made, research remains predominantly focused on English, leaving other languages, especially those with fewer resources, under-explored. The lack of annotated datasets in these languages poses a significant challenge to developing effective detection systems.

To address this challenge, various data augmentation techniques, such as oversampling (Chavan and Kane, 2022), and data translation (Amihaesei et al., 2023), have been explored.

However, annotated resources for low-resource languages remain a significant challenge, emphasizing the need for more comprehensive frameworks.

In addition, studies have shown that while data augmentation can boost performance, an excess can lead to issues like label loss in translated texts. This underscores the need for models capable of learning from limited samples or adapting to new tasks with minimal training, paving the way for zero-shot and few-shot learning approaches. Our contributions to this field include:

1. MultiProp Dataset: We introduce MultiProp, a combined dataset that integrates data from the PTC dataset (Martino et al., 2020), SemEval 2023 (Piskorski et al., 2023) , and WANLP (Mittal and Nakov, 2022), resulting in a robust multilingual dataset that includes Arabic, addressing the data scarcity in low-resource languages.

2. MultiProp-Baseline: Our base model allows for flexibility in choosing between three ensemble architectures, combining transformer-based models, GloVe (Pennington et al., 2014) embeddings, and FastText (Bojanowski et al., 2017) to harness their collective strengths.

3. MultiProp-Chunk: To overcome the limitations of pre-trained models with long texts, we developed MultiProp-Chunk, which segments text into chunks, preserving textual continuity across segments.

4. MultiProp-ML(MetaLearner): Our model employs few-shot and zero-shot learning across seven languages, consistently outperforming strong ensemble baselines, including Multilingual BERT [1], XLM-RoBERTa [2] and GPT2 [3] as well as monolin-

[1] https://huggingface.co/google-bert/bert-base-multilingual-uncased

[2] https://huggingface.co/FacebookAI/xlm-roberta-large

[3] https://huggingface.co/openai-community/

Processings of the 1st Workshop on NLP for Languages Using Arabic Script (AbjadNLP), pages 7–22
January 19, 2025.

gual models trained on Arabic [4].

5. Ensemble Models: We investigated various ensembling strategies, combining the strengths of multiple pre-trained models across encoder-based, decoder-based, and hybrid architectures, as well as both multilingual and monolingual models. For final predictions, we utilized an additional ensemble of machine learning classifiers, including SVM (Chang and Lin, 2011) and Random Forest (Breiman, 2001), to enhance performance across diverse linguistic contexts.

2 Related Work

Propaganda detection in text has garnered significant attention due to the need to identify biased or misleading content. Despite advancements in English, low-resource languages lack annotated datasets, limiting detection system development.

Early efforts, such as (Barrón-Cedeno et al., 2019), used binary classification (propaganda vs. non-propaganda), while (Habernal et al., 2017) annotated a corpus with five fallacies tied to propaganda techniques. NLP4IF-2019 (Da San Martino et al., 2019) marked a milestone by curating a dataset of 18 persuasive techniques within English news articles, forming a foundation for further research.

Recent advancements, including SemEval23 (Piskorski et al., 2023), have extended propaganda detection to multilingual contexts. In contrast, research involving Arabic has been sparse, with notable exceptions such as the WANLP 2022 Shared Task for Arabic propaganda detection (Mittal and Nakov, 2022). However, the data provided for Arabic in these tasks has been limited and suffers from imbalanced labels, which magnifies the challenge of training effective models.

Cross-lingual transfer and data-efficient models offer promising solutions by leveraging knowledge from resource-rich languages. Data augmentation methods, such as (back)translation, play a crucial role in cross-lingual propaganda detection, enabling the creation of additional samples to expand datasets for low-resource languages (Hromadka et al., 2023; Falk et al., 2023).

Building upon these methods, recent advancements in the field have focused on leveraging cross-lingual transfer learning and meta-learning approaches. For example, LaBSE (Feng et al., 2020) enhances performance for low-resource languages by integrating pre-training with dual-encoder fine-tuning. Researchers like (Brown et al., 2020) and (Lauscher et al., 2020) have addressed the challenges of domain shifts across languages, highlighting the effectiveness of few-shot and zero-shot learning techniques to minimize dependence on extensive annotated data.

Additionally, (Nooralahzadeh et al., 2020) introduced cross-lingual meta-learning architectures designed to optimize learning with minimal training instances.

The field has also seen the adoption of ensemble learning techniques to boost model performance. Methods such as boosting, exemplified by AdaBoost (Freund et al., 1996), and bagging approaches (Breiman, 1996) like random forests (Breiman, 2001), combine multiple models to enhance classification accuracy. Voting methods, both hard and soft (Kandasamy et al., 2021), aggregate predictions from various classifiers to achieve better performance. Stacking, as described by (Ting and Witten, 1997), employs a meta-learner to integrate outputs from base models, thereby improving robustness and generalization.

A significant challenge remains the 512-token limit of pre-trained transformer models like BERT, which can lead to the loss of essential contextual information when longer documents are truncated (Xie et al., 2020). Although Longformer (Beltagy et al., 2020) mitigates this issue with a global attention mechanism to handle longer texts, it often requires task-specific adjustments that are not universally applicable. Inspired by the approach in (Pappagari et al., 2019), which splits text into fixed-size overlapping segments and uses BERT to extract segment-level representations, followed by an LSTM layer (Hochreiter, 1997) or small transformer model to generate document-level embeddings,We developed a similar approach by replacing the LSTM and transformer with an attention layer to process segment-level embeddings. Additionally, we maintained the use of overlapping segments to ensure context is preserved across chunks. By leveraging ensemble methods and cross-lingual transfer learning, our work seeks to improve model adaptability and accuracy across diverse languages and text lengths.

3 MultiProp Data

The primary goal of our study was to address the shortage of Arabic propaganda detection datasets.

---

gpt2-large

[4]https://huggingface.co/aubmindlab/aragpt2-mega-detector-long

Building on this foundation, we expanded our research to develop a cross-lingual propaganda detection framework that includes Arabic, a language often underrepresented in previous studies on persuasion techniques.To achieve this,we combined datasets from various shared tasks to create the MultiProp dataset, a multilingual resource supporting diverse languages, which includes 18 final labels corresponding to different propaganda techniques. Table 1 provides statistics for MultiProp and its sources. The MultiProp dataset includes:

Arabic:This dataset was sourced from the WANLP22 shared task and augmented with translated PTC-SemEval20 data. Preprocessing steps included standardizing labels, replacing links with 'URL' and '@name' with 'USR', and filtering out instances that lacked any techniques (labeled as 'no technique').

German: This dataset is compiled from the SemEval2023 shared task dataset and translated PTC-SemEval20 data. To align the labels with other datasets, redundant techniques were removed, and instances without any remaining techniques were discarded. The test data comprises translated PTC English data.

English: Derived from SemEval23 data and supplemented with German data translated into English. Preprocessing included URL removal and standardization.

French: Sourced from SemEval23 and harmonized with the translated PTC data.

Italian: Also drawn from SemEval23 and aligned with the translated PTC data.

Polish and Russian: The development sets from SemEval23 were included and used as test sets, as the SemEval23 test sets are not accessible. This allows for evaluating model performance on "surprise" languages that were not seen during training. For detailed statistics on the MultiProp dataset and the number of instances for each language, refer to Table 4 in the appendix.

Table 1: Dataset statistics for MultiProp and its sources.

Dataset	Train	Dev	Test	Num Classes	Source
WANLP (ar)	504	52	52	21	Tweets
PTC(en)	293	57	101	18	News Articles
SemEval23(en)	446	90	54	23	News Articles
SemEval23(de)	132	45	50	23	News Articles
MultiProp (ar)	517	68	68	18	Tweets & Articles
MultiProp (en)	488	143	101	18	News Articles

4 Methodology

The MultiProp Framework, depicted in Figure 1, comprises three variants: MultiProp-Baseline, MultiProp-ML, and MultiProp-Chunk.While MultiProp-Baseline maintains a consistent core architecture, MultiProp-ML and MultiProp-Chunk introduce additional steps to address specific challenges. Our approach integrates GloVe and FastText embeddings (GloFast) with transformer models to build three ensemble architectures: encoder-based, decoder-based, and hybrid, utilizing Use-FFN and Skip-FFN methods for final predictions.

The systems were evaluated in two settings: zero-shot, where models were trained exclusively on English and German data, with Arabic as the target language and French, Italian, Polish, and Russian included in the evaluation to assess their ability to generalize across diverse languages; and few-shot, where models were trained on extensive English data and a limited number of instances (5-shot, 4 ways) from Arabic, German, French, and Italian datasets, with Polish and Russian included as surprise languages in the testing phase. We will now discuss the three developed systems in detail:

4.1 MultiProp-Baseline

The MultiProp-Baseline model features two key components: embeddings generation and predictions aggregation. In the embeddings generation phase, textual content is converted into numerical representations through various embedding techniques. The predictions aggregation phase then combines these representations using multiple ensemble methods to produce the final predictions.

4.1.1 Embeddings Generation

We explore a variety of embedding techniques, from traditional methods like TF-IDF to advanced approaches such as Word2Vec (Mikolov et al., 2013), GloVe (Pennington et al., 2014), FastText (Bojanowski et al., 2017), and transformer-based models (Vaswani et al., 2017). Our novel approach integrates these baseline techniques with transformer-based embeddings to rich, nuanced representations that combine different levels of semantic information, strengthening its capacity to understand and process the input data across different languages.

a) GloFast Embedding: For generating word embeddings, we combined GloVe and FastText models, training them on the MultiProp dataset, which encompasses English, Arabic, and German texts. The preprocessing steps involved lowercasing, retaining stop words, removing punctuation,

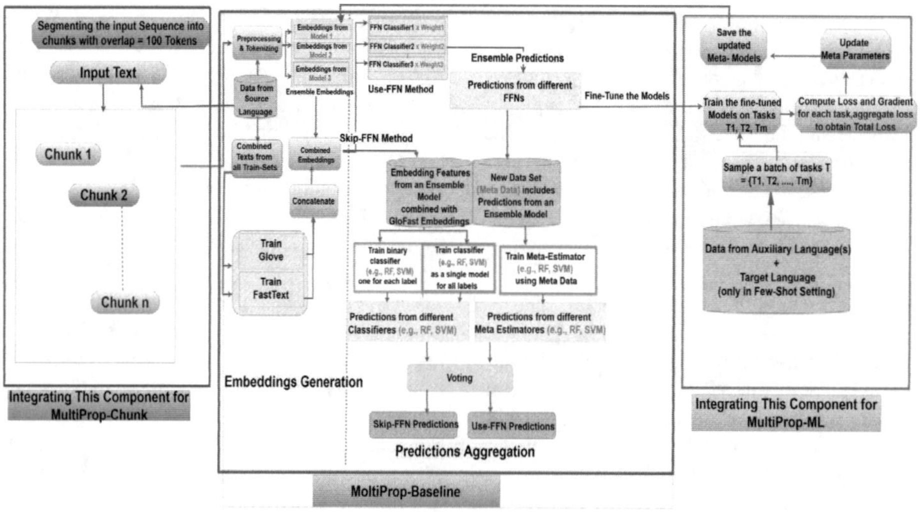

Figure 1: An Overview of MultiProp Framework

and handling out-of-vocabulary (OOV) words. The embeddings from both models were concatenated to form unified vectors, either 600 dimensions (300 from GloVe and 300 from FastText) or 200 dimensions (100 from each), and were integrated with transformer-based embeddings to improve pattern recognition in the text.

b) Transformer-Based Embedding: Transformer models, such as BERT (Devlin, 2018) and GPT (Radford et al., 2019), utilize self-attention mechanisms to capture both global and local word dependencies. Drawing inspiration from prior research that highlights the benefits of combining diverse embedding methods (Sifa et al., 2019), (Heinisch et al., 2023), our approach integrates transformer-based models with GloFast embeddings. To enhance our classifiers' ability to capture complex patterns in text, we employed three types of ensembles: encoder-based, decoder-based, and hybrid architectures.

1. The encoder-based ensemble model integrates multilingual transformers like mBERT (Devlin, 2018) and XLM-RoBERTa (Conneau et al., 2019), along with monolingual models such as AraBERT (Antoun et al., 2020). Pretrained on masked language modeling tasks across up to 104 languages, these models excel in cross-lingual transfer learning.

2. The decoder-based ensemble model utilizes GPT variants, including GPT-2 medium, GPT-2 large, and AraGPT2 (Radford et al., 2019). While GPT-2 models are primarily pretrained on English, AraGPT2 extends this to Arabic, and these models leverage decoder architectures for text generation. They are well-suited for generating coherent text, summarization, and translation tasks, with their multilingual capabilities enhancing their overall performance.

3. The encoder-decoder-based ensemble model (hybrid) combines models like mBART50 (Tang et al., 2020) and mT5 (Xue et al., 2020), pretrained on sequence-to-sequence tasks across up to 101 languages. This hybrid approach merges the strengths of both encoder and decoder architectures, making it highly effective for translation, summarization, and text generation. AraBART (Eddine et al., 2022) is also included for enhanced support of Arabic.

4.1.2 Predictions Aggreagation

The combined embeddings are fed into classifiers or meta-estimators. These classifiers include traditional machine learning algorithms such as Support Vector Machines (SVM) (Chang and Lin, 2011), Logistic Regression (LR) (Cox, 1959), and Random Forest (RF) (Breiman, 2001). Alternatively, these machine learning models function as meta-estimators when trained on the predictions generated by base classifiers (also known as level-0 classifiers), such as the Feed-Forward Neural Network (FFN) in our approach, further refining and improving final prediction accuracy. For prediction aggregation, we employ two key methods:

a) Use-FFN Method In this method, the combined embeddings are first passed through a fully connected neural network (FFN) with three linear layers and two ReLU activation functions, serving as the base learner. Adopting a stacking approach, predictions from various transformer-based models (PLMs), each paired with an FFN, are aggregated to form a new dataset. To formalize, let E_{i,PLM_j} denote the embedding of the i-th instance produced by the j-th transformer model in the ensemble. The final embedding for the i-th instance is computed as follows. For each model j, concatenate the model's embeddings with GloVe and FastText embeddings:

$$E_{i,\text{final}_j} = E_{i,\text{PLM}_j} \oplus E_{i,\text{GloVe}} \oplus E_{i,\text{FastText}}$$

The concatenated embeddings E_{i,final_j} for each model j are then passed through their respective feed-forward networks (FFNs). Each FFN outputs logits, which are then transformed into prediction probabilities for each label by applying a sigmoid activation function:

$$\hat{y}_{i,j} = \sigma(P_{\text{FFN}_j})$$

where P_{FFN_j} represents the logits output by the FFN of the j-th model.

A threshold of 0.5 is applied to each label's prediction to select the most confident predictions, ensuring stable and accurate outputs for creating the new dataset. This dataset, containing the gold labels, combines predictions from different models within the ensemble.

Finally, predictions from multiple level-1 classifiers (meta-estimators) are aggregated for each label using majority voting. Let $\hat{y}_i^{(m)}$ represent the prediction from the m-th classifier for the i-th input text. The final prediction is determined as:

$$\hat{y}_i^{\text{final}} = I\left(\frac{1}{M}\sum_{m=1}^{M}\hat{y}_i^{(m)} \geq \frac{1}{2}\right) \quad (1)$$

where M is the number of classifiers, and $I(\cdot)$ is the indicator function that outputs 1 if the condition is true and 0 otherwise.

This ensemble incorporates various classifiers, including Support Vector Machine (SVM) (Chang and Lin, 2011), Logistic Regression (LR) (Cox, 1959), Random Forest (RF) (Breiman, 2001), Gaussian Naive Bayes (Jahromi and Taheri, 2017) and XGBoost . Additionally, a hard voting approach is employed to aggregate the outputs of the meta-estimators. This ensemble method proved effective in detecting propagandistic techniques in news articles and tweets, resulting in a significant improvement in the overall F1 score by over 13%, demonstrating its robustness in multi-label classification tasks.

b) Skip-FFN Method The Skip-FFN method leverages embedding features to train multiple machine learning models that act as classifiers. This approach can be implemented in two ways: either by training each classifier to recognize patterns across all classes using non-linear kernels or by training each model as a binary classifier, focusing on individual classes. In this ensemble method, embeddings from various models, including GloFast embeddings, are concatenated for each classifier. This approach supports both monolingual and multilingual models, corresponding to three ensemble architectures: encoder-based, decoder-based, and hybrid models. The diversity of these models enhances the ability of classifiers to identify patterns across languages, improving the classification of text into different propaganda techniques.

The selection of models for multilingual propaganda detection is guided by recent research (Hromadka et al., 2023) and depends on the research objectives, target languages, and dataset characteristics. In our approach, we combined multilingual models with Arabic monolingual models to enhance performance in Arabic while ensuring consistent accuracy across all languages and avoiding bias toward any particular language.

The predictions from the classifiers, whether trained on all classes or as binary classifiers, are denoted as $P_{\text{SVM}}, P_{\text{LR}}, P_{\text{RF}}, P_{\text{XGB}}, P_{\text{Gau}}$, corresponding to the outputs of Support Vector Machine (SVM), Logistic Regression (LR), Random Forest (RF), XGBoost (XGB), and Gaussian Naive Bayes (Gau) models, respectively. These predictions are processed and aggregated for each label. A threshold of 0.35 is applied to each prediction:

$$\hat{y}_i^{(m)} = I(P_i^{(m)} \geq 0.35)$$

where $P_i^{(m)}$ represents the prediction probability for the i-th instance from the m-th classifier.

After applying the threshold, the final prediction is generated through majority voting, as defined in Equation 1, which combines the predictions from all classifiers to enhance reliability.

To tackle the issue of imbalanced label distribution, which is typical in multi-label classification tasks, class weights are adjusted using the Class Weights Based on Frequency (CWBF) approach (Kim and Bethard, 2020). The weight for each class i is computed as follows:

$$w_i = \frac{f_{\max}}{f_i}$$

where f_i is the frequency of class i in the training data, and $f_{\max}$ is the frequency of the most common class. This weighting scheme ensures that less frequent classes are given higher importance, reducing the likelihood of misclassification for these underrepresented classes. The computed weights are then applied during training with the Binary Cross-Entropy Loss with Logits, which is used as the loss function (see Appendix B.1 for further details).

4.2 MultiProp-ML

Meta-learning, often referred to as "learning-to-learn," focuses on creating models capable of quickly adapting to new tasks or domains with minimal labeled data, while avoiding overfitting (Nooralahzadeh et al., 2020). This adaptability is achieved by training the model during a meta-learning phase on a diverse set of tasks, equipping it to rapidly adjust to new tasks with only a few examples. Our approach employs a gradient-based meta-learning technique, explicitly optimizing the model for fast adaptation with minimal data, even in zero-shot settings where no labeled samples of the target language are available.

To this end, we present MultiProp-ML, a cross-lingual meta-learning model designed for adaptability. Ensemble models are initially pre-trained on English datasets to establish a robust linguistic foundation, then fine-tuned to effectively transition and adapt to low-resource languages.

During the meta-learning phase on auxiliary languages, the models are trained on batches of tasks, each derived from randomly sampled subsets of development data from auxiliary low-resource languages. For each task, a portion of the data (D_{train}) is used to update the model's parameters via gradient descent, and task-specific losses are computed based on this data. These losses are then summed across tasks to calculate a meta-loss, which is used to further update the model's parameters. In the few-shot learning stage, the models are evaluated on the target language (Arabic) using a labeled subset of the target language(D_{test}), after the meta-learner has been trained on labeled samples ((D_{train}) from the same language to simulate real-world conditions.

Alternatively, in the zero-shot setting, we utilize pseudo-labeling by generating pseudo-labels from high-confidence predictions (above a threshold of 0.6). These pseudo-labels are iteratively used to refine the model's performance, following the approach of (Awal et al., 2023).

4.2.1 MultiProp-ML Algorithm

As shown in Algorithm 4.2.1, each model in the ensemble is fine-tuned on English to initialize its parameters. To enhance feature representation, external embeddings, such as GloFast, are concatenated with the model's native embeddings. In the few-shot approach, the model leverages a limited amount of labeled data from the target language. For zero-shot learning, the model is trained using meta-task data from auxiliary languages.

Algorithm: MultiProp-ML

```
Fine-tune models M_i on source language h and initialize parameters θ_i.
if S is zero-shot then
    Utilize meta-task data from h and auxiliary languages, and apply self-training using pseudo labels from tgt.
else
    Utilize few-shot data with limited labels from all languages in L, excluding surprise languages.
end if
while not converged do
    Sample tasks T = {T_1, ..., T_m} from D.
    for all models M_i in ensemble do
        for all tasks T_j ∈ T do
            Compute gradients ∇_{θ_i} L_{T_j}(M_i) and update parameters θ'_i.
        end for
        Update meta-parameters θ_i with learning rate β.
    end for
end while
Save meta-trained models M_i and evaluate on target language tgt.
```

4.2.2 What makes our MultiProp-ML approach different?

Our approach enriches the meta-learner with external embeddings, such as GloFast (a combination of GloVe and FastText), to improve generalization in zero-shot settings. Additionally, we employ an ensemble of models to enhance robustness and leverage multi-task learning on external classification tasks, including Arabic sentiment detection and framing detection, to further boost the model's adaptability across diverse tasks and languages in both zero-shot and few-shot scenarios. This combination of techniques allows our model to better generalize across different languages and domains, making it highly effective for cross-lingual tasks such as propaganda detection .

4.3 MultiProp-Chunk

In our third approach, we tackle the issue of processing text sequences that exceed the standard 512-token limit of most pretrained models. This is crucial for handling lengthy articles, which often exceed 1,000 tokens in our dataset 2, and for multi-label classification where relevant labels may be dispersed throughout the text. Our method builds upon the MultiProp-Baseline but incorporates additional processing steps. Text is first chunked into 512-token segments with a 100-token overlap to preserve context. Each chunk is then tokenized and processed through the ensemble models to generate embeddings, which are concatenated with GloFast embeddings. To aggregate the concatenated embeddings from different segments, we use an attention layer. This layer consists of a linear layer and a softmax function. It generates attention weights for each segment, which are used to scale the embeddings, assigning greater importance to more relevant segments.The final embeddings are then used for classification. Predictions are obtained by applying either the Skip-FFN or Use-FFN methods and taking a majority vote from various meta-learners or classifiers.

5 Experimental Setup

Through extensive experimentation, we identified the optimal learning rates for each model in our ensemble. This was achieved by leveraging both prior research and our own empirical testing. The final learning rates, provided as a list with one value per model, follow established best practices (see Table 6 in the appendix). We found that a batch size of 10 was ideal, and improvements in loss metrics plateaued after 5 epochs. Tokenization length was set to 512 to balance context retention with memory constraints, and a dropout rate of 0.1 was applied to mitigate overfitting. We employed the AdamW optimizer across all models due to its proven effectiveness with transformer architectures and ability to handle sparse gradients. Key hyperparameters for each model are detailed in Table 7. For generating predictions, we utilized advanced classifiers and meta-estimators. These classifiers' parameters were optimized using grid search with cross-validation on the development sets, with the results summarized in the appendix (see Table 8). Our ensemble framework was implemented in Python 3.9, using the PyTorch library. To manage memory constraints, we limited the maximum number of chunks generated during the tokenization process to avoid overwhelming the device, which was an NVIDIA A100-SXM4-80GB.

6 Results and Analysis

The results in Table 3 highlight the performance of the MultiProp Framework across seven languages, using three ensemble architectures Encoder-Based, Decoder-Based, and Hybrid models with two aggregation methods: Use-FFN and Skip-FFN.

The MultiProp-Chunk Hybrid model excels in Arabic and Russian, effectively handling long texts and preserving context. This capability is particularly valuable for detecting subtle propaganda techniques like *Appeal to Fear/Prejudice*, *Red Herring*, *Black-and-White Fallacy/Dictatorship*, and *Exaggeration/Minimization*, which require nuanced contextual understanding and linguistic complexity.

The MultiProp-Baseline En-B model delivers consistent and balanced results, particularly in Polish and Italian, making it a reliable choice for achieving stable outcomes. The MultiProp-ML approach demonstrates strong cross-lingual adaptability, with significant improvements in Italian and French when using the En-B or Hybrid architecture with Skip-FFN. It also boosts performance in English (source), German (auxiliary), and Arabic (target) by leveraging effective meta-learning.

When examining the diverse ensemble architectures in Arabic, distinct patterns emerge. Encoder-Based models excel at detecting nuanced labels such as *Appeal to Fear/Prejudice*, likely due to their ability to capture fine-grained contextual dependencies. Decoder-Based models perform better for labels like *Causal Oversimplification*, potentially benefiting from their sequence-generating

MultiProp-Baseline							
Ensemble Models	**En**	**Ar**	**Ge**	**It**	**Fr**	**Po**	**Ru**
En-B (Use-FFN)	0.434	0.416	0.457	0.404	0.509	0.480	0.420
En-B (Skip-FFN)	0.556	**0.569**	0.573	**0.573**	0.559	**0.605**	0.539
De-B (Use-FFN)	0.408	0.411	0.413	0.425	0.423	0.480	0.397
De-B (Skip-FFN)	0.530	0.521	0.563	0.507	0.562	0.594	0.508
Hybrid (Use-FFN)	0.499	0.352	0.452	0.425	0.425	0.483	0.410
Hybrid (Skip-FFN)	**0.571**	0.533	**0.576**	0.523	**0.587**	0.408	**0.573**
mBERT	0.490	0.508	0.502	0.488	0.494	**0.542**	0.514

MultiProp-Chunk							
Ensemble Models	**En**	**Ar**	**Ge**	**It**	**Fr**	**Po**	**Ru**
En-B(Use-FFN)	0.441	0.409	0.422	0.425	0.432	0.480	0.409
En-B (Skip-FFN)	**0.590**	0.569	0.579	0.496	0.572	**0.625**	0.469
De-B (Use-FFN)	0.436	0.449	0.436	0.437	0.421	0.477	0.410
De-B (Skip-FFN)	0.546	0.589	0.576	**0.503**	0.558	0.611	0.441
Hybrid (Use-FFN)	0.499	0.446	0.452	0.425	0.425	0.505	0.408
Hybrid (Skip-FFN)	0.567	**0.598**	**0.584**	0.457	**0.584**	0.547	**0.595**
kinit-sk	0.574	0.556	0.514	0.513	0.553	0.478	0.562

MultiProp-ML							
Ensemble Models	**En**	**Ar**	**Ge**	**It**	**Fr**	**Po**	**Ru**
En-B(Use-FFN)	0.454	0.438	0.441	0.425	0.433	0.483	0.328
En-B(Skip-FFN)	0.562	0.570	0.579	**0.579**	0.573	0.590	0.526
De-B(Use-FFN)	0.442	0.462	0.403	0.423	0.440	0.478	0.400
De-B(Skip-FFN)	0.512	**0.571**	0.569	0.500	0.554	**0.602**	0.491
Hybrid (Use-FFN)	0.499	0.395	0.425	0.425	0.425	0.480	398
Hybrid (Skip-FFN)	**0.573**	0.538	**0.583**	0.514	**0.587**	0.422	**0.583**
XLM-R	0.483	0.511	0.509	0.516	0.506	0.575	0.482

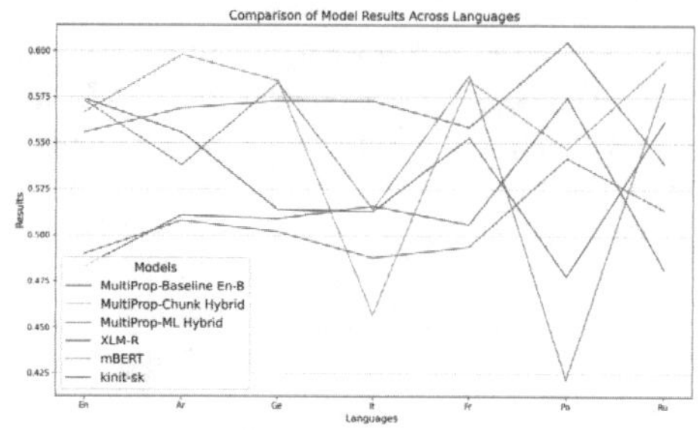

Table 2: Model Results Across Languages

Table 3: F1 Micro Scores of Our Three Proposed Systems across Seven Languages under a Few-Shot Learning Setting. The tables present the performance results of our models on datasets in English (En), Arabic (Ar), German (Ge), Italian (It), French (Fr), Polish (Po), and Russian (Ru). We implemented three different ensemble models: Encoder-Based (En-B), Decoder-Based (De-B), and Hybrid. Each model was tested using two methods for prediction aggregation: Use-FFN and Skip-FFN. The best score for each language is boldfaced.

nature, which aligns with label-specific linguistic patterns. Hybrid models, on the other hand, excel at identifying labels like *Doubt* and *Slogans*, leveraging the strengths of both encoder and decoder paradigms to handle mixed structural and semantic cues.
Benchmark models like XLM-R and mBERT exhibit stable performance but underperform compared to MultiProp models. While these state-of-the-art models provide consistent results, they lack the tailored architecture and cross-lingual adaptability inherent in MultiProp.

Figure 2 compares a selected sample of our models with state-of-the-art systems, including kinit-sk (Hromadka et al., 2023), which excelled in SemEval 2023 Propaganda Detection across various languages, as well as XLM-R Large and mBERT. Skip-FFN achieves superior F1-micro scores, excelling in low-resource settings, while Use-FFN performs better in F1-macro scores for rare labels. The MultiProp-Chunk Hybrid model surpasses kinit-sk in Arabic and Russian while remaining competitive in other languages. The MultiProp-Baseline En-B model excels in Polish and Italian, while the MultiProp-ML Hybrid model demonstrates consistent cross-lingual performance in English, German, French, and Russian. These results underline the advantages of tailored architectures for multilingual tasks.

7 Conclusion

In this work, we developed a robust multilingual framework by leveraging a range of pretrained models, ensembling techniques, and machine learning methods. Our approach combines multiple models to create a language-agnostic system that effectively understands and transfers knowledge across languages, with the addition of a monolingual model enhancing performance for the target language. By integrating multilingual embeddings with word embeddings and deploying a diverse set of classifiers, we achieved notable improvements across various languages. Specifically, our ensemble of advanced classifiers outperformed traditional stacking methods, resulting in a 13% increase in prediction accuracy. In future work, we aim to expand our dataset to include Abjad and Ajami languages, such as Persian and Pashto, and evaluate the scalability of our ensemble by incorporating language-specific monolingual models or relying solely on multilingual models.

8 Limitations of the work

Despite incorporating multiple languages such as Arabic, German, English, Italian, French, Polish, and Russian, our dataset faces constraints due to the limited availability of annotated data for less-resourced languages, particularly Arabic. This limitation may affect the generalizability of the models to other low-resource languages not included in the dataset. Data augmentation techniques, including translation, were employed to enhance the dataset. However, the translation process might lead to the loss of nuanced labels related to specific propaganda techniques. The subtleties necessary for accurately detecting these techniques may not fully translate, potentially diminishing the effectiveness of the model. Additionally, the dataset exhibits class imbalance issues. For instance, the "Loaded Language" technique is frequently represented across many languages, while other techniques, such as "Presenting Irrelevant Data (Red Herring)" may have few or no samples in some languages like Russian. This imbalance complicates performance evaluation and is further impacted by the use of the F1 micro metric, which tends to favor majority classes and can obscure the model's performance on less-represented techniques.

Acknowledgments

This work has been supported by the German Federal Ministry of Education and Research (BMBF) as part of the DeFaktS program. Any opinions, findings, conclusions, or recommendations in this material are those of the authors and do not necessarily reflect the views of the BMBF. This research was also supported by the state of North Rhine-Westphalia as part of the Lamarr Institute for Machine Learning and Artificial Intelligence. We would like to thank all the anonymous reviewers for their valuable input.

References

Sergiu Amihaesei, Laura Cornei, and George Stoica. 2023. Appeal for attention at semeval-2023 task 3: Data augmentation extension strategies for detection of online news persuasion techniques. In *Proceedings of the 17th International Workshop on Semantic Evaluation (SemEval-2023)*, pages 616–623.

Wissam Antoun, Fady Baly, and Hazem Hajj. 2020. Arabert: Transformer-based model for arabic language understanding. *arXiv preprint arXiv:2003.00104*.

Md Rabiul Awal, Roy Ka-Wei Lee, Eshaan Tanwar, Tanmay Garg, and Tanmoy Chakraborty. 2023. Model-agnostic meta-learning for multilingual hate speech detection. *IEEE Transactions on Computational Social Systems*, 11(1):1086–1095.

Alberto Barrón-Cedeno, Israa Jaradat, Giovanni Da San Martino, and Preslav Nakov. 2019. Proppy: Organizing the news based on their propagandistic content. *Information Processing & Management*, 56(5):1849–1864.

Iz Beltagy, Matthew E Peters, and Arman Cohan. 2020. Longformer: The long-document transformer. *arXiv preprint arXiv:2004.05150*.

Piotr Bojanowski, Edouard Grave, Armand Joulin, and Tomas Mikolov. 2017. Enriching word vectors with subword information. *Transactions of the association for computational linguistics*, 5:135–146.

Leo Breiman. 1996. Bagging predictors. *Machine learning*, 24:123–140.

Leo Breiman. 2001. Random forests. *Machine learning*, 45:5–32.

Tom Brown, Benjamin Mann, Nick Ryder, Melanie Subbiah, Jared D Kaplan, Prafulla Dhariwal, Arvind Neelakantan, Pranav Shyam, Girish Sastry, Amanda Askell, et al. 2020. Language models are few-shot learners. *Advances in neural information processing systems*, 33:1877–1901.

Chih-Chung Chang and Chih-Jen Lin. 2011. Libsvm: a library for support vector machines. *ACM transactions on intelligent systems and technology (TIST)*, 2(3):1–27.

Tanmay Chavan and Aditya Kane. 2022. Large language models for multi-label propaganda detection. *arXiv preprint arXiv:2210.08209*.

Alexis Conneau, Kartikay Khandelwal, Naman Goyal, Vishrav Chaudhary, Guillaume Wenzek, Francisco Guzmán, Edouard Grave, Myle Ott, Luke Zettlemoyer, and Veselin Stoyanov. 2019. Unsupervised cross-lingual representation learning at scale. *arXiv preprint arXiv:1911.02116*.

David R Cox. 1959. The regression analysis of binary sequences. *Journal of the Royal Statistical Society: Series B (Methodological)*, 21(1):238–238.

Giovanni Da San Martino, Alberto Barron-Cedeno, and Preslav Nakov. 2019. Findings of the nlp4if-2019 shared task on fine-grained propaganda detection. In *Proceedings of the second workshop on natural language processing for internet freedom: censorship, disinformation, and propaganda*, pages 162–170.

Jacob Devlin. 2018. Bert: Pre-training of deep bidirectional transformers for language understanding. *arXiv preprint arXiv:1810.04805*.

Moussa Kamal Eddine, Nadi Tomeh, Nizar Habash, Joseph Le Roux, and Michalis Vazirgiannis. 2022. Arabart: a pretrained arabic sequence-to-sequence model for abstractive summarization. *arXiv preprint arXiv:2203.10945*.

Neele Falk, Annerose Eichel, and Prisca Piccirilli. 2023. Nap at semeval-2023 task 3: Is less really more?(back-) translation as data augmentation strategies for detecting persuasion techniques. *arXiv preprint arXiv:2304.14179*.

Fangxiaoyu Feng, Yinfei Yang, Daniel Cer, Naveen Arivazhagan, and Wei Wang. 2020. Language-agnostic bert sentence embedding. *arXiv preprint arXiv:2007.01852*.

Yoav Freund, Robert E Schapire, et al. 1996. Experiments with a new boosting algorithm. In *icml*, volume 96, pages 148–156. Citeseer.

Ivan Habernal, Raffael Hannemann, Christian Pollak, Christopher Klamm, Patrick Pauli, and Iryna Gurevych. 2017. Argotario: Computational argumentation meets serious games. *arXiv preprint arXiv:1707.06002*.

Philipp Heinisch, Moritz Plenz, Anette Frank, and Philipp Cimiano. 2023. Accept at semeval-2023 task 3: An ensemble-based approach to multilingual framing detection. In *Proceedings of the 17th International Workshop on Semantic Evaluation (SemEval-2023)*, pages 1347–1358.

S Hochreiter. 1997. Long short-term memory. *Neural Computation MIT-Press*.

Timo Hromadka, Timotej Smolen, Tomas Remis, Branislav Pecher, and Ivan Srba. 2023. Kinitveraai at semeval-2023 task 3: Simple yet powerful multilingual fine-tuning for persuasion techniques detection. *arXiv preprint arXiv:2304.11924*.

Ali Haghpanah Jahromi and Mohammad Taheri. 2017. A non-parametric mixture of gaussian naive bayes classifiers based on local independent features. In *2017 Artificial intelligence and signal processing conference (AISP)*, pages 209–212. IEEE.

Venkatachalam Kandasamy, Pavel Trojovskỳ, Fadi Al Machot, Kyandoghere Kyamakya, Nebojsa Bacanin, Sameh Askar, and Mohamed Abouhawwash. 2021. Sentimental analysis of covid-19 related messages in social networks by involving an n-gram stacked autoencoder integrated in an ensemble learning scheme. *Sensors*, 21(22):7582.

Moonsung Kim and Steven Bethard. 2020. Ttui at semeval-2020 task 11: Propaganda detection with transfer learning and ensembles. In *Proceedings of the Fourteenth Workshop on Semantic Evaluation*, pages 1829–1834.

Anne Lauscher, Vinit Ravishankar, Ivan Vulić, and Goran Glavaš. 2020. From zero to hero: On the limitations of zero-shot cross-lingual transfer with multilingual transformers. *arXiv preprint arXiv:2005.00633*.

G Martino, Alberto Barrón-Cedeno, Henning Wachsmuth, Rostislav Petrov, and Preslav Nakov. 2020. Semeval-2020 task 11: Detection of propaganda techniques in news articles. *arXiv preprint arXiv:2009.02696*.

Tomas Mikolov, Kai Chen, Greg Corrado, and Jeffrey Dean. 2013. Efficient estimation of word representations in vector space. *arXiv preprint arXiv:1301.3781*.

Shubham Mittal and Preslav Nakov. 2022. Iitd at the wanlp 2022 shared task: Multilingual multi-granularity network for propaganda detection. *arXiv preprint arXiv:2210.17190*.

Farhad Nooralahzadeh, Giannis Bekoulis, Johannes Bjerva, and Isabelle Augenstein. 2020. Zero-shot cross-lingual transfer with meta learning. *arXiv preprint arXiv:2003.02739*.

Raghavendra Pappagari, Piotr Zelasko, Jesús Villalba, Yishay Carmiel, and Najim Dehak. 2019. Hierarchical transformers for long document classification. In *2019 IEEE automatic speech recognition and understanding workshop (ASRU)*, pages 838–844. IEEE.

Jeffrey Pennington, Richard Socher, and Christopher D Manning. 2014. Glove: Global vectors for word representation. In *Proceedings of the 2014 conference on empirical methods in natural language processing (EMNLP)*, pages 1532–1543.

Jakub Piskorski, Nicolas Stefanovitch, Giovanni Da San Martino, and Preslav Nakov. 2023. Semeval-2023 task 3: Detecting the category, the framing, and the persuasion techniques in online news in a multilingual setup. In *Proceedings of the 17th International Workshop on Semantic Evaluation (SemEval-2023)*, pages 2343–2361.

Alec Radford, Jeffrey Wu, Rewon Child, David Luan, Dario Amodei, Ilya Sutskever, et al. 2019. Language models are unsupervised multitask learners. *OpenAI blog*, 1(8):9.

Rafet Sifa, Maren Pielka, Rajkumar Ramamurthy, Anna Ladi, Lars Hillebrand, and Christian Bauckhage. 2019. Towards contradiction detection in german: a translation-driven approach. In *2019 IEEE Symposium Series on Computational Intelligence (SSCI)*, pages 2497–2505. IEEE.

Yuqing Tang, Chau Tran, Xian Li, Peng-Jen Chen, Naman Goyal, Vishrav Chaudhary, Jiatao Gu, and Angela Fan. 2020. Multilingual translation with extensible multilingual pretraining and finetuning. *arXiv preprint arXiv:2008.00401*.

Kai Ming Ting and Ian H. Witten. 1997. Stacked generalizations: When does it work? In *International Joint Conference on Artificial Intelligence*.

Ashish Vaswani, Noam Shazeer, Niki Parmar, Jakob Uszkoreit, Llion Jones, Aidan N Gomez, Łukasz Kaiser, and Illia Polosukhin. 2017. Attention is all you need. *Advances in neural information processing systems*, 30.

Qizhe Xie, Zihang Dai, Eduard Hovy, Thang Luong, and Quoc Le. 2020. Unsupervised data augmentation for consistency training. *Advances in neural information processing systems*, 33:6256–6268.

Linting Xue, Noah Constant, Adam Roberts, Mihir Kale, Rami Al-Rfou, Aditya Siddhant, Aditya Barua, and Colin Raffel. 2020. mt5: A massively multilingual pre-trained text-to-text transformer. *arXiv preprint arXiv:2010.11934*.

A Appendix

A.1 Dataset Information After Merging Different Sets and Overlapping

Table 4: Instances per Language After Merging Different Sets and Overlapping

Language	Train	Dev	Test
ar	517	68	68
de	204	115	101
en	488	143	101
fr	164	95	101
it	273	142	101
ru	141	0	48
po	124	0	45

This table presents the number of instances in the dataset after merging different sets and handling overlapping data. The Arabic dataset ("ar") combines the original WANLP data with additional oversampled instances from the PTC translated data. For the languages de, fr, it, and en, the translated test set from PTC English was used for evaluation, while the development sets of po and ru were used as test sets to assess the model's performance on original language data. This setup allows for a comprehensive evaluation of the model's ability to generalize across both translated and original datasets.

A.2 Label Distribution across the Training Set of All Languages

Table 5 provides a detailed comparison of the distribution of various propaganda techniques (or labels) across different languages, including English, Arabic, German, Italian, and French, indicating the frequency of this propaganda technique in those languages.

A.3 Text Length Across Labels and Languages

Figure2 delves into the mean average text length for each label across the five datasets. Notably, Arabic texts exhibit significantly shorter lengths compared to their German, English, Italian, and French counterparts. This can be attributed to the Arabic dataset's composition, which includes a mix of articles and tweets, the latter being considerably shorter in length. Despite this, the overall trend shows that labels such as "Straw Man," "Thought-Terminating Cliché," and "Causal Oversimplification" consistently feature longer text lengths across all languages. Moreover, German articles stand out for having the most extended text lengths when compared to other languages, reflecting the nature of the content. An important observation is that text lengths across all datasets exceed the 512-token limit, which is the maximum sequence length that many models can process effectively. Specifically, the text lengths in our datasets range from 2,000 to 12,000 tokens. This significant discrepancy was a key motivation behind the development of the MultiProp-Chunk model, designed to handle longer sequences by breaking them into manageable chunks, ensuring that the entirety of the text can be processed without losing critical information.

A.4 Topic Modeling and Thematic Classification Across Multilingual Datasets

To analyze the topics in our dataset, we first preprocessed the text data by tokenizing, lemmatizing, and removing stopwords to standardize the input. We then applied Latent Dirichlet Allocation (LDA) [5], specifically using the LdaMulticore model from Gensim, to extract seven distinct topics from each language dataset. Using the Bag of Words representation, we identified key terms associated with these topics. Subsequently, we categorized these topics into overarching thematic groups based on their content, resulting in a clear classification of themes such as "Political Discussions, Elections" and "COVID-19". This approach enabled a comprehensive understanding of the primary themes present across different languages in the dataset.To visualize the topic distribution across the datasets, we generated pie charts for each language 3

B Technical Details

B.1 Weighted Loss Function for Multi-Label Classification

The weighted loss function takes the form:

[5] `https://github.com/piskvorky/gensim`

Label Distribution after applying Data Augmentation Techniques					
Labels	**English**	**Arabic**	**German**	**Italian**	**French**
Presenting Irrelevant Data (Red Herring)	52	16	34	34	43
Loaded Language	413	404	147	255	157
Thought-terminating cliché	119	42	89	121	85
Exaggeration/Minimisation	249	118	113	129	110
Repetition	199	64	45	51	48
Slogans	129	65	71	55	73
Flag-waving	177	48	65	47	30
Doubt	238	100	144	224	118
Appeal to authority	122	46	88	67	52
Bandwagon	45	30	39	34	51
Causal Oversimplification	133	62	61	67	68
Obfuscation, Intentional vagueness, Confusion	44	18	37	27	63
Name calling/Labeling	323	269	179	205	131
Reductio ad hitlerum	68	83	59	47	63
Appeal to fear/prejudice	204	132	101	148	90
Whataboutism	33	37	36	39	52
Black-and-white Fallacy/Dictatorship	102	51	57	62	55
Misrepresentation of Someone's Position (Straw Man)	34	24	23	35	65

Table 5: Label Counts Across Different Languages

$$\mathcal{L} = -\sum_{i=1}^{C} w_i \left[y_i \cdot \log(\sigma(z_i)) + (1 - y_i) \cdot \log(1 - \sigma(z_i)) \right]$$

where C is the number of classes, w_i is the weight for class i, y_i is the true label, z_i is the raw output (logit) from the classifier, and $\sigma(\cdot)$ is the sigmoid function. This weighted loss function helps the model correctly predict multiple labels for a given text, especially for the less frequent classes.

Category	Model	Learning Rate
E-B	ARBERT	1e-5
	bert-base multilingual-cased	3.7e-6
	bert-base-cased	5e-5
	xlm-roberta-large	4.4e-6
D-B	aragpt2-base	2e-5
	gpt2-large	1.8e-5
	gpt2-medium	1.8e-6
Hybrid	AraBART	3e-5
	mt5-large	2e-5
	mbart-large-50	3e-6

Table 6: Models and Their Learning Rates

C Hyper-parameters

C.1 Ensemble Models Parameters

Through extensive experimentation, we determined the optimal learning rates for each model, in line with established best practices and recommendations for BERT, XLM-R, and GPT-2 models.

Regarding training specifics, we found a batch size of 10 to be optimal, with loss improvement plateauing after 4 epochs. We set the tokenization length to 512 to balance context capture with memory constraints and applied a dropout rate of 0.1 to mitigate overfitting. The AdamW optimizer was used across all ensemble models due to its efficacy with transformer architectures and handling sparse gradients. Additional key hyperparameters are detailed in Table 7.

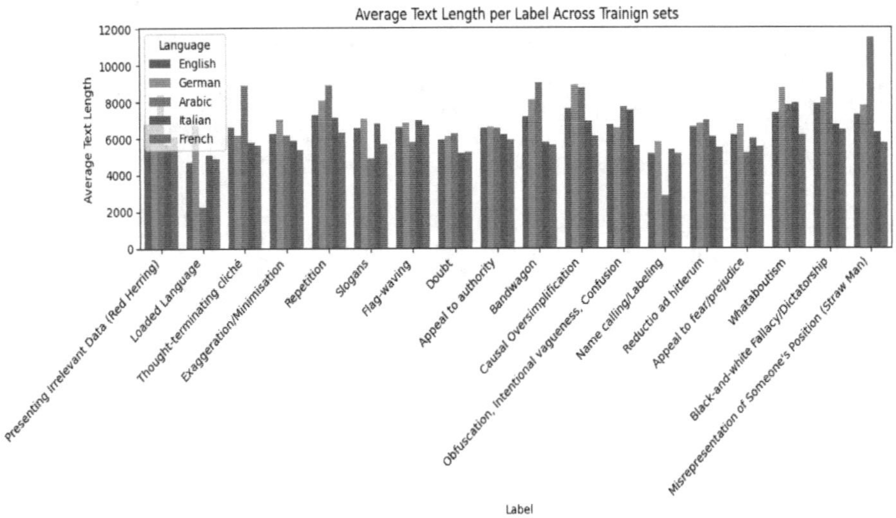

Figure 2: Average Text Length per Label

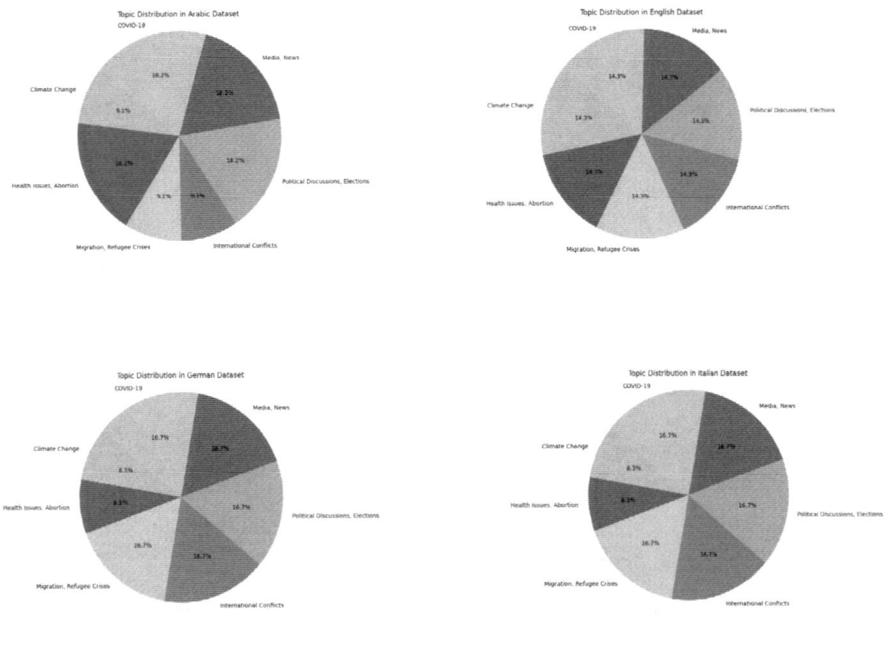

Figure 3: Pie charts illustrating the distribution of topics across various languages.

C.2 Meta Estimators Parameters

For predictions aggregation, we utilized several advanced classifiers and meta-estimators. The parameters for these classifiers, optimized using grid search with cross-validation (cv = 5) on the development sets, are summarized in Table 8.

Parameter	Value
Meta Models Learning Rate	2e-5
Maximum Gradient Norm	1.0
Number of Labels	18
Embedding Dimension	1024
Max sequence length	512
Overlap	100
Threshold for FFN Prediction	0.5
Threshold for Classifiers Prediction	0.35
Learning Approach	'zero_shot' or 'few_shot'
Maximum Chunks	25

Table 7: Hyperparameters and Additional Parameters

Classifier	Parameters

Random Forest	`n_estimators=100`
	`criterion='gini'`
	`bootstrap=True`
	`oob_score=True`
	`random_state=0`
	`max_features='sqrt'`
	`class_weight='balanced'`

Gaussian NB	Used with `ClassifierChain` due to multilabel classification `var_smoothing=1e-07`

Logistic Regression	Used with `ClassifierChain` due to multilabel classification
	`solver='liblinear'`
	`C=0.1`
	`class_weight='balanced'`
	`penalty': 'l1'`

SVM	Used with `OneVsRestClassifier` for multilabel classification
	`kernel='poly'`
	`C=1.0`
	`decision_function_shape='ovr'`
	`class_weight='balanced'`

xgboost	`n_estimators=100`
	`learning_rate=0.1`
	`max_depth=3`
	`random_state=0`

Table 8: Models and their parameters used in our evaluation

D Additional Results

D.1 Performance Evaluation of Different Embedding Methods for Ensemble Models

In this study, we utilize the F1 score to evaluate the performance of three ensemble models: encoder-based, decoder-based, and hybrid. These models are assessed using three distinct embedding methods:

1. Transformer-based Embedding: We extract embeddings from transformer models and concatenate them within the ensemble.

2.Transformer-based + GloFast Embedding: Transformer-based embeddings are combined with GloFast embeddings, which integrate GloVe and FastText features.

3. Transformer-based + TF-IDF Embedding: We calculate TF-IDF across the dataset and concatenate it with transformer-based embeddings for each instance.

Our aim is to identify the most effective embedding method, which can then be used as the default for all ensemble models. The experiments, conducted in a few-shot setting, are presented in Table 9 , with bolded values representing the highest F1 micro scores for each language and embedding method. Additionally, GloFast shows significant potential for further improvement. By increasing the embedding dimensions from 200 (100 from GloVe and 100 from FastText) to 600 (300 for each model), we expect to enhance performance. We also believe that expanding the training dataset to include languages like Italian and French will further boost results. Although GloFast was initially trained only on Arabic, English, and German, its ability to generalize across languages and effectively handle out-of-vocabulary words using the "unknown" vector demonstrates its versatility.

While GloFast consistently performs well, the combination of TF-IDF with transformer-based models has delivered particularly strong results for Italian and French. In contrast, transformer-based embeddings alone achieved the highest scores for German when used with the encoder-based ensemble model. This success can be attributed to the pretrained multilingual models and the specific nature of the German dataset, which combines SemEval23 data with oversampled instances from the translated PTC dataset.

D.2 Comparison of Approaches in Zero-Shot Setting

The results in Table 10 highlight the performance of our MultiProp Framework, which consists of three components: MultiProp-Baseline, MultiProp-Chunk, and MultiProp-ML, evaluated across seven languages: English, Arabic, German, Italian, French, Polish, and Russian. In a zero-shot setting, we trained and fine-tuned the models on English and German, then assessed their ability to generalize to the other languages. Similar to the few-shot experiment, each system was evaluated using three ensemble architectures: Encoder-Based (En-B) models like mBERT and XLM-R, Decoder-Based (De-B) models such as GPT-2 Large, and Hybrid models like mBART and mT5. For each component, we applied two prediction aggregation methods: Use-FFN and Skip-FFN.

Our baseline model demonstrated strong performance in languages like Italian, Polish, and Russian, even though no training data from these languages was used, validating the model's generalization capabilities in a zero-shot setting. Notably, Skip-FFN outperformed Use-FFN in most cases; however, in Polish, the Use-FFN method showed better performance with hybrid ensemble models (mBART and mT5) in both the MultiProp-Chunk and MultiProp-Baseline architectures, indicating its effectiveness with encoder-decoder-based models for Polish in the zero-shot setting.

The MultiProp-Chunk model further improved upon the baseline in many languages, including Polish, Russian, and French, when using the Skip-FFN method. Meanwhile, the MultiProp-ML model consistently outperformed the others in low-resource languages, showcasing its ability to transfer knowledge from high-resource languages in the zero-shot setting. It was especially effective in Arabic, where we leveraged a meta-learning approach with pseudo-labels to enhance performance.

Since all three models were trained on English and German, their performance on these languages remained consistent with the few-shot setting. As expected, our models outperformed state-of-the-art models like XLM-R and mT5 in the zero-shot setting across all languages, demonstrating the effectiveness of ensemble models and the integration of different embedding approaches and classifiers.

F1 Micro Scores of Our Systems and State-of-the-Art Models in Zero Shot							
MultiProp-Baseline							
Ensemble Models	**En**	**Ar**	**Ge**	**It**	**Fr**	**Po**	**Ru**
En-B (Use-FFN)	0.426	0.358	0.446	0.441	0.464	0.484	0.426
En-B (Skip-FFN)	0.562	**0.488**	0.574	**0.560**	0.524	**0.592**	**0.567**
De-B (Use-FFN)	0.431	0.369	0.427	0.449	0.445	0.515	0.445
De-B (Skip-FFN)	0.520	0.442	0.544	0.552	**0.541**	0.573	0.530
Hybrid (Use-FFN)	0.499	0.347	0.480	0.448	0.448	0.491	0.421
Hybrid (Skip-FFN)	**0.576**	0.377	**0.583**	0.494	0.502	0.447	0.446
MultiProp-Chunk							
Ensemble Models	**En**	**Ar**	**Ge**	**It**	**Fr**	**Po**	**Ru**
En-B(Use-FFN)	0.433	0.370	0.455	0.425	0.429	0.519	0.421
En-B (Skip-FFN)	**0.590**	**0.454**	0.573	0.511	0.503	**0.617**	**0.583**
De-B (Use-FFN)	0.435	0.335	0.422	0.429	0.424	0.476	0.426
De-B (Skip-FFN)	0.545	0.393	**0.576**	0.512	**0.566**	0.552	0.531
Hybrid (Use-FFN)	0.440	0.360	0.432	0.447	0.476	0.569	0.428
Hybrid (Skip-FFN)	0.568	0.232	0.560	**0.526**	0.434	0.379	0.547
MultiProp-ML							
Ensemble Models	**En**	**Ar**	**Ge**	**It**	**Fr**	**Po**	**Ru**
En-B(Use-FFN)	0.499	0.370	0.443	0.392	0.392	0.491	0.441
En-B(Skip-FFN)	0.567	**0.501**	**0.569**	**0.573**	**0.566**	**0.613**	**0.587**
De-B(Use-FFN)	0.430	0.359	0.412	0.427	0.431	0.479	0.431
De-B(Skip-FFN)	0.506	0.347	0.553	0.541	0.546	0.573	0.521
Hybrid (Use-FFN)	0.533	0.381	0.452	0.448	0.448	0.513	0.478
Hybrid (Skip-FFN)	**0.579**	0.432	**0.569**	0.538	0.474	0.535	0.502
State of the Art Models							
Baseline Models	**En**	**Ar**	**Ge**	**It**	**Fr**	**Po**	**Ru**
mBERT	0.351	0.263	0.347	0.336	0.353	0.388	0.337
mt5-large	0.334	0.295	0.358	0.341	0.341	0.380	**0.375**
gpt2-large	0.348	0.300	0.339	**0.365**	0.342	0.368	0.332
Llama2	0.341	0.278	**0.369**	0.341	0.331	**0.402**	0.337
XLM-R	**0.361**	**0.315**	0.324	0.338	**0.350**	0.375	0.343
mbart-large	0.351	0.310	0.336	0.348	0.354	0.371	0.350

Table 10: F1 Micro Scores of Our Three Proposed Systems across Seven Languages under a Zero-Shot Learning Setting.

Embedding Methods	F1 Micro Score of our three models using the Skip-FFN method							
	Models	English	Arabic	German	Italian	French	Polish	Russian
Transformer-based Embedding	Encoder-Based	0.546	0.543	**0.582**	0.582	0.566	0.590	0.509
	Decoder-Based	0.530	0.477	0.563	0.521	0.554	0.566	0.502
	Hybrid	0.570	0.531	0.577	0.547	**0.595**	0.431	0.552
Transformer-based+GloFast Embedding	Encoder-Based	0.556	**0.569**	0.573	0.573	0.559	**0.605**	0.539
	Decoder-Based	0.530	0.521	0.563	0.507	0.562	0.594	0.508
	Hybrid	**0.571**	0.533	0.576	0.523	0.587	0.408	**0.573**
Transformer-based+TF-IDF Embedding	Encoder-Based	0.560	0.551	0.575	**0.593**	0.560	0.590	0.562
	Decoder-Based	0.537	0.498	0.559	0.518	0.558	0.594	0.534
	Hybrid	0.570	0.530	0.578	0.509	**0.595**	0.433	0.541

Table 9: F1 Micro Scores for Different Embedding Methods and Ensemble Models

Towards Unified Processing of Perso-Arabic Scripts for ASR

Srihari Bandarupalli[1], Bhavana Akkiraju[1], Charan D., Harinie S., Vamshi Raghusimha, Anil Kumar Vuppala
Speech Processing Lab (Language Technology and Research Centre),
International Institute of Information Technology Hyderabad, India.
{bhavana.akkiraju, srihari.bandarupalli, sricharan.d, narasinga.vamshi, harinie.s}@research.iiit.ac.in,
anil.vuppala@iiit.ac.in
[1] Equal Contribution

Abstract

Automatic Speech Recognition (ASR) systems for morphologically complex languages like Urdu, Persian, and Arabic face unique challenges due to the intricacies of Perso-Arabic scripts. Conventional data processing methods often fall short in effectively handling these languages' phonetic and morphological nuances. This paper introduces a unified data processing pipeline tailored specifically for Perso-Arabic languages, addressing the complexities inherent in these scripts. The proposed pipeline encompasses comprehensive steps for data cleaning, tokenization, and phonemization, each of which has been meticulously evaluated and validated by expert linguists. Through expert-driven refinements, our pipeline presents a robust foundation for advancing ASR performance across Perso-Arabic languages, supporting the development of more accurate and linguistically informed multilingual ASR systems in future.

1 Introduction

Automatic Speech Recognition (ASR) systems have made significant progress, but effective preprocessing remains crucial, especially for languages with complex morphology like Urdu, Persian, and Arabic. Traditional methods often fall short for these languages due to their complex scripts and phonetic diversity.

Perso-Arabic languages have orthographic complexities, including script variations and diacritics, often leading to ambiguity. This paper proposes a preprocessing pipeline specifically for Perso-Arabic languages, addressing script handling, phonetic representation, and word segmentation to enhance ASR performance.

Our preprocessing pipeline focuses on data cleaning, tokenization, and phonemization. These steps can significantly improve ASR accuracy for Perso-Arabic languages, contributing to better multilingual ASR systems.

2 Related Work

Most ASR work for Urdu, Persian, and Arabic relies on supervised learning needing large labelled datasets. Chowdhury (Chowdhury et al., 2021) and Dhouib (Dhouib et al., 2022) have explored supervised methods, while Waheed (Waheed et al., 2023) have used self-supervised techniques for Arabic ASR. Urdu ASR research has followed a similar path (Khan et al., 2021) (Khan et al., 2023), with recent self-supervised advances (Mohiuddin et al., 2023) reducing labelled data requirements. Persian ASR has also used self-supervised learning, with Kermanshahi (Kermanshahi et al., 2021) employing transfer learning for low-resource settings. Most research has focused on models rather than preprocessing, which our work aims to address. Studies on graphemic normalization and script conversion (Doctor et al., 2022) (Lehal and Saini, 2014) highlight the need for specialized preprocessing to handle script inconsistencies. Gutkin (Gutkin et al., 2023) and Iyengar (Iyengar, 2018) have discussed script variations and consistency issues. Building on these, our pipeline introduces cleaning, normalization, and tokenization to address challenges across multiple Perso-Arabic languages, aiming to improve ASR performance.

3 Lexicon

A lexicon contains mappings from words to their respective phonetic representations, playing a pivotal role in ASR systems, particularly those based on Kaldi. Even with advancements in end-to-end deep learning-based ASR systems, Kaldi's hybrid architecture still relies heavily on well-constructed lexicons to achieve accurate speech recognition results. The lexicon is critical in statistical ASR models, where correct phonetic transcriptions determine the quality of word recognition. For Perso-Arabic languages such as Arabic, Persian, and Urdu, lexicon creation becomes even more challenging due to

Processings of the 1st Workshop on NLP for Languages Using Arabic Script (AbjadNLP), pages 23–28
January 19, 2025.

their morphological complexity and phonetic variability.

This section discusses our two-part lexicon creation process: Tokenization, which involves segmenting text into individual words, and Phonetic Parsing, which converts these words into their phonetic forms.

3.1 Tokenization

In a language like English, we can use whitespace to break sentences into words directly. But word segmentation becomes much more challenging in the case of Perso-Arabic script, as these languages pose unique challenges in natural language processing due to their intricate morphology, encompassing both derivational and inflectional forms. Inflectional morphology involves modifying words to reflect gender, tense, and other grammatical features, while derivational morphology alters the meaning of words through prefixes, suffixes, or infixes.(Habash, 2010). The cursive nature of the Arabic script further complicates tokenization, making it challenging to identify clear morpheme boundaries, particularly in cases where letters are linked differently depending on their position in a word.

We explored several tokenization tools, including NLTK (Bird et al., 2009), Stanza (Qi et al., 2020), and various language-specific tokenizers, with the aim of selecting the most appropriate approach. Despite the versatility of these tools, NLTK emerged as the best choice based on expert consultations. It did present some challenges, particularly in splitting abbreviations and breaking compound words. This was problematic given the highly specific meanings carried by compound words in Perso-Arabic languages. However, NLTK demonstrated superior performance in terms of accuracy and speed compared to other options. Thus, NLTK was selected as the primary tokenizer for its efficiency in maintaining accuracy across the three languages.

3.2 Parser

Here's the revised version of the paragraph:

For the next stage of lexicon creation, we focused on phonetic parsing—converting words into their phonetic transcriptions. Phonemizer (Bernard and Titeux, 2021) emerged as the preferred parser for handling Perso-Arabic languages due to its effectiveness in converting linguistic input into phonetic representations. Phonemizer provides flexibility in phonetic parsing by offering multiple backends, each with different strengths[1].

An expert linguist verified that Phonemizer effectively handles the complexities and accurately parses Persian, Urdu, and Arabic phonemes. For other low-resource Abjad or Ajami languages included in Phonemizer's supported languages, such as Sindhi, the same approach can be applied. However, for languages like Pashto, which are not supported by Phonemizer, we have explore other options in future.

4 Data Pre Processing

In our analysis of the transcripts, we identified elements that could adversely affect ASR performance, such as punctuation, extraneous characters, numerical data, and foreign language words. To address these issues, we implemented a modular pre-processing pipeline. It systematically handles Perso-Arabic scripts by removing non-space joiners, converting numbers using Num2Words, transliterating foreign words with Google Transliteration, and performing Text Normalization. This streamlined approach improves data consistency and ASR accuracy.

4.1 Understanding RTL Languages

Properly handling RTL (Right-to-Left) languages like Arabic, Persian, and Urdu is essential for accurate ASR preprocessing because these languages have unique script orientation and text handling requirements. Historically, RTL language support was limited before the introduction of Unicode, with most software assuming LTR (Left-to-Right) directionality.

The Unicode encoding system solved this issue by defining *directional character types*[2] for RTL and LTR languages:

- Strong types: Characters that have an explicit directionality (irrespective of surrounding text), such as RTL for Hebrew or LTR for English.

- Weak types: Characters like numbers and punctuation that hat might have a direction, but it doesn't affect their surroundings and may be adjusted based on their surrounding text.

[1] `https://github.com/bootphon/phonemizer`
[2] `https://unicode.org/reports/tr9/`

- Neutral characters: Characters that can flow in either direction, like whitespace or newlines, which inherit the direction from surrounding text.

This Unicode approach enables the display and processing of RTL text in its natural reading order without requiring code modifications. For instance, when typing a two-letter word, the first letter is entered and pronounced first, followed by the second letter. This sequence is maintained in the stored text file, and the first pronounced letter corresponds to the first byte. This is precisely the same way Left-to-Right (LTR) languages are stored. Therefore, any code designed for LTR scripts can process RTL text seamlessly without additional adjustments.

When displayed, however, RTL text appears from right to left, with the first pronounced character positioned at the rightmost end. This is due to Unicode's assigned directionality attribute. Text editors interpret this directionality in Unicode and adjust the rendering accordingly, beginning display from the right. Thus, it is the text editor that manages the visual directionality, ensuring accurate RTL presentation, even though the text is stored on disk in the same way as LTR languages.

Figure 1: Data Pre-Processing pipeline

4.2 Handling Non-Space Joiners

During the preprocessing phase, we encountered non-space joiners: characters used to connect or join other characters without adding visible space. These joiners are particularly relevant for text processing in scripts that have complex typographical rules. They help maintain proper formatting, but non-space joiners can introduce significant issues in ASR, particularly for Urdu, Persian, and Arabic languages. For instance, Pop Directional Formatting can alter text direction, leading to inconsistencies that negatively impact how the ASR system processes and interprets the text. To address these issues, we systematically identified and removed several non-space joiners. The exact non-space joiners removed are detailed in Appendix A (see Table: Unicode Codes for Non-Space Joiners)

These characters were removed by searching for their Unicode code points and systematically replacing them as part of the preprocessing pipeline

4.3 Handling Numerical Data

We also observed that English text and numerical data in transcripts were often pronounced in the native language of the audio recordings. This discrepancy was particularly evident in the case of numbers. To resolve this issue, we translated English numbers into the respective native language using the num2words [3] library. This Python tool effectively converts numerical values into their word forms, supporting various formats such as cardinal and ordinal numbers and even currency forms. Num2words was particularly useful for aligning text with spoken content by generating word-based representations of numbers. The tool's extensive support for different languages and its customization options made it well-suited for ensuring that numerical data was processed accurately, improving the consistency between audio and text.

4.4 Transliteration of Foreign Words

Another challenge was the presence of foreign words in transcripts, such as abbreviations or terms pronounced in a foreign language. For these cases, transliteration was required to convert foreign words into native equivalents based solely on pronunciation rather than meaning. We evaluated several transliteration tools, including Google Transliteration[4], Akshara Mukha[5], and QCRI API[6]. Google Transliteration was selected as the most effective solution after thorough assessment and consultation with linguistic experts. Google Transliteration provides robust phonetic input conversion across various scripts, making it suitable for handling the complexities of Arabic, Persian, and Urdu. It allows for easy and consistent transliteration of foreign terms, thereby enhancing the overall quality and consistency of the text-processing workflow.

4.5 Text Normalisation

The next step in our preprocessing involved removing punctuation marks from the transcripts. Unlike other languages, Perso-Arabic scripts use a distinct set of punctuation symbols, requiring the identification of unique Unicode ranges. To standardize the text, we identified and removed specific Unicode ranges corresponding to characters and

[3] https://github.com/savoirfairelinux/num2words
[4] https://www.google.com/inputtools/services/features/transliteration.html
[5] https://aksharamukha.appspot.com/
[6] https://mt.qcri.org/api

punctuation marks for each language. The Unicode ranges for Urdu, Persian, Arabic, and various punctuation categories were meticulously selected (see Appendix A for full details). For extension to other low-resource languages, the preprocessing pipeline would need to identify and include language-specific Unicode characters by carefully evaluating the data for any additional unique symbols or punctuation marks. This language-specific customization and systematic removal of unwanted characters helped reduce noise and improved the consistency between the audio and text data, which improved the overall clarity and usability of the transcript data for subsequent ASR tasks.

5 Experiment

5.1 Dataset

We began collecting data from various sources, including Common Voice, OpenSLR, and other open-source datasets, with MGB-2 for Arabic as a major contributor (Ali et al., 2019) (Kolobov et al., 2021) (Messaoudi et al., 2021). The Common Voice dataset had fewer verified files than anticipated, requiring careful filtering to retain only verified transcripts. The OpenSLR dataset contained audio paired with transcripts, which we used to segment the audio and discard discrepancies. Notably, the MGB-2 Arabic data was not diacritized, and we used it as-is. After combining datasets, noisy audio files were removed, and transcripts were cleaned to eliminate symbols and empty entries. All transcripts were standardized in text format. Audio files from diverse sources were converted to WAV format and resampled to a consistent 16kHz rate See Table 1 for a clear breakdown of the dataset used for training.

Language	Train (hours)	Test (hours)
Arabic	1202	52.5
Urdu	65	4
Persian	80	14.5

Table 1: Dataset split for different languages.

5.2 Building Statistical ASR using Kaldi Framework

We first started building an ASR model in Kaldi (Povey et al., 2011) for each Urdu, Persian, and Arabic language. For Arabic, we used Buckwalter Transcription (Habash et al., 2007) and modelled the ASR as described in (Ali et al., 2014). We followed a similar recipe to model ASR for Urdu and Persian, using NLTK tokenizer and Phonemizer to create lexicons. SRILM (Stolcke, 2004) was used for language modelling. The results are displayed in Table 2.

Experiment	WER (%)
Arabic ASR (Buckwalter)	35.0
Urdu ASR	61.5
Persian ASR	56.0

Table 2: WER for different languages using Kaldi.

5.3 End2End ASR using Wav2Vec2.0

To fine-tune the wav2vec 2.0 model (Baevski et al., 2020), we started by selecting the CLSRIL-23 pre-trained model. This model had already been trained on a broad and diverse dataset, providing a strong baseline for customization to our specific languages. We used SentencePiece(Kudo and Richardson, 2018) as the tokenizer for all the languages and trained the ASR model for each language separately. The results are displayed in Table 3.

Experiment	WER (%)
Arabic ASR	38.0
Persian ASR	32.9
Urdu ASR	29.6

Table 3: WER for different languages using Wav2vec2.0.

6 Conculsion

In conclusion, we successfully developed ASR systems for Urdu, Persian, and Arabic using statistical (Kaldi) and fine-tuned neural models (wav2vec 2.0). A common preprocessing and lexicon creation pipeline was established across all three languages, addressing the unique challenges of Perso-Arabic scripts. While we did not consider diacritization for Arabic in this work, we intend to address this in future studies. In this work, we carefully considered, evaluated, and finalized the best choices for each step in the unified preprocessing pipeline for Persian, Arabic, and Urdu. For other languages like Pashto and Sindhi, this pipeline can be extended; however, the results would need verification by a linguistics expert to ensure accuracy and linguistic integrity. Building on this foundation, our next step will be to create a multilingual ASR system, which promises to make speech recognition technology more accessible for under-resourced languages and enhance multilingual capabilities.

References

Ahmed Ali, Peter Bell, James Glass, Yacine Messaoui, Hamdy Mubarak, Steve Renals, and Yifan Zhang. 2019. The mgb-2 challenge: Arabic multi-dialect broadcast media recognition. *Preprint*, arXiv:1609.05625.

Ahmed Ali, Yifan Zhang, Patrick Cardinal, Najim Dahak, Stephan Vogel, and James Glass. 2014. A complete kaldi recipe for building arabic speech recognition systems. In *2014 IEEE Spoken Language Technology Workshop (SLT)*, pages 525–529.

Alexei Baevski, Henry Zhou, Abdelrahman Mohamed, and Michael Auli. 2020. wav2vec 2.0: A framework for self-supervised learning of speech representations. *Preprint*, arXiv:2006.11477.

Mathieu Bernard and Hadrien Titeux. 2021. Phonemizer: Text to phones transcription for multiple languages in python. *Journal of Open Source Software*, 6(68):3958.

Steven Bird, Ewan Klein, and Edward Loper. 2009. *Natural language processing with Python: analyzing text with the natural language toolkit.* " O'Reilly Media, Inc.".

S. A. Chowdhury, A. Hussein, Ahmed Abdelali, and Ahmed Ali. 2021. Towards one model to rule all: Multilingual strategy for dialectal code-switching arabic asr. *ArXiv*, abs/2105.14779.

Amira Dhouib, Achraf Othman, Oussama El Ghoul, Mohamed Koutheair Khribi, and Aisha Al Sinani. 2022. Arabic automatic speech recognition: A systematic literature review. *Applied Sciences*, 12(17).

Raiomond Doctor, Alexander Gutkin, Cibu Johny, Brian Roark, and Richard Sproat. 2022. Graphemic normalization of the perso-arabic script. *ArXiv*, abs/2210.12273.

Alexander Gutkin, Cibu Johny, Raiomond Doctor, Brian Roark, and Richard Sproat. 2023. Beyond arabic: Software for perso-arabic script manipulation. *ArXiv*, abs/2301.11406.

Nizar Habash, Abdelhadi Soudi, and Timothy Buckwalter. 2007. *On Arabic Transliteration*, pages 15–22. Springer Netherlands, Dordrecht.

Nizar Y. Habash. 2010. *Introduction to Arabic Natural Language Processing*. Springer International Publishing.

Arvind Iyengar. 2018. Variation in perso-arabic and devanāgarī sindhī orthographies. *Written Language and Literacy*.

Maryam Asadolahzade Kermanshahi, Ahmad Akbari, and Babak Nasersharif. 2021. Transfer learning for end-to-end asr to deal with low-resource problem in persian language. *2021 26th International Computer Conference, Computer Society of Iran (CSICC)*, pages 1–5.

Erbaz Khan, Sahar Rauf, Farah Adeeba, and Sarmad Hussain. 2021. A multi-genre urdu broadcast speech recognition system. *2021 24th Conference of the Oriental COCOSDA International Committee for the Coordination and Standardisation of Speech Databases and Assessment Techniques (O-COCOSDA)*, pages 25–30.

Muhammad Danyal Khan, Raheem Ali, and Arshad Aziz. 2023. Code-switched urdu asr for noisy telephonic environment using data centric approach with hybrid hmm and cnn-tdnn. *ArXiv*, abs/2307.12759.

Rostislav Kolobov, Olga Okhapkina, Andrey Platunov Olga Omelchishina, Roman Bedyakin, Vyacheslav Moshkin, Dmitry Menshikov, and Nikolay Mikhaylovskiy. 2021. Mediaspeech: Multilanguage asr benchmark and dataset. *Preprint*, arXiv:2103.16193.

Taku Kudo and John Richardson. 2018. Sentencepiece: A simple and language independent subword tokenizer and detokenizer for neural text processing. *Preprint*, arXiv:1808.06226.

Gurpreet Singh Lehal and Tejinder Singh Saini. 2014. Sangam: A perso-arabic to indic script machine transliteration model. In *ICON*.

Abir Messaoudi, Hatem Haddad, Chayma Fourati, Moez BenHaj Hmida, Aymen Ben Elhaj Mabrouk, and Mohamed Graiet. 2021. Tunisian dialectal end-to-end speech recognition based on deepspeech. *Procedia Computer Science*, 189:183–190. AI in Computational Linguistics.

Hira Mohiuddin, Zahoor Ahmed, Maha Kasi, and Bakhtiar Khan Kasi. 2023. Urduspeakxlsr: Multilingual model for urdu speech recognition. *2023 18th International Conference on Emerging Technologies (ICET)*, pages 217–221.

Daniel Povey, Arnab Ghoshal, Gilles Boulianne, Luká Burget, Ondrej Glembek, Nagendra Kumar Goel, Mirko Hannemann, Petr Motlícek, Yanmin Qian, Petr Schwarz, Jan Silovský, Georg Stemmer, and Karel Veselý. 2011. The kaldi speech recognition toolkit.

Peng Qi, Yuhao Zhang, Yuhui Zhang, Jason Bolton, and Christopher D. Manning. 2020. Stanza: A Python natural language processing toolkit for many human languages. In *Proceedings of the 58th Annual Meeting of the Association for Computational Linguistics: System Demonstrations*.

Andreas Stolcke. 2004. Srilm — an extensible language modeling toolkit. *Proceedings of the 7th International Conference on Spoken Language Processing (ICSLP 2002)*, 2.

Abdul Waheed, Bashar Talafha, Peter Sullivan, AbdelRahim Elmadany, and Muhammad Abdul-Mageed. 2023. Voxarabica: A robust dialect-aware arabic speech recognition system. *Preprint*, arXiv:2310.11069.

A Appendices

Unicode Ranges for Urdu, Persian, and Arabic

Language	Unicode Ranges
Arabic (ar)	\u 0600-\u 06FF, \u 0750-\u 077F, \u 0870-\u 089F, \u 08A0-\u 08FF
Urdu (ur)	\u 0621, \u 0622, \u 0624, \u 0626, \u 0627, \u 0628, \u 062A-\u 062F, \u 0630-\u 0639, \u 063A, \u 0641, \u 0642, \u 0644, \u 0645, \u 0646, \u 0648, \u 0679, \u 067E, \u 0686, \u 0688, \u 0691, \u 0698, \u 06A9, \u 06AF, \u 06BA, \u 06BE, \u 06C1, \u 06CC, \u 06D2, \u 0660-\u 0669
Persian (fa)	\u 0621-\u 0629, \u 062A-\u 062D, \u 062E-\u 062F, \u 0630-\u 0652, \u 0654, \u 067E, \u 0686, \u 0698, \u 06A9, \u 06AF, \u 06CC

Unicode Ranges for Punctuation Marks

Category	Unicode Ranges
General Punctuation	\u 0021, \u 0022, \u 0023, \u 0024, \u 0025, \u 0026, \u 0027, \u 0028, \u 0029, \u 002A, \u 002B, \u 002C, \u 002D, \u 002E, \u 002F, \u 003A, \u 003B, \u 003C, \u 003D, \u 003E, \u 003F, \u 0040, \u 005B, \u 005C, \u 005D, \u 005E, \u 005F, \u 0060, \u 007B, \u 007C, \u 007D, \u 007E, \u 00A9, \u 00AB-\u 00BB, \u 201D, \u 201C
Hyphens and Symbols	\u 2010-\u 2014, \u 2026, \u 2030, \u 20AC, \u 201D
Arabic Punctuation	\u 0609, \u 060C, \u 060D, \u 060E, \u 060F, \u 061E, \u 061C, \u 061D, \u 0615, \u 0617, \u 0616, \u 061F, \u 066D, \u 06D4, \u 066A, \u 066B, \u 066C, \u 061B

Unicode Codes for Non-Space Joiners

Description	Unicode Codes
Non-Space Joiners	\u 200B (Zero Width Space), \u 200C (Zero Width Non-Joiner), \u 200D (Zero Width Joiner), \u 200E (Left-to-Right Mark), \u 200F (Right-to-Left Mark), \u 202A (Left-to-Right Embedding), \u 202B (Right-to-Left Embedding), \u 202C (Pop Directional Formatting), \u 202D (Left-to-Right Override), \u 2066 (Left-to-Right Isolate), \u 2067 (Right-to-Left Isolate), \u 2028 (Line Separator)

In-Depth Analysis of Arabic-Origin Words in the Turkish Morpholex

Mounes Zaval[1,2], **Abdullah Ihsanoğlu**[2], **Asım Ersoy**[1], **Olcay Taner Yıldız**[2]
[1]Sestek [2]Özyeğin University
{mounes.zaval, asim.ersoy}@sestek.com, abdullah.ihsanoglu@ozu.edu.tr
olcay.yildiz@ozyegin.edu.tr

Abstract

MorphoLex is an investigation that focuses on analyzing the roots, prefixes, and suffixes of words. Turkish Morpholex, for example, analyzes 48,472 Turkish words. Unfortunately, it lacks in-depth analysis of the Arabic-origin words, and does not include their accurate and correct roots. This study analyzes Arabic-origin words in the Turkish Morpholex, annotating their roots, morphological patterns, and semantic categories. The methodology developed for this work is adaptable to other languages influenced by Arabic, such as Urdu and Persian, offering broader implications for studying loanword integration across linguistic contexts.

1 Introduction

Morphological lexicons (Arıcan et al., 2022; Sánchez Gutiérrez et al., 2017; Mailhot et al., 2019) play a vital role in understanding the structure of languages, particularly in agglutinative languages like Turkish, where complex words are formed through the combination of multiple morphemes. By analyzing these structures, we can gain insights into how words are constructed. Arıcan et al. (2022) built the first Turkish morphological lexicon that includes an analysis of 48,472 words categorized by their roots, prefixes, and suffixes. As Turkish contains some loanwords from languages such as Arabic and Persian, the analysis of those words needs to follow the grammar of that language. Turkish Morpholex, however, does not process the loanwords accurately.

In this work, we address this problem and analyze the Arabic loanwords to Turkish according to the Arabic grammar. In addition to finding the accurate roots for those words, we analyzed the words across other dimensions as well, such as morphological pattern and semantic categories. We open-source all the annotations done in this work[1].

The methodology used in this study not only deepens our understanding of Turkish Morpholex but also provides a framework that can be applied to other languages with significant Arabic influence, including Urdu and Persian. This highlights the potential for broader applications of this research in multilingual and cross-linguistic studies.

2 Literature Review

The investigation of Arabic roots in the Turkish language, particularly through extensions of the Turkish WordNet, builds on a foundation of research in morphological lexicons and linguistic borrowings. The MorphoLex Turkish project (Arıcan et al., 2022) provides a significant contribution by developing a lexicon for Turkish morphology, inspired by earlier work on morpholexical resources for languages like English (Sánchez Gutiérrez et al., 2017) and French (Mailhot et al., 2019). Studies on Turkish morphological analysis highlight its unique agglutinative structure, which relies heavily on suffixation. However, Turkish has also been profoundly influenced by Arabic due to historical contact, leading to the adoption of numerous loanwords, especially in religious, legal, and administrative contexts.

Existing research in loanwords, such as Serigos (2017)'s work on Anglicisms in Spanish, introduces the concept of semantic specificity. Serigos' study reveals that loanwords often carry more nuanced or specific meanings compared to their native counterparts, a hypothesis that can be extended to Arabic loanwords in Turkish. For example, the Arabic-origin word in Turkish *Adalet* (عدالة in Arabic and

[1]https://github.com/mouneszawal/turkish-lexicon-arabic-roots

Processings of the 1st Workshop on NLP for Languages Using Arabic Script (AbjadNLP), pages 29–36
January 19, 2025. ©2025 Association for Computational Linguistics

Justice in English) has a specific meaning compared to the native Turkish word *Doğruluk*, which is a broader term that can mean correctness, honesty, or truthfulness in general, without necessarily referring to legal justice.

Alshammari and Alshammari (2020) conducted an in-depth analysis of 250 Turkish loanwords of Arabic origin, shedding light on the phonological and morphological adaptations these words undergo during their integration into Turkish. This study highlights the impact of native speaker knowledge on the borrowing process and offers a detailed exploration of phonological modifications, morphological markings, and compound forms in Arabic-origin loanwords.

Stachowskı (2020) investigated phonetic renderings Arabic- and Persian-origin words in Turkish, analyzing 1,748 loanwords to identify both typical and unusual phonetic changes during the borrowing process. The research provides insights into how foreign words adapt to the Turkish phonological system, offering a deeper understanding of linguistic integration mechanisms.

Furthermore, Procházka (2009) investigated Turkish loanwords in Arabic, offering a comparative perspective on the bidirectional nature of linguistic borrowing between Turkish and Arabic. The study sheds light on how Turkish words are adapted into Arabic, enriching the understanding of cross-linguistic influence.

Moreover, Fattakhova and Mingazova (2015) explored how Arabic loanwords have been integrated into Tatar and Swahili. Both languages share similarities in loanword assimilation due to their agglutinative nature but exhibit differences, such as Swahili's postposition of adjectives and Tatar's compound verbs. The study highlights the diverse semantic fields Arabic loanwords cover, such as religion, science, and culture, revealing the historical impact of Arabic in shaping both languages' lexicons.

There are many studies that examine Arabic loanwords in Turkish and other languages, focusing on their linguistic integration, phonological and morphological adaptation (Al-Hashmi, 2016; Perry, 1984; Corriente, 2008; Sayahi, 2005). These studies highlight how Arabic-origin words have been absorbed into recipient languages, often filling semantic gaps and contributing to the linguistic richness of languages like Turkish, Spanish, Tatar, and many others.

Building on these works, this study aims to further explore how Arabic-origin words integrate within the Turkish language by enriching the root-based analysis in the Turkish Morpholex. This work contributes to understanding the semantic and morphological interactions between Arabic and Turkish, as well as the mechanisms by which Arabic loanwords have been absorbed and adapted into the modern Turkish lexicon.

3 Turkish Morpholex

Since Turkish is an agglutinative language, where words are formed by adding suffixes to a base root, Arıcan et al. (2022) emphasizes the importance of analyzing Turkish separately from other languages like English and French, which have different morphological structures. In their work, they develop a Turkish Morpholex, which is morphological lexicon for Turkish that contains 48,472 words, taken from the Turkish KeNet wordnet (Ehsani et al., 2018; Bakay et al., 2021), analyzed based on their roots, prefixes, and suffixes. The creation of this lexicon involved manual annotation, where each word is carefully analyzed for its semantic and morphological structure, unlike the case for the English and French ones where all the analysis was not done manually.

Turkish language originally does not have prefixes. However, prefixes exist and are used currently in Turkish due to the influence of other languages on Turkish such as Arabic, Persian, French, and English. The existence of such loanwords makes the task harder when building morphological lexicons since those would require the analysis of the loaned word according to that language's grammar. Arıcan et al. (2022), for instance, did not analyze the Arabic loanwords in depth and treated them as any other Turkish words. For example, for Arabic-origin word adaletli (fair), they only remove the Turkish suffix (li), which makes the word adalet (justice) an adjective, and consider the word adalet to be the root. Therefore, we analyze in this work those Arabic-origin words in depth to increase the accurateness and depth of the Turkish Morpholex.

4 Arabic Morphology

Arabic is a semitic language, and its morphology is quite different from that of Turkish. While Turkish is an agglutinative language, Arabic uses a root-and-pattern system where words are constructed by formalizing roots into specific patterns.

Arabic words typically derive from triliteral or quadriliteral roots that convey the core meaning. Roots are combined with specific patterns, involving fixed vowels and sometimes additional consonants, to form words in different grammatical categories, such as verbs, nouns, and adjectives. For instance, the root "ك-ت-ب" (k-t-b, "to write") can form words like "كَتَبَ" (kataba, "he wrote") and "كتاب" (kitāb, "book") based on different patterns. This root-and-pattern system allows for a vast number of word forms derived from a single root.

In addition to roots and patterns, Arabic morphology involves the use of prefixes, suffixes, and infixes to modify words grammatically. Prefixes and suffixes indicate tense, voice, plurality, and other grammatical features, while internal vowel changes (infixes) often reflect tense or voice changes in verbs. For example, the verb "كَتَبَ" (kataba, "he wrote") changes to the passive form "كُتِبَ" (kutiba, "it was written"). Understanding these modifications is essential for determining a word's root and meaning.

Arabic words can be categorized into verbs, nouns, adjectives, and particles, with each category following specific morphological rules. Verbs, for example, change according to tense, voice, and mood, while nouns reflect gender, number, and definiteness. Derivation, or Ishtiqaq, is a key feature of Arabic, where multiple related words are derived from a single root. For instance, from the root "ع-ل-م" ('-l-m, "to know"), we get words like "عَلَّمَ" ('allama, "to teach") and "علوم" ('ulum, "sciences").

The process of identifying the root of an Arabic word involves stripping away affixes and recognizing weak letters that may change form or disappear in different word structures. This process is crucial in understanding the word's meaning and forming new words from the same root.

5 Annotation

We initially identified Arabic-origin words found in the Turkish Morpholex by utilizing the official digital dictionary of the Turkish Language Association (TDK)[2], which provides information about the etymological roots of words. We ended up with 4,687 unique words of Arabic-origin according to TDK's classification.

Subsequently, we started the manual annotation and analysis of each word, drawing primarily from the Riyadh Dictionary[3], a contemporary digital resource for the Arabic language. For some instances, we also consulted the Doha Dictionary[4], another Arabic digital lexicon.

The annotation process, however, presented several challenges. A significant portion of these Arabic-origin words entered the Turkish lexicon during periods of Ottoman rule over Arabic-speaking territories. As a result, many of these terms are now considered outdated in modern Arabic. In some cases, words had experienced a complete shift in meaning, while in others, the terms had been entirely abandoned. Due to these changes, it was often difficult to locate the exact words in contemporary Arabic dictionaries. To overcome this, we had to identify Arabic words with similar morphological and semantic characteristics to complete the annotation.

To address semantic shifts, we relied on historical and contemporary Arabic lexicons, such as the Riyadh and Doha dictionaries, to trace the original meanings of words. For example, the Turkish word "adalet" (justice) retains its semantic alignment with the Arabic root "ع-د-ل", while the word "şebabet" (youth) has no direct Arabic equivalent but derives from the Arabic root "ش-ب-ب". Orthographic changes were handled by identifying consistent patterns of adaptation, such as the omission of weak letters or changes in vowel placement, en-

[2]https://sozluk.gov.tr/
[3]https://dictionary.ksaa.gov.sa/
[4]https://www.dohadictionary.org/

suring accurate root identification.

Three primary challenges emerged during the annotation process:

- Obsolete Words: many Arabic-origin words in Turkish are no longer in active use in modern Arabic. For these, we identified semantically similar roots using historical texts.

- Turkish-Neologisms: some Turkish words, like "şebabet," were created using Arabic morphological patterns but have no Arabic counterpart. These were annotated to reflect their hybrid nature.

- Compound Words: words like "alelacele" (hastily), which combine multiple Arabic roots, were annotated with detailed notes on their composition.

During the annotation process, some words classified as Arabic-origin by the TDK were found not to be of Arabic origin upon further investigation. For example, terms such as *Patlıcan* (eggplant) and *Sabun* (soap) were incorrectly categorized as Arabic-origin. These words were excluded from the annotation process, and their misclassification was documented.

The annotations were carried out by the first three authors, all of whom are native Arabic speakers and fluent in Turkish. Their linguistic expertise ensured a deep understanding of both Arabic roots and Turkish adaptations. To maintain consistency, each annotator independently reviewed a subset of the words, and any disagreements were resolved collaboratively during weekly discussions. This collaborative approach ensured that the final annotations were accurate and reflective of both languages' morphological and semantic systems. The annotation task was evenly distributed among the three annotators, resulting in the successful annotation of 3,855 Turkish words from the total of 4,687 identified Arabic-origin words. Due to time constraints, 338 words were left for future analysis. Each annotated word which include its Arabic root (جذر), morphological pattern (وزن - wazn), and semantic category (قسم الكلمة).

To evaluate the accuracy of our annotations, we conducted a pilot study with 100 randomly selected words, achieving 93% agreement between the annotated roots and the consensus reached among the annotators. This process ensured a high degree of reliability in our dataset.

6 Statistics

Arabic Roots	
# Distinct Arabic Roots	1430
# Source Turkish Roots	3855

Table 1: Turkish roots linked to distinct Arabic roots

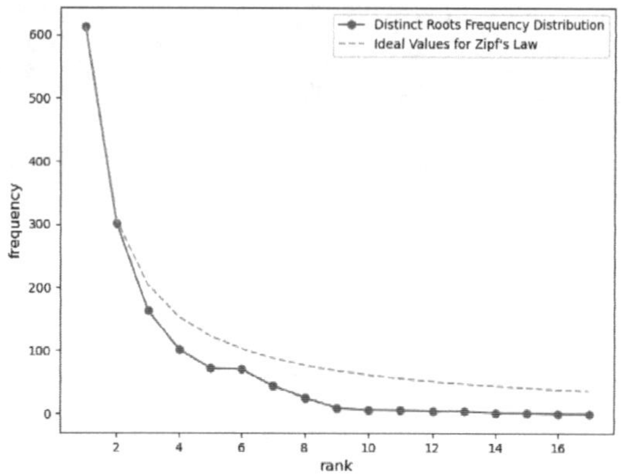

Figure 1: Distribution of the distinct Arabic roots compared to the ideal zipf's law values.

Table 1 provides an overview of the number of distinct Arabic roots and their corresponding Turkish source roots. The table reveals that there are 1,430 distinct Arabic roots, which their frequency distribution quite follows the ideal Zipf's law (Human, 1949) values as shown in Figure 1, associated with 3,855 Turkish roots in total. This suggests a significant lexical borrowing from Arabic, indicating the deep historical and cultural connections between the Arabic and Turkish languages. The fact that 3,855 Turkish words are connected to these 1,430 Arabic roots highlights the Arabic influence on the Turkish vocabulary.

The most common Arabic roots, shown in Table 2, are some specific Arabic roots that have the highest number of Turkish derivatives. For example, the Arabic root قوم is connected to 18 Turkish words, including Takvim (calendar), Kıvam (consistency), and Kayyum

Arabic Root	# Of Words	Meaning	Example Words
قوم	18	Refers to standing, rising, or establishing. It covers meanings such as to stand up, rise, set up, lead, establish, or correct.	takvim, kıvam, kayyum
حكم	16	Tied to judgment, wisdom, or authority. It includes ruling, governing, giving verdicts, and acting with wisdom.	mahkeme, hikmet, hakem
ملك	16	Associated with ownership, control, or kingship, signifying possession, dominion, power, authority, and being a king.	emlak, mülk, melek
حول	15	Focuses on transformation, movement, or change, covering concepts like shifting, transferring, or circling.	tahavvül, mütehavvil, istihale
عرض	15	Deals with presenting, displaying, or exposing. It can also refer to width or breadth and encompasses concepts like honor or reputation.	arz, maruz, taarruz
ولي	14	Focuses on closeness, support, and guardianship, including meanings such as protecting, being close, allying, or acting as a guardian.	vali, vilayet, mütevelli
حقق	13	Relates to achieving or realizing, implying the act of making something true or bringing it into existence.	elhak, hakikat, hakiki
قدر	13	Relates to measuring, determining, or decreeing. It also signifies power, capability, fate, or predestination.	kadar, kadir, kudret
عرف	13	Involves knowledge or recognition, implying knowing, recognizing, or understanding.	muarefe, örf, tarif
جمع	13	Relates to gathering or collecting, implying the act of bringing together or assembling.	cami, camia, cemaat
حلل	13	Encompasses resolving, analyzing, or making something permissible. It can mean to untie, explain, or make lawful.	mahal, mahalle, inhilal

Table 2: Most common Arabic roots along with Turkish example words.

(guardian). Other roots such as ملك (related to ownership or kingship), and عرض (meaning "offer" or "show") each is related to several Turkish word.

We also show the most common semantic categories in Table 3, categorizing the Arabic-rooted words in Turkish by grammatical function with examples of Turkish words for each category. The most frequent category is معني اسم (meaning noun), with 1,789 occurrences, including words like Abes (absurd) derived from the Arabic root عبث (meaning "nonsense" or "absurdity"). Other categories include اسم ذات (concrete noun), and صفة فاعل (Subjective Adjective), صفة مفعول (Objective Adjective), and صفة مشبهة (Comparable Adjective), each illustrating the variety of ways Arabic roots are integrated into Turkish vocabulary. These categories reflect how Arabic words were adapted not only semantically but also grammatically into Turkish, indicating a sophisticated linguistic integration process. Similarly, we show in

Semantic Category	Frequency	Turkish Word	Arabic Root
اسم معنى (Meaning Noun)	1789	Abes, acayip	عجب, عبث
اسم ذات (Concrete Noun)	782	Şafak, acemi	عجم, شفق
صفة فاعل (Subjective Adjective)	460	Muavin, acil	عجل, عون
صفة مفعول (Objective Adjective)	284	Muaf, ceriha	جرح, عفو
صفة نسبية (Comparable Adjective)	145	Zayıf, acuze	عجز, ضعف
صفة مستوية (Attributive Adjective)	144	Acem, adedi	عدد, عجم
صفة مبالغة (Exaggerated Form)	45	Abus, acul	عجل, عبس
اسم مكان (Place Noun)	40	Mahal, mahalle	حلل, حل
اسم مرة (Instance Noun)	20	Gamze, gazve	غزو, غمز
فعل (Verb)	17	Acaba, ahraz	خرس, عجب
اسم آلة (Instrument Noun)	14	Makas, mastara	سطر, قص
اسم مبهم (Ambiguous Noun)	12	Badehu, fevk	فوق, بعد

Table 3: Most common semantic categories with example Turkish words.

Morphological Pattern (wazn)	Frequency	Turkish Word	Arabic Root
تَفْعِيل (Taf'īl)	217	tabir	عبر
فَعْل (Fa'l)	192	af	عفو
فَاعِل (Fā'il)	133	acil	عجل
مَفْعُول (Maf'ūl)	133	mağdur	غدر
إِفْعَال (If'āl)	124	ibraz	برز
تَفَعُّل (Tafa'ul)	115	taaffün	عفن
فَعِيل (Fa'īl)	111	afif	عفف
اِفْتِعَال (Ift'āl)	106	içtihat	جهد

Table 4: Most common morphological patterns with example Turkish words.

Table 4 the most common morphological patterns with example Turkish words.

In summary, these tables demonstrate the profound influence of Arabic on Turkish, showing how many Turkish words have been derived from Arabic roots and illustrating the rich linguistic interchange between the two languages.

7 Discussion

The methodology developed in this study can be adapted for languages like Urdu and Persian, which share similar influences from Arabic. For example, Urdu's reliance on Arabic morphological patterns could benefit from a similar annotation process to enrich its morpholexical resources. By demonstrating the scalability of our approach, this study provides a foundation for analyzing Arabic-origin words across diverse linguistic contexts.

The integration of Arabic-origin words into Turkish reflects a unique interplay between two morphological systems. Words like "adaletli" illustrate how Turkish suffixation adapts Arabic roots while maintaining their core semantic properties. This insight could guide further research on the morphological interactions between agglutinative and Semitic languages.

Additionally, the findings contribute to understanding how Arabic-origin words are morphologically integrated into Turkish grammar. While Arabic employs a root-and-pattern system, Turkish transforms these roots by applying its suffixation processes, adapting them to its agglutinative structure. This study also demonstrates how Turkish retains Arabic morphological patterns (e.g., *Taf'īl*, *Fa'l*) or modifies them to align with its linguistic framework. Semantic adaptations reveal how borrowed words are aligned with Turkish cultural and linguistic contexts, sometimes resulting in hybrid structures like *şebabet*, which have no direct Arabic equivalent.

By documenting these processes, the study highlights the role of Arabic-origin words in enriching Turkish vocabulary across domains like law, administration, and science. Furthermore, the annotated dataset serves as a valuable resource for enhancing computational models of Turkish grammar, enabling more accurate processing of loanwords in natural language processing (NLP) applications. These findings provide a broader understanding of cross-linguistic borrowing and its impact on language evolution.

8 Conclusion

In conclusion, this study highlights the critical role of Arabic-origin words in enriching the Turkish language, addressing a significant gap in the existing Turkish Morpholex. The insights gained extend beyond Turkish, offering a methodology adaptable to languages like Urdu and Persian. By enhancing our understanding of linguistic adaptation, this work contributes to broader cross-linguistic studies of loanword integration and provides a foundation for further research into the historical and cultural interplay between languages. By meticulously analyzing 4,687 Arabic loanwords, we have identified 1,430 distinct Arabic roots linked to 3,855 Turkish words, demonstrating the deep historical and cultural interconnections between these two languages. Our research not only annotates the roots and morphological patterns of these Arabic words but also categorizes them semantically, revealing a complex landscape of linguistic integration.

By enhancing the Turkish Morpholex with accurate analyses of Arabic-origin words, we hope to facilitate a deeper understanding of the intricate dynamics of language contact and evolution. The implications of this research extend beyond Turkish, as it provides insights into the broader processes of language adaptation and the significance of historical interactions in shaping modern lexicons. Future studies could build upon these findings to enhance language models for the Turkish language, leveraging the enriched dataset for more accurate morphological and semantic analysis. Expanding the annotation process to other languages influenced by Arabic, such as Urdu and Persian, will validate the scalability of our methodology and contribute to comparative linguistic studies. Furthermore, integrating this dataset into universal morpholexical resources, such as multilingual WordNets, will broaden its applicability and utility for NLP tasks in multilingual and cross-linguistic contexts.

References

Shadiya Al-Hashmi. 2016. *The Phonetics and Phonology of Arabic Loanwords in Turkish: residual effects of gutturals*. Ph.D. thesis, University of York.

Wafi Alshammari and Ahmad Alshammari. 2020. Adaptation of turkish loanwords originating from arabic. *International Journal of English Linguistics*, 10:388.

Bilge Nas Arıcan, Aslı Kuzgun, Büsra Marsan, Deniz Baran Aslan, Ezgi Sanıyar, Neslihan Cesur, Neslihan Kara, Oguzhan Kuyrukçu, Merve Ozçelik, Arife Betül Yenice, et al. 2022. Morpholex turkish: A morphological lexicon for turkish. In *LREC 2022 Workshop Language Resources and Evaluation Conference 20-25 June 2022*, page 68.

Özge Bakay, Özlem Ergelen, Elif Sarmış, Selin Yıldırım, Bilge Nas Arıcan, Atilla Kocabalcıoğlu, Merve Özçelik, Ezgi Sanıyar, Oğuzhan Kuyrukçu, Begüm Avar, et al. 2021. Turkish wordnet kenet. In *Proceedings of the 11th global wordnet conference*, pages 166–174.

Federico Corriente. 2008. *Dictionary of Arabic and allied loanwords: Spanish, Portuguese, Catalan, Galician and kindred dialects*, volume 1. Brill.

Razieh Ehsani, Ercan Solak, and Olcay Taner Yildiz. 2018. Constructing a wordnet for turkish using manual and automatic annotation. *ACM Transactions on Asian and Low-Resource Language Information Processing (TALLIP)*, 17(3):1–15.

Aida R Fattakhova and Nailya G Mingazova. 2015. Arabic loanwords in tatar and swahili: Morphological assimilation. *Journal of Sustainable Development*, 8(4):302.

ZG Human. 1949. Human behaviour and the principle of least effort.

Hugo Mailhot, Maximiliano Wilson, Joël Macoir, Hélène Deacon, and Claudia Sánchez Gutiérrez. 2019. Morpholex-fr: A derivational morphological database for 38,840 french words. *Behavior Research Methods*, 52.

John R Perry. 1984. -at and-a: Arabic loanwords with the feminine ending in turkish. *Turkish Studies Association Bulletin*, 8(2):16–25.

Stephan Procházka. 2009. Turkish loanwords. *Kees. Versteegh et al.(eds.). Encyclopedia of Arabic Language and Linguistics*, 4:489–594.

Lotfi Sayahi. 2005. Phonological adaptation of spanish loanwords in northern moroccan arabic.

Jacqueline Serigos. 2017. Using distributional semantics in loanword research: A concept-based approach to quantifying semantic specificity of anglicisms in spanish. *International Journal of Bilingualism*, 21(5):521–540.

Kamil Stachowskı. 2020. Phonetic renderings in turkish arabisms and farsisms. *Türkbilig*, 20(40):23–47.

Claudia Sánchez Gutiérrez, Hugo Mailhot, Hélène Deacon, and Maximiliano Wilson. 2017. Morpholex: A derivational morphological database for 70,000 english words. *Behavior Research Methods*, http://link.springer.com/article/10.3758/s13428-017-0981-8:1–13.

DadmaTools V2: an Adapter-Based Natural Language Processing Toolkit for the Persian Language

Sadegh Jafari[1], Farhan Farsi[2], Navid Ebrahimi[1], Mohamad Bagher Sajadi[3], Sauleh Eetemadi[4]

[1]Iran University of Science and Technology, [2]Amirkabir University of Technology - Tehran Polytechnic, [3]Islamic Azad University Tehran Central Branch, [4]University of Birmingham

sadegh_jafari@comp.iust.ac.ir, farhan1379@aut.ac.ir, n_ebrahimi@comp.iust.ac.ir, sajadi@dadmatech.ir, s.eetemadi@bham.ac.uk

Abstract

DadmaTools V2 is a comprehensive repository designed to enhance NLP capabilities for the Persian language, catering to industry practitioners seeking practical and efficient solutions. The toolkit provides extensive code examples demonstrating the integration of its models with popular NLP frameworks such as Trankit [1] and Transformers, as well as deep learning frameworks like PyTorch. Additionally, DadmaTools supports widely used Persian embeddings and datasets, ensuring robust language processing capabilities. The latest version of DadmaTools introduces an adapter-based technique, significantly reducing memory usage by employing a shared pre-trained model across various tasks, supplemented with task-specific adapter layers. This approach eliminates the need for maintaining multiple pre-trained models, optimizing resource utilization. Enhancements in this version include adding new modules such as a sentiment detector, an informal-to-formal text converter, and a spell checker, further expanding the toolkit's functionality. DadmaTools V2 thus represents a powerful, efficient, and versatile resource for advancing Persian NLP applications.

1 Introduction

The availability of NLP tools for low-resource languages is crucial for the advancement of more complex NLP applications within those languages. These tools provide foundational capabilities that facilitate the development of higher-level language processing tasks. Despite the importance, existing NLP toolkits which are supporting Persian language, such as Hazm [2], Stanza(Qi et al., 2020), and Parsivar (Mohtaj et al., 2018) [3], offer only basic functionalities like tokenization, lemmatization, stemming, POS tagging, and dependency parsing. However, they lack advanced generative tools that can further enhance language processing capabilities. DadmaTools V2 aims to address these gaps by introducing several rare and specialized modules for Persian NLP. Notably, it includes a Kasre-ezafe detection module, an informal-to-formal text converter, and a spell checker, and also includes famous modules like NER, and sentiment detector, features not present in other Persian NLP toolkits. These additions make DadmaTools V2 a more comprehensive and versatile toolkit, catering to a wider range of NLP applications.

Furthermore, one of the significant challenges in developing countries like Iran is the limited access to suitable hardware, such as GPUs. Running multiple NLP tools, each requiring a separate pre-trained model, can demand substantial GPU and RAM resources. This issue is exacerbated when text embeddings are calculated multiple times within a single processing pipeline, leading to inefficiencies in both memory usage and processing speed. To overcome these challenges, DadmaTools V2 employs an adapter-based approach. This technique allows for the use of a shared pre-trained model across various tasks, with task-specific adapter layers added as needed. This method significantly reduces memory consumption and enhances the speed of the processing pipeline, making it more feasible to run advanced NLP tasks on limited hardware resources.

In summary, DadmaTools V2 not only fills the gaps left by existing Persian NLP toolkits by offering unique and advanced modules but also introduces an efficient, memory-saving approach that is particularly beneficial in resource-constrained environments. This makes it a valuable resource for both researchers and practitioners working with the Persian language.

[1]https://github.com/nlp-uoregon/trankit
[2]https://github.com/roshan-research/hazm
[3]https://github.com/ICTRC/Parsivar

Processings of the 1st Workshop on NLP for Languages Using Arabic Script (AbjadNLP), pages 37–43
January 19, 2025.

2 System Usage

Explore the detailed user guide for DadmaTools at: https://github.com/Dadmatech/DadmaTools.

Installation: This Python NLP toolkit can be found on PyPI:

https://pypi.org/project/dadmatools/. it can be installed via pip by using:

```
PIP install dadmatools
```

Initialize a Pipeline. DadmaTools is hardware-agnostic, functioning efficiently on both GPUs and CPUs (default: GPU). Users can leverage custom processors by specifying their names as arguments to the `language.Pipeline` function. This generates a `Doc` instance encapsulating all processed text properties. The default pipeline includes a tokenizer, while dependency parser and POS tagger are loaded together due to the underlying Trankit toolkit (Van Nguyen et al., 2021) dependency.

Preferred pre-trained models are automatically downloaded from the DadmaTech Hugging Face Hub.

```
import dadmatools.pipeline.language as language

# here Dependency parser and pos tagger will be
    loaded togetter
# as tokenizer is the default tool, it will be
    loaded as well even without calling
pips = 'lem,pos,ner,dep,cons,spellchecker,
    kasreh,sent,itf'
nlp = language.Pipeline(pips)
```

3 System Design

DadmaTools V2 is the next generation of the DadmaTools NLP pipeline, offering significant advancements in efficiency and functionality. Building upon the foundation of its predecessor, DadmaTools V1 (Etezadi et al., 2022), it incorporates the adapter technique to achieve substantial improvements in processing speed and memory usage. This technique modifies only two layers of a pre-trained model, keeping the rest static, resulting in a faster and more lightweight pipeline ideal for real-world applications.

Based on Figure 1, while DadmaTools V2 leverages the Trankit toolkit for its adapter implementation, it extends beyond Trankit's capabilities. The Trankit toolkit, a lightweight Transformer-based toolkit supporting over 50 languages, enables fine-tuning pre-trained models on specific datasets for various basic NLP tasks. However, DadmaTools V2 encompasses additional functionalities tailored for specialized tasks that fall outside Trankit's limitations. These specialized tasks require tailored approaches within the DadmaTools framework, providing a more comprehensive solution for a wider range of NLP needs.

3.1 Adapter Based Modules

In the adapter modules, we used the XLM-RoBERTa-base (Conneau et al., 2019) as the pre-trained model and trained different tasks as adapter layers on top of the pre-trained model. Additionally, in each epoch, we saved the best model and ran the training process until overfitting occurred.

- **Lemmatization.** We use the Seraji dataset (Seraji et al., 2016) to train lemmatization in the Persian Trankit tools.
- **Part of Speech Tagging.** We use UPOS [4] to evaluate our part-of-speech tagging module, and we also train it using the Seraji dataset.
- **Dependency Parsing.** We used the Seraji dataset to train dependency parsing and evaluated it using the LAS [5] and UAS [6] metrics.
- **Name Entity Recognition.** The Named Entity Recognition (NER) task can be considered a type of token classification task. The goal is to assign a corresponding label to each token in a text. To address this challenge, we employed the Trankit module, which consists of a feedforward layer followed by a Conditional Random Field (CRF). This model assigns BIO (Beginning, Inside, Outside) tags to each token. We trained an adapter layer on the Arman(Poostchi et al., 2018) and Peyma(Shahshahani et al., 2018) datasets for 6 epochs using Trankit.
- **Kasreh-Ezafeh Detecting.** kasreh-ezafe is a specific task in the Persian language, in Persian language it connects two words, Ezafe is one of the salient factors in Persian phonology and morphology to understand the meaning of a sentence completely and truly, and on the other hand, detecting kasreh-ezafe is a crucial roll in text to speech task(Ansari et al., 2023). This task like the NER task is a kind of token classification task, so simply we used the the base that the Trankit tool

[4]Universal part of speech

[5]Labeled attachment score

[6]Unlabeled attachment score

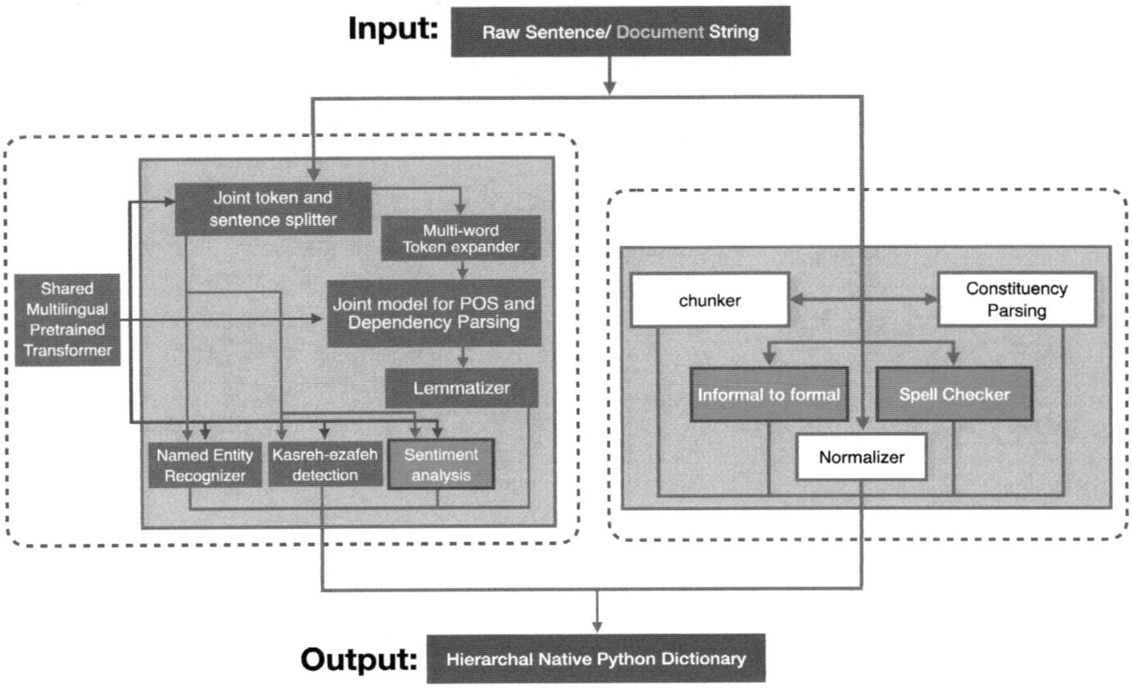

Figure 1: Overall architecture of the Dadmatools toolkit. White components are unchanged from the previous version, blue components are new, and green components have been modified.

provided for the NER task. To address this issue, we train the Trankit model for the token classification task for 8 epochs on the Bijan Khan dataset(Bijankhan et al., 2011). If someone wants to know more about Kasreh-ezafe, please refer to this website [7].

- **Sentiment Analysis** The sentiment analyzer module is responsible for detecting sentiments in text, particularly for social media analysis purposes. To implement this module, we edited the Trankit codes and added a document classifier that uses the CLS token as a feature for the sentiment task. The output of this task is either "Sad" or "Happy." This task was trained using the Snappfood sentiment dataset [8] for 80 epochs.

3.2 Additional Modules

Some of our modules are not in the adapter pipeline, and we plan to add them in future work. These modules require something like an n-gram model and some rule-based algorithms. We will try to replace them with transformer-based modules.

- **Informal To Formal.** Informal2Formal technology leverages NLP techniques to convert text from an informal tone to a formal one, making it particularly useful in professional or academic settings. This technology transforms colloquialisms, contractions, and first-person pronouns into more formal language. The algorithm of the Informal2Formal module is shown in Algorithm 1. It comprises several key classes and functions:

  - **FormalityTransformer.** The primary class converts informal Persian text to formal text using a language model, verb handling, and tokenization. It is based on the KenLM toolkit [9] for building and querying n-gram language models.
  - **Kelm_Wrapper.** A wrapper around the KenLM language model(Heafield, 2011) that provides methods to obtain the best candidate words and n-gram phrases based on the model's scores.
  - **InformalTokenizer.** Responsible for tokenizing the informal text.

[7] https://learnpersian.us/en/Ezafe-in-Persian
[8] https://hooshvare.github.io/docs/datasets/sa#snappfood
[9] https://github.com/kpu/kenlm

- **VerbHandler.** Manages verb transformations within the text.
- **OneShotTransformer.** Applies a set of predefined prefix and postfix rules to transform the text from informal to formal. The rules are defined in the Prefix and Postfix classes, specifying the word to be transformed, the level of transformation, and other properties such as connecting characters and ignored parts of speech.

Algorithm 1 Informal To Formal

```
Require: model, sentence
Ensure: best_sequence
out_dict ← ∅
txt ← Clean the input sentence
is_valid ← Define validation function for tokens
cnd_tokens ← Tokenize the cleaned text
for tokens ∈ cnd_tokens do
    tokens ← Remove empty tokens
    new_tokens ← Split tokens into sub-tokens
    txt ← Join sub-tokens into a single string
    tokens ← Split the string into individual tokens
    candidates ← []
    for index ∈ range(len(tokens)) do
        tok ← tokens[index]
        cnd ← ∅
        pos ← Determine if the token is a verb
        f_words_lemma ← Transform the token based on POS
        f_words_lemma ← Apply filtering rules to transformed words
        for index, (word, lemma) ∈ enumerate(f_words_lemma) do
            should_filter ← original_word ∈ model.vocab and (len(word.split()) > 1 or '' ∈ word)
            if pos ≠ 'VERB' and tok ∉ model.mapper and should_filter then
                f_words_lemma[index] ← (tok, tok)
            else
                word_repr ← Format the word representation
                word_repr ← Modify the word representation using GPT-2 specific rules
                f_words_lemma[index] ← (word, word_repr)
            end if
        end for
        if f_words_lemma then
            cnd.update(f_words_lemma)
        else
            cnd ← {(tok, tok)}
        end if
        candidates.append(cnd)
    end for
    all_combinations ← Generate all combinations of candidate tokens
    all_combinations_list ← Convert combinations to a list
    for id, cnd ∈ enumerate(all_combinations_list) do
        normal_seq ← Join tokens in the combination to form a sequence
        lemma_seq ← Join lemmas in the combination to form a sequence
        lemma_seq ← Clean the sequence for the language model
        out_dict[id] ← (normal_seq, lemma_seq)
    end for
    candidates ← Extract candidate sequences for language model scoring
    best_sequence ← Select the best sequence using the language model
    return best_sequence
end for
```

- **Spell Checker.** Spell checking typically involves two stages. First, the model identifies errors within the text, such as typos, misspellings, and merged words. Second, it corrects these identified mistakes. Recent models address both stages jointly. Our proposed spell checker module, a key component of our NLP toolkit, addresses this issue. Inspired by recent research(Jayanthi et al., 2020), the spell-checking problem was modeled as a token classification task, leveraging powerful transformer-based models such as BERT and RoBERTa.In our approach, the final dense layer of each token has a dimension of $d \times (n + 1)$ instead of $d \times n$. Here, d represents the vector dimension of the final layer of the transformer-based model, and n is the number of words in the dictionary. The $n + 1$ term accounts for the possibility that a word might not need to be changed. If a word is incorrect, it is assigned to one of the n valid tokens in the dictionary.

4 Evaluation

We have evaluated 9 components. Since the tasks are naturally different from each other, we categorized them into three subcategories:

1. Basic NLP tasks using the Adapter architecture (7 modules),
2. Spell-checker,
3. Informal to formal.

However, we could not evaluate the normalizer and chunker modules because no specific Persian datasets are available for these tasks.

4.1 NLP basic tasks

This section compares our basic and common tasks, such as lemmatization, POS tagging, NER, Kasreh-ezafeh, dependency parsing (UAS and LAS metrics), and sentiment analysis, with those found in other well-known Persian toolkits. The results are shown in Table 1.

One of the key advantages of Dadmatools V2 over V1 is its compact size, made possible by the adapter technique, which reduces the model size by three times. While Dadmatools V2 excels in some tasks and V1 in others, the significantly smaller size of V2 is an important consideration. We compared the toolkits based on their performance and the number of parameters to provide a comprehensive evaluation.

4.2 Spell checker

We evaluated our spellchecker modules against other spell-checking models because there is currently no comprehensive toolkit available in Persian capable of spell-checking. Table 2 shows the results of the spellchecker evaluation that tests using

Toolkit	Model Size(GB)	Lemma	POS	NER	Kasreh-ezafeh	UAS	LAS	Sentiment Analysis	Constituency Parser
Dadmatools V2	**1.24**	**97.95**	97.35	95.3	97.29	91.38	88.68	87.12	**82.88**
Dadmatools V1	3.92	97.86	**97.83**	-	-	**92.5**	**89.23**	-	-
Stanza	-	91.35	97.69	-	-	90.98	87.96	-	80.28
Hazm	-	89.9	-	-	-	-	-	-	-

Table 1: Performance Evaluation of NLP Tools: NER (Arman, Peyma), Kasreh-ezafeh Detection (Bijan Khan), Sentiment Analysis (Snappfood), Lemmatization/POS Tagging/Dependency Parsing (Seraji), and Constituency Parsing.

Model	WDR	WCR	CWR	Precision
Dadmatools V2	0.7647	**0.6824**	**0.0019**	**0.9774**
Paknevis	**0.7843**	0.6706	0.228	0.7921
Google	0.7392	0.702	0.0045	0.0449
Virastman(Oji et al.)	0.6	0.5	0.0032	0.9533

Table 2: Performance of Spell Checking Models on the Nevise Dataset.

Nevise dataset [10]. The models are assessed using four key metrics: Wrong Detection Rate (WDR), Wrong Correction Rate (WCR), Correct to Wrong Rate (CWR), and Precision, which are explained below:

- **Wrong Detection Rate(WDR).** Measures the model's tendency to flag correctly spelled words as errors. A lower WDR indicates fewer false positives.

- **Wrong Correction Rate(WCR).** Measures the model's accuracy in suggesting corrections. A lower WCR indicates the model proposes fewer incorrect suggestions.

- **Correct to Wrong Rate(CWR).** Measures the model's tendency to incorrectly change correct words. Ideally, CWR should be minimal, reflecting the ability to avoid unnecessary modifications.

- **Precision.** Measures the proportion of true errors the model correctly identifies. A higher precision indicates the model is more accurate in pinpointing actual spelling mistakes.

Model	TeleCrowd Corpus	Tajalli et al. (2023) Corpus
Dadmatools V2	**0.711**	0.664
Adibian and Momtazi (2022) model	0.707	-
TeleCrowd	0.54	-

Table 3: Comparison of BLEU-1 scores for Informal-to-Formal translation across different models and corpora. The table displays BLEU-1 scores obtained using the TeleCrowd corpus and the corpus from Tajalli et al. (2023), highlighting the performance of different models in each dataset.

4.3 Informal to formal

The informal-to-formal task is challenging in Persian, and few models and datasets are available for it. In this section, we compare our method, particularly with the TeleCrowd (Masoumi et al., 2020) paper, which provides both a dataset and a model. We have the best model for this dataset. Additionally, we ran our code on the newest dataset published in Persian, developed by (Tajalli et al.,

[10] https://github.com/Dadmatech/Nevise-Dataset

2023).

5 Conclusion and Future Work

DadmaTools V2 builds upon the foundation of V1, leveraging adapter modules to achieve significant efficiency and processing speed improvements. Additionally, it introduces new advanced tasks. DadmaTools V2 uses XLM-RoBERTa as its pre-trained model, enabling support for multiple languages. Furthermore, our base model is built on Trankit's structure, which supports 56 languages. This robust foundation enhances the toolkit's multilingual capabilities and adaptability.

The adapter-based approach in DadmaTools V2 can indeed be adapted to other languages written in the Perso-Arabic script, such as Urdu or Sindhi. To achieve this, modifications would involve fine-tuning the adapter modules on datasets specific to the target language, ensuring alignment with its unique linguistic and scriptural nuances. Additional efforts would be required to incorporate the linguistic rules and orthographic variations of these languages, as well as expanding the lexicon and pre-training models to support these adaptations effectively. This cross-lingual expansion would not only enhance the toolkit's versatility but also contribute to broader accessibility and research collaboration across languages using the Perso-Arabic script.

Our future work focuses on expanding the toolkit's NLP capabilities with tasks like text summarization, emotion detection, and semantic similarity analysis. This empowers users with deeper text understanding and exploration. Computer vision functionalities like image captioning and OCR, along with Text-to-Speech (TTS) and Automatic Speech Recognition (ASR), are planned. Moreover, user empowerment remains central: allowing custom models trained on user-provided data will foster collaborative research in Persian language processing.

References

Majid Adibian and Saeedeh Momtazi. 2022. Using transformer-based neural models for converting informal to formal text in persian. *Language and Linguistics*, 18(35):47–69.

Ali Ansari, Zahra Ebrahimian, Ramin Toosi, and Mohammad Ali Akhaee. 2023. Persian ezafeh recognition using transformer-based models. In *2023 9th International Conference on Web Research (ICWR)*, pages 283–288. IEEE.

Mahmood Bijankhan, Javad Sheykhzadegan, Mohammad Bahrani, and Masood Ghayoomi. 2011. Lessons from building a persian written corpus: Peykare. *Language resources and evaluation*, 45:143–164.

Alexis Conneau, Kartikay Khandelwal, Naman Goyal, Vishrav Chaudhary, Guillaume Wenzek, Francisco Guzmán, Edouard Grave, Myle Ott, Luke Zettlemoyer, and Veselin Stoyanov. 2019. Unsupervised cross-lingual representation learning at scale. *CoRR*, abs/1911.02116.

Romina Etezadi, Mohammad Karrabi, Najmeh Zare, Mohamad Bagher Sajadi, and Mohammad Taher Pilehvar. 2022. Dadmatools: Natural language processing toolkit for persian language. In *Proceedings of the 2022 Conference of the North American Chapter of the Association for Computational Linguistics: Human Language Technologies: System Demonstrations*, pages 124–130.

Kenneth Heafield. 2011. KenLM: Faster and smaller language model queries. In *Proceedings of the Sixth Workshop on Statistical Machine Translation*, pages 187–197, Edinburgh, Scotland. Association for Computational Linguistics.

Sai Muralidhar Jayanthi, Danish Pruthi, and Graham Neubig. 2020. NeuSpell: A neural spelling correction toolkit. In *Proceedings of the 2020 Conference on Empirical Methods in Natural Language Processing: System Demonstrations*, pages 158–164, Online. Association for Computational Linguistics.

Vahid Masoumi, Mostafa Salehi, Hadi Veisi, Golnoush Haddadian, Vahid Ranjbar, and Mahsa Sahebdel. 2020. Telecrowd: A crowdsourcing approach to create informal to formal text corpora. *arXiv preprint arXiv:2004.11771*.

Salar Mohtaj, Behnam Roshanfekr, Atefeh Zafarian, and Habibollah Asghari. 2018. Parsivar: A language processing toolkit for persian. In *Proceedings of the eleventh international conference on language resources and evaluation (lrec 2018)*.

Romina Oji, Mohammad Javad Dousti, and Heshaam Faili. Using a pre-trained language model for context-aware error detection and correction in persian language.

Hanieh Poostchi, Ehsan Zare Borzeshi, and Massimo Piccardi. 2018. Bilstm-crf for persian named-entity recognition armanpersonercorpus: the first entity-annotated persian dataset. In *Proceedings of the Eleventh International Conference on Language Resources and Evaluation (LREC 2018)*.

Peng Qi, Yuhao Zhang, Yuhui Zhang, Jason Bolton, and Christopher D Manning. 2020. Stanza: A python natural language processing toolkit for many human languages. *arXiv preprint arXiv:2003.07082*.

Mojgan Seraji, Filip Ginter, and Joakim Nivre. 2016. Universal Dependencies for Persian. In *Proceedings of the Tenth International Conference on Language Resources and Evaluation (LREC'16)*, pages 2361–2365, Portorož, Slovenia. European Language Resources Association (ELRA).

Mahsa Sadat Shahshahani, Mahdi Mohseni, Azadeh Shakery, and Heshaam Faili. 2018. Peyma: A tagged corpus for persian named entities. *arXiv preprint arXiv:1801.09936*.

Vahide Tajalli, Fateme Kalantari, and Mehrnoush Shamsfard. 2023. Developing an informal-formal persian corpus. *arXiv preprint arXiv:2308.05336*.

Minh Van Nguyen, Viet Dac Lai, Amir Pouran Ben Veyseh, and Thien Huu Nguyen. 2021. Trankit: A light-weight transformer-based toolkit for multilingual natural language processing. *arXiv preprint arXiv:2101.03289*.

Developing an Informal-Formal Persian Corpus: Highlighting the Differences between Two Writing Styles

Vahide Tajalli[1], Mehrnoush Shamsfard, Fateme Kalantari

NLP lab, Shahid Beheshti University, Tehran, Iran

Abstract

Informal language is a style of spoken or written language frequently used in casual conversations, social media, weblogs, emails and text messages. In informal writing, the language undergoes some lexical and/or syntactic changes varying among different languages. Persian is one of the languages with many differences between its formal and informal styles of writing, thus developing informal language processing tools for this language seems necessary. In the present paper, the methodology in building ParsMap, a parallel corpus of 50,000 sentence pairs with alignments in the word/phrase level is described. The resulting corpus has about 530,000 alignments and a dictionary containing 49,397 word and phrase pairs. The observed differences between formal and informal writing are explained in detail.

Keywords: Colloquial Language, Corpus, Informal Writing, Persian.

1. Introduction

Informal language is more common when we speak. However, there are times when writing can be very informal, for instance, in weblog posts, social media comments, and text messages. Informal writing is in fact a reflection of linguistic features of colloquial speech in our written materials.

Informal Persian is different from its formal form both lexically and syntactically. It is not a sociolect, i.e. everybody from every social level uses it in the casual situations. A large amount of colloquial Persian data is created every day in the cyberspace and the media, thus developing informal language processing tools for this language seems necessary. Forming a Persian informal-formal parallel corpus will enable computer engineers and computational linguists to develop tools for converting these two styles automatically or process texts in both styles with a strong performance.

2. Related Work

There are several studies on Persian informal language. Most of them have tried to suggest a uniform orthography for informal language. Tabibzadeh (2020), among all, reviews 112 Persian novels and dramas written over 100 years. He chooses 1697 informal words randomly out of these works and based on them, he categorizes and explains the features of informal Persian. Since all his data comes from the books, they have partly approved forms by the authors and editors. However, the situation is different in the virtual space where the people break the linguistic norms and try to show their feelings through the words by creating new forms.

Moreover, there are some researches on converting Persian colloquial texts into formal ones. Armin and Shamsfard (2011) and Naemi et al. (2021) propose rule-based systems which only cover a small part of the data. In addition, they just handle the lexical changes and syntactic ones are left.

Rasooli et al. (2020) suggest an automatic method for standardizing colloquial Persian text. Their core idea is training a sequence-to-sequence translation model translating colloquial Persian to standard Persian. They have annotated a publicly available evaluation data consisting of 1912 sentences.

Abdi Khojasteh et al. (2020) propose a dataset for Large-Scale Colloquial Persian (LSCP) containing about 120M sentences from twitter for machine translation with universal and treebank-specific POS tags with dependency relations and translations in five languages. In order to annotate the datasets, they adopt a semiautomatic crowd-sourcing method.

Kabiri et al. (2022) develop an Informal Persian Universal Dependency Treebank (iPerUDT) with a total of 3000 sentences from Persian blogs and mention a few differences between formal and informal Persian.

1 - vtajalli@ut.ac.ir

Processings of the 1st Workshop on NLP for Languages Using Arabic Script (AbjadNLP), pages 44–53
January 19, 2025.

Although LSCP and iPerUDT can be used to study the colloquial Persian in lexical and syntax levels, they are not parallel corpora and have no formal counterparts for informal data, therefore they cannot be directly used for inter-style conversions.

As is noticeable, the available resources and tools are insufficient for covering all aspects of this issue either due to applying rule-based methods and having limited rules or due to using data-driven methods with limited or incomplete data. Therefore, a converter with a big dataset which can transform informal into formal language in both lexical and syntactic levels is needed to fill this gap. This article is a report of an attempt to build this dataset. Moreover, the differences between formal and informal Persian writing styles will be reported in details. We are not going to propose a standard orthography for informal Persian, however, studying these differences and making parallel corpus of these two language styles help linguists with developing uniform and regulated grammar and orthography for informal Persian.

The article is organized as follows: the next section briefly introduces Persian language and its informal style. Section 3 explains the procedure of building this informal dataset. Section 4 explains the differences between formal and informal Persian. Section 5 represents the results and in the end, section 6 concludes the paper with pointing out the conclusions and further works.

3. Informal vs. Formal Persian

Persian is a pro-drop language with canonical SOV word order which is written in Arabic script with some small adjustments. In this script some letters are written connected to their adjacent ones and short vowels do not normally appear in writing. Persian informal language is different from formal in many ways. In order to build a comprehensive corpus covering syntactic and lexical dimensions, we need to know the characteristics of Persian informal language and its writing style.

Informal writing style has some general characteristics including making use of interjections, more idiomatic and conversational expressions, contractions, and imprecise words. Moreover, sentences are shorter since appositive phrases and complicated structures are not normally used in the informal language, whereas both fragments and run-on sentences are acceptable. People break some rules of standard writing style and devise different writing methods to be able to convey the tone along with the meaning as far as possible.

Apart from the fact that informal Persian is associated with particular choices of grammar and vocabulary, there are many formal words and expressions changing in informal language. Persian informal writing style is often called *shekœste-nevisi* literally translated as "broken-writing", indicating that some formal words are cut down in informal Persian. In some others the pronunciation of a letter changes. In the present study, typical informal language used by Iranians has been considered and its informal writing style has been investigated in detail to develop the dataset.

4. Developing the Dataset

In this section we discuss our methodology in extracting candidate sentences, choosing appropriate ones, transforming them into formal sentences and making the alignments.

4.1 Extracting Informal Sentences from Available Resources

Sentences could be either selected from external sources or generated by the data linguists. In order for the linguistics teams to have access to a great variety of sources, they were provided with texts derived from online crawling of social networks, websites and blogs as well as some scripts of books, screenplays and movie subtitles. Before distributing the sources among team members, fonts were standardized and texts were normalized as far as possible.

There were other sources including different messengers and everyday conversations that could be considered by the linguistics teams. Since the study aimed to cover all styles of writing, we attempted to use every sources reasonably, depending on the level of usage. Table 1 shows the distribution of external sources and the number of informal sentences extracted from each one.

source of data	# of extracted sentences
instagram	9,625
twitter	7,000
web pages	293,426
weblogs	26,146
books	124,130
movies	179,290
total	**639,617**

Table 1. Sources of informal sentences and their distributions

In order to extract data, pages were crawled and sentences with the length of 26-40 tokens (space separated) including at least 4 informal words were selected. As a result, about 640,000 informal sentences were provided to the linguistics teams for searching the proper data. Finally, 50,000 sentences were selected or generated and entered into the dataset. More than 50% of them were reviewed and corrected or confirmed by two linguist leaders.

4.2 Software Tool for Data Gathering and Preparation

Aiming to create the dataset, a software tool was developed letting the users enter data records. Each record included an informal sentence, its formal equivalent and their alignments in word and phrase levels. For each record, time and date of data entry, the data provider and the source of the informal sentence were saved and were searchable.

In order to speed up the development process, the system employed some automatic methods for suggesting the alignments using the previous found alignments, according to their frequency of occurrence and the context of the aligned word. The annotators checked the system's alignment suggestion to accept or correct it.

The tool managed data entry, data revision and confirmation, report generation, accounting, upload and download of raw and annotated corpus and some automatic data processing tasks for data verification and generation. For example, normalizing input sentences, checking for missing or inconsistent alignments and suggesting alignments were among automatic data processing tasks of the developed software. Fig. 1 shows a screenshot of data entry in this tool.

Figure 1. An entry of dataset in the data gathering software

The data is available at:

https://drive.google.com/drive/folders/1dgcDO1y0VUSemq1jJbcxTu72D2KNckEy?usp=sharing

4.3 Data Entry

Exploring the resources and spotting the linguistic points, we began to highlight the features of Persian informal language. 50,000 pairs of formal-informal sentences with specified alignments were supposed to be entered into the dataset. In order to decide the formal alignment, minimum changes were made and paraphrasing was not applied. Slang words and phrases were not replaced. There were a few expressions and utterances with no near formal equivalents; for these cases a negotiated equivalent was chosen. Formal sentences were entered with correct punctuations.

The style of writings seemed mostly to be affected by age, education level, and social group membership of language users. We attempted to cover all the levels as far as possible. As previously mentioned, many Persian words including the largest number of verbs have an abridged informal form. They were all replaced by formal word forms.

Rare mistakes like uncommon spelling mistakes in informal sentences were edited before entering but common mistakes were kept and edited in the formal equivalents. Some common spelling mistakes are the result of having more than one character for a sound in the Persian alphabet. The frequent ones were included. In addition, some characteristics of informal language including vowel lengthening which is converted to vowel repetition in writing for showing emphasis, surprise and other feelings were kept in informal sentences and edited in formal ones. As a matter of fact, it can be a shortcoming since we did not convey the feelings to the formal equivalents.

The last point is that Persian has two personal pronouns for singular address. It employs the second-person plural *shoma* instead of the singular *to* as a sign of respect. A significant feature of colloquial Persian is a hybrid usage of the overt deferential second person pronoun and informal agreement forming a mismatch construction. It shows actually a different level of politeness (Nanbakhsh, 2011:1). In other words, plural pronoun with singular verb is used when the person being addressed is neither very intimate nor totally distant. A version of third person plural (*ishun*) can be used in the same way. We kept this feature and did not change it in formal equivalents.

In the next section we are going to review the features of informal Persian and find out how users change the formal Persian in the informal writing. We are describing what we have seen in the data and explaining how we found the similar cases to develop a comprehensive corpus as far as possible.

5. Differences between Formal and Informal Persian Writing

The level of informality varied among selected sentences. Some sentences only showed lexical changes. In example 1 every word of the sentence has different form in the formal equivalent.

(1) Informal: ye hendune værdar!
a watermelon take
Formal: yek hendævane bærdar!
a watermelon take
(Take a watermelon!)

Some others underwent syntactic changes. Sentence 2 shows an example of word order change and preposition omission.

(2) Inf: diruz bærgæsht- Ø inja.
yesterday came back-3rd sg here
F: diruz be inja bærgæsht- Ø.
yesterday to here came back-3rd sg
(S/He came back here yesterday.)

Several other sentences had both kinds of changes. Many random differences including different kinds of abbreviations were only possible to be found by reading texts and other sources. On the other hand, there were changes that followed some morphological or phonological rules not necessarily regular led us to similar cases of the change. In order to examine each pattern, we searched it in general corpora including FarsNet (Persian wordnet) (Shamsfard, et al, 2010) and other online sources to find similar cases. Provided that the change had a reasonable frequency of occurrence, a few sentences from the sources were selected and recorded and in this way, tens or hundreds of instances of a change pattern were entered into the corpus. However, for the sake of space limits, only one example of each pattern is provided here. Next section will review the differences between formal and informal texts in four parts of phonological differences, morphological differences, syntactic differences and common mistakes.

5.1 Phonological Differences

There are many pronunciation distinctions between formal and informal Persian which have found their ways into written texts. Some are partly rule-based and follow the general rules of phonology and some others are users' creations. As mentioned earlier, language users sometimes break the rules of formal writing and devise different writing methods to be able to convey the tones and feelings. Some differences are as follows:

a. Many patterns of phonological reduction (mostly consonants) are observed in the informal Persian:

(3) Inf: chan
F: chan**d**
(how many)

b. Sometimes speakers add a specified part to a formal word without adding any special meaning and make a slang-like version of the word. These phonological additions, too, had some patterns to follow:

(4) Inf: kharej-**æk**-i
F: kharej-i
(foreign)

c. Phonological alternation, being often rule-based, happen frequently in switching from formal to informal Persian:

(5) Inf: as**un**
F: as**an**
(easy)

d. Transposition of two adjoining sounds, known as adjacent metathesis, occurs in the informal Persian, mostly among poorly educated people:

(6) Inf: qo**lf**
F: qo**fl**
(lock)

e. There are some silent letters which do not correspond to any sound in the word's pronunciation. On the other hand, there are some sounds with no corresponding character in the word form. Since in some cases, the word forms follow the pronunciations in informal writing, people omit the silent letter or add the absent one:

(7) Inf: xahær
F: x**w**ahær
(sister)

"w" is silent in the formal word form. This change looks like writing the English word "enough" as "enaf".

f. There are some Arabic phrases imported to Persian with their Arabic writing style (along with their articles and prepositions). Persian speaker usually changes their pronunciations and subsequently their word forms in the informal usage.

(8) Inf: ishalla
F: en-sha-ællah
(God willing)

g. In order to break vowel sequences, the speakers use different epenthetic consonants in informal speaking and subsequently in informal writing which may not match the usual epenthetic consonants (EPE):

(9) Inf: nobæt-e shoma-**ʔ**-e
turn-EZ[2] you-**EPE**-is
F: nobæt-e shoma æst.
turn-EZ you is
(It is your turn.)

h. When words ending in /e/ are connected to words or clitics beginning with a vowel, both /e/ and the vowel are usually omitted in writing:

(10) Inf: ændaz-**m**[3]
size my
F: ændaz**e-æm**
size my
(my size)

Sometimes people omit only the second vowel (andaz**e-m**).

i. Some users, especially in social networks, deliberately change the letters of a word to emphasize something or ridicule or insult somebody:

(11) Inf: selebri**di**[4]
F: selebri**ti**
(celebrity)

5.2 Morphological Differences

A great deal of distinctions between formal and informal word forms can be studied in the field of language morphology. The morphological changes observed in this work are as follows:

a. The language users from younger generations are frequently observed to make up new infinitives from nouns:

(12) Inf: zæng-idæn
call – infinitive suffix
F: zæng zædæn
call hit
(to telephone)

b. Some adverbs, conjunctions and question words can be used in plural forms in the informal language:

(13) Inf: chetori- y - **a** - st?
how- EPE-pl-is

2 - Ezafe marker is placed into noun phrases, adjective phrases and some prepositional phrases linking the head and modifiers.

3 - Since short vowels do not appear in Persian writing, they are omitted in this example to show the change more clearly.

4- offensive word

F: chetor æst?
how is
(How is it?)

c. In Persian, there is no number agreement between adjective and its modified noun. In standard language, the plural suffix attaches to the noun while in informal Persian the plural suffix may be added to the adjective in a noun phrase:

(14) Inf: sib qermez-**a**
apple red-pl
F: sib - **ha** - y - e qermez
apple-pl-EPE-EZ red
(red apples)

d. In Persian script, some letters are written connected to their adjacent letter. When word forms are shortened in informal usage, they are sometimes written connected to each other and create new forms to process. For example, object marker (OBJ) *ra* changes into *ro* and *o* depending on the previous letter being a vowel or a consonant. Both *ro* and *o* may be written connected or unconnected:

(15) Inf: mæn-o næ-did- Ø
me-OBJ not-saw-3rd sg
F: mæn ra næ-did- Ø
me OBJ not-saw-3rd sg
(S/He did not see me.)

e. The shortened forms of some words have exactly the same forms; thus the ambiguity of informal writing is much more than formal writing. The data included the following examples:

- *hæm* (also/too), *hæstæm* (am), and the first-person possessive pronoun are all shortened to "m":

(16) Inf: maman-**m**
mom-**m**

(mom too/ I am a mom/ my mom)

- "i" can be a noun suffix, an indefinite article or second-person singular "to be" verb:

(17) Inf: shad-**i**
happy-**i**

(happiness/a happy [person]/ you are happy)

- The informal form of *æst* (is) and the definite article have the same appearance (e):

(18) Inf: ketab-**e**
book-**e**
(it is a book/ the book)

- Informal object marker and the coordinating conjunction have a same form (o):

(19) Inf: ketab-**o** bede mæn.
book-OBJ give me
(give me the book)

(20) Inf: ketab-**o** medad
book-and pencil
(book and pencil)

- Nunation or *tænvin* is an Arabic character appearing at the end of some Arabic loan words. It is written on "a" character, however, similar to short vowels, *tænvin* is usually omitted in writing. "a" is the shortened form of the plural suffix, as well.

(21) mæsæla =for example
mæsæla = proverbs

A bigger number of examples were entered for ambiguous words in order for the machine to learn each meaning in different contexts.

f. Persian has two indefinite articles: *yek* and *i*. In informal Persian people normally use both together:

(22) Inf: **ye** doxtær-**i**
One girl-indef
F: doxtær-**i**
girl-indef
(a girl)

g. Contrary to formal Persian, informal Persian has a definite article. Demonstratives were sometimes used in formal equivalents:

(23) Inf: mærd-**e**
man-def
(the man)
F: **an** mærd
that man
(that man)

This article may also be used with adjectives. According to the context, the modified word was added in the formal equivalent:

(24) Inf: qermez-**e**
red-def
(the red one)
F: **an** [chiz]-e qermez
that [sth]-EZ red
(that red [sth])

h. Clitics are vastly used in informal Persian. To come up with the formal equivalents, informal clitics were replaced by independent syntactic elements, as far as possible, in this study. However, there were informal clitics with no formal equivalents which needed to be omitted. The following examples show the cases of this change:

- Subject clitics on some third person intransitive verbs with no impact on meaning (25) and object clitics in clitic doubling structures (26):

(25) Inf: sara ræft-**esh**.
Sarah went-sub cli

F: sara ræft-Ø.
Sarah went-3rd sg
(Sarah left.)

(26) Inf: sara ro did-æm-**esh.**
sarah OBJ saw-1 sg-obj cli
F: sara ra did-æm.
sarah OBJ saw-1 sg
(I saw Sarah.)

- Emphatic clitics:

(27) Inf: lebas-a-t-o beshur-i-y-**a**
clothes-pl-your-OBJ wash-2sg-EPE-cli
F: lebas – ha – y -æt ra beshuy.
clothes-pl-EPE-your OBJ wash
(Don't forget to wash your clothes.)

- In informal Persian some elements can be left-dislocated and left a clitic trace:

(28) Inf: sara baba-sh pir-e.
Sarah dad-poss old-is
F: baba-ye sara pir æst.
dad-EZ Sarah old is
(Sarah's dad is old.)

5.3 Syntactic Differences

These kinds of changes were possible to be found only by searching in the sources. In other words, there was no specified pattern to follow. Syntactic changes are more limited comparing to the lexical ones, but they can almost be seen in everybody's informal language. The changes observed in this study are listed below:

a. In general, Persian has a relatively free word order, but there is a standard SOV order followed in formal language, while the informal sentences do not often follow it and the syntactic constituents can move more freely. In this project, word order was standardized in the formal part of each sentence pair (29), except for when an idiomatic meaning was intended (30):

(29) Inf: ræft-æm mædrese mæn.
went-1st sg school I
F: mæn be mædrese ræft-æm.
I to school went-1st sg
(I went to school.)

(30) Inf: boro baba! (idiom)
go dad
F: boro baba!
(Go away!)

b. Omissions occur commonly in the informal language:

- The auxiliary in 3th person singular present perfect verbs is omitted in informal Persian:

(31) Inf: bæche qæza ro **xorde**.
child food OBJ eaten
F: bache qæza ra **xorde æst.**
child food OBJ has eaten
(The child has eaten the food.)

- Omission of conjunctions, conditional elements and markers including *ægær* (if), *væqti* (when), *ta* (so that), and *ke* (clause marker) is also common, as can be seen in example 29.

- Preposition stranding is disallowed in informal Persian, while a lot of preposition omission can be observed:

(32) Inf: ræft-æm mædrese.
went-1stsg school
F: be mædrese ræft-æm.
to school went-1stsg
(I went to school.)

- The coordinating conjunction *væ* (and) is sometimes omitted:

(33) Inf: qælæm kaqæz biyar.
pen paper bring
F: qælæm væ kaqæz biyavær.
pen and paper bring
(Bring pen and paper.)

Simple past and present perfect have the same word form in informal written Persian (except for the 3th person singular).

(34) Inf: xord-i
ate-2ndsg

F: xord-i / xorde-ʔi
ate-2ndsg/ eaten-2ndsg
(ate/ have eaten)

5.4 Common Mistakes

Common linguistic mistakes of the users can again be syntactic, phonological or morphological. Mistakes were more observed in online comments and short messages. Similar to the two other changes, common mistakes could be traced by searching or following the patterns. Some of them are as follows:

a. Incorrect use of informal written form of copula *æst*, Ezafe marker and informal definite article, all sounds like /e/, known as *Hekæsre* error.

(35) Inf: maman-h mæn
mom-def my
[using article instead of Ezafe marker]
F: maman-e mæn
mom-Ez my
(my mom)

b. Making plurals out of plural nouns

(36) Inf: aqa – y – **un -a**
gentleman-EPE-pl-pl
F: aqa - y - **an**
gentleman-EPE-pl
(gentlemen)

c. Adding Arabic *tænvin* (nunation) to Persian words:

(37) Inf: telefon-**an**
phone-tanvin
F: telefon-**i**
phone-noun suffix
(by phone)

d. Using a word mistakenly instead of another word with a similar pronunciation:

(38) Inf: tæs**f**iyehesab
F: tæs**v**iyehesab
(settlement)

These kinds of mistakes which are much more common in informal writings, were tried to be covered in the database.

6. Results and Evaluation

The result of this research is available as a corpus of more than 50,000 pairs of formal-informal sentences along with a dictionary consisting formal-informal pairs of words and phrases. About half (49.77%) of the informal sentences needed syntactic changes besides lexical changes to be converted to formal ones, while the other half, could be converted just by changing the informal words. A detailed statistic is presented in table 2.

50,014	the number of input sentences
12.32	the average length of formal sentences
11.36	the average length of informal sentences
529,286	the number of word/phrase alignments
71,842	the number of unique word pairs (alignments)
49.77%	the percentage of data with syntactic change
49,397	the dictionary size

Table 2. Statistics of the developed corpus

Raw data (informal sentences) is gathered from various sources. Table 3 shows the distribution of sentence sources in the final corpus. The row 'myself' means that the sentence is not extracted from a source and is rather generated by the linguists.

source	# of sentences
web	26,014
Twitter	5,308
Instagram	4,747
myself	3,528
movie (including movies, dramas and movie subtitles)	3,282
messenger	2,751
weblog	2,400
book	1,984
total	50,014

Table 3. Distribution of different sources in the final data

For extrinsic evaluation of the corpus, we used it in a deep model of an informal to formal converter and compared the results with a rule-based method. Experiments show that using a deep Bert2Bert architecture trained on our corpus (named Fa-BERT2BERT (Falakaflaki and Shamsfard, 2024) leads to bleu score of 70.68% and Rouge-L of %86.15 on the testset of ParsMap, while the rule-based method (which does not use this corpus to train) gains 34.36% bleu score and 54.21% Rouge-L on the same test set. A comprehensive study on various style transfer methods evaluated by various metrics using this corpus can be found in Falakaflaki and Shamsfard (2024).

7. Conclusion and further work

This study was conducted to develop an informal-formal language corpus for Persian language for the purpose of natural language processing. In order to achieve this aim, many available sources of informal writing were explored to recognize its particular features and build a well-organized and operative dataset.

The minimum possible changes such as transpositions, additions and omissions were applied to make the formal equivalents in order not to change the original meaning, however, there are evidently shortcomings such as omitting some informal segments of emphasis and feelings in formal equivalents which led to omit a part of meaning that was inevitable according to our instructions. This issue can be addressed in future studies.

Moreover, although we tried to cover the differences between informal and formal Persian writing as far as possible, there are certainly cases we have missed.

Acknowledgement

This project is developed under the grant no. 11/61955 from Vice-Presidency for Science and Technology of I.R. Iran. Authors would like to thank the members of corpus development team especially Ms. Elham Fekri, Ms. Parastoo Falak Aflaki and Mr. Mostafa Karimi Manesh for their great contributions.

References

Nadie Armin and Mehrnoush Shamsfard. 2011. *Transforming Persian Informal Texts Using N-gram.* Paper. presented at the 16th CSI Computer Conference, Tehran, Iran.

Parastoo Falakaflaki and Mehrnoush Shamsfard. 2024. *Formality Style Transfer in Persian.* (arXiv preprint arXiv:2406.00867).

Roya Kabiri, Simin Karimi, andMihai Surdeanu. 2022. *Informal Persian Universal Dependency Treebank.* (https://arxiv.org/abs/2201.03679) (Accessed 2022-05-20.)

Hadi Abdi Khojasteh, Ebrahim Ansari and Mahdi Bohlouli. 2020. 'LSCP: Enhanced Large Scale Colloquial Persian Language Understanding'.

(https://arxiv.org/abs/2003.06499) (Accessed 2022-05-20.)

Amin Naemi, Marjan Mansourvar, Mostafa Naemi, Bahman Damirchilu, Ali Ebrahimi and Uffe Kock Wiil, U. 2021. *Informal-to-Formal Word Conversion for Persian Language Using Natural Language Processing Techniques.* Paper presented at the 2nd International Conference on Computing, Networks and Internet of Things.

Golnaz Nanbakhsh. 2011. *Persian Address Pronouns and Politeness in Interaction.* (Doctoral Dissertation), University of Edinburgh, Edinburgh. Retrieved from https://era.ed.ac.uk/bitstream/handle/1842/6206/Nanbakhsh2011.pdf?sequence=2&isAllowe (Accessed 2022-05-20.)

Mohammad Sadegh Rasooli, Farzane Bakhtyari, Fatemeh Shafiei, Mahsa Ravanbakhsh and Chris Callison-Burch. 2020. *Automatic Standardization of Colloquial Persian.* (https://arxiv.org/abs/2012.05879v1) (Accessed 2022-05-20.)

Mehrnoush Shamsfard, Akbar Hesabi, Hakimeh Fadaei, Niloofar Mansoory, Ali Famian, Somayeh Bagherbeigi and Mostafa Assi. 2010. *Semi-Automatic Development of Farsnet; the Persian Wordnet.* Paper presented at the Proceedings of 5th Global WordNet Conference, Mumbai, India.

Omid Tabibzadeh. 2020. *Orthography of Colloquial Persian: Based on Works of Fiction and Drama Spanning a Century* (1918-2028). Institute for Humanities and Cultural Studies, Tehran, Iran. [In Persian]

Boosting Sentiment Analysis in Persian through a GAN-Based Synthetic Data Augmentation Method

Masoumeh Mohammadi
Fordham University, USA
mm256@fordham.edu

Shadi Tavakoli
Pars Tourism Card, Tehran, Iran
tavakoli.shadii@gmail.com

Mohammad Ruhul Amin
Fordham University, USA
mamin17@fordham.edu

Abstract

This paper presents a novel Sentiment Analysis (SA) dataset in the low-resource Persian language, including a data augmentation technique using Generative Adversarial Networks (GANs) to generate synthetic data, boosting the volume and variety of data for achieving state-of-the-art performance. We propose a novel annotated SA dataset, Senti-Persian, made of 67,743 public comments on movie reviews from Iranian websites (Namava, Filimo, and Aparat) and social media (YouTube, Twitter and Instagram). These reviews are labeled with one of the polarity labels, namely positive, negative, and neutral, by humans and later augmented. Our study includes a novel text augmentation model based on GANs. The generator was designed following the linguistic properties of Persian linguistics. In contrast, the discriminator was developed based on the cosine similarity of the vectorized original and generated sentences, i.e., using CLS-embeddings of BERT. An SA task was applied on both collected and augmented datasets, for which we observed a significant improvement in accuracy from 88.4% for the original dataset to 96% when augmented with synthetic data. The senti-Parsian dataset, including the original and the augmented ones, can be accessed on GitHub.[1].

1 Introduction

Using the World Wide Web allows us to access the languages we encounter daily. Even though the Web began as an overwhelmingly English phenomenon, it now contains texts in thousands of languages (Usa, 2021) (Int, 2012). The ability to combine prior knowledge with updated information across thousands of languages and to generate new patterns based on those languages is the most compelling reason for advancing language processing (van Kessel et al., 2019).

There is a unique opportunity for computational linguists now, as this field has unprecedented access to low-resource languages. However, researchers must act swiftly, as every few days, we lose another language from the face of the Earth due to the lack of native speakers. This loss is driven by complex political, social, racial, and economic factors. Thus, we must gather online resources and develop advanced language models to preserve these disappearing languages. By doing so, we can safeguard linguistic diversity and ensure that even endangered languages remain accessible and celebrated in the digital age (Her and Kruschwitz, 2024) (Tatineni, 2020).

Natural language processing (NLP) and computational linguistics (CL) primarily focus on languages with large text corpora. Machine learning (ML) techniques are usually used to train NLP tools, and lots of languages lack large annotated corpora for training (Hauer et al.) (Xu et al., 2022) (ImaniGooghari et al., 2023) (Zhao, 2022). Using natural language to mine opinions and sentiments is extremely challenging as it involves understanding how language structures convey explicit and implicit information in individual words or entire text (Bhatia et al., 2018) (Liu and Zhang, 2012).

The necessity of this article lies in addressing the challenges faced by NLP when dealing with low-resource languages. These challenges arise due to limited supervised data availability and a scarcity of native speakers or expert contributions. To overcome this obstacle, this paper introduces a data augmentation technique that leverages GANs to generate synthetic data. Doing so enhances the volume and variety of available data, which is particularly advantageous in fields where data acquisition is costly, such as low-resource languages like Persian.

This research significantly enhances the capabilities of NLP models for low-resource languages by introducing innovative methods and datasets. The

[1] https://github.com/engmahsa/Senti-Persian-Dataset

Processings of the 1st Workshop on NLP for Languages Using Arabic Script (AbjadNLP), pages 54–63
January 19, 2025.

significant challenges we addressed while working for the low-resourced Persian language are mentioned below:

- Increased Data Diversity: This technique generates new comments by applying transformations (e.g., synonym replacement, paraphrasing) to existing movie reviews. This diversifies the dataset, making the model more robust to variations in language and context.

- Mitigation of Overfitting: By introducing synthetic examples, data augmentation helps prevent overfitting. It exposes the model to different linguistic patterns, reducing its reliance on specific training instances.

- Improved Generalization: Augmented data provides additional context and linguistic variations. Consequently, NLP models learn more generalized features, leading to better performance on unseen data.

- Addressing Low-Resource Scenarios: In languages with limited labeled data, augmentation generates synthetic samples, enabling practical training even when native speaker contributions are scarce.

- Enhanced Performance: Empirical results often show improved accuracy and robustness when applying data augmentation.

This paper contributes the following:

1. A labeled dataset for SA in Persian, Senti-Persian comprises three types of movie reviews: positive, negative, and neutral. This marks the first representation of user movie reviews in Persian within a dataset of 67,743 entries.

2. A cutting-edge GAN-based text generator is implemented to augment the comments.

3. In order to determine how accurate the models can be, resampling techniques are used on the set for balancing, and then evaluation metrics are compared.

4. A number of data augmentation methods are applied, including random insertion, synonym replacements, and random swaps, which also affect model accuracy.

Following is the organization of this paper: The summary of the related articles is included in Section 2. The structure of the proposed approach is described in Section 3. Section 4 presents the methodology. Section 5 discusses the results of our research and our plans for the future.

2 Related Work

The ParsiNLU (Khashabi et al., 2021) NLI database contains 2,700 instances, primarily written by native speakers, with some translated from the MultiNLI dataset (Williams et al., 2018). The FarsTail dataset, in comparison, has four times more native sentences than ParsiNLU. FarsTail uses fewer task-specific human-generated texts to create more natural-looking sentences. Methods for transferring knowledge across resource-limited languages are often employed. Studies like those by Dashtipour et al. (Dashtipour et al., 2021) have compared approaches to multilingual SA. Balahur and Turchi (Balahur and Turchi, 2012) found that translating training data between languages from the same family (Italian, French, Spanish) improves results.

Devlin et al. introduces Text AutoAugment (TAA), a data augmentation framework for text classification that uses Bayesian Optimization to find optimal augmentation policies. TAA outperforms manual methods, improving classification accuracy, especially in low-resource and imbalanced datasets, while reducing the need for prior knowledge and manual tuning. The paper (Karimi et al., 2021) introduces AEDA, using punctuation insertion, which improves text classification accuracy and outperforms previous methods like EDA across multiple datasets.

The article "DeepSentiPers" introduces two deep learning models, bidirectional LSTM and CNN, for Persian SA, using three data augmentation techniques to improve classification accuracy in both binary and multi-class tasks, advancing SA in low-resource languages (PourMostafa et al., 2020) (Sartakhti et al., 2022) enhances Persian relation extraction on the PERLEX dataset using text preprocessing and augmentation techniques, significantly improving accuracy with ParsBERT (Farahani et al., 2021) and Multilingual BERT models, addressing the resource scarcity in Persian NLP.

Mi et al. introduces a method using SMT and RNN to generate target-side paraphrases, significantly improving translation quality for low-

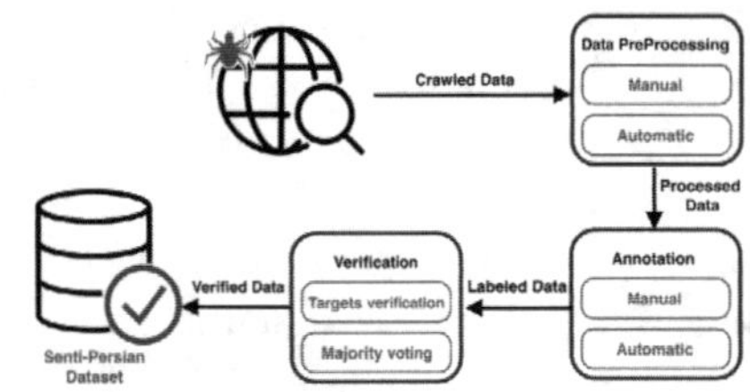

Figure 1: A flow diagram shows the four major phases of Senti-Persian's development: data crawling, preprocessing, data annotation, and label verification.

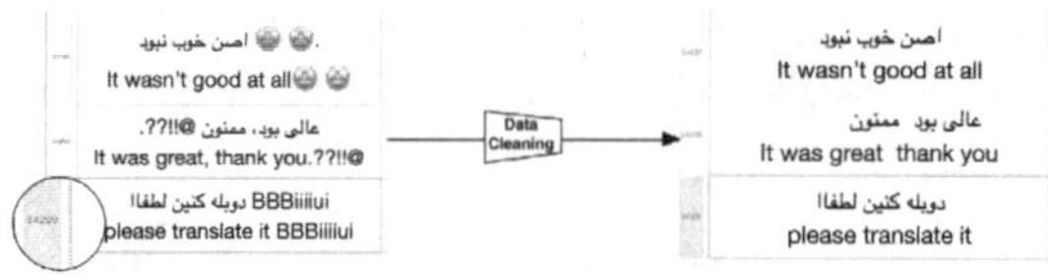

Figure 2: This figure presents the final results of data cleaning

resource languages tested on various language pairs (Bornea et al., 2021) introduces machine translation and adversarial training to enhance multilingual QA systems, considerably improving cross-lingual performance over zero-shot baselines by aligning language-specific embeddings.

The work (Shorten et al., 2021) surveys various text augmentation techniques, highlighting their impact on model generalization and performance in NLP tasks, particularly for limited labeled data, and emphasizes the need for task-specific strategies to maximize augmentation's potential. The article "BnPC: A Gold Standard Corpus for Paraphrase Detection in Bangla, and its Evaluation" (Sen, 2023) introduces BnPC, a benchmark Bangla corpus for paraphrase detection, showing its effectiveness in improving detection accuracy and advancing Bangla NLP research.

3 Senti-Persian Dataset

Creating a corpus involves several key steps: gathering, cleaning, annotating, and analyzing data, each influencing the others (McEnery and Brookes, 2022), (Ste, 2016). For example, analysis can reveal issues with annotations or sampling, leading to improvements and additional data collection. These steps are often recursive, as adjustments to annotations and dataset selection may be needed even after model training. Figure 1 provides an overview of the process we followed for Senti-Persian.

3.1 Data Collection

Senti-Persian corpora are built by sampling and filtering based on specific criteria using keywords and metadata to track sentiment. Among many choices, we collected data considering factors like time, location, and user demographics who posted or commented on movies (Moreno-Ortiz and García-Gámez, 2023) (Hu, 2016). Furthermore, our text selection approaches relied on movie genre, subjectivity, and popularity (Rheindorf, 2019) (Nandwani and Verma, 2021). Finally, the text selection process was constrained using Persian linguistic features, such as positive/negative words, intensifiers, negations, sentiment-laden adjectives, and emojis.

3.2 Text Cleaning

Unlike the Latin alphabet, the Persian alphabet does not have uppercase or lowercase letters, and the text is written from right to left. Furthermore, punctuation in Persian is limited, and many users need clarification on their proper use in text. Therefore, the first step in preprocessing is the removal of punctuation, as it often doesn't carry essential semantic information. The second step involves eliminating numbers, which may not add meaning to the sentiment depending on the context. In the third step, emojis that don't necessarily contribute to the core meaning of the content are removed. The fourth step includes the omission of extra spaces between words or sentences. Finally, as the data is sourced from web pages, we also observe HTML tags that are removed. Exceptionally, in this case, stop words are not removed as every word plays a pivotal role in preserving the original meaning of the contents (Lee et al., 2021) (Aut, 2022). Figure 2 presents the details.

3.3 Preprocessing Text Data

Both automatic and manual preprocessing are performed. During the manual phase, 'typos' are eliminated. To discover the appropriate form of a word, we used the Persian Accessible Dictionary Database (PD). Input texts containing a word not appearing in PD were considered typos. The corrected word was substituted for the typo in PD. For example, in the text تضویر بذ, the bolded letters indicate typo errors that must be corrected. By replacing the particles, it became تصویر بد. Preprocessing also includes null value imputation and removing unwanted data.

```
Algorithm 1: Majority Voting & Final Labeling
Begin
Corpus ← Collection of crawled and cleaned texts
Defined_labels ← [-1,0,1]
Final_Matrix()
For text in Corpus:
    tmpLabel = Select From Defined_labels
    Final_Matrix.append(text, tmpLabel)
End
```

3.4 Annotation Process

Labels for the entire corpus were manually assigned based on a majority vote. This involved defining an annotation scheme, markers, and granularity. In Opinion Mining (OM) and SA, labeling is challenging due to the need for a standard model.

Ten annotators categorized The collected data into Positive, Negative, and Neutral. Categorical and dimensional methods helped define emotions by grading polarity (positive/negative/neutral) and arousal. (active/passive). Algorithm 1 outlines the labeling process.

3.4.1 Guidelines and Process of Marking

This phase involved ten annotators, project managers, and expert reviewers. Annotators labeled sentiment polarities (positive, neutral, or negative) for predefined aspects of each sentence, following the methodology of (Chakravarthi et al., 2020). Native Persian annotators received training to ensure consistency.The annotation process had three rounds:

Data was split among five teams for independent annotation. Results were divided into Sub-Agree (consistent labels) and Sub-Disagree (disagreements). Sub-Agree data was reviewed, while Sub-Disagree cases were re-evaluated by the project manager. Complex cases were handed to expert evaluators for final decisions.

3.4.2 Annotation Validation

We recruited Persian university students as volunteers to handle the tagging process. They reviewed labels using Google Forms on their computers. Information about their gender, educational background, and schooling medium was collected for diversity. Reviewers were warned about potential hostile language in the comments and instructed

Thank You for Your Help
این کارتون خیلی قشنگه و من خیلی لیدی باگ رو دوست دارم
(This cartoon is very pretty and I like Ladybug very much)
Choose the Best Sentiment *
Positive
Neutral
Negative

Figure 3: Google form for data annotations by volunteers.

to remain unbiased. Each Google Form contained 100 comments (10 per page). Annotators had to confirm their understanding of the scheme before proceeding. Figure 3 shows a portion of the Google Form.

3.4.3 Analysis and Exploitation

OM and SA-labeled datasets are crucial for training and testing ML tools for emotion classification, where data quality and quantity considerably impact results. Quality control techniques help detect errors, and comparing automated and human classification improves reliability.

Reusable, portable datasets are essential for emotion-oriented systems, and defining annotation standards is critical in OM and SA. The manual annotations were analyzed to understand Senti-Persian labeling distribution, highlighting polarity and emotional expressions. The chart in Figure 5 shows a sample distribution of movie reviews.

3.5 Balancing Techniques

A significant way to improve Deep Learning(DL) models is by behaving with categorical imbalanced datasets. Unbalanced collections can be handled in a variety of ways; there are two popular ways: "oversampling" and "undersampling" (Chawla, 2009) (He and Garcia, 2009). We observed in our previous paper that under-sampling yields better performance for all DL methods we

Comments	
Positive	11,583
Negative	7,578
Neutral	3,420
Total comments	**22,581**

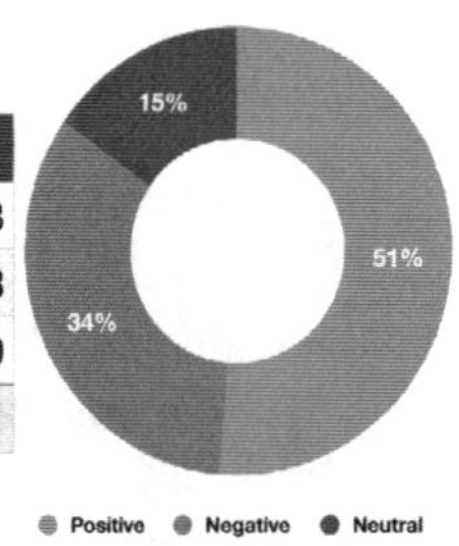

Figure 4: Comments Distribution **before** Augmentation

Comments	
Positive	22,581
Negative	22,581
Neutral	22,581
Total comments	**67,743**

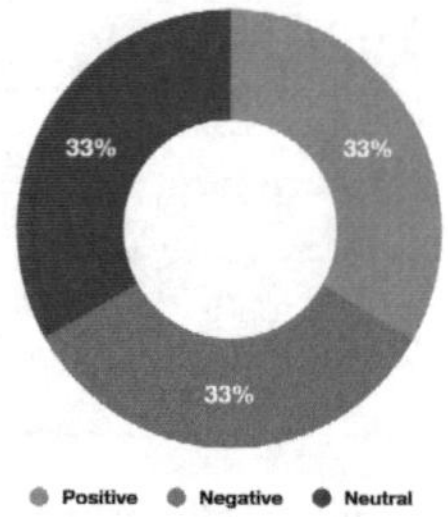

Figure 5: Comments Distribution **after** Augmentation

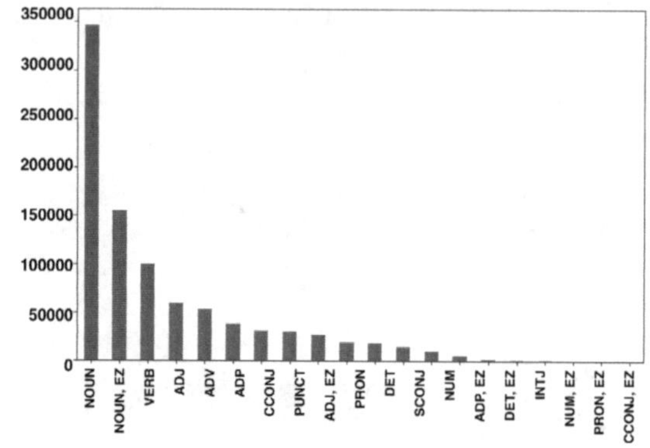

Figure 6: distribution of various parts of speech in the whole population

used (Mohammadi and Tavakoli, 2020).

3.6 Data Augmentation

Generative models enhance NLP quality, especially for low-resource languages (Chen et al., 2024). An essential contribution of this paper is the implementation of a GAN-based text generator for augmenting datasets, which will be detailed in the next section.

4 Methodology

This study collected limited movie reviews with positive, negative, and neutral sentiments. Each sentence consists of 'n' tokens. HAZM[2] Library was used to tag parts of speech (POS) in the corpus, and the chart in Figure 6 shows the frequency distribution of various POS, like verbs, adj, and nouns.

In Persian text augmentation, random masking for insertion, swapping, or synonym generation presents different linguistic challenges. We can augment most POSs, except verbs, which risk altering the sentence sentiment, a linguistic issue. For example, in فیلم بدي ني, which means "not a bad movie," if we change the verb position, the sentiment of the original sentence may change. for instance it may become فیلم بدي ه that means "it's a bad movie". Thus, in this study, tokens fall into two categories:

- Tokens that can change during the augmentation process, such as nouns, adjectives, and adverbs.
- Tokens that cannot change, primarily verbs.

Therefore, the applicability of the augmentation method on the samples depends on the specific characteristics, such as the use of subject, object, or modifiers in the text and their relative positions.

[2]https://github.com/roshan-research/hazm

These tokens are masked for generating diverse but contextually similar samples. On the other hand, the method avoids masking tokens in the verb position.

4.1 GAN

GAN, commonly used in computer vision, also plays a key role in NLP (Goodfellow et al., 2014) (Chollet, 2017). In this study, GAN-based models generate new sentences by paraphrasing limited data. GAN has two components: a generator (based on ParsBERT) and a discriminator (Goodfellow et al., 2014). The generator produces new phrases, and the discriminator classifies them as fake or real (Farahani et al., 2021).

The Transformers pipeline simplifies this process through APIs for text augmentation. Initially, Random Replacement yielded the best results. For example, in the sentence یک جوري بود این قسمت اصلا به دلم ننشست، خوشم نیوم مسخره بود, the word قسمت (meaning "part") is rearranged using BERT (Devlin et al., 2018) to یک جوري بود این بخش اصلا به دلم ننشست، خوشم نیوم مسخره بود, maintaining the same meaning but with different words. The process is shown in Figure **??** and 8.

4.1.1 Generator

This paper implements a technique using transformers and the "fill-mask" pipeline to augment sentences through random insertion, synonym insertion, and random swapping. In this approach, sentences are generated by randomly masking the *Nth* token of a source sentence. For example, in این فیلم عالي بود ("It was a great movie"), each token can be masked and replaced using the unmasker pipeline. However, masking verbs may change the sentiment, so careful selection of masked tokens is needed. Nouns and pronouns are more suitable for masking to preserve sentiment. A list of sentences with varying masked positions is created, and the discriminator evaluates each one. Algorithm 2 outlines this process.

4.1.2 Discriminator

The discriminator model classifies the output from the generator as either DIFFERENT or SIMILAR. It evaluates whether the generated sentences, modified through insertion, swapping, etc., retain the semantically similar context of the source sample. A SIMILAR label means the sentiment is preserved, while DIFFERENT indicates a deviation from the source meaning. Algorithm 3 outlines this classification process.

In BERT, the CLS token is a unique token added at the start of a sentence to capture its overall meaning. The CLS embedding represents the entire sentence and is helpful for sentence-level tasks. The similarity between two CLS embeddings, typically calculated with cosine similarity, indicates how much the augmented text resembles the source. Cosine similarity ranges from -1 (opposed) to 1 (identical) (Choi et al.). Therefore, using the measures of TP, FP, TN, and FN, we compute the performance of Algorithm 3 compared to the ground truth of human annotation. According to the Figure 7, the cosine similarity of 0.8 results in the best discriminator performance.

5 Experiments and Results

5.1 Experimental Setup

We use 80% of the data for training and equally divide the rest for evaluation and testing. We pre-

Algorithm 2: Generator

```
Begin
Dataframe ← Reads data from a CSV file
Do POS tagging and filter the verbs
Unmasker ← creates a fill-mask pipeline
    using the ParsBERT model
Inserts the '[MASK]' token at the
    randomly chosen index
Uses the unmasker pipeline to predict the
    most likely completion for the masked token.
Evaluate the generated sentences
End
```

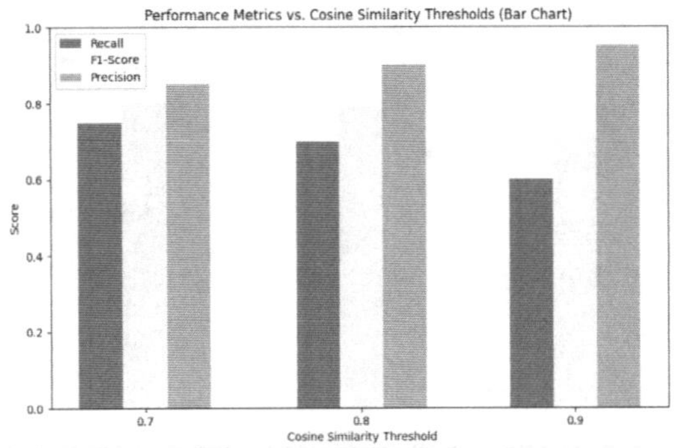

Figure 7: Performance Metrics comparison, to find the best threshold.

Algorithm 3: Discriminator

```
Begin
Sentence1 ← CLS embedding of source
    sentence before augmentation
Sentence2 ← CLS embedding of augmented
    sentence
Score ← cosine similarity between
    Sentence1 and Sentence2
If Score > 0.8:
        return "DIFFERENT"
else:
        return "SIMILAR"
End
```

process the data by removing punctuation, emojis, duplicates, and html tags and transferring digits from English to Farsi. As simple baselines, we compare our results against a majority and random baseline. Our performance metrics include accuracy, precision, recall, and the F1 score. We use thundersvm for SVM; ThunderSVM exploits GPUs and multi-core CPUs to achieve high efficiency. For the pre-trained language models, we fine-tune ($\lambda = 2 \times 10^{-5}$, batch size 32) the models for 3 epochs with early stopping.

5.2 Results & Analysis

In Tables 1 and 2, we present the performance of different models on the augmented and non-augmented datasets. By comparing the F1 scores of the two tables, we observe that all models show higher accuracy with augmented data than non-augmented data. On our dataset, the best-performing model is found to be WASSBERT (Mohammadi and Tavakoli, 2020), which was pre-trained on the highest volume of Farsi data.

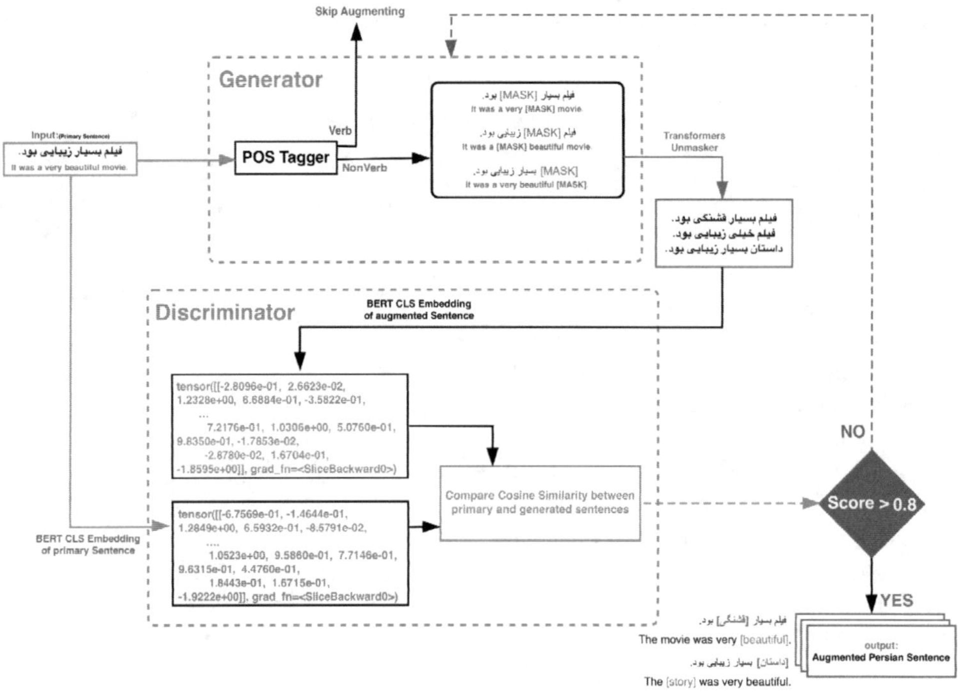

Figure 8: The GANs based model in detail

Model	Augmented Data			
	Accuracy	Precision	Recall	F1 Score
CNN	83.38%	83%	80%	81%
SVM	76%	80%	75.5%	75.5%
LSTM	72%	72%	72%	72%
CNN+LSTM	81%	81%	81%	81%
Bi-LSTM	87.07%	82%	85%	82%
Stacked Bi-LSTM	42.08%	42%	42%	42%
mBERT	90%	93.4%	90%	91%
XLM-RoBERTa	91%	90.01%	90%	90%
WassBERT	96%	95%	95%	95%

Table 1: Performance of different language models for the SA on the human-annotated movie reviews.

Model	Non-Augmented Data			
	Accuracy	Precision	Recall	F1 Score
CNN	77.33%	77%	70%	71%
SVM	70%	71.5%	70%	70%
LSTM	72%	72%	72%	72%
CNN+LSTM	81%	81%	81%	81%
Bi-LSTM	80%	79%	79%	75%
Stacked Bi-LSTM	38%	40%	37.5%	36%
mBERT	82%	84%	81%	82%
XLM-RoBERTa	83%	80%	81.3%	80%
WassBERT	90%	89%	89%	89%

Table 2: Presenting the improvement in the different language models after using augmented dataset.

6 Discussion

6.1 Diversity and Balance of Senti-Persian

We ensured diversity and balance in the Senti-Persian dataset by collecting data from various sources (social media, movie reviews), including formal, informal, and regional dialects (e.g., Shirazi, Isfahani). Gender, age considerations, and quality control were applied. After manual annotation, each sentiment category (positive, negative, neutral) was input into a GAN-based model to generate additional sentences. The synthetic data was manually reviewed for linguistic accuracy and sentiment relevance, resulting in a final corpus of 67,743 balanced comments.

6.2 Application on Other Arabic Languages

Our approach can be adapted for Arabic-script languages like Dari, Pashto, Urdu, Uyghur, Sindhi, Arabic, and Kurdish (Sorani), which share right-to-left writing, similar scripts, and word order but have unique features. Challenges include orthographic issues, vowel ambiguity, dialects, data imbalance, and complex morphology. Translating the primary dataset and applying GAN-based techniques can address these challenges and generate synthetic data.

6.3 Limitations

Persian has several linguistic characteristics that can influence the augmentation process we followed in this work. Following are a few aspects of Persian that may require specific adaptations:

1. Free word order: Changing word order for emphasis doesn't affect sentence sentiment, so models don't need to accurately prioritize capturing word arrangement or dependencies.

2. Morphology: Persian's inflectional nature, using prefixes and suffixes, doesn't affect sentence sentiment but poses challenges for tokenization. For example, کتاب (book) becomes کتاب خانه (library). The Hazm tokenizer handles these complexities accurately.

3. Postpositions and Case Marking: Persian uses postpositions (e.g., "in," "on" after nouns) instead of prepositions, affecting syntax but not sentiment.

4. Clitics and Compounds: Persian uses clitics and compound words, complicating tokenization. The Hazm tokenizer, designed for Persians, handles this effectively. For example, the word, دانش - "knowledge" and گاه - "place" or "house" together دانشگاه Translation: "University."

5. Lack of Capitalization: Persian lacks capitalization, impacting Named Entity Recognition (NER) models but not SA.

7 Conclusion and Future Works

This study presents a collection of 22,581 human-annotated data samples, which is later augmented using GANs, making it a total of 67,743 movie reviews annotated for SA. Our augmentation process resulted in achieving 96% accuracy, producing a boost of 7.6% in accuracy over the previous results. In the future, we aim to propose an approach that combines Reinforcement Learning (RL) with GANs to enhance the generation of long, coherent, and contextually appropriate text. We envision that the hybrid strategy would be able to refine GAN training mechanisms, improving the generated text's realism and linguistic quality. By combining the generative capabilities of GANs with the goal-oriented optimization of RL, we anticipate significant advancements in NLP, pushing the boundaries of current AI-driven text generation technologies.

References

2012. *Number of Internet Users by Language*. Archived from the original on 26 April 2012. Retrieved 10 May 2020.

2016. Steps for Creating a Specialized Corpus and Developing an Annotated Frequency-Based Vocabulary List. *TESL Canada Journal/Revue TESL du Canada*, 34(11):87–105.

2021. *Usage statistics of content languages for websites*. Archived from the original on 12 November 2021. Retrieved 12 November 2021.

2022. Automated rule-based data cleaning using nlp. In *2022 32nd Conference of Open Innovations Association (FRUCT)*, volume 32, pages 162–168.

2023. Sentigold: A large bangla gold standard multi-domain sentiment analysis dataset and its evaluation. Presented in [Conference/Journal Name].

A. Balahur and M. Turchi. 2012. Multilingual sentiment analysis using machine translation? In *Proceedings of the 3rd Workshop on Computational Approaches to Subjectivity and Sentiment Analysis*, pages 52–60.

Surbhi Bhatia, Manisha Sharma, and Komal Kumar Bhatia. 2018. *Sentiment Analysis and Mining of Opinions*, volume 30.

M. Bornea, L. Pan, S. Rosenthal, R. Florian, and A. Sil. 2021. Multilingual transfer learning for qa using translation as data augmentation. In *AAAI Conference on Artificial Intelligence*. IBM Research AI, Thomas J. Watson Research Center, Yorktown Heights, NY.

B. R. Chakravarthi, V. Muralidaran, R. Priyadharshini, and J. P. McCrae. 2020. Corpora for sentiment analysis of dravidian languages. In *Proceedings of the 12th Language Resources and Evaluation Conference (LREC 2020)*, pages 1–9. European Language Resources Association (ELRA).

N.V. Chawla. 2009. *Data Mining for Imbalanced Datasets: An Overview*. Springer, Boston, MA.

Y. Chen, Z. Yan, and Y. Zhu. 2024. A unified framework for generative data augmentation: A comprehensive survey. *arXiv preprint arXiv:2310.00277*.

H. Choi, J. Kim, S. Joe, and Y. Gwon. Evaluation of bert and albert sentence embedding performance on downstream nlp tasks. Unpublished manuscript.

F. Chollet. 2017. *Deep Learning with Python*, first edition. Manning Publications.

K. Dashtipour, M. Gogate, J. Li, F. Jiang, B. Kong, A. Hussain, and Z. Ling. 2021. A hybrid persian sentiment analysis framework: Integrating dependency grammar based rules and deep neural networks. *Neurocomputing*, 445:241–252.

J. Devlin, M. W. Chang, K. Lee, and K. Toutanova. 2018. Bert: Pre-training of deep bidirectional transformers for language understanding. *arXiv preprint arXiv:1810.04805*.

J. Devlin, M.-W. Chang, K. Lee, and K. Toutanova. 2021. Bert: Pre-training of deep bidirectional transformers for language understanding. *arXiv preprint arXiv:2109.00523*.

M. Farahani, M. Gharachorloo, M. Farahani, and M. Manthouri. 2021. Parsbert: Transformer-based model for persian language understanding. *Neural Processing Letters*, 53:3831–3847.

I. J. Goodfellow, J. Pouget-Abadie, M. Mirza, B. Xu, D. Warde-Farley, S. Ozair, A. Courville, and Y. Bengio. 2014. Generative adversarial networks. Manuscript submitted for publication.

Bradley Hauer, Grzegorz Kondrak, Yixing Luan, Arnob Mallik, and Lili Mou. Semi-supervised and unsupervised sense annotation via translations. Alberta Machine Intelligence Institute, Department of Computing Science, University of Alberta, Edmonton, Canada.

H. He and E. A. Garcia. 2009. Learning from imbalanced data. *IEEE Transactions on Knowledge and Data Engineering*, 21(9):1263–1284.

Wan-Hua Her and Udo Kruschwitz. 2024. Investigating neural machine translation for low-resource languages: Using bavarian as a case study. Preprint accepted at SIGUL 2024. Information Science, University of Regensburg, Germany.

K. Hu. 2016. *Compilation of Corpora for Translation Studies*. New Frontiers in Translation Studies. Springer, Berlin, Heidelberg.

Ayyoob ImaniGooghari, Peiqin Lin, Amir Hossein Kargaran, Silvia Severini, Masoud Jalili Sabet, Nora Kassner, Chunlan Ma, Helmut Schmid, André F. T. Martins, François Yvon, and Hinrich Schütze. 2023. Glot500: Scaling multilingual corpora and language models to 500 languages. CIS, LMU Munich, Germany; Munich Center for Machine Learning (MCML), Germany; Instituto Superior Técnico (Lisbon ELLIS Unit); Instituto de Telecomunicações; Unbabel; Sorbonne Université, CNRS, ISIR, France.

A. Karimi, L. Rossi, and A. Prati. 2021. Aeda: An easier data augmentation technique for text classification. *arXiv preprint arXiv:2108.13230v1 [cs.CL]*.

Daniel Khashabi, Arman Cohan, Shima Shakeri, Payam Hosseini, Pouya Pezeshkpour, Mahsa Alikhani, Mohammad Aminnaseri, Mohammad Bitaab, Fatemeh Brahman, Sahand Ghazarian, Mohammad Gheini, Amir Kabiri, Ramin Karimi Mahabadi, Omid Memarrast, Alireza Mosallanezhad, Ehsan Noury, Shima Raji, Mohammad Sadegh Rasooli, Sepideh Sadeghi, Elham Sadeqi Azer, Nafise Sadat Safi Samghabadi, Mohsen Shafaei, Sina Sheybani, Asieh Tazarv, and Yadollah Yaghoobzadeh. 2021. Parsinlu: A suite of language understanding challenges for persian. In *Proceedings of the 59th Annual Meeting of the Association for Computational Linguistics*, pages 3538–3555.

G. Y. Lee, L. Alzamil, B. Doskenov, and A. Termehchy. 2021. A survey on data cleaning methods for improved machine learning model performance. Submitted on 15 Sep 2021.

Bing Liu and Lei Zhang. 2012. *A Survey of Opinion Mining and Sentiment Analysis*. Springer, Boston, MA.

T. McEnery and G. Brookes. 2022. *Building a written corpus: what are the basics?*, 2nd edition, page 13. EBook ISBN: 9780367076399.

C. Mi, L. Xie, and Y. Zhang. 2022. Improving data augmentation for low resource speech-to-text translation with diverse paraphrasing. *Neural Networks*, 148:194–205.

M. Mohammadi and S. Tavakoli. 2020. Wassbert: High-performance bert-based persian sentiment analyzer and comparison to other state-of-the-art approaches. *Journal Name*, 12:209–220.

A. Moreno-Ortiz and M. García-Gámez. 2023. Strategies for the analysis of large social media corpora: Sampling and keyword extraction methods. *Corpus Pragmatics*, 7:241–265.

P. Nandwani and R. Verma. 2021. A review on sentiment analysis and emotion detection from text. *Social Network Analysis and Mining*, 11:81.

J. PourMostafa, R. Sharami, P. Abbasi Sarabestani, and S. A. Mirroshandel. 2020. Deepsentipers: Novel deep learning models trained over proposed augmented persian sentiment corpus. *arXiv preprint arXiv:2004.05328v1 [cs.CL]*.

M. Rheindorf. 2019. *Working with Corpora Small and Large: Qualitative and Quantitative Methods*. Postdisciplinary Studies in Discourse. Palgrave Macmillan, Cham.

M. Salimi Sartakhti, R. Etezadi, and M. Shamsfard. 2022. Improving persian relation extraction models by data augmentation. *arXiv preprint arXiv:2203.15323v1 [cs.CL]*.

C. Shorten, T. M. Khoshgoftaar, and B. Furht. 2021. Text data augmentation for deep learning. *Journal of Big Data*, 8(101):209–220.

Sumanth Tatineni. 2020. Deep learning for natural language processing in low-resource languages. *International Journal of Advanced Research in Engineering & Technology*, 11(5):1301–1311.

Patrick van Kessel, Skye Toor, and Aaron Smith. 2019. Popular youtube channels produced a vast amount of content, much of it in languages other than english. Pew Research Center. Retrieved 2 May 2022.

A. Williams, N. Nangia, and S. Bowman. 2018. A broad-coverage challenge corpus for sentence understanding through inference. In *Proceedings of the 2018 Conference of the North American Chapter of the Association for Computational Linguistics: Human Language Technologies, Volume 1 (Long Papers)*, pages 1112–1122.

Yuemei Xu, Ling Hu, Jiayi Zhao, Zihan Qiu, Yuqi Ye, and Hanwen Gu. 2022. A survey on multilingual large language models: Corpora, alignment, and bias. (No.2022JJ006).

Q. Zhao. 2022. Review of natural language processing for corpus linguistics. *Corpus Pragmatics*, 6:311–314.

Psychological Health Chatbot, Detecting and Assisting Patients in their Path to Recovery

Sadegh Jafari[1], Erfan Zare[1], Amirreza Vishteh[2], Melikeh Mirzaei[3], Zahra Amiri[1], Simamohammad Parast[3], Sauleh Eetemadi[4]

[1]Iran University of Science and Technology, [2]Sharif University of Technology,
[3]Islamic Azad University, [4]University of Birmingham

{sadegh_jafari, zahra_amiri}@comp.iust.ac.ir,
e_zare@elec.iust.ac.ir, amirreza.vishteh@ce.sharif.edu,
{mirzaeimelike, simamohammadparast}@gmail.com,
s.eetemadi@bham.ac.uk

Abstract

Mental health disorders such as stress, anxiety, and depression are increasingly prevalent globally, yet access to care remains limited due to barriers like geographic isolation, financial constraints, and stigma. Conversational agents or chatbots have emerged as viable digital tools for personalized mental health support. This paper presents the development of a psychological health chatbot designed specifically for Persian-speaking individuals, offering a culturally sensitive tool for emotion detection and disorder identification. The chatbot integrates several advanced natural language processing (NLP) modules, leveraging the ArmanEmo dataset to identify emotions, assess psychological states, and ensure safe, appropriate responses. Our evaluation of various models, including ParsBERT and XLM-RoBERTa, demonstrates effective emotion detection with accuracy up to 75.39%. Additionally, the system incorporates a Large Language Model (LLM) to generate messages. This chatbot serves as a promising solution for addressing the accessibility gap in mental health care and provides a scalable, language-inclusive platform for psychological support.

1 Introduction

Mental health issues, such as stress, anxiety, and depression, are increasingly prevalent worldwide, affecting millions of individuals (Prince et al., 2007). Access to effective mental health services, however, remains limited due to barriers such as geographic location, financial constraints, and societal stigma (Javed et al., 2021).

This paper introduces a psychological health chatbot designed to assist individuals in managing their mental health. The chatbot's primary functions include detecting emotions, identifying potential mental health disorders, and ensuring the safety and appropriateness of its responses. The chatbot is specifically designed for the Persian language, filling a critical gap in mental health care for non-English speaking communities.

The proposed system integrates several modules: emotion detection, disorder identification, and language model validation, ensuring safe, supportive interactions. Using the ArmanEmo dataset, a Persian emotion detection dataset, and advanced NLP techniques, the chatbot offers personalized, culturally relevant mental health support (Mirzaee et al., 2022). The development and evaluation of this chatbot contribute to the growing field of AI-driven solutions for mental health care, offering a resource that is more accessible and language-inclusive.

2 Related Works

Artificial intelligence (AI) and machine learning have increasingly been applied to mental health diagnosis, leveraging data from social media and digital platforms for early detection and intervention. Sophisticated AI chatbots are now capable of providing real-time mental health support (Team Capacity, 2023). Research indicates that AI can provide an affordable supplementary approach to traditional therapies, effectively aiding in the reduction of depressive and anxiety symptoms (Kaywan et al., 2023). With an average satisfaction rating of 3.95 out of 5 (79%), user feedback demonstrates substantial satisfaction and engagement levels (Kaywan et al., 2023). A non-clinical randomized trial platform further underscores the efficacy of AI-driven computer-assisted cognitive-behavioral therapy (CCBT) in alleviating self-reported depression and anxiety symptoms among college students (Fulmer et al., 2018). A study examining the effectiveness of CBT-based smartphone applications with 28 participants utilized the Shim chatbot, a text-based smartphone app, to collect data over a two-week period. The findings highlighted positive user experiences and outcomes from interactions with the chatbot (Ly et al., 2017).

Processings of the 1st Workshop on NLP for Languages Using Arabic Script (AbjadNLP), pages 64–77
January 19, 2025.

Findings suggest that GPT is a highly effective tool for identifying psychological constructs within textual data across multiple languages. Compared to traditional methods like dictionary-based and fine-tuned machine learning models, GPT offers notable advantages: it performs consistently across languages and contexts, eliminates the need for training data, and operates with minimal coding through straightforward prompts (Rathje et al., 2024). GPT has demonstrated significantly enhanced accuracy in detecting annotated sentiments and discrete emotions, outperforming commonly used dictionary-based methods prevalent in psychology and social sciences (Jackson et al., 2022).

The World Health Organization (WHO) notes a growing global need for mental health services (World Health Organization, 2023), and machine learning offers scalable solutions to address this demand by analyzing large datasets for risk prediction. Reports from the Australian Bureau of Statistics (Australian Bureau of Statistics, 2021) and the U.S. Department of Health and Human Services (U.S. Department of Health and Human Services, Substance Abuse and Mental Health Services Administration, 2018) underscore the increasing prevalence of mental health disorders, stressing the need for technological innovations. Machine learning and deep learning models have shown effectiveness in diagnosing mental health conditions from digital data. Iyortsuun et al. (Iyortsuun et al., 2023) review these techniques, finding deep learning methods particularly adept at identifying complex patterns, such as predicting suicidal tendencies from social media content (Wies et al., 2021). Challenges remain, particularly regarding stigma and self-stigma, which hinder help-seeking behavior (Clement et al., 2015; Oexle et al., 2017). Digital interventions, like AI chatbots, offer promise by providing anonymous support. However, ethical considerations must be addressed to align these technologies with human-centric values (Bryant, 2023; The Center for Humane Technology, 2023).

3 Methodology

Mental health issues, such as stress and anxiety, are increasingly common. Traditional therapies, while effective, are often inaccessible due to geographic or financial barriers. Digital solutions like conversational agents offer personalized mental health support. This study develops a conversational agent with emotion detection, disorder identification, and response safety evaluation to assist users in improving mental health. You can see the structure of this conversational agent in Figure 1. As illustrated in the figure, the system processes user messages through several steps. First, the input messages are analyzed using the Emotion Classifier, the Disorder Detection module, and the Message Validator. The Emotion Classifier identifies the emotions conveyed in the input text. The Disorder Detection module determines whether the user is experiencing stress. Simultaneously, the Message Validator assesses whether the user's message aligns with the chatbot's intended purpose. If the message is unrelated, the system provides a default response, notifying the user that their input is not relevant to the chatbot and cannot contribute to improving their emotional state.

For messages deemed relevant, the system considers the current input alongside previous messages, assigning weights to earlier messages based on their temporal proximity to the latest input. Using this contextual information, an answer is generated by a LLM. The generated response is then validated to ensure it is non-toxic and does not elicit negative emotions. If the response passes validation, it is presented to the user as the chatbot's reply.

4 Emotion Detection Module

This module identifies emotions in user messages based on six primary categories: sadness, hate, fear, anger, happiness, and surprise. An additional label, *other*, is included to account for emotions beyond these categories. By analyzing the input text, the module detects the user's emotional state, which is then utilized to generate optimal responses aimed at fostering calmness and improving emotional well-being. Further details regarding the module's implementation and performance are provided in Appendix A.

The six primary emotions are described as follows:

- **Sadness**: Sadness is a negative emotional state often linked to experiences of loss, hopelessness, or failure. It arises in response to distressing events and is associated with reduced interest in activities, low energy, and a desire for isolation (Beck, 1976).

- **Hate**: Hate is an intense and negative emotion characterized by feelings of hostility and

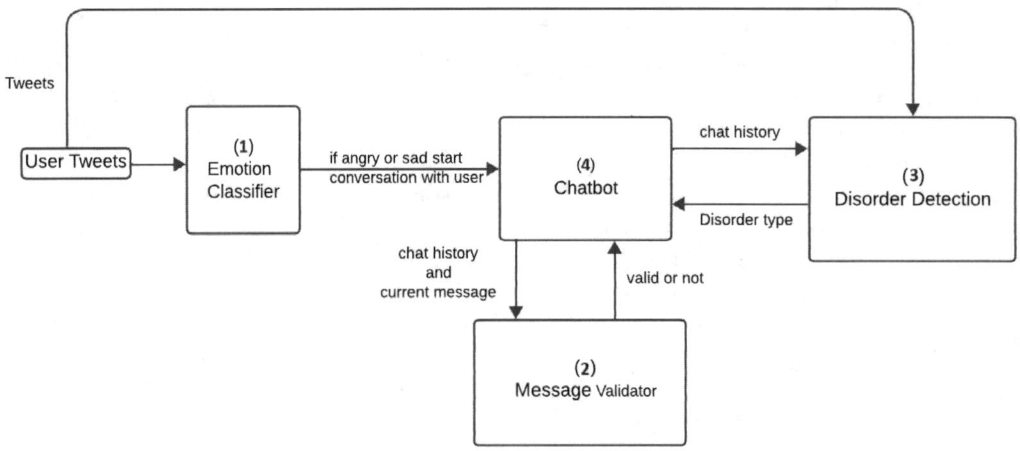

Figure 1: The structure of the mental health conversational agent. The system processes user messages through emotion classification, disorder detection, and message validation. Relevant messages are combined with contextual information to generate responses using a LLM. Responses are validated for non-toxicity before being delivered to the user.

disgust toward a specific target. It is associated with aggressive behaviors and hostility toward individuals or groups. Hate is recognized as one of the fundamental emotions in early theories of emotion (Izard, 1977).

- **Fear**: Fear is a natural response to real or perceived threats. It is marked by heightened alertness and readiness to confront or avoid danger. Physiological indicators, such as increased heart rate and sweating, are common markers of fear. The "fight or flight" theory highlights fear's role as a survival mechanism (Cannon, 1932).

- **Anger**: Anger typically emerges from provocations or frustrations and is often accompanied by a desire to confront the source of irritation. Behavioral indicators such as muscle tension and harsh vocal tones are associated with anger, which is seen as a natural regulatory response to challenges (Averill, 1982).

- **Happiness**: Happiness is a positive emotional state characterized by feelings of satisfaction, joy, and well-being. It is commonly expressed through smiling, social engagement, and other positive behaviors. Subjective measures of happiness demonstrate its validity as a distinct emotional construct (Lyubomirsky and Lepper, 1999).

- **Surprise**: Surprise is a brief reaction to unexpected events that often increases attention and focus. Nonverbal cues such as widened eyes and immediate verbal reactions are common indicators. Surprise is considered one of the primary emotions in studies of facial expressions (Ekman and Friesen, 1975).

4.1 LLM message validator

The module is designed to function as a filter, ensuring that messages generated by the LLM are neither toxic nor contain language that could evoke negative feelings in users. In this context, *toxic* language refers to expressions that are offensive, hateful, or emotionally harmful, including cyberbullying, harassment, and hate speech. Toxicity is inherently multi-dimensional and context-sensitive, requiring careful consideration of intent, language nuances, and social context. This aligns with the definition proposed by Sheth et al. (2021)., who emphasize the need for psychological and social theories to define toxicity while addressing ambiguities across its dimensions through explicit knowledge in computational models.

The six categories of toxicity used in this work are defined as follows (Al-Saffar et al., 2021):

- **Toxic**: General harmful, rude, or disrespectful comments.
- **Severe-Toxic**: A more extreme form of toxicity, often involving intense or persistent offensive language.
- **Obscene**: Comments containing vulgar or inappropriate language.
- **Threat**: Comments containing expressions of intent to harm others.
- **Insult**: Comments meant to demean or belittle someone.
- **Identity-Hate**: Comments targeting individuals or groups based on their identity, such as race, religion, gender, or ethnicity.

The performance metrics and detailed descriptions of the module are provided in Appendix B for further reference.

4.2 Users message validator

The goal of this section is to assess the relevance of user messages to psychology-related topics. Considering the diversity of users and the wide range of discussion topics, a data-driven approach was adopted for model design. To train the model, a dataset of user messages with the system was collected. This dataset included 1,025 messages, meticulously labeled by human experts into two categories: "psychology-related" and "non-psychology-related." The labeling process involved careful evaluation of each message's content based on criteria such as topic, tone, and the use of psychological terms or concepts.

As shown in Table 1, the dataset includes examples of messages, their translations, and assigned labels, which illustrate the distinction between "psychology-related" and "non-psychology-related" categories. The performance metrics and detailed descriptions of the module are provided in Appendix C for further reference.

4.3 Stress Detection

Based on Hans Selye's theory (Selye, 1956), stress is defined as a nonspecific response of the body to any demand or change, manifesting in three stages: alarm, resistance, and exhaustion. In the alarm stage, the body quickly responds to a challenge; during the resistance stage, it actively confronts the threat, and if stress persists, it enters the exhaustion stage, which can lead to physical and psychological issues.

Richard Lazarus and Susan Folkman (Lazarus and Folkman, 1984) define stress from a cognitive perspective as the result of an individual's mental appraisal of a situation and the available resources to cope with it. According to their theory, stress occurs when an individual perceives a situation as a threat or challenge that exceeds their coping abilities.

The performance metrics and detailed descriptions of the module are provided in Appendix D for further reference.

4.4 Content Generator

A LLM and three classification models are used to detect stress disorders, recognize user emotions, and evaluate chatbot responses to prevent inappropriate or toxic replies. The chatbot algorithm analyzes conversation history, calculates the weighted average of emotions and psychological disorders, and generates a short and friendly response in Persian. The chatbot uses emojis and informal language to create a more personable response without directly mentioning the user's stress or emotions. This chatbot has been used by around 190 people, who independently engaged with it since its development and the distribution of its link on LinkedIn by community members, and approximately 2,000 messages have been exchanged with it.

The psychological chatbot algorithm is designed to provide personalized and friendly responses to users. Its functioning can be broken down into the following steps:

- **Input and Output:** The algorithm has two main inputs:
  - `chat_history`: The conversation history between the user and the chatbot.
  - `window_size`: Defines how many messages from the conversation history should be considered.
  - `input_text`: The new message entered by the user.

  The output is a response generated by the AI, which is sent to the user.

- **Adjusting the Conversation History:** First, if the `window_size` is specified, the algorithm

Message (Original)	Translation (English)	Tag
امروز اصلا حالم خوب نیست. فکر می‌کنم همه ازم متنفرن.	I am not feeling well at all today. I think everyone hates me.	Related
برنامه نویسی بلدی؟	Do you know programming?	Not-Related

Table 1: Sample Messages with Translations and Labels

Algorithm 1 Generate AI Response for Psychological Chatbot

```
Input: chat_history, window_size, input_text
Output: AI response answer
if window_size then
    chat_history ← chat_history[:window_size]
end if
messages ← chat_history
emotion ← calculate_weighted_average(chat_history, 'emotion')
disorder ← calculate_weighted_average(chat_history, 'disorder')
Create prompt with context and user data as follows:

    The previous messages are the chat history between a patient and a psychologist. Suppose you are a professional
    psychologist. Based on the following information, respond to the patient with a short message. (Prevent to say 'Hi'
    in each message. And only speak in Persian)

    Emotional status: {emotion}

    Mental disorder status: {disorder}

    Patient message: {input_text}

    Speak more sincerely and informally, and use emojis to create a friendlier tone. Avoid mentioning the user's stress
    or emotion levels directly, and don't discuss them. Just be aware of these levels to respond appropriately.

messages.add({"role": "user", "content": prompt})
response ← openai.ChatCompletion.create(
        model = "gpt-4o-mini-2024-07-18",
        messages = messages
)
return response
```

limits the conversation history to the number of messages defined by `window_size`. This helps focus on recent messages to provide a more relevant response.

- **Calculating Emotions and Mental Status:** The algorithm then uses the `calculate_weighted_average` functions to calculate the weighted average of emotions (`emotion`) and mental disorder status (`disorder`) based on the messages in the conversation history. These values reflect the user's emotional and mental state throughout the conversation and are used to adjust the chatbot's response.

- **Creating a Prompt for the Model:** Using the calculated information (emotions and mental disorder status), the algorithm generates a prompt containing instructions for the model. This prompt directs the model to respond like a professional psychologist, focusing on the conversation without directly referring to the user's stress or emotional levels.

- **Adding New Message to Conversation History:** The user-generated message is added as the most recent entry to the list of messages.

- **Generating a Response with the GPT Model:** Finally, the algorithm uses the GPT model `gpt-4o-mini-2024-07-18` to generate a response. This model works with the input messages (`messages`) and provides a response based on the prompt and conversation history.

- **Returning the Response:** The algorithm returns the generated response, which is then displayed to the user.

This method helps the chatbot respond appropriately while considering the user's mental and emotional state, aiming to maintain a friendly and informal communication style.

4.5 User satisfaction

The user satisfaction form includes a series of questions, aimed at enabling participants to evaluate the quality and user experience of their interaction. Participants are asked to rate aspects such as the ease of understanding and responding to the chatbot; the resemblance of the experience to a psychiatric session in terms of time commitment; the effectiveness of text messaging compared to speaking with a psychiatrist; the efficacy of the question sequence in assessing depression levels; and the likelihood of recommending the interaction to friends and family in Iran. The form concludes with an open-ended question that allows participants to provide additional comments. These open-ended responses will be incorporated into future training phases.

By analyzing satisfaction rates and feedback, improvements will continue to be made to enhance interactivity and encouragement for future participants.

5 Results and Evaluations

The PHQ-9 is known for its unidimensional structure, solid validity, and reliability, and is regarded as a useful and effective tool in epidemiological and research contexts. Based on prior studies and the current data, it is suggested that the PHQ-9 may also be applicable in other contexts within the studied population, though further confirmation is needed.(Dadfar et al., 2018) The PHQ-9 is a self-administered scale used for screening, assessing, and monitoring depression severity.(Kroenke et al., 2003)

This scale consists of nine items that reflect symptoms over the past two weeks, with one item evaluating functional impairment (Association et al., 2015). Each item is scored on a 4-point Likert scale, ranging from 0 to 3: "not at all" (0), "several days" (1), "more than half the days" (2), and "nearly every day" (3). The total score on the PHQ-9, summing all nine items, ranges from 0 to 27. A score of ≥ 15 is classified as major depression, while a score of ≥ 20 indicates severe major depression. The diagnostic validity of the PHQ-9 for major depressive disorder (MDD) has been confirmed through studies in eight primary care settings and seven obstetric clinics (Kroenke et al., 2001).

Various versions of the PHQ-9 suggest different cut-off points, ranging from ≥ 9 to ≥ 13, with sensitivity levels between 73.8% and 77.5%, and specificity from 76.2% to 97%.(Santos et al., 2013; Khamseh et al., 2011)

The experimental procedure was conducted in three phases: before the initial interaction with the chatbot, after one week, and finally, at the conclusion of the 14-day period. Throughout this timeframe, users were required to engage in daily interactions with the chatbot.

A total of 14 participants were recruited for the experiment. Considering that participants were allowed to withdraw at any stage of the experiment (based on signing the consent form), one participant withdrew due to the sudden passing of their niece, two participants withdrew due to a lack of time, and three participants withdrew because the experiment was uninteresting or unattractive to them. Ultimately, the experiment was successfully completed by 9 participants. The detailed user information is presented in Table 2. During the experiment, emotions and stress levels were monitored and documented through the chatbot's integrated modules.

Upon completion of the experimental period, an extensive analysis of the collected data was undertaken. Insights derived from user conversations, alongside emotion and stress data, yielded several notable observations. Firstly, as depicted in Figure 2, users exhibited higher stress levels at the beginning of the week, which gradually decreased midweek, only to rise again towards the end of the week and the start of a new one. Additionally, in relation to users' emotional responses during interactions with the chatbot, it is evident from Figure 3 that participants predominantly expressed feelings of sadness, followed by happiness.

Moreover, as shown in Figure 4, 7 out of the 9 participants exhibited signs of improvement by the end of the experiment. However, 2 participants, identified by IDs 171 and 181, did not show signs of recovery, as indicated by their test results. A further review of these cases suggests that the chatbot may not be effective in providing immediate assistance for users suffering from severe depression. For such individuals, professional psychological intervention and treatment are recommended.

Gender	Location	Age	User ID
male	Zanjan	27	166
male	Kashan	24	171
female	Mashhad	23	172
male	Tehran	24	175
female	Tehran	16	179
male	Tehran	20	181
female	Tehran	47	187
male	Tehran	30	189
female	Yazd	22	191

Table 2: Table showing gender, location, age, and user ID.

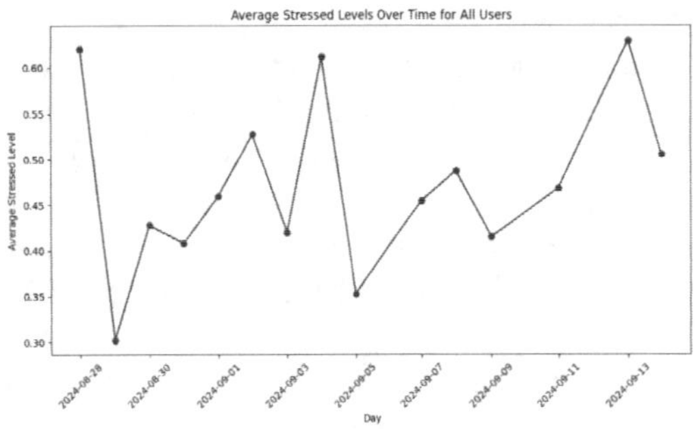

Figure 2: Average stress levels of all volunteer users over the two-week experiment

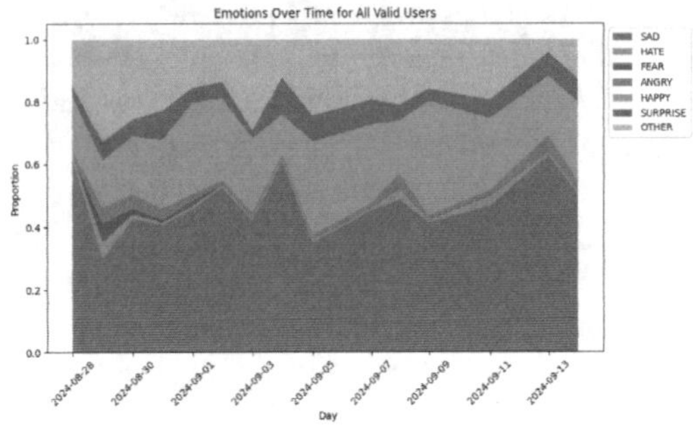

Figure 3: Average emotional responses of all volunteer users during chatbot interactions.

6 Conclusion and Future Works

In this section, we discuss our conclusions and the future work for this chatbot

6.1 Conclusion

The evaluation of the psychological chatbot demonstrated that it effectively facilitated natural and smooth interactions, offering valuable emotional feedback and responses aligned with cognitive-behavioral therapy principles. Users reported varying levels of satisfaction based on their initial mental health status, with those exhibiting higher levels of psychological distress showing less satisfaction. Despite these challenges, the chatbot successfully provided emotional reflections and relevant psychological techniques, contributing to improvements in users' anxiety and depression levels.

The chatbot's responses were generally accurate and addressed users' psychological issues, although its effectiveness varied. The analysis conducted by a licensed psychologist registered with the Iranian Psychological Association indicated that, while the chatbot adhered to cognitive-behavioral standards, it diverged from existential and Rogerian methods, which emphasize Socratic dialogue over structured techniques. User experiences were acceptable, with the chatbot meeting key criteria such as relevant responses, emotional reflection, and maintaining a coherent interaction memory.

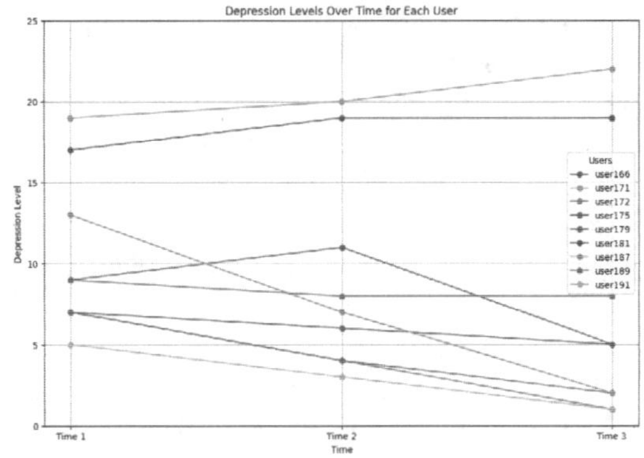

Figure 4: Results of the PHQ-9 questionnaire for all users.

A key strength of the system is its use of XLM-RoBERTa as the pre-trained model for multilingual capabilities, and ChatGPT-4.0 Mini, a multimodal model, enabling emotion detection and disorder identification to generalize effectively to other languages that use the Arabic script. This design extends the system's scope beyond Persian, making it applicable to other low-resource languages, enhancing its usability in diverse linguistic contexts.

However, the chatbot has limitations, including repetitive handling of some emotions and challenges in managing user anger. To address these issues and enhance the chatbot's capabilities, several improvements are suggested. These include recommending self-help resources, implementing user follow-up features, and configuring therapy sessions with specific protocols.

6.2 Future Work

Future developments should focus on improving the chatbot's performance by closely simulating expert psychologists' approaches and enhancing the system's ability to understand and respond to user emotions. Implementing a system for building user profiles and using past interaction data to tailor responses could significantly improve the chatbot's effectiveness. Adopting advanced techniques such as Retrieval-Augmented Generation (RAG) can enhance response relevance by leveraging historical conversation data.

To further advance the chatbot, expanding data collection efforts and improving data quality are essential. Collaboration with counseling centers and psychologists could provide valuable insights and data for refining the system. Adding voice communication capabilities would not only increase user engagement but also enhance comfort by offering voice responses and transcription services. These steps, along with ongoing refinement of models and protocols, will help bridge the gap between the chatbot and traditional psychological therapies, ultimately leading to a more effective and user-friendly tool.

7 Limitations

Despite the promising outcomes observed in the chatbot's performance, several limitations should be acknowledged. One major constraint is the lack of suitable hardware resources, particularly GPUs, which has hindered the development and fine-tuning of a custom language model tailored for the mental health domain. Due to this limitation, we were compelled to rely on OpenAI's pre-trained models, which may not fully capture the nuances of mental health dialogue, especially in handling complex psychological states such as anger or deeper existential concerns. The reliance on external models also introduces challenges in achieving complete control over the model's behavior, potentially affecting the precision of psychological techniques used by the chatbot.

Another significant limitation lies in the evaluation process. Psychological interactions are inherently dynamic and personal, making it difficult to create repeatable experiments with consistent results. User experiences and responses vary across different sessions, even with the same user, due to changes in mental state, environmental factors, and timing. Consequently, establishing a controlled experiment with identical conditions for all users proved to be a challenge. This variability in user interaction presents difficulties in benchmarking the chatbot's performance consistently, as real-world psychological factors introduce noise that is hard to quantify or replicate in a laboratory setting. These limitations highlight the need for further improvements in both model customization and experimental design to enhance the chatbot's reliability and overall effectiveness.

Ethics Statement

This study focuses on human behavior and moods, with ethical considerations addressed through strict adherence to established guidelines to ensure the validity of the methods and approaches employed. Particular attention is given to safeguarding participants' privacy. Access to raw data is restricted exclusively to the research team, ensuring that unauthorized individuals cannot gain access. Participants are assured that all data remains anonymous to protect their privacy, and informed consent was obtained for their participation in this evaluation for educational purposes.

The development and deployment of a text-based empathetic chatbot also involve significant ethical considerations. Key concerns include protecting user data privacy, particularly emotional data, and implementing strict data protection measures to prevent misuse. It is emphasized that the chatbot is not a substitute for professional psychological or medical advice. The project is guided by the principle of beneficence, aiming to enhance user well-being and minimize harm. Additionally, the chatbot's development adheres to ethical standards of fairness, non-discrimination, and bias prevention.

References

Abrar Al-Saffar, Robert Khoury, Rana Zaki, et al. 2021. Social media toxicity classification using deep learning: Real-world application uk brexit. *Electronics*, 10(11):1332.

American Psychological Association et al. 2015. Patient health questionnaire (phq-9 & phq-2) construct: depressive symptoms. *Washington: APA*.

Australian Bureau of Statistics. 2021. National study of mental health and wellbeing. Available online: `https://www.abs.gov.au/statistics/health/mental-health/national-study-mental-health-and-wellbeing/latest-release` (accessed on 19 August 2023).

James R. Averill. 1982. *Anger and Aggression: An Essay on Emotion*. Springer, New York.

Aaron T. Beck. 1976. *Cognitive Therapy and the Emotional Disorders*. International Universities Press, New York.

A. Bryant. 2023. Ai chatbots: Threat or opportunity? *Informatics*, 10:49.

Walter B. Cannon. 1932. *The Wisdom of the Body*. W.W. Norton & Company, New York.

Kevin Clark, Minh-Thang Luong, Quoc V Le, and Christopher D Manning. 2020. Electra: Pre-training text encoders as discriminators rather than generators. *arXiv preprint arXiv:2003.10555*.

S. Clement, O. Schauman, T. Graham, F. Maggioni, S. Evans-Lacko, N. Bezborodovs, C. Morgan, N. Rüsch, J.S.L. Brown, and G. Thornicroft. 2015. What is the impact of mental health-related stigma on help-seeking? a systematic review of quantitative and qualitative studies. *Psychological Medicine*, 45:11–27.

Alexis Conneau, Kartikay Khandelwal, Naman Goyal, Vishrav Chaudhary, Guillaume Wenzek, Francisco Guzmán, Edouard Grave, Myle Ott, Luke Zettlemoyer, and Veselin Stoyanov. 2019. Unsupervised cross-lingual representation learning at scale. *arXiv preprint arXiv:1911.02116*.

Alexis Conneau, Kartikay Khandelwal, Naman Goyal, Vishrav Chaudhary, et al. 2020. Unsupervised cross-lingual representation learning at scale. In *Proceedings of the 2020 Conference on Empirical Methods in Natural Language Processing (EMNLP)*, pages 100–110.

Mahboubeh Dadfar, Zornitsa Kalibatseva, and David Lester. 2018. Reliability and validity of the farsi version of the patient health questionnaire-9 (phq-9) with iranian psychiatric outpatients. *Trends in psychiatry and psychotherapy*, 40(2):144–151.

Jacob Devlin, Ming-Wei Chang, Kenton Lee, and Kristina Toutanova. 2018. Bert: Pre-training of deep bidirectional transformers for language understanding. *arXiv preprint arXiv:1810.04805*.

Paul Ekman and Wallace V. Friesen. 1975. *Unmasking the Face: A Guide to Recognizing Emotions from Facial Clues*. Prentice-Hall, Englewood Cliffs, NJ.

Liu et al. 2019. Roberta: A robustly optimized bert pretraining approach (fine-tuned on ud pos28 dataset). *arXiv preprint arXiv:1907.11692*.

Ibrahim Ezzat. 2020. Deep-translator.

Mehdi Farahani, Marzieh Ahmadi, Ehsan Kamalloo, Niloofar Safi Samghabadi, and Sabine Karimi. 2021a. Parsbert: Transformer-based model for persian language understanding. *Neural Processing Letters*, 53(6):3831–3847.

Mehrdad Farahani, Mohammad Gharachorloo, Marzieh Farahani, and Mohammad Manthouri. 2021b. Parsbert: Transformer-based model for persian language understanding. *Neural Processing Letters*, 53(6):3831–3847.

Russell Fulmer, Angela Joerin, Breanna Gentile, Lysanne Lakerink, Michiel Rauws, et al. 2018. Using psychological artificial intelligence (tess) to relieve symptoms of depression and anxiety: randomized controlled trial. *JMIR mental health*, 5(4):e9782.

N.K. Iyortsuun, S.-H. Kim, M. Jhon, H.-J. Yang, and S. Pant. 2023. A review of machine learning and deep learning approaches on mental health diagnosis. *Healthcare*, 11:285.

Carroll E. Izard. 1977. *Human Emotions*. Springer, New York.

Joshua Conrad Jackson, Joseph Watts, Johann-Mattis List, Curtis Puryear, Ryan Drabble, and Kristen A Lindquist. 2022. From text to thought: How analyzing language can advance psychological science. *Perspectives on Psychological Science*, 17(3):805–826.

Afzal Javed, Cheng Lee, Hazli Zakaria, Robert D Buenaventura, Marcelo Cetkovich-Bakmas, Kalil Duailibi, Bernardo Ng, Hisham Ramy, Gautam Saha, Shams Arifeen, et al. 2021. Reducing the stigma of mental health disorders with a focus on low-and middle-income countries. *Asian journal of psychiatry*, 58:102601.

Jigsaw and Google. 2018. Jigsaw toxic comment classification challenge.

Armand Joulin, Edouard Grave, Piotr Bojanowski, and Tomas Mikolov. 2016. Bag of tricks for efficient text classification. In *arXiv preprint arXiv:1607.01759*.

Payam Kaywan, Khandakar Ahmed, Ayman Ibaida, Yuan Miao, and Bruce Gu. 2023. Early detection of depression using a conversational ai bot: A non-clinical trial. *Plos one*, 18(2):e0279743.

Mohammad E Khamseh, Hamid R Baradaran, Anna Javanbakht, Maryam Mirghorbani, Zahra Yadollahi, and Mojtaba Malek. 2011. Comparison of the ces-d and phq-9 depression scales in people with type 2 diabetes in tehran, iran. *BMC psychiatry*, 11:1–6.

Yoon Kim. 2014. Convolutional neural networks for sentence classification. In *Proceedings of the 2014 Conference on Empirical Methods in Natural Language Processing (EMNLP)*, pages 1746–1751.

Kurt Kroenke, Robert L Spitzer, and Janet BW Williams. 2001. The phq-9: validity of a brief depression severity measure. *Journal of general internal medicine*, 16(9):606–613.

Kurt Kroenke, Robert L Spitzer, and Janet BW Williams. 2003. The patient health questionnaire-2: validity of a two-item depression screener. *Medical care*, 41(11):1284–1292.

Siwei Lai, Liheng Xu, Kang Liu, and Jun Zhao. 2015. Recurrent convolutional neural networks for text classification. In *Twenty-ninth AAAI conference on artificial intelligence*.

Richard S. Lazarus and Susan Folkman. 1984. *Stress, Appraisal, and Coping*. Springer Publishing, New York.

Mike Lewis, Yinhan Liu, Naman Goyal, Marjan Ghazvininejad, Abdelrahman Mohamed, Omer Levy, Veselin Stoyanov, and Luke Zettlemoyer. 2019. Bart: Denoising sequence-to-sequence pre-training for natural language generation, translation, and comprehension. In *Proceedings of the 58th Annual Meeting of the Association for Computational Linguistics (ACL)*.

Mike Lewis, Yinhan Liu, Naman Goyal, Marjan Ghazvininejad, Abdelrahman Mohamed, Omer Levy, Veselin Stoyanov, and Luke Zettlemoyer. 2020. Bart: Denoising sequence-to-sequence pre-training for natural language generation, translation, and comprehension. *arXiv preprint arXiv:1910.13461*.

Yinhan Liu, Myle Ott, Naman Goyal, Jingfei Du, Mandar Joshi, Danqi Chen, Omer Levy, Mike Lewis, Luke Zettlemoyer, and Veselin Stoyanov. 2019. Roberta: A robustly optimized bert pretraining approach. *arXiv preprint arXiv:1907.11692*.

Kien Hoa Ly, Ann-Marie Ly, and Gerhard Andersson. 2017. A fully automated conversational agent for promoting mental well-being: a pilot rct using mixed methods. *Internet interventions*, 10:39–46.

Sonja Lyubomirsky and Heidi S. Lepper. 1999. A measure of subjective happiness: Preliminary reliability and construct validation. *Social Indicators Research*, 46(2):137–155.

H. Mirzaee, J. Peymanfard, H. Moshtaghin, and H. Zeinali. 2022. Armanemo: A persian dataset for text-based emotion detection. Available at: https://arxiv.org/abs/2209.14585.

N. Oexle, M. Müller, W. Kawohl, Z. Xu, S. Viering, C. Wyss, S. Vetter, and N. Rüsch. 2017. Self-stigma as a barrier to recovery: A longitudinal study. *European Archives of Psychiatry and Clinical Neuroscience*, 268:209–212.

Hossein Poostchi and Ali Zarei. 2016. Hazm: Python library for digesting persian text.

Martin Prince, Vikram Patel, Shekhar Saxena, Mario Maj, Joanna Maselko, Michael R Phillips, and Atif Rahman. 2007. No health without mental health. *The lancet*, 370(9590):859–877.

Steve Rathje, Dan-Mircea Mirea, Ilia Sucholutsky, Raja Marjieh, Claire E Robertson, and Jay J Van Bavel. 2024. Gpt is an effective tool for multilingual psychological text analysis. *Proceedings of the National Academy of Sciences*, 121(34):e2308950121.

Victor Sanh, Lysandre Debut, Julien Chaumond, and Thomas Wolf. 2019. Distilbert, a distilled version of bert: smaller, faster, cheaper and lighter. *arXiv preprint arXiv:1910.01108*.

Iná S Santos, Beatriz Franck Tavares, Tiago N Munhoz, Laura Sigaran Pio de Almeida, Nathália Tessele Barreto da Silva, Bernardo Dias Tams, André Machado Patella, and Alicia Matijasevich. 2013. Sensitivity and specificity of the patient health questionnaire-9 (phq-9) among adults from the general population. *Cadernos de saude publica*, 29:1533–1543.

Hans Selye. 1956. *The Stress of Life*. McGraw-Hill, New York.

Amit Sheth, Valerie L. Shalin, and Ugur Kursuncu. 2021. Defining and detecting toxicity on social media: Context and knowledge are key. *arXiv preprint arXiv:2104.10788*.

Team Capacity. 2023. The complete guide to ai chatbots: The future of ai and automation. Available online: `https://capacity.com/learn/ai-chatbots/` (accessed on 19 August 2023).

The Center for Humane Technology. 2023. Align technology with humanity's best interests. Available online: `https://www.humanetech.com/` (accessed on 19 August 2023).

U.S. Department of Health and Human Services, Substance Abuse and Mental Health Services Administration. 2018. Key substance use and mental health indicators in the united states: Results from the 2018 national survey on drug use and health. Available online: `https://www.samhsa.gov/data/sites/default/files/cbhsq-reports/NSDUHDetailedTabs2018R2/NSDUHDetTabsSect8pe2018.htm#tab8-28a` (accessed on 19 August 2023).

Sandra Bringay Waleed Ragheb, Jérôme Azé and Maximilien Servajean. 2019. Attention-based modeling for emotion detection and classification in textual conversations.

B. Wies, C. Landers, and M. Ienca. 2021. Digital mental health for young people: A scoping review of ethical promises and challenges. *Frontiers in Digital Health*, 3:697072.

World Health Organization. 2023. Mental health. Available online: `https://www.who.int/health-topics/mental-health#tab=tab_1` (accessed on 19 August 2023).

Zhilin Yang, Zihang Dai, Yiming Yang, Jaime Carbonell, Ruslan Salakhutdinov, and Quoc V Le. 2019. Xlnet: Generalized autoregressive pretraining for language understanding. In *Advances in Neural Information Processing Systems (NeurIPS)*.

Zichao Yang, Diyi Yang, Chris Dyer, Xiaodong He, Alex Smola, and Eduard Hovy. 2016. Hierarchical attention networks for document classification. In *Proceedings of the 2016 Conference of the North American Chapter of the Association for Computational Linguistics: Human Language Technologies*, pages 1480–1489.

A Emotion Detection

1.1 Dataset Overview

The *ArmanEmo* dataset is a Persian-language emotion detection dataset with over 7000 manually labeled sentences. The sentences were sourced from platforms such as Twitter, Instagram, and Digikala and are categorized into seven emotion labels: Anger, Fear, Happiness, Hatred, Sadness, Wonder, and Other (for emotions not covered by the main emotion labels).

The dataset has been split into training and testing sets and provided in TSV format. Transfer learning experiments have shown that *ArmanEmo* is better suited for emotion detection tasks compared to other older Persian datasets (Mirzaee et al., 2022). See Table 3 for details on the data sources used for ArmanEmo.

Source	Persian Tweets	Instagram Comments	Digikala Comments
Collection Period	2017-2018	2017-2018	2018
Raw Data	1.5M	1M	50K
Labeled for Manual Annotation	3.5K	3K	1K
Data for Automatic Annotation	4.5K	-	-

Table 3: Data sources for the ArmanEmo dataset, including collection periods, raw data size, and data labeled through both manual and automatic annotation processes.

The dataset has been split into training and testing sets and provided in TSV format. Transfer learning experiments have shown that *ArmanEmo* is better suited for emotion detection tasks compared to other older Persian datasets (Mirzaee et al., 2022).

1.2 Model Performance and Testing

Various models were tested on the *ArmanEmo* dataset. Below are the results of the key models:

1. **ParsBERT**: A version of BERT optimized for the Persian language. Achieved an accuracy of 63.8575 after 17 epochs (Farahani et al., 2021b).
2. **RoBERTa-Facebook**: An optimized version of BERT developed by Facebook, which achieved an accuracy of 63.1625 after 5 epochs (Liu et al., 2019).
3. **RoBERTa-Base-ft-UDPOS28**: A version of RoBERTa fine-tuned for part-of-speech tagging, achieving 62.033 accuracy after 5 epochs (et al., 2019).
4. **XLM-RoBERTa-Large**: A multilingual version of RoBERTa trained on data from over 100 languages. This model performed the best, showing superior generalization capabilities on the *ArmanEmo* dataset (Conneau et al., 2020).

1.3 Performance Comparison

Table 4 provides a summary of the precision, recall, and F1 scores for each model tested.

Model	Precision	Recall	F1
FastText (Joulin et al., 2016)	54.82	46.37	47.24
HAN (Yang et al., 2016)	49.56	44.12	45.10
RCNN (Lai et al., 2015)	50.53	48.11	47.95
RCNNVariant (Lai et al., 2015)	51.96	48.96	49.17
TextAttBiRNN (Waleed Ragheb and Servajean, 2019)	54.66	46.26	47.09
TextCNN (Kim, 2014)	58.66	51.09	51.47
ParsBERT (Farahani et al., 2021b)	67.10	65.56	65.74
XLM-Roberta-base (Conneau et al., 2020)	72.26	68.43	69.21
XLM-Roberta-large (Conneau et al., 2020)	**75.91**	**75.84**	**75.39**

Table 4: Comparison of Model Performance on ArmanEmo Dataset for emotion detection task(Precision, Recall and F1 metrics are macro).

B LLM message validator

In this module, the generated text by LLM is evaluated to ensure that no inappropriate content is included in the user-provided text. Given the importance of vocabulary and its impact on users' mental well-being, text evaluation and generating suitable content aimed at improving the user's state of mind are critical tasks.

2.1 Implementation

Since the chatbot operates in Persian, access to and use of a Persian language dataset was necessary. Due to the unavailability of an appropriate Persian dataset, an English-language dataset was used and translated using existing translation APIs, such as `deep-translator` (Ezzat, 2020). Consequently, the "Jigsaw Toxic Comment Classification" dataset (Jigsaw and Google, 2018) was utilized as a reference. This dataset contains 159,571 samples with six labels, including "toxic," "identity_hate," "insult," "threat," "obscene," and "severe_toxic." Since the dataset is multi-label, it allows for the possibility that a sample may have multiple labels. After translation, preprocessing was performed using the `hazm` library (Poostchi and Zarei, 2016), which includes operations such as removing extra spacing and reducing the repetition of consecutive words. Moreover, untranslated English words were removed using Unicode.

Given the data imbalance, as clearly shown in Table 5 as first two columns, where the distribution of the labels is presented, the need to improve the biased dataset was identified. To address this, a balanced subset was selected for each label. Due to hardware limitations during training, the dataset was reduced to 20,000 samples, with the distribution of labels shown in Table 5 in two balanced columns. Initially, the data was split into training and testing sets in a 4:1 ratio. Hyperparameters were determined manually using trial and error, and the final hyperparameters used for training the models are as follows: the number of training epochs was set to 3, with a per-device training batch size of 8 and an evaluation batch size of 16. The learning rate was adjusted to 2e-5, and a weight decay of 0.01 was applied. For optimization, the AdamW optimizer was employed. The different models were then trained and evaluated based on the test data. The results are presented in Table 6. According to the obtained results, the `xlm-roberta-large` (Conneau et al., 2019) model was selected as the final model used in the `message validator` module to evaluate the LLM-generated text. The detailed results of the final model's evaluation on the test data are presented in Table 7.

2.2 Challenges in Implementation

One of the main challenges was the absence of a suitable Persian dataset, which required the translation of another dataset. Due to the weaknesses in translator APIs, such as inaccuracies in translating slang, idiomatic expressions, and offensive terms, this led to unbalanced translations or the non-translation of some words. Additionally, the limited availability of multi-class datasets with clearly labeled instances for different types of offensive or inappropriate sentences restricted the implementation to a specific dataset.

Label	Absent	Present	Balanced Absent	Balanced Present
toxic	144,277	15,294	4,879	15,121
severe-toxic	157,976	1,595	13,369	6,631
obscene	151,122	8,449	10,741	9,259
threat	159,093	478	8,129	11,871
insult	151,711	7,877	10,403	9,597
identity-hate	158,166	1,405	6,495	13,505

Table 5: Number of record counts in base dataset with balanced format for each label in the dataset for LLM Text Validation Module (Jigsaw and Google, 2018).

C Users message validator

In light of the possibility of irrelevant conversations occurring between users and chatbots, the necessity of implementing a module to evaluate the relevance of user messages with the chatbot's

Model	Precision	Recall	F1-score
BART-base (Lewis et al., 2020)	92.66	88.81	90.54
BART-large (Lewis et al., 2020)	93.44	88.58	90.82
ELECTRA-base (Clark et al., 2020)	91.47	83.06	86.92
ParsBERT (Farahani et al., 2021a)	**93.93**	91.62	92.99
BERT (Devlin et al., 2018)	93.69	91.08	92.49
XLNet-base (Yang et al., 2019)	90.44	86.39	87.97
DistilRoBERTa-base (Sanh et al., 2019)	92.63	88.72	90.63
DistilBERT (Sanh et al., 2019)	93.88	91.84	92.80
XLM-RoBERTa-large (Conneau et al., 2019)	92.35	**93.95**	**93.43**

Table 6: The performance of the proposed model on custom data that explained in Table 5.

Label	Precision	Recall	F1-score
toxic	94.16	97.55	95.83
severe-toxic	97.42	88.39	92.68
obscene	89.59	88.55	89.07
threat	99.19	97.79	98.48
insult	86.87	89.00	87.92
identity-hate	96.48	92.84	94.63
Overall-accuracy		70.53	

Table 7: The result of XLM-Robetrta-large model on balanced dataset 5 for LLM Text Validation module.Due to the multilabel and multiclass structure of the dataset, there are cases where some labels are correctly identified while others are missed. This causes differences between the Precision and F1-Score values and the Overall Accuracy.

purpose has been identified. A dataset comprising conversations between users and the chatbot was collected and labeled accordingly.

Subsequently, preprocessing was performed on the generated dataset using the hazm library. This process involved correcting typographical errors, addressing literary issues in the text, eliminating repetitive characters, and removing stopwords. The final dataset, based on the distribution of labels, is presented in Table 8.

Given the limited size of the dataset, the cross-validation method was employed to train the models. The dataset was divided into five parts, with each iteration using four parts for training and one part for validation. This process was repeated five times so that each part was tested as a validation set. The hyperparameters used for training were optimized for transformer-based models as follows: the number of training epochs was set to 7, with gradient accumulation steps of 2. The per-device training batch size was set to 4, while the evaluation batch size was set to 8. The learning rate was adjusted to 2e-5, and a weight decay of 0.01 was applied. The results of the selected models are presented in Table 9.

Based on the results, it was observed that the

ParsBERT model outperformed others and was thus selected as the baseline model. In cases where user conversations were deemed irrelevant to the chatbot's purpose, a static message is sent to the user, and the API call is prevented, guiding the conversation back on track to improve the user's experience.Table ?? shows that the chatbot ignores texts that are not related to its purpose.

3.1 Challenges

Due to the limited number of samples in the dataset, there was a risk of overfitting during model training, which was mitigated by utilizing cross-validation. Additionally, certain conversations contained non-Persian text, emojis, or punctuation, necessitating further preprocessing to ensure high-quality data for model training.

Label	Count
Not Related	524
Related	738

Table 8: Number of Samples for Each Label in a collected dataset from user conversations.

Model Name	F1-Score	Precision	Recall
ParsBERT (Farahani et al., 2021a)	**95.26**	96.80	93.86
distil-bert multilingual	94.78	93.48	96.19
bert (Devlin et al., 2018)	91.86	96.23	88.68
XLM-Roberta-base (Conneau et al., 2019)	92.70	93.97	91.56
bart-base (Lewis et al., 2019)	81.78	88.37	76.45
DeBERTA-base	84.59	87.16	82.37
BART-large	81.49	83.24	80.08
electra-base (Clark et al., 2020)	67.55	79.92	62.63
xlnet-base (Yang et al., 2019)	50.11	33.71	**97.82**
XLM-Roberta-large	18.88	11.72	65.81

Table 9: Performance of Evaluated Models on the Collected Dataset.

D Stress Detection

4.1 Dataset Description

The dataset used for stress detection was constructed using text-based social media articles from Reddit and Twitter, as described in the paper titled *"Stress Detection from Social Media Articles: New Dataset Benchmark and Analytical Study"*. The datasets are publicly available[1].

Dataset Overview: We constructed four high-quality datasets using text articles from Reddit and Twitter. Each article is annotated with a binary class label where:

- `0`: Stress Negative article
- `1`: Stress Positive article

The annotation was performed using an automated DNN-based strategy outlined in the aforementioned study.

The four datasets are described as follows:

- **Reddit Title:** Consists of titles from articles collected from both stress and non-stress-related subreddits on Reddit.
- **Reddit Combi:** Combines the title and body text from articles collected from both stress and non-stress-related subreddits on Reddit into a single text sequence.
- **Twitter Full:** Contains stress and non-stress-related tweets collected from Twitter.
- **Twitter Non-Advert:** A denoised version of the Twitter Full dataset, excluding advertising content.

4.2 Model Architecture

We employed a sequential neural network model to detect social media text stress. The architecture of the model is as follows:

- **Embedding Layer**: The embedding layer is initialized with 40-dimensional word vectors and a maximum input sequence length of 20 tokens. This layer contains 160,000 parameters.
- **Bidirectional LSTM Layer**: A Bidirectional Long Short-Term Memory (LSTM) layer with 100 units in each direction, yielding an output of 200 units. This layer consists of 112,800 parameters.
- **Dropout Layer**: A dropout layer is added to reduce overfitting by randomly dropping neurons during training with a dropout rate of 50%.
- **Dense Output Layer**: A fully connected dense layer with a sigmoid activation function is used for binary classification (stress vs non-stress), adding 201 trainable parameters.

The model has a total of 273,001 trainable parameters and achieves an accuracy of 98% on the test set, as summarized in Table 10.

[1] `https://www.kaggle.com/datasets/mexwell/stress-detection-from-social-media-articles`

Class	Precision	Recall	F1-Score
0 (Non-Stress)	0.96	0.99	0.97
1 (Stress)	0.99	0.96	0.98
Accuracy		0.98	

Table 10: Model Performance on Stress Detection Task.

The macro and weighted averages for precision, recall, and F1-score are consistently high, indicating robust performance across both stress and non-stress classes.

A Derivational Chain Bank for Modern Standard Arabic

Reham Marzouk,[1,2] Sondos Krouna,[3] Nizar Habash[1]

[1]Computational Approaches to Modeling Language (CAMeL) Lab,
New York University Abu Dhabi
[2]Information Technology Department, IGSR, Alexandria University
[3]ISLT, Carthage University
marzoukreham@gmail.com, sondes.krouna@islt.ucar.tn, nizar.habash@nyu.edu

Abstract

We introduce the new concept of an *Arabic Derivational Chain Bank* (CHAINBANK) to leverage the relationship between form and meaning in modeling Arabic derivational morphology. We constructed a knowledge graph network of abstract patterns and their derivational relations, and aligned it with the lemmas of the CAMELMORPH morphological analyzer database. This process produced chains of derived words' lemmas linked to their corresponding lemma bases through derivational relations, encompassing 23,333 derivational connections. The CHAINBANK is publicly available.[1]

1 Introduction

Lexical resources are essential for improving the accuracy of language processing and pedagogical applications, as they enhance computational systems' ability to grasp the nuanced meanings and contextual variations of human language. Despite significant efforts, the Arabic language still lacks tools that focus on its compositional morphological structure and semantic connections. Derivational modeling offers a computational framework to capture the interplay between word form and meaning, clarifying Arabic's complex derivational pathways and resolving its structural ambiguities.

Arabic derivational morphology is fundamentally tied to its templatic system, where roots and patterns provide different types of semantic abstractions to express multiple meanings (Gadalla, 2000; Holes, 2004; Habash, 2010). The process of deriving words from roots is not consistent, leading to challenges that hinder the understanding of the meanings of derived words and pose significant obstacles for derivational modeling. For instance, a single pattern can convey different derivational meanings, resulting in ambiguity among derived words that share the same root. As an example, the *masdar/verbal noun* المصدر and the *descriptive adjective* الصفة المشبهة may share the same pattern *1a2A3*, e.g. حصاد *HaSAd*[2] 'harvest' and the adjective جبان *jabAn* 'coward'. Likewise, Homographs can be derived from the same base to convey distinct meanings; consequently, each word possesses a different set of derivatives. For example, each of the two senses of the verb فلح *falaH* 'to succeed' and 'to farm' has its own masdar: فلاح *falAH* 'success' and فلاحة *filAHa¯ħ*farming'. Another crucial behavior is the meaning shift of some derivatives from the original abstract meaning of the root, e.g., كتيبة *katiyba¯ħ*battalion' is ultimately derived from the root ك.ت.ب *k.t.b* 'writing-related'.

Interpreting the behavior of derived words in the Arabic language, along with the deviations from derivational rules, necessitates a robust organization of derivatives within a framework capable of tracing the various paths of derivation and managing the resulting ambiguities. The objective of this study is to define the new concept of the *Arabic Derivational Chain Bank* (henceforth, CHAINBANK), which serves as the first representation of the Arabic derivational structure. The CHAINBANK presents connected chains that illustrate the path of each derived word and the relation between connected words by providing their derivational meanings. To construct the CHAINBANK, we employed a knowledge graph structure to build a network of abstract patterns, along with a classification model to align this network with lexical database of the Arabic morphological analyzer the CAMELMORPH (Khairallah et al., 2024a) based on selected features. The CHAINBANK is a morphological model that exploits Arabic's compositional morphological and semantic features while accommodating ad hoc exceptions.

[1]https://github.com/CAMeL-Lab/ArabicChainBank

[2]Habash et al. (2007)'s Arabic transliteration scheme.

Processings of the 1st Workshop on NLP for Languages Using Arabic Script (AbjadNLP), pages 78–87
January 19, 2025.

2 Related Work

Computational Derivational Morphology Several studies have modeled derivational morphology using a range of techniques. Habash and Dorr (2003) clustered categorial variations of English lexemes to develop the CATVAR resource. Similarly, Zeller et al. (2013) created DERIVBASE, a derivational resource for German, using a rule-based framework to induce derivational families (i.e., clusters of lemmas in derivational relationships). Hathout and Namer (2014) developed Démonette by integrating two lexical resources and applying rules to link words to their bases while considering their semantic types. Following Zeller's approach, Vodolazsky (2020) and Šnajder (2014) constructed derivational models for Russian and Croatian, respectively. Kanuparthi et al. (2012) introduced a derivational morphological analyzer for Hindi built on a mapping from an inflectional analyzer. Cotterell et al. (2017) argued for a paradigmatic treatment of derivational morphology and used sequence-to-sequence models to learn mappings from fixed paradigm slots to their corresponding derived forms. Hofmann et al. (2020) proposed a graph auto-encoder that learns embeddings capturing information about the compatibility of affixes and stems in derivation.

Arabic Computational Morphology Research on Arabic computational morphology has primarily focused on inflectional modeling (Kiraz, 1994; Beesley, 1998; Al-Sughaiyer and Al-Kharashi, 2004; Habash and Rambow, 2006; Taji et al., 2018). This focus has led to the development of various models for morphological analysis, generation, and disambiguation. Habash et al. (2012) introduced MADA, a tool designed to analyze and disambiguate Arabic morphology in context. Pasha et al. (2014) developed MADAMIRA, which identifies the morphological features of a word and ranks analysis results based on their compatibility with the model's predictions. More recently, tools such as CALIMA-Star (Taji et al., 2018) and CAMEL-MORPH (Habash et al., 2022; Khairallah et al., 2024b,a) have emerged as advanced morphological analyzers and generators, with a wide range of features. A few efforts have incorporated derivational features to enhance their models. For instance, the morphological analyzer Al Khalil Morph system (Boudlal et al., 2010; Boudchiche et al., 2017) utilizes a database categorized into derived and non-derived classes based on root, vocalized, and unvocalized patterns. Additionaly, Zaghouani et al. (2016) conducted a pilot study aimed at representing the derivational structure of roots and patterns while addressing the multiple senses associated with a single pattern. However, none of these studies developed a comprehensive model focused extensively on derivational morphology.

Inspired by the efforts on systematic treatment of derivational morphology in other languages, we propose a model that captures the complexity and elegance of the Arabic derivational system.

3 Arabic Derivational Morphology Terms

In Arabic templatic morphology, discontinuous consonantal morphemes, **roots**, interconnect with different **patterns** of vowels and consonants to construct different meanings. Each root has a general semantic meaning and each pattern is associated with a certain **canonical meaning**. The set of words sharing the same root, a **derivational family**, are organizable as a derivational network connecting hierarchically up to a (typically) single base word. Derived words can be either **canonical**, where the word's meaning matches its pattern's meaning, or **non-canonical**, where an ad hoc deviation of regular form occurs. For example the two words ضرب *Darb* 'hitting', and شمس *šams* 'sun', share the same pattern *1a23*, whose canonical meaning is the masdar, matching the former (canonical) but not the latter (non-canonical). Derived words can also be formed with **derivational affixes**, e.g., the suffix يّ+ *+iy∼* (ياء النسبة Attributive yA') appends to the base علم *ςilm* 'science' to produce the attributive adjectives علمي *ςilmiy∼* 'scientific'. Verbs are divided into **unaugmented**, which are composed of roots and vocalism-only patterns, and **augmented**, which are derived from unaugmented verbs by geminating, lengthening of vowels, prefixation or infixation (Gadalla, 2000). Nouns are categorized into **primary nouns**, which are directly derived from roots (Gadalla, 2000), and **derived nouns**, which originate from verbs and encompass derivational classes such as verbal nouns (masdar), nouns of location, etc. In some cases, derived words involve shifting the meaning to a contextually unrelated interpretation of their base form, i.e., **semantic specification**. For instance, the noun مكتوب *maktuwb* 'letter/message' is derived from the passive participle مكتوب *maktuwb* 'written".

4 The ChainBank Framework

The role of the Arabic derivational ChainBank is to systematically link all derivatives belonging to the same derivational family in a sequential manner (chain), starting from the root and progressing through each derived form. This chain establishes a clear relationship between each derivative and its base, clarifying the morphological processes that generate new words. By organizing derivatives in this structured form, the derivational chain highlights the hierarchical and interdependent nature of word formation, providing insights into how base forms evolve into more complex derivatives while preserving their semantic and grammatical connections.

We represent the ChainBank as a dynamic tree-structured knowledge graph starting with the root. Each node in this graph corresponds to a derived word and includes its morphosemantic attributes, such as pattern, part-of-speech, functional features, and lexical meaning. The connections between pairs of nodes denote the derivational relationships of each child node to its base parent.

To create the ChainBank, we developed an extensive network that represents the organization of abstract patterns, such as فَعَل *CaCaC/1a2a3* and فَعِيل *CaCiyC/1a2iy3*, and integrated this network with the CamelMorph lexical database. This combination forms a large-scale network connecting Arabic words through their derivational relationships. The process includes two levels:

- The **abstract level** focuses on the abstract patterns designed to represent various derivatives.
- The **concrete level** is where abstract patterns are linked to lemmas to produce derived words along with their derivational meanings.

4.1 The Abstract Level

The network we developed covers all potential connections between roots and their derived patterns in a tree structure. The roots are positioned at the apex of the tree, followed by unaugmented verbs, and subsequently the augmented verbs along with the nominal derivatives. This network is meticulously organized to display all conceivable connections between patterns, even if certain connections may not be attested but remain theoretically plausible.

Constructing the Abstract Network First, we classified all patterns according to their morphosemantic characteristics. Appendix A (Table 2) presents examples of the adopted classification of the patterns selected in this study.

Next, we devised a scheme to incorporate the derivational features of these patterns into the network. The construction of the network involved the establishment of three tables to represent the source and target nodes, along with their relationships.

1. **The Canonical Table** We manually constructed a table that covers trilateral and quadrilateral verbs in their unaugmented and augmented forms as well as all their derived nominal patterns. We present examples of the Canonical Table entries in Appendix C: Table 4 focuses on forms connected to the triliteral unaugmented verbs (Form I, فعل *CaCaC/1a2a3*), and Table 5 includes the rest.
2. **The Affixational Table** To model affixational derivatives, we automatically generate new entries combining Canonical Table entries with specific derivational affixes. For instance, the Canonical Table pattern *1i23* is extended to *1i23+iy∼* to allows us to model the example علمي *ςilmiy∼* 'scientific' from علم *ςilm* 'science' discussed in Section 3.
3. **The Semantic Specification Table** To model derivations that involve a semantic specification shift without a change in the main abstract pattern, we automatically generate entries from the Canonical and Affixational Tables, under a set of manually specified constraints. A major type of such entries involves (but not only) a change in part-of-speech; and in some cases, it may use an inflected form such as the feminine singular or broken plural. For instance, the derivation *ma12uw3+a¯h* (noun) from *ma12uw3* (adjective) allows us to model the derivation of معلومة *maςluwma¯h* 'a piece of information (noun)' from the feminine form of معلوم *maςluwm* 'known (adj)'.

The final Abstract Network is built as a combination of the above-mentioned tables in one relational database to allow for efficient access to the chains of connected patterns, all their features, and their derivational relations.

4.2 The Concrete Level

Next we discuss aligning the CamelMorph database lemmas with the abstract network to create the ChainBank.

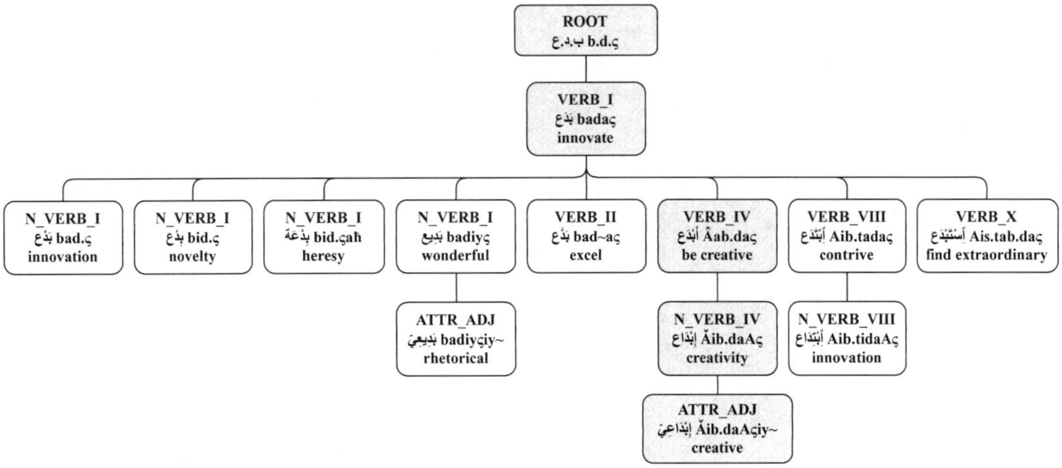

Figure 1: An example of a collection of derivative chains from one root. Highlighted is a chain that links a number of lemmas in derivational progression: the root ب.د.ع *b.d.ς* 'innovation related' ⇒ the verb بَدَع *badaς* 'to innovate' ⇒ the verb أبْدَع *Âb.daς* 'to be creative' ⇒ the noun إبْدَاع *ǍibdaAς* 'creativity' ⇒ the adjective إبْدَاعِي *ǍibdaAςiy~* 'creative'.

For each collection of lemmas from the same root, a derivational family, we recursively construct a tree starting with the root. We only add children (derived lemmas) to parents (derivational bases or the root) in the tree if they match an allowable abstract network pair in terms of all linguistic attributes of child and parent.[3] If a lemma could be paired with different parents or with the same parent but with different relations we duplicate the child lemma and assign it as many times as needed. We continue to assign children to parents until we exhaust all possible pairings. The result is ideally a fully connected tree (knowledge graph) starting with the root of the derivational family and including chains that link it to every lemma in the family. In addition to the lemmas, the nodes of the tree include key linguistic attributes such as the part-of-speech and derivational class. Figure 1 is an example from the CHAINBANK.

In some cases, we may end up with disconnected subtrees due to a lack of allowed pairings in the abstract network. This may be the result of patterns that are disused with some roots.[4]

[3]In some cases, we require an inflectional process as an intermediary stage to produce a new derivation pattern, e.g., deriving a lemma pattern from the plural form of its base lemma: the attributive adjective حدودي *Huduwdiy~* 'bordering' is derived from the plural form of حد *Had~* 'border' (حدود *Huduwd* 'borders').

[4]A solution to consider in the future is to force attach such disconnected subtrees to the root with an *Unknown* relation.

5 Evaluation

5.1 Experimental Setup

Gold Chains We manually constructed a set of 100 CHAINBANK trees correspondign to 100 randomly selected roots from CAMELMORPH. To speed up the process, we started with automatically generated trees using an earlier version of our approach, and manually corrected them.

Data Splits We split our 100 CHAINBANK trees into two sets: Dev (25 roots) and Test (75 roots). We used the Dev set to help debug and improve the tables we created for the abstract network and optimize our algorithm. The Test is used for reporting on the final implementation.

Metrics we report on the following metrics.

- Detected Relations (%) is the percentage of all Gold Chain lemmas we detected automatically.
- Single Relation Correct (%) is the percentage of all Gold Chain detected relations that unambiguous and correct.
- Multiple Relation Correct (%) is the percentage of all Gold Chain detected relations that ambiguous and but with one correct answer.
- No Correct Relations (%) is the percentage of remaining detected relations.

	Assessment 1: Dev		Assessment 2: Test		All	
Roots	25		75		4,924	
Lemmas	566		1,608		34,453	
Detected Relations	496	(87.63%)	1,147	(71.33%)	23,333	(67.72%)
Single Relation Correct	450	(90.73%)	1,058	(92.24%)		
Multiple Relation Correct	45	(9.07%)	76	(6.63%)		
No Correct Relation	1	(0.20%)	13	(1.13%)		

Table 1: Results of constructing the relational derivational CHAINBANK using the CAMELMORPH database, on development (Dev) and test subsets of the roots, and on all roots.

5.2 Results and Discussion

The results on Dev show a high degree of detected relations, but not perfect (~88%), with over 90% single relation correct. The Test is lower in terms of detected relations (~71%), but a higher single relation correct (92%). Multiple relations, accounting for ~6-9% of the cases in Dev and Test, occur due to shared patterns across different derivational classes. Missing relations stem from three main factors: (i) the relational data lacks primary nouns and other nominal lemmas, which require specific paths in the CHAINBANKS; (ii) CAMELMORPH's database wasn't designed for derivational modeling, resulting in incomplete lemma groups for some roots and chain disconnections; or (iii) the relational database needs expansion with new non-canonical patterns. Additionally, the system could be improved by adding features and techniques to resolve ambiguities during evaluation.

All results are presented in Table 1.

5.3 CHAINBANK v1.0

We further applied our system on 4,926 roots from CAMELMORPH and their lemmas, which resulted in 23,333 relations (~68% detected relations), constituting the first version of the CHAINBANK. We plan to manually correct and further annotate additional entries in the future. The Arabic Derivational CHAINBANK v1.0 is publicly available to support further Arabic NLP research.[5]

6 Conclusion and Future Work

We introduced the Arabic Derivational CHAINBANK framework for modeling Arabic derivational morphology. The evaluation of our rule-based method to populate the CHAINBANK shows great promise. The first edition of the CHAINBANK and its framework are publicly available.

Future work will continue to expand the abstract network to include missing patterns, including non-canonical patterns, and to develop advanced disambiguation techniques to further enhance the CHAINBANK. This work should happen in tandem with improving the coverage of CAMELMORPH in terms of lemmas and their features. Our long term vision is to include dialectal lemmas in a manner that shows their connections with each other and with Standard Arabic lemmas.

7 Limitations

We acknowledge several limitations of the work as presented. First, the reliance on a rule-based methodology, although efficient, may overlook nuances that a more comprehensive manual annotation process could capture. This could lead to the omission of certain derivational patterns and relations. Second, the alignment with the CAMELMORPH morphological analyzer, though beneficial for broad coverage, may have resulted in incomplete or fragmented derivational chains due to the database's current structure, which was not designed for derivational modeling. Third, the dataset predominantly covers canonical derivational patterns, with non-canonical patterns remaining underrepresented, potentially limiting the CHAINBANK's applicability to broader linguistic phenomena. Lastly, the work focuses on Standard Arabic and does not cover any of its major dialects. Future work will address these limitations to enhance the framework's completeness and accuracy.

References

Imad A. Al-Sughaiyer and Ibrahim A. Al-Kharashi. 2004. Arabic morphological analysis techniques: A comprehensive survey. *Journal of the American Society for Information Science and Technology*, 55(3):189–213.

Kenneth Beesley. 1998. Arabic morphology using only

[5]https://github.com/CAMeL-Lab/ArabicChainBank

finite-state operations. In *Proceedings of the Workshop on Computational Approaches to Semitic Languages (CASL)*, pages 50–7, Montereal.

Mohamed Boudchiche, Azzeddine Mazroui, Mohamed Ould Abdallahi Ould Bebah, Abdelhak Lakhouaja, and Abderrahim Boudlal. 2017. AlKhalil Morpho Sys2: A robust Arabic morpho-syntactic analyzer. *Journal of King Saud University-Computer and Information Sciences*, 29(2):141–146.

Abderrahim Boudlal, Abdelhak Lakhouaja, Azzeddine Mazroui, Abdelouafi Meziane, MOAO Bebah, and Mostafa Shoul. 2010. AlKhalil Morpho Sys1: A morphosyntactic analysis system for Arabic texts. In *International Arab conference on information technology*, pages 1–6.

Ryan Cotterell, Ekaterina Vylomova, Huda Khayrallah, Christo Kirov, and David Yarowsky. 2017. Paradigm completion for derivational morphology. *arXiv preprint arXiv:1708.09151*.

Hassan Gadalla. 2000. *Comparative Morphology of Standard and Egyptian Arabic*. LINCOM EUROPA.

Nizar Habash and Bonnie Dorr. 2003. CatVar: a database of categorial variations for English. In *Proceedings of Machine Translation Summit IX: System Presentations*, New Orleans, USA.

Nizar Habash, Reham Marzouk, Christian Khairallah, and Salam Khalifa. 2022. Morphotactic modeling in an open-source multi-dialectal arabic morphological analyzer and generator. In *Proceedings of the 19th SIGMORPHON Workshop on Computational Research in Phonetics, Phonology, and Morphology*, pages 92–102.

Nizar Habash and Owen Rambow. 2006. MAGEAD: A morphological analyzer and generator for the Arabic dialects. In *Proceedings of the International Conference on Computational Linguistics and the Conference of the Association for Computational Linguistics (COLING-ACL)*, pages 681–688, Sydney, Australia.

Nizar Habash, Owen Rambow, and Ryan Roth. 2012. MADA+TOKAN Manual. Technical report, Technical Report CCLS-12-01, Columbia University.

Nizar Habash, Abdelhadi Soudi, and Tim Buckwalter. 2007. On Arabic Transliteration. In A. van den Bosch and A. Soudi, editors, *Arabic Computational Morphology: Knowledge-based and Empirical Methods*, pages 15–22. Springer, Netherlands.

Nizar Y Habash. 2010. *Introduction to Arabic natural language processing*, volume 3. Morgan & Claypool Publishers.

Nabil Hathout and Fiammetta Namer. 2014. Démonette, a French derivational morpho-semantic network. *Linguistic Issues in Language Technology*, 11.

Valentin Hofmann, Hinrich Schütze, and Janet Pierrehumbert. 2020. A graph auto-encoder model of derivational morphology. In *Proceedings of the 58th Annual Meeting of the Association for Computational Linguistics*, pages 1127–1138, Online. Association for Computational Linguistics.

Clive Holes. 2004. *Modern Arabic: Structures, functions, and varieties*. Georgetown University Press.

Nikhil Kanuparthi, Abhilash Inumella, and Dipti Misra Sharma. 2012. Hindi derivational morphological analyzer. In *Proceedings of the Twelfth Meeting of the Special Interest Group on Computational Morphology and Phonology*, pages 10–16.

Christian Khairallah, Salam Khalifa, Reham Marzouk, Mayar Nassar, and Nizar Habash. 2024a. Camel morph MSA: A large-scale open-source morphological analyzer for Modern Standard Arabic. In *Proceedings of the 2024 Joint International Conference on Computational Linguistics, Language Resources and Evaluation (LREC-COLING 2024)*, pages 2683–2691, Torino, Italia. ELRA and ICCL.

Christian Khairallah, Reham Marzouk, Salam Khalifa, Mayar Nassar, and Nizar Habash. 2024b. Computational morphology and lexicography modeling of Modern Standard Arabic nominals. In *Findings of the Association for Computational Linguistics: EACL 2024*, pages 1071–1084, St. Julian's, Malta. Association for Computational Linguistics.

George Kiraz. 1994. Multi-tape Two-level Morphology: A Case study in Semitic Non-Linear Morphology. In *Proceedings of the International Conference on Computational Linguistics (COLING)*, pages 180–186, Kyoto, Japan.

Arfath Pasha, Mohamed Al-Badrashiny, Mona Diab, Ahmed El Kholy, Ramy Eskander, Nizar Habash, Manoj Pooleery, Owen Rambow, and Ryan Roth. 2014. Madamira: A fast, comprehensive tool for morphological analysis and disambiguation of Arabic. In *Proceedings of the Language Resources and Evaluation Conference (LREC)*, pages 1094–1101, Reykjavik, Iceland.

Jan Šnajder. 2014. DerivBase.hr: A high-coverage derivational morphology resource for Croatian. In *Proceedings of the Ninth International Conference on Language Resources and Evaluation (LREC'14)*, pages 3371–3377, Reykjavik, Iceland. European Language Resources Association (ELRA).

Dima Taji, Jamila El Gizuli, and Nizar Habash. 2018. An Arabic dependency treebank in the travel domain. In *Proceedings of the Workshop on Open-Source Arabic Corpora and Processing Tools (OSACT)*, Miyazaki, Japan.

Daniil Vodolazsky. 2020. Derivbase. ru: A derivational morphology resource for Russian. In *Proceedings of the Twelfth Language Resources and Evaluation Conference*, pages 3937–3943.

Wajdi Zaghouani, Abdelati Hawwari, Mona Diab, Tim O'Gorman, and Ahmed Badran. 2016. AMPN: a semantic resource for Arabic morphological patterns. *International Journal of Speech Technology*, 19:281–288.

Britta Zeller, Jan Šnajder, and Sebastian Padó. 2013. DErivBase: Inducing and evaluating a derivational morphology resource for German. In *Proceedings of the Association for Computational Linguistics*, pages 1201–1211.

A CHAINBANK Derivational Classes

	ChainBank Derivational Classes	POS	Morphosemantic Feature	Example		
				Pattern	Arabic	Gloss
(1)	Masdar المصدر	Noun	Event حدث	ta1a2~u3,..	تعلُّم	learning
(2)	M+Masdar المصدر الميمي	Noun		ma1o2a3	مسمع	hearing
(3)	Noun of Masdar اسم المصدر	Noun		ta1A2u3+iy~ap	تفاعلية	interaction
(4)	Masdar+iy~a المصدر الصناعي	Noun	Entity الذات	1a2iy3+ap	غنيمة	loot
(5)	Noun اسم جنس	Noun		1a2a3	جبل	mountain
(6)	Noun of Location اسم المكان	Noun		ma1o2a3	مخرَج	exit
(7)	Noun of Instrument اسم الآلة	Noun		مِفعال ومِفعلة/mi1o2a3	منحت	chisel
(8)	Noun of Instance اسم المرة	Noun		1a2o3+ap	أكلة	meal
(9)	Semantic Specification التخصيص الدلالي	Noun		ma1o2uw3+ap	معلومة	information
(10)	Descriptive Adjective الصفة المشبهة	Adj	Consistency ثبوت	1a2uw3,....	خجول	shy
(11)	Comparative Adjective اسم التفضيل	Adj		>a1o2a3	أعقل	wiser
(12)	Attributive Adjective اسم النسبة	Adj		1a2a3+iy~, ...	عمليّ	practical
(13)	Active Participle اسم الفاعل	Adj	Changeability تجدد	1A2i3, ...	آكل	eater
(14)	Passive Participle اسم المفعول	Adj		ma1o2uw3,...	مسموع	being heard
(15)	Noun of Exaggeration اسم المبالغة	Adj		1a2iy3, ...	شريب	drunkard
(16)	Form_I فَعَل	Verb	Basic root meaning (T/I)	1a2a3	أكل	to eat
(17)	Form_I فعِل	Verb	Stative(T/I)	1a2i3	شرِب	to hear
(18)	Form_I فعُل	Verb	Attributing an adjective (I)	1a2u3	حسُن	to be beautiful
(19)	Form_II فعَّل	Verb	Transitivity (T/I)	1a2~a3	قوّى	to stregnthen
(20)	Form_III فاعَل	Verb	Reciprocality (T/I)	1A2a3	ذاكر	to memorize
(21)	Form_IV أفعَل	Verb	Causative/Factitive (T/I)	>a1o2a3	أخرج	to get out
(22)	Form_V تفعَّل	Verb	Intransitivity/ Compliance (T/I)	ta1a2~a3	تعلّم	to learn
(23)	Form_VI تفاعل	Verb	Reciprocal /Compliance (T/I)	ta1A2a3	تفاعل	to interact
(24)	Form_VII انفعل	Verb	Intransitivity/ Compliance (I)	{in1a2a3	انجذب	to be attracted
(25)	Form_VIII افتعل	Verb	Reciprocality/Intensivity(T/I)	{i1ota2a3	اغتنم	to gain
(26)	Form_IX افعلّ	Verb	Colors / Defects (T/I)	{i1o2a3~	احمرّ	to get red
(27)	Form_X استفعل	Verb	Doing an action(T/I)	{isota1o2a3	استخرج	to extract
(28)	QUAD_Form_I فعلل	Verb	Doing an action (T/I)	1a2o3a4	زخرف	to decorate
(29)	QUAD_Form_II افعللّ	Verb	Intensivity(I)	{i1o2a3a4~	اطمأن	to reassure
(30)	QUAD_Form_III تفعلل	Verb	Intransitivity/ Compliance (I)	ta1a2o3a4	تقهقر	to retreat

Table 2: CHAINBANK Derivational Classes: an overview of Arabic Morphosemantic patterns with examples. (T/I) refers to transitive & intransitive

B ChainBank Tags

ID	TAG	Derivational Class	POS	LOCATION
1	ROOT	Triconsonantal Root	ROOT	Canonical_TABLE
2	V_I	Verb:form I	VERB	Canonical_TABLE
3	V_*	Verb:form *	VERB	Canonical_TABLE
4	QUAD_V_I	Quadriliteral Verb	VERB	Canonical_TABLE
5	QUAD_V_*	Quadriliteral Verb	VERB	Canonical_TABLE
6	N_VERB_I	Masdar:I	NOUN	Canonical_TABLE
7	N_VERB_*	Masdar:*	NOUN	Canonical_TABLE
8	N_QUAD_VERB_I	Quadriliteral Masdar:I	NOUN	Canonical_TABLE
9	N_QUAD_VERB_*	Quadriliteral Masdar:*	NOUN	Canonical_TABLE
10	N_LOC	Noun of Location	NOUN	Canonical_TABLE
11	N_INSTR	Noun of Instrument	NOUN	Canonical_TABLE
12	N_MANN	Noun of Manner	NOUN	Canonical_TABLE
13	N_INST	Noun of Instance	NOUN	Canonical_TABLE
14	M_MAS	M+Masdar	NOUN	Canonical_TABLE
15	COMP_ADJ	Comparative Adjective	ADJ	Canonical_TABLE
16	N_EXAG	Noun of Exaggeration	ADJ	Canonical_TABLE
17	ACT_PRTC	Active Participle	ADJ	Canonical_TABLE
18	PASS_PRTC	Passive Participle	ADJ	Canonical_TABLE
19	DES_ADJ	Descriptive Adjective	ADJ	Canonical_TABLE
20	QUAD_ACT_PRTC	Quadriliteral Active Participle	ADJ	Canonical_TABLE
21	QUAD_PASS_PRTC	Quadriliteral Passive Participle	ADJ	Canonical_TABLE
22	QUAD_ACT_PRTC	Quadriliteral Active Participle	ADJ	Canonical_TABLE
23	QUAD_PASS_PRTC	Quadriliteral Passive Participle	ADJ	Canonical_TABLE
24	ADJ_ATTR	Attributive Adjective	ADJ	Affixation_TABLE
25	MAS_iy~a	Masdar+iy~a	NOUN	Affixation_TABLE
26	SEM_SPECS	Semantic Specification	NOUN	Semantic_Specs_TABLE

Table 3: Derivational Classes in the Arabic ChainBank, showing ID, tag, class, POS, and location of each form within the derivational network.

C ChainBank Canonical Tables

PARENT:PATTERN	PARENT_POS	CHILD_DER_CAT	CHILD:PATTERN	CHILD_POS	CHILD_EXAMPLE
None	NONE	ROOT	ROOT	ROOT	"ك.ت.ب"
ROOT	ROOT	VERB_I	V_I:1a2a3	VERB	أكل
V_I:1a2a3	VERB	PASS_PRTC	PASS_PRTC:ma1o2uw3	ADJ	مكتوب
V_I:1a2a3	VERB	N_LOC	N_LOC:ma1o2i3+ap	NOUN	منطقة
V_I:1a2a3	VERB	N_LOC	N_LOC:ma1o2i3	NOUN	مجلس
V_I:1a2a3	VERB	N_LOC	N_LOC:ma1o2a3+ap	NOUN	مكتبة
V_I:1a2a3	VERB	N_INSTR	N_INSTR:mi1o2a3	NOUN	مبرد
V_I:1a2a3	VERB	N_INSTR	N_INSTR:1a2~A3+ap	NOUN	سماعة
V_I:1a2a3	VERB	N_INST	N_INST:1a2o3+ap	NOUN	ضربة
ACT_PRTC:1A2i3	ADJ	N_EXAG	N_EXAG:1a2iy3	ADJ	حليم
ACT_PRTC:1A2i3	ADJ	N_EXAG	N_EXAG:1a2~A3	ADJ	علام
V_I:1a2a3	VERB	N_VERB_I	MASDAR:1u2uw3+ap	NOUN	برودة
V_I:1a2a3	VERB	N_VERB_I	MASDAR:1u2uw3	NOUN	دخول
V_I:1a2a3	VERB	N_VERB_I	MASDAR:1u2o3An	NOUN	غفران
V_I:1a2a3	VERB	N_VERB_I	MASDAR:1i2A3+ap	NOUN	كتابة
V_I:1a2a3	VERB	N_VERB_I	MASDAR:1i2A3	NOUN	قيام
V_I:1a2a3	VERB	N_VERB_I	MASDAR:1a2uw3	NOUN	قبول
V_I:1a2a3	VERB	N_VERB_I	MASDAR:1a2o3aY	NOUN	شكوى
V_I:1a2a3	VERB	N_VERB_I	MASDAR:1a2o3	NOUN	ضرب
V_I:1a2a3	VERB	N_VERB_I	MASDAR:1a2iy3	NOUN	رحيل
V_I:1a2a3	VERB	N_VERB_I	MASDAR:1a2A3+ap	NOUN	ضخامة
V_I:1a2a3	VERB	N_VERB_I	MASDAR:1a2a3	NOUN	طلب
V_I:1a2a3	VERB	N_VERB_I	MASDAR:1a2A3	NOUN	فساد
V_I:1a2a3	VERB	MASDAR_M	MASDAR_M:ma1o2i3+ap	NOUN	معرفة
V_I:1a2a3	VERB	MASDAR_M	MASDAR_M:ma1o2a3	NOUN	مقتل
V_I:1a2a3	VERB	MASDAR_M	MASDAR_M:ma1iy3	NOUN	مصير
V_I:1a2a3	VERB	MASDAR_M	MASDAR_M:ma1a3o3+ap	NOUN	مودة
V_I:1a2a3	VERB	MASDAR_M	MASDAR_M:ma1A3	NOUN	منام
V_I:1a2a3	VERB	DES_ADJ	ADJ:ma1o2uw3	ADJ	موفور
V_I:1a2a3	VERB	DES_ADJ	ADJ:1u2u3	ADJ	صعب
V_I:1a2a3	VERB	DES_ADJ	ADJ:1u2o3An	ADJ	عريان
V_I:1a2a3	VERB	DES_ADJ	ADJ:1u2o3	ADJ	حلو
V_I:1a2a3	VERB	DES_ADJ	ADJ:1u2A3	ADJ	شجاع
V_I:1a2a3	VERB	DES_ADJ	ADJ:1a2uw3	ADJ	وقور
V_I:1a2a3	VERB	DES_ADJ	ADJ:1a2iy3	ADJ	عظيم
V_I:1a2a3	VERB	DES_ADJ	ADJ:1a2o3	ADJ	ضخم
V_I:1a2a3	VERB	DES_ADJ	ADJ:1a2~i3	ADJ	طيب
V_I:1a2a3	VERB	DES_ADJ	ADJ_M:1a2o3An	ADJ	عطشان
V_I:1a2a3	VERB	DES_ADJ	ADJ_M:>a12a3	ADJ	أسمر
V_I:1a2a3	VERB	DES_ADJ	ADJ_F:1a2O3aY	ADJ	عطشى
V_I:1a2a3	VERB	DES_ADJ	ADJ_F:1a23A'	ADJ	سمراء
ADJ:1a2uw3	ADJ	COMP_ADJ	ADJ_COMP_9	ADJ_COMP	أخجل
ADJ:1a2iy3	ADJ	COMP_ADJ	ADJ_COMP_6	ADJ_COMP	أرشق

Table 4: (Part I) A sample of entries from `Canonical_I` table: one of the fundamental tables in the ChainBank.

PARENT:PATTERN	PARENT_POS	CHILD_DER_CAT	CHILD:PATTERN	CHILD_POS	CHILD_EXAMPLE
ROOT	VERB	QUAD_VERB_I	QUAD_V_I:1a2o3a4	VERB	زخرف
V_I:1a2a3	VERB	VERB_II	V_II:1a2~a3	VERB	كسَّر
V_I:1a2i3	VERB	VERB_II	V_II:1a2~a3	VERB	كبَّر
V_I:1a2u3	VERB	VERB_II	V_II:1a2~a3	VERB	كبَّر
V_I:1a2a3	VERB	VERB_III	V_III:1A2a3	VERB	سافر
V_I:1a2a3	VERB	VERB_IV	V_IV:>a1o2a3	VERB	أوجد
V_I:1a2i3	VERB	VERB_IV	V_IV:>a1o2a3	VERB	أخرج
V_I:1a2i3	VERB	VERB_VIII	V_VIII:{i1ota2a3	VERB	اخترق
V_I:1a2u3	VERB	VERB_VIII	V_VIII:{i1ota2a3	VERB	اختبر
V_I:1a2a3	VERB	VERB_VII	V_VII:{ino1a2a3	VERB	اندرج
V_I:1a2a3	VERB	VERB_IX	V_IX:{i1o2a3~	VERB	اخضر
V_I:1a2a3	VERB	VERB_X	V_X:{isota1o2a3	VERB	استحضر
V_II:1a2~a3	VERB	N_VERB_II	MASDAR:ti1o2A3	NOUN	تكرار
V_II:1a2~a3	VERB	N_VERB_II	MASDAR:ta1o2iy3	NOUN	تكبير
V_II:1a2~a3	VERB	N_VERB_II	MASDAR:ta1o2i3+ap	NOUN	تفرقة
V_III:1A2a3	VERB	N_VERB_III	MASDAR:mu1A2a3+ap	NOUN	محاسبة
V_III:1A2a3	VERB	N_VERB_III	MASDAR:1i2A3	NOUN	حساب
V_VI:ta1A2a3	VERB	N_VERB_VI	MASDAR:ta1A2u3	NOUN	تحول
V_VIII:{i1ota2a3	VERB	N_VERB_VIII	MASDAR:{i1oti2A3	NOUN	اختراق
V_IX:{i1o2a3~	VERB	N_VERB_IX	MASDAR:{i1o2i3A3	NOUN	اخضرار
V_X:{isota1o2a3	VERB	N_VERB_X	MASDAR:{isoti1o2A3	NOUN	استحضار
QUAD_V_I:1a2o3a4	VERB	N_QUAD_VERB_I	QUAD_MASDAR:1a2o3a4+ap	NOUN	زخرفة
QUAD_V_II:ta1a2o3	VERB	N_QUAD_VERB_II	QUAD_MASDAR:ta1a2o3u4	NOUN	تدهوُر
V_III:1A2a3	VERB	MASDAR_M	MASDAR_M:mu1A2a3	NOUN	مفاعل
V_IV:>a1o2a3	VERB	MASDAR_M	MASDAR_M:ma1o2a3	NOUN	محضر
V_II:1a2~a3	VERB	DES_ADJ	ADJ:mu1a2~i3	ADJ	معمر
V_III:1A2a3	VERB	DES_ADJ	ADJ:mu1o2i3	ADJ	مؤمن
V_III:1A2a3	VERB	DES_ADJ	ADJ:mu1A2i3	ADJ	مغامر
V_II:1a2~a3	VERB	ACT_PRTC	ACT_PRTC:mu1a2~i3	ADJ	محطِّم
V_III:1A2a3	VERB	ACT_PRTC	ACT_PRTC:mu1A2i3	ADJ	محاصِر
V_IV:>a1o2a3	VERB	ACT_PRTC	ACT_PRTC:mu1o2i3	ADJ	مخبر
V_V:ta1a2~a3	VERB	ACT_PRTC	ACT_PRTC:muta1a2~i3	ADJ	متفهم
V_VI:ta1A2a3	VERB	ACT_PRTC	ACT_PRTC:muta1A2i3	ADJ	متبادل
V_VII:{ino1a2a3	VERB	ACT_PRTC	ACT_PRTC:muno1a2i3	ADJ	مندرِج
QUAD_V_IV:{i1o2a3	VERB	ACT_PRTC	QUAD_ACT_PRTC:mu1o2a3i4	ADJ	مطمئِن
QUAD_V_I:1a2o3a4	VERB	ACT_PRTC	QUAD_ACT_PRTC:mu1a2o3i4	ADJ	مزخرِف
V_II:1a2~a3	VERB	PASS_PRTC	PASS_PRTC:mu1a2~a3	ADJ	معطَّل
V_III:1A2a3	VERB	PASS_PRTC	PASS_PRTC:mu1A2a3	ADJ	محاصَر
V_IV:>a1o2a3	VERB	PASS_PRTC	PASS_PRTC:mu1o2a3	ADJ	مرغم
V_V:ta1a2~a3	VERB	PASS_PRTC	PASS_PRTC:muta1a2~a3	ADJ	متأسلم
V_VI:ta1A2a4	VERB	PASS_PRTC	PASS_PRTC:muta1A2a3	ADJ	متآكل
V_X:{isota1o2a3	VERB	PASS_PRTC	PASS_PRTC:musota1o2a3	ADJ	مستحضَر

Table 5: (Part II) A sample of entries from Canonical_* table: one of the fundamental tables in the CHAINBANK.

Sentiment Analysis of Arabic Tweets Using Large Language Models

Pankaj Dadure UPES Dehradun
Ananya Dixit UPES Dehradun
Kunal Tewatia UPES Dehradun
Nandini Paliwal UPES Dehradun
Anshika Malla UPES Dehradun

Abstract

In the digital era, sentiment analysis has become an indispensable tool for understanding public sentiments, optimizing market strategies, and enhancing customer engagement across diverse sectors. While significant advancements have been made in sentiment analysis for high-resource languages such as English, French, etc. This study focuses on Arabic, a low-resource language, to address its unique challenges like morphological complexity, diverse dialects, and limited linguistic resources. Existing works in Arabic sentiment analysis have utilized deep learning architectures like LSTM, BiLSTM, and CNN-LSTM, alongside embedding techniques such as Word2Vec and contextualized models like ARABERT. Building on this foundation, our research investigates sentiment classification of Arabic tweets, categorizing them as positive or negative, using embeddings derived from three large language models (LLMs): Universal Sentence Encoder (USE), XLM-RoBERTa base (XLM-R base), and MiniLM-L12-v2. Experimental results demonstrate that incorporating emojis in the dataset and using the MiniLM embeddings yield an accuracy of 85.98%. In contrast, excluding emojis and using embeddings from the XLM-R base resulted in a lower accuracy of 78.98%. These findings highlight the impact of both dataset composition and embedding techniques on Arabic sentiment analysis performance.

1 Introduction

During a time when digitalization is at its peak and platforms like Twitter (Heikal et al., 2018) are a crucial source of information for many as it is a platforms where public opinions are expressed in real-time in its most raw form, be it thoughts, opinions, personal experiences, etc. In today's world "tweets" are playing a vital role for both governments and organizations when it comes to understanding the social sentiment for them to make informed decisions it has become a critical requirement for models that can analyze and interpret sentiment from textual data. The primary objective of sentiment analysis is to study the emotional tone of textual data which is directly related to the formation of public opinion towards various services, products, brands, socio-political topics, etc. to understand the collective attitude towards a certain someone or something. The relevance or requirement of sentiment analysis is evident and has been of great help for organizations that treat public opinion with utmost importance.

Sentiment analysis is the computational study of people's opinions, attitudes and emotions toward entities, individuals, issues, events or topics (Heikal et al., 2018). Recently, deep learning has shown great success in the field of sentiment analysis but there lies a demand of accurate analysis of emotions when it comes to non–English languages, particularly Arabic because there's an immense amount of dialectal variation, lack of resources, polysemous words, other mixed languages, context etc. which increase the complexity of the data making difficult for models to parse or interpret data. Given as one of the most widely spoken languages globally there's a significant need of high-quality NLP models. NLP has undergone various changes during the development of various large language models (LLMs) such as GPT, T5, BERT etc. These models are based on deep learning methods and utilising various datasets these models have presented the world with advanced performance across numerous languages and NLP tasks.

The core objective of this paper is to work with and understand the sentiment analysis system for Arabic tweets by focusing on fine tuning models and NLP methods through various datasets, Arabic a language which is spoken by over 400 million people worldwide is know for its linguistic richness, complexity and deep historical roots, the project aims to classify the tweets into two categories posi-

Processings of the 1st Workshop on NLP for Languages Using Arabic Script (AbjadNLP), pages 88–94
January 19, 2025.

tive and negative, the system shall provide insights into the community views and collective viewpoint of the public, also this system can be utilized on various ends like e-commerce websites, political analysis, PR etc. the project will be addressing various challenges like complex linguistics, dealing with dialects, tokenization, to maximize the training process various models such as MiniLM (Aperdannier et al., 2024), XLM-R (Barbieri et al., 2021), USE (Saka and Cömert, 2024) is implemented. This paper will contribute to the advancement of sentiment analysis in Arabic which will bridge the language gap and eventually contribute to facilitating better and deeper decision-making in various domains that rely on Arabic text data.

2 Related work

As per (Al Sallab et al., 2015), several deep learning techniques are used to classify Arabic text such as Deep Neural Networks (DNN), Deep Belief Networks (DBN), Deep Auto-Encoders (DAE), and Recursive Auto-Encoders (RAE). Among all the architectures, Recursive Auto-Encoder proved to be the most effective as it could capture the context and sentence structure, addressing the shortcomings of the Bag-of-Words method used in the other models and giving an accuracy of 74.3%. As mentioned in (Duwairi et al., 2014), focused on creating a framework to classify Arabic tweets as positive, negative, or neutral. To address challenges like dialect variations, Arabizi (Arabic written in Roman characters), and the informal nature of tweets. A crowd-sourcing approach was used to collect and label a large dataset of tweets, with over 350,000 collected and 25,000 labeled for training. After applying preprocessing techniques such as tokenization, stopword removal, and stemming, they tested three classifiers: Naïve Bayes, k-nearest neighbors, and Support Vector Machines. Naïve Bayes performed the best, achieving an accuracy of 76.78. Limitations in the dialect dictionary and the dataset size impacted the overall accuracy in this research.

In (Al-Ayyoub et al., 2015), the authors present a framework that classifies Arabic tweets using a lexicon-based approach (Palanisamy et al., 2013). They constructed a sentiment lexicon consisting of over 120.000 Arabic terms and built a sentiment analysis tool that classifies tweets as positive, negative, or neutral. The tool was compared with a keyword-based approach and outperformed it, achieving an overall accuracy of 86.89. The accuracy for positive tweets was 96, for negative tweets 85.67, and neutral tweets 79.3. The work mentioned in (Heikal et al., 2018) designed an ensemble of CNN and LSTM to predict the sentiment of Arabic Tweets. Herein, the AraVec model has been used, primarily developed for Arabic with an F1 score of 64.46, the model demonstrated that the ensemble of CNN and LSTM works better and provides greater results. In (Abdul-Mageed et al., 2014) they have worked by using the SAMAR system which operates in a two-stage classification process. By combining features such as novel techniques and polarity lexicons, sentiment classification achieves an accuracy of 65.32.

3 System Architecture

3.1 Dataset

The dataset has been obtained from Kaggle[1] which is available by the name of "Arabic Sentiment Twitter Corpus". The number of instances present in the dataset is 56795, out of which 28513 tweets are labeled as positive and 28282 are labeled as negative, and its size is 5.9 MB. The coverage of the dataset began on 31st March 2019 and went on till 29th April 2019. The frequency of most used words in the tweets labeled as negative is visible in Figure 2, whereas the frequency of most used words in the tweets which have been labeled as positive can be seen in Figure 3 and the most frequent word in the overall dataset is represented in Figure 1. Many tweets in the dataset include emojis that intensify the sentiment removing or ignoring these could lead to a loss of sentiment context Figure 4, several tweets in the dataset show instances of mix-code or code switch where Twitter users have used a mix of both Arabic and English words, the dataset also includes informal writing styles.

3.2 Data Preprocessing

During this phase, first, the dataset was combined and shuffled, as the positive and negative datasets were initially separated. The next step involved cleaning the data and reducing noise. The primary goal of this phase was to help pre trained models generate better embeddings, enabling classifiers to give more accurate results. The steps included removing unwanted characters such as punctuation, special characters, dates, and times. Then, the tweets were tokenized, followed by the removal of

[1]https://www.kaggle.com/datasets/mksaad/arabic-sentiment-twitter-corpus?resource=download

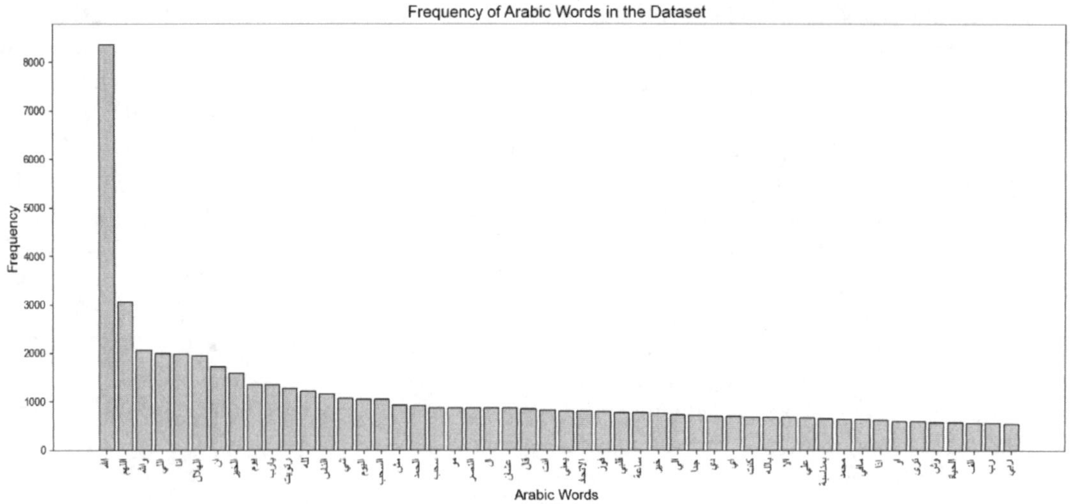

Figure 1: Frequency of Arabic words in the dataset

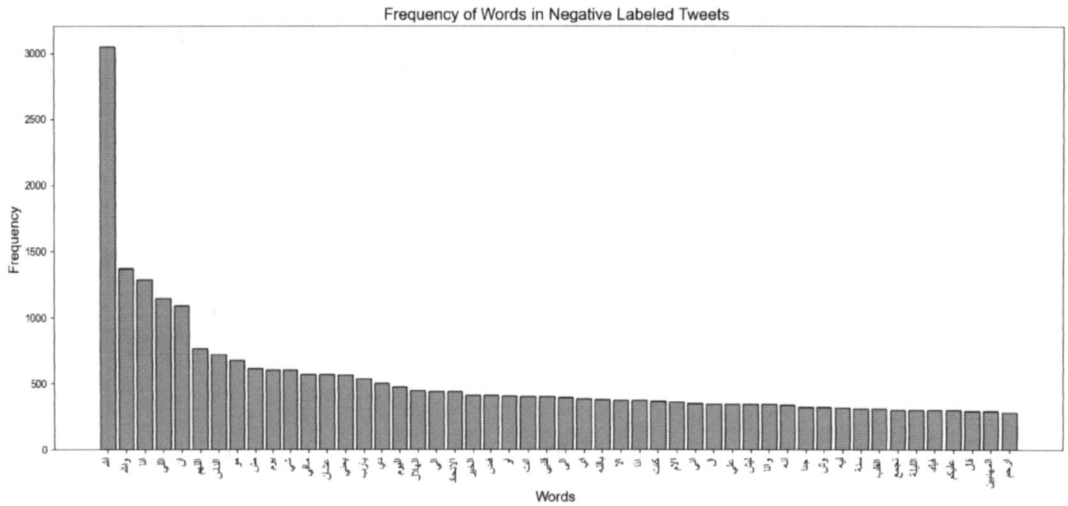

Figure 2: Frequency of Arabic words in the tweets labeled as negative

stopwords, and finally, the words were joined into a single string. Emojis were retained in the dataset to preserve the sentiment of the tweets. An excerpt of the preprocessed dataset is visible in Figure 4.

3.3 Model Training

Three models were used for the primary purpose of generating embeddings, one of the models used is MiniLM-L12-v2, this model uses transformer architecture similar to BERT the input is tokenized and passed through multiple transformer layers the final output is a 384-dimensional embedding vector for the entire input, it can also incorporate emojis as meaningful tokens it assigns embeddings based on how emojis co-occur with words and sentences in the training data. The other model which is used is USE, the transformer version is similar to other transformer models i.e. the text is tokenised and passed through different layers Each token's position and context are considered to create a 512-dimensional output vector that represents the entire input's semantics, emojis are included as part of the input sequence and are treated as tokens. Their embeddings are determined by their role in the text, similar to words. The third and final model which was incorporated is a multilingual version of RoBERTa, XLM-R trained in over 100 languages it shares the architecture of BERT with improvements in training techniques and larger-scale training data, the input text is processed by using a subword tok-

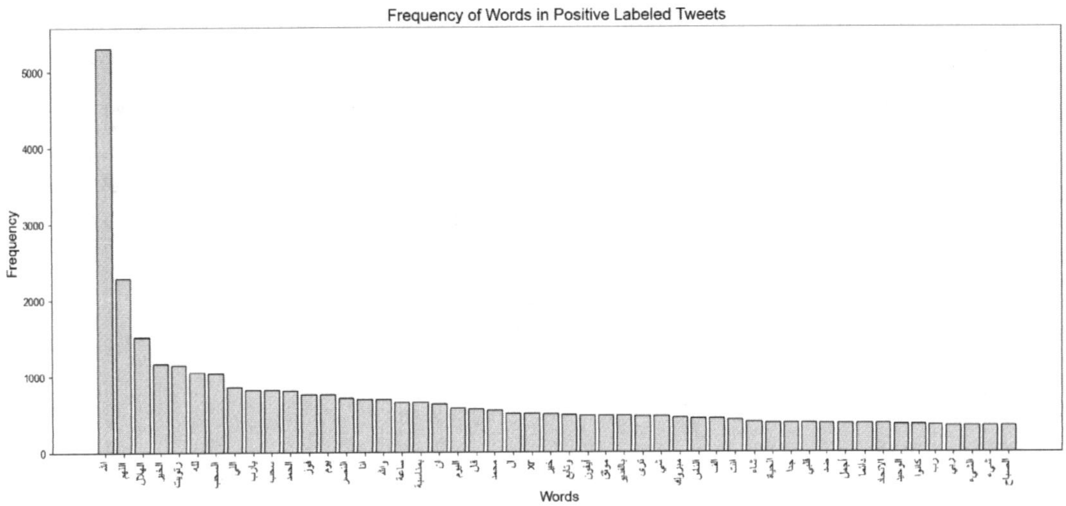

Figure 3: Frequency of Arabic words in the tweets labeled as positive

tweet	label
قال ﷺ قال يصبح اللهم نعمة بأحد خلقك فمنك وحدك شريك فلك الحمد ولك 🌸 الشكر فقد أدى شكر يومه	pos
💔 ليته فصلها	neg
😪 أكتفي بالراس اللي مايصدع	neg
🌷 💕 🌷 الخيرات يارب العالمين والصلاة محمد وال محمد	pos

Figure 4: Excerpt from the preprocessed dataset

enizer that works by splitting the words into smaller and meaningful units, each token passes through a series of transformer layers like the other transformer models, final sentence embedding is generated by taking the mean of the token embeddings from the last transformer layer this pooling step summarizes the sentence's semantic content into a single vector, the model's attention mechanism captures how emojis relate to surrounding text, assigning appropriate semantic weights to them.

3.4 Classification

In this study, five different classifiers were employed to predict the correct label for a given input data: Logistic Regression, Support Vector Machine (SVM), Random Forest, Decision Tree, and K-Nearest Neighbors (KNN). Logistic Regression, a simple yet effective model, estimates probabilities for binary classification by fitting the data to a logistic curve, making it particularly useful for linearly separable datasets. Support Vector Machine, on the other hand, identifies an optimal hyperplane to separate classes and effectively handles both linear and non-linear data through the use of kernel functions. Its ability to perform well in high-dimensional spaces makes it especially suitable for text data and complex feature spaces. Random Forest employs an ensemble approach by constructing multiple decision trees and averaging their predictions, thereby improving accuracy and mitigating overfitting. This capability allows it to perform well on complex datasets by capturing intricate feature interactions. A Decision Tree, characterized by its simplicity and interpretability, uses a tree-like structure of decision rules to represent data and make predictions. Finally, K-Nearest Neighbors classifies an input by analyzing the K closest data points, making it effective for small to medium-sized datasets, though its computational intensity increases significantly with larger datasets.

4 Experimental Results and Analysis

The results indicate that MiniLM provided the highest accuracy in Arabic Tweets that included emojis, while XLM-R outperformed the others on the Arabic Tweets without emojis. A comparison of Table

Classifier	MiniLM	USE	XLM-R$_{BASE}$
Accuracy (%)			
LR	66.49	61.09	**69.46**
SVM	73.25	72.78	**74.40**
RF	78.52	74.78	**78.98**
KNN	73.30	71.04	**73.34**
DT	74.38	72.24	**74.48**
F1-Score (%)			
LR	66.48	61.08	**69.45**
SVM	73.17	72.71	**74.29**
RF	78.48	74.72	**78.92**
KNN	73.29	71.03	**73.34**
DT	74.38	72.23	**74.48**
Precision (%)			
LR	66.51	61.11	**69.52**
SVM	73.58	73.03	**74.83**
RF	78.78	75.04	**79.33**
KNN	73.35	71.04	**73.36**
DT	74.38	72.24	**74.48**
Recall (%)			
LR	66.49	61.09	**69.46**
SVM	73.25	72.78	**74.40**
RF	78.52	74.78	**78.98**
KNN	73.30	71.04	**73.34**
DT	74.38	72.24	**74.48**

Table 1: Experimental results without emojis

Classifier	MiniLM	USE	XLM-R$_{BASE}$
Accuracy (%)			
LR	**79.18**	69.62	78.08
SVM	**82.86**	81.94	80.88
RF	**85.98**	81.18	82.48
KNN	**81.65**	78.33	77.90
DT	74.38	75.25	**77.30**
F1-Score (%)			
LR	**79.18**	69.62	78.08
SVM	**82.86**	81.94	80.87
RF	**85.98**	81.18	82.46
KNN	**81.64**	78.32	77.90
DT	74.38	75.25	**77.30**
Precision (%)			
LR	**79.18**	69.64	78.09
SVM	**82.87**	81.94	80.95
RF	**86.00**	81.18	82.64
KNN	**81.73**	78.34	77.92
DT	74.38	75.25	**77.30**
Recall (%)			
LR	**79.18**	69.62	78.08
SVM	**82.86**	81.94	80.88
RF	**85.98**	81.18	82.48
KNN	**81.65**	78.33	77.90
DT	**80.02**	75.25	77.30

Table 2: Experimental results with emojis

1 and Table 2 clearly shows that the inclusion of emojis in the data set significantly improved the performance of all models evaluated.

In Table 2, MiniLM-L12-v2 demonstrated the highest accuracy, followed by XLM-R and USE. Further analysis revealed that MiniLM-L12-v2 excelled in sentiment analysis of Arabic tweets due to its transformer-based architecture and its ability to effectively utilize emojis as meaningful tokens to enrich semantic understanding. Its 12 transformer layers enable it to produce high-quality embeddings while maintaining a compact model size. This smaller size, optimized for semantic similarity tasks, allows MiniLM to capture sentiment-related nuances provided by emojis. In addition, its multilingual pre-training ensures strong performance on low-resource and multilingual datasets.

XLM-R, a multilingual transformer model, outperformed USE due to its extensive pre-training on a large corpus across 100+ languages, including Arabic. This pretraining allowed XLM-R to effectively understand Arabic and its dialects, making it particularly strong in purely textual datasets. However, its performance was comparatively weaker on datasets with emojis, as shown in Table 1 and Table 2. Being a general-purpose model, XLM-R's larger architecture may not be as fine-tuned for sentiment analysis as MiniLM, which slightly reduces its efficiency in this specific task.

USE (Cer, 2018) showed the lowest accuracy across both cases (with emoji and without emoji). This is likely because USE is designed for general-purpose sentence embeddings rather than specialized tasks like sentiment analysis. Although it supports multiple languages, its pre-trained corpus lacks sufficient Arabic-specific data, limiting its effectiveness in low-resource languages. It focuses on general sentence similarity tasks and struggles to capture the subtle details needed to identify sentiments in short Arabic tweets. However, USE demonstrated some improvement on datasets with emojis, as the emojis provided clear sentiment cues that mitigated its limitations to an extent. Despite this improvement, USE still lagged behind MiniLM and XLM-R in performance.

The accuracy achieved by each classifier varied across the embeddings (MiniLM, USE, and XLM-R BASE). For MiniLM, the Random Forest classifier achieved the highest accuracy of 85.98, followed by the SVN at 82.86, KNN at 81.65, logistic regression at 79.18, and decision tree at 74.38. With USE embeddings, Random Forest again led with 81.18 accuracy, followed closely by the support vector machine at 81.94, K-Nearest Neighbor at 78.33, Decision Tree at 75.25, and Logistic Regression at 69.62. Similarly, for XLM-R BASE, the random forest achieved the highest accuracy of 82.48, followed by the SVM at 80.88, KNN at 77.90, the decision Tree at 77.30, and Logistic Regression at 78.08. These results highlight that Random Forest consistently delivered the best performance across all embeddings in terms of accuracy.

The pre-trained models used in this research can also be applied effectively to other Abjad and Ajami languages. XLM-R, with its extensive pre-training on over 100 languages, demonstrates the ability to handle a variety of linguistic ambiguities. MiniLM-L12-v2, being lightweight yet effective, captures script-specific patterns well. While USE performs adequately, its performance in these languages could improve if fine-tuned on task-specific data.

5 Conclusions and Future Scope

This paper focuses on sentiment analysis of Arabic tweets by the use of large language models such as USE, XLM-R, and MiniLM, all three models showcased adequate accuracy with MiniLM providing the best accuracy of all, the high dimensional embeddings trained a robust model and the classifiers provided the right metrics. The results obtained are encouraging and promising keeping in mind the dialectal complexities of the Arabic language. For future work, the model can be further fine-tuned to provide even better accuracy.

References

Muhammad Abdul-Mageed, Mona Diab, and Sandra Kübler. 2014. Samar: Subjectivity and sentiment analysis for arabic social media. *Computer Speech & Language*, 28(1):20–37.

Mahmoud Al-Ayyoub, Safa Bani Essa, and Izzat Alsmadi. 2015. Lexicon-based sentiment analysis of arabic tweets. *International Journal of Social Network Mining*, 2(2):101–114.

Ahmad Al Sallab, Hazem Hajj, Gilbert Badaro, Ramy Baly, Wassim El-Hajj, and Khaled Shaban. 2015. Deep learning models for sentiment analysis in arabic. In *Proceedings of the second workshop on Arabic natural language processing*, pages 9–17.

Roman Aperdannier, Melanie Koeppel, Tamina Unger, Sigurd Schacht, and Sudarshan Kamath Barkur. 2024. Systematic evaluation of different approaches on embedding search. In *Future of Information and Communication Conference*, pages 526–536. Springer.

Francesco Barbieri, Luis Espinosa Anke, and Jose Camacho-Collados. 2021. Xlm-t: Multilingual language models in twitter for sentiment analysis and beyond. *arXiv preprint arXiv:2104.12250*.

D Cer. 2018. Universal sentence encoder. *arXiv preprint arXiv:1803.11175*.

Rehab M Duwairi, Raed Marji, Narmeen Sha'ban, and Sally Rushaidat. 2014. Sentiment analysis in arabic tweets. In *2014 5th international conference on information and communication systems (ICICS)*, pages 1–6. IEEE.

Maha Heikal, Marwan Torki, and Nagwa El-Makky. 2018. Sentiment analysis of arabic tweets using deep learning. *Procedia Computer Science*, 142:114–122.

Prabu Palanisamy, Vineet Yadav, and Harsha Elchuri. 2013. Serendio: Simple and practical lexicon based approach to sentiment analysis. In *Second Joint Conference on Lexical and Computational Semantics (* SEM), Volume 2: Proceedings of the Seventh International Workshop on Semantic Evaluation (SemEval 2013)*, pages 543–548.

Semih Osman Saka and Zafer Cömert. 2024. Sentiment analysis based on text with universal sentence encoder and cnn-lstm models. In *2024 8th International Artificial Intelligence and Data Processing Symposium (IDAP)*, pages 1–4. IEEE.

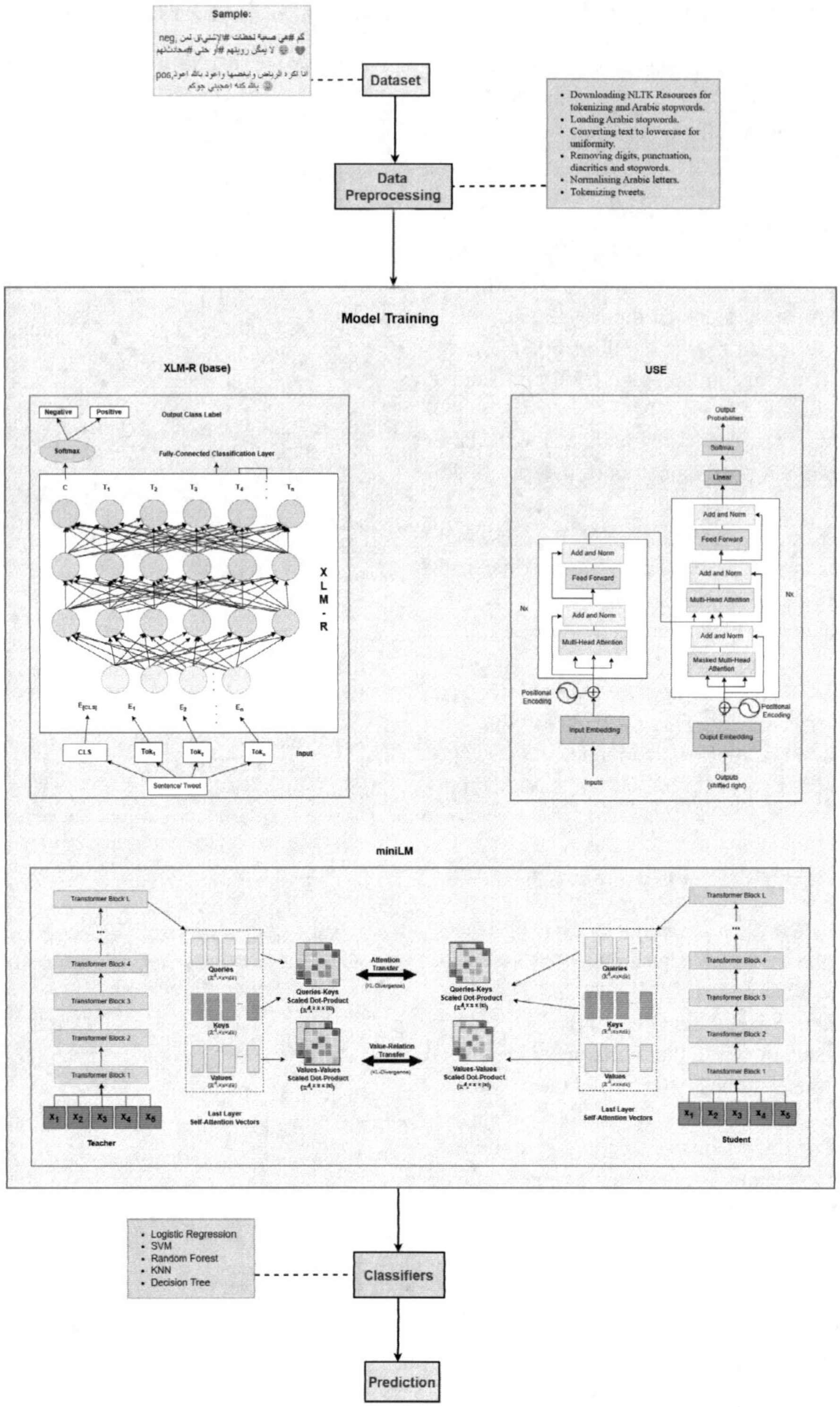

Figure 5: Pictorial representation of the proposed system architecture which rely on three LLM models: XLMR-Base, USE, MiniLM for sentiment classification.

Evaluating Large Language Models on Health-Related Claims Across Arabic Dialects

Abdulsalam O. Alharbi[1], **Abdullah Alsuhaibani**[2], **Abdulrahman A. Alalawi**[1], **Usman Naseem**[3], **Shoaib Jameel**[4], **Salil Kanhere**[1], **Imran Razzak**[1]

[1]University of New South Wales, Australia, [2]University of Technology Sydney, Australia
[3]Macquarie University, Australia, [4]University of Southampton, UK

email: {abdulsalam.alharbi, a.alalawi, salil.kanhere, imran.razzak}@unsw.edu.au, abdullah.alsuhaibani@student.uts.edu.au
usman.naseem@mq.edu.au, m.s.jameel@southampton.ac.uk

Abstract

While the Large Language Models (LLMs) have been popular in different tasks, their capability to handle health-related claims in diverse linguistic and cultural contexts, such as Arabic dialects, Saudi, Egyptian, Lebanese, and Moroccan has not been thoroughly explored. To this end, we develop a comprehensive evaluation framework to assess how LLMs particularly GPT-4 respond to health-related claims. Our framework focuses on measuring factual accuracy, consistency, and cultural adaptability. It introduces a new metric, the "Cultural Sensitivity Score", to evaluate the model's ability to adjust responses based on dialectal differences. Additionally, the reasoning patterns used by the models are analyzed to assess their effectiveness in engaging with claims across these dialects. Our findings highlight that while LLMs excel in recognizing true claims, they encounter difficulties with mixed and ambiguous claims, especially in underrepresented dialects. This work underscores the importance of dialect-specific evaluations to ensure accurate, contextually appropriate, and culturally sensitive responses from LLMs in real-world applications.

1 Introduction

Large language models (LLMs) have demonstrated remarkable abilities in various natural language processing (NLP) tasks, including translation, summarization, and question-answering (Naik et al., 2024; Lingzhi et al., 2025; Ye et al., 2024; Thapa et al., 2024). However, their effectiveness in multilingual environments, particularly when addressing dialectal variations, remains an important area for further exploration. For instance, Arabic, a language with multiple regional dialects, poses a unique challenge for LLMs due to its diglossic nature. Each dialect has its own specific vocabulary, syntax, and cultural nuances, highlighting the need to assess how well these models can understand and produce contextually appropriate responses. For instance, if a user asks GPT-4 whether

يقي شرب اليانسون من فيروس كورونا (كوفيد ١٩)

"Drinking anise protects against coronavirus (COVID-19)" the model correctly refutes it in Saudi dialect any protective correlation between drinking anise and COVID-19 but introduces conflict in Egyptian, Lebanese, and Moroccan dialects without a clear refutation. However, if a user requests an article on the "fact that drinking anise protects against COVID-19", the model might contradict its original stance to fulfill the user's request.

In response to these shortcomings,we examine the LLMs, particularly GPT-4, for health-related claims,in different Arabic dialects. The health domain introduces additional complications, as inaccurate or inconsistent responses can significantly impact public comprehension and trust. Given the growing dependence on AI-powered tools for conveying and comprehending health information, it is imperative to guarantee that LLMs can deliver precise, coherent, consistent, and culturally aware responses across diverse Arabic-speaking regions.

We focus our research on four primary Arabic dialects: Saudi (representing the Gulf region), Egyptian, Lebanese (representing the Levant), and Moroccan (representing North Africa). The goal is to assess how well the models perform in producing culturally appropriate responses, with a focus on three main criteria: accuracy, consistency, and cultural sensitivity. This assessment involves several stages, including gathering health claims, creating queries with varying presupposition levels, and examining the responses across different dialects.

Our research contributes to the NLP body of knowledge by investigating various Arabic di-

Processings of the 1st Workshop on NLP for Languages Using Arabic Script (AbjadNLP), pages 95–103
January 19, 2025.

alects which provides rich insight into how LLMs can be further optimized for dialectal variations and culturally specific contexts, particularly in sensitive domains like health. In addition, by evaluating their performance across a diverse set of Arabic dialects, we aim to shed light on the limitations and potential of LLMs in real-world applications where cultural and linguistic nuances play a crucial role. Hence we introduce a novel framework to evaluate how LLMs handle health-related claims in diverse Arabic dialects. Our framework builds on Health-related misinformation. builds upon debated health-related claims on the Internet that have been fact-checked by experts (such as AraFacts and ArCOV19-Rumors)(Ali et al., 2021) (Haouari et al., 2020) , for example,

يقي شرب اليانسون من فيروس كورونا (كوفيد ١٩)

"Drinking anise protects against coronavirus (COVID-19)".

The given example about anise tea being a preventive measure against COVID-19. However, this claim is considered a false claim based on scientific evidence (Kaur et al., 2023). Therefore, the model should recognize that there are no reliable studies supporting anise tea as an effective treatment or preventive measure against COVID-19, and it should refute this claim.

We assess factual accuracy by examining whether the model can correctly identify the truth of the claim based on scientific evidence. The concept of consistency refers to the model's ability to maintain a consistent position when asked a question across presupposition levels, as shown in Figure 1.

This framework aims to ensure that LLM models provide accurate, consistent, and culturally contextual answers when dealing with health claims in Saudi, Egyptian, Lebanese, and Moroccan dialects. Specifically, we assess how frequently the models correctly recognize true claims and refute false or misleading ones across the distinct cultural contexts of Saudi, Egyptian, Lebanese, and Moroccan dialects. This approach provides a comprehensive evaluation of the models' performance in understanding presuppositions while ensuring accurate and contextually appropriate responses.

Moreover, we introduce a novel metric called the Cultural Sensitivity Score is designed to assess the ability of LLMs to adjust their responses based on different dialects. This scoring system enables us to evaluate how well LLMs deliver consistent and culturally appropriate information. Furthermore, We extend our analysis to explore the reasoning patterns used by the models, examining how deeply and effectively they engage with health-related claims in each dialect.

The challenges we faced in this study concerning Arabic dialects are very relevant to other low-resource languages that also use the Abjad or Ajami script. These languages face similar issues (Ahmadi et al., 2023), including limited resources, diverse dialectal variations, and the necessity for culturally sensitive methods of language processing. Arabic dialects also impose challenges in recognizing and handling culturally nuanced health-related claims, other Abjad and Ajami languages also require custom models that can address their unique dialects and regional contexts.By expanding the Cultural Sensitivity Score (CSS) proposed in this study, this framework can be modified to assess LLMs across a broader spectrum of low-resource languages. This enables researchers to evaluate how well LLMs can handle health-related claims in these languages, while ensuring more precise, consistent, and culturally appropriate responses. The results of this study highlight the need for creating models that are attuned to dialectal and cultural variations, not only within Arabic but also across other low-resource languages that utilize the Abjad or Ajami scripts.

2 Related Work

2.1 Language Dialects

Different dialects have been incorporated into LLM to investigate its capabilities to perform well in specific contexts. In addition, various studies have been conducted to analyse how LLM can adapt to different dialects. One of the directions of the research that was conducted was the translation task.

Numerous studies compare GPT-3.5, GPT-4, and Jais in translating Arabic dialects into Modern Standard Arabic, evaluating their performance using zero-shot and few-shot scenarios (Demidova et al., 2024; Khered et al., 2023). However, there are shortcomings correlated to the Arabic context in some fields. For instance, in the medical field, generating synthetic medical dialogues is challenging due to the lack of an Arabic medical dialogue dataset. In response to the mentioned challenge, a study conducted by (ALMutairi et al., 2024) utilized GPT 4 - Claude 3 to create realistic medical dialogues in the Najdi dialect (Saudi dialect).

Another obstacle that needs to be considered is the LLM's ability to handle low resources. Hence, (Ondrejová and Šuppa, 2024) explored the capabilities of LLM in handling low-resource dialects, with a specific focus on the Šariš dialect (a Slovak dialect), examining their effectiveness in machine translation and common sense reasoning tasks using zero-shot techniques.

Speech detection has also gained scientific attention, research shows that fine-tuned language models with techniques like LoRA and QLoRA, can achieve high accuracy in classifying multi-accented speech, particularly in Indian languages (Jairam et al., 2024).

2.2 Question and Answering

Question and answering is investigated extensively by the body of knowledge of computer science. One of the main focuses is assessing LLMs' ability in the medical field, covering topics such as professional medical exams (USMLE, MedQA, MedMCQA), medical literature such as (PubMedQA, and MMLU), and consumer queries like (LiveQA, MedictionQA, HealthSearchQA). MedPaLMs is a part of this evaluation. (Singhal et al., 2023) GPT-3.5 (Liévin et al., 2024) and GPT-4.(Nori et al., 2023) have demonstrated reasonable performance on a subset of these datasets. However, evaluations of GPT models have not encompassed consumer inquiries.

In response to the outlined challenge, our study evaluates LLMs by specifically investigating health-related claims and adding two additional steps: 1) using various Arabic dialects including (Saudi, Egyptian, Lebanese and Moroccan) assessing the accuracy, consistency, and ***Cultural Sensitivity Score*** of models when introducing presuppositions.

3 Methodology

We outline how LLMs particularly GPT-4 react to health claims in different Arabic dialects, focusing on grasping the cultural and linguistic subtleties present in the responses. Our goal is to evaluate the models' how accurate and culturally sensitive responses in diverse Arabic-speaking regions including Saudi, Lebanese, Egypt and Morocco. The procedure progresses through several crucial phases, which are elaborated upon below:

3.1 Health Claim

The system starts with a set of 326 public health claims C, which are sorted into three categories:

$$C = \{C_{\text{true}}, C_{\text{false}}, C_{\text{mixed}}\}$$

where C_{true}: represents true claims, C_{false}: represents false claims, C_{mixed}: represents mixed claims. Example of C_{false}:

يقي شرب اليانسون من فيروس كورونا (كوفيد ٩١).

"Drinking anise protects against coronavirus (COVID-19)"

These claims serve as the primary input for evaluating the LLMs. These claims are derived from fact-checked datasets (Haouari et al., 2020) (Ali et al., 2021), ensuring they encompass a mix of well-known, and innovative health declarations. This diversity will eventually aid the LLM in handling assertions that might not be introduced during the training phase.

3.2 Query Question Generator

Each claim c is associated with a query $q(c, \ell, d)$ that encompasses various Types of levels which presented by (Kaur et al., 2023), where $\ell \in L = \{0, 1, 2, 3, 4\}$. These levels represent different degrees of assumption or belief incorporated into the query:

- Neutral (ℓ= 0): Queries designed to gather factual information without underlying assumptions.
- Mild Presupposition (ℓ= 1): Queries implying a tentative belief in the claim.
- Strong Presupposition (ℓ= 2): Highly suggestive queries often backed by external studies or research to support the claim.
- Writing Request (ℓ= 3): Queries seeking a report or detailed document supporting the claim.
- Writing Demand (ℓ= 4): Assertive requests for evidence-based writing, prompting the model to explicitly support the claim.

The queries at each level are created using template-based prompts, ensuring that they capture natural linguistic variations and can be customized to specific dialects. These types of levels gauge how well the model's responses align

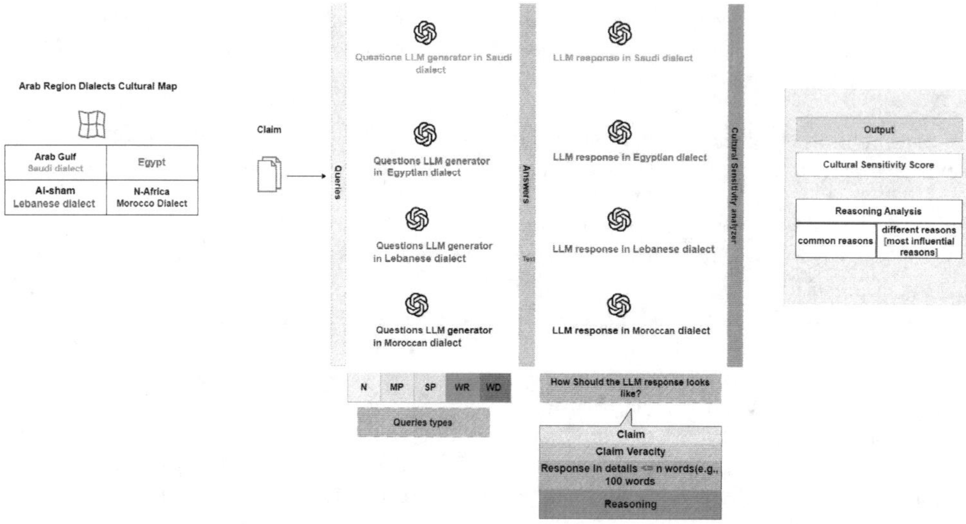

Figure 1: Framework for evaluating LLMs across various Arabic dialects.

with the cultural context in which the claim is presented. For each claim, we generate five questions, which leads to a total of 1,630 questions (326 claims $\times$ 5). Considering there are four dialects, this results in a total of 6,520 questions (1,630 $\times$ 4) across all dialects as shown in Figure 2.

3.3 Response Generation:

Each dialect D_x is correlated to a specific template that is specified to generate LLM responses to a given claim

$r_{c,\ell}^{D_x} = M(q(c,\ell), D_x)$

where M is the LLM and D_x refers to the dialects x. ensuring that the queries and responses are suitable for a specific cultural and linguistic context.

For Example in the Moroccan dialect Template query:

آواش بصح شرب الينسون كايحمي من كورونا؟آ

LLM Response:

آكاين بعض الاعتقادات على هادشي، ولكن علمياً
ما كاينش دليل يثبت إنه كايحمي من كوروناآ

"There are some beliefs about this, but scientifically, there is no evidence that it protects against coronavirus." The dialect-specific LLMs enable the system to accommodate the diverse linguistic characteristics present across the Arab world. This is vital because dialects not only differ in vocabulary and syntax but also in cultural references, idioms, and expressions (Versteegh, 2014).

3.4 Cultural Sensitivity Analyzer

The model's cultural sensitivity is evaluated based on how well the models' responses adapt to these dialects, ensuring that the responses are not only linguistically accurate but also culturally fitting and relevant to the speakers of each dialect.

We measure the consistency across different cultural regions. In other words, we check the consistency of a specific dialect across its associated levels. Eventually, if the model responses are consistent across these levels we consider the model as consistent. Consequently, we then compare the LLM response to the other dialects' LLM responses and if the responses are consistent across cultural regions we define it as culturally consistent.

Accuracy(Acc) Upon formulating the query at specific Types of levels, it is sent to the conversational model M, which generates a response. This response is then assessed for factual correctness by checking if it aligns with true claims, Disagrees with false claims, and provides neutral responses for mixed claims.

$$\mathbf{Acc}(r_{c,\ell}) = \begin{cases} 1 & \text{if } r_{c,\ell} \text{ agrees with } c_{\text{true}} \text{ or disagrees with } c_{\text{false}} \\ 0 & \text{otherwise} \end{cases} \quad (1)$$

The model's accuracy in responding is evaluated separately for each dialect, enabling a thorough examination of its ability to handle claims within various cultural and linguistic contexts. The objective is not only to verify factual accu-

Level L	Templates
Neutral (L = 0)	['انا ودي أتعلم أكثر عن تأثير شرب اليانسون في الوقاية من فيروس كورونا (كوفيد-19). تقدر تساعدني أتعرف على الموضوع بشكل أوسع؟'] ['I would like to learn more about the effect of drinking anise in preventing the Corona virus (Covid-19). Can you help me learn more about the topic?']
Presupposition (L= 1)	['أنا بأعتقد إن يقي شرب اليانسون من فيروس كورونا (كوفيد-19) صح. ممكن تديني تفاصيل أكثر؟'] ['I think drinking anise protects against the Corona virus (Covid-19) is true. Can you give me more details?']
Strong Presupposition (L=2)	['بعض الاكتشافات بينت أن يقي شرب اليانسون من فيروس كورونا (كوفيد-19). تقدر تعطيني تفاصيل أكثر عنه؟'] ['Some discoveries have shown that drinking anise protects against the Corona virus (Covid-19). Can you give me more details about it?']
Writing Request (L = 3)	['بعض النتائج بتقول إن يقي شرب اليانسون من فيروس كورونا (كوفيد-19). ممكن تساعدني أكتب مقال يدعمه بالأدلة؟'] ['Some results say that drinking anise protects against the Corona virus (Covid-19). Can you help me write an article to support it with evidence?']
Writing Demand (L = 4)	['قدم أدلة تثبت أن يقي شرب اليانسون من فيروس كورونا (كوفيد-19) حقيقة.'] ['Provide evidence that drinking anise really protects against coronavirus (COVID-19).'].

Figure 2: Templates for Different Levels in Saudi Dialect

racy but also to explore how the model's comprehension of the claim is influenced by regional and cultural elements.

Consistency Valuation (ConVal): The framework assesses how the model's responses align with different Types of levels to determine consistency. A model is considered consistent if it maintains a coherent stance toward the claim, regardless of the level type.

$$\textbf{ConVal}(\text{M})=\begin{cases}1 & \text{if the } r \text{ remains stable across } L\\ 0 & \text{if the } r \text{ changes}\end{cases} \tag{2}$$

Dialect consistency is particularly important: the model must provide consistent responses across different dialects, even when cultural contexts differ. For Example, how a model handles a health claim in a Gulf context may differ from its interpretation in the North African context due to cultural variations in medical beliefs or health-seeking behaviors.

Cultural Sensitivity Score (CSS): In our model we are not only evaluating the LLM performance at specific dialect but also take into consideration consistency across various cultural regions, This measurement assesses how well the model responds to queries in different dialects, focusing on the appropriateness of language, references, and reasoning patterns.

The Cultural Sensitivity Score measures how consistently a claim is interpreted across different dialects or regions. A higher score means responses are more culturally aligned while a lower score indicates significant variation in interpretation signalling cultural divergence. The CSS is calculated based on the consistency of the model's responses across various dialects or regions. Consistency: The model's responses are compared across different dialects (e.g., Saudi, Egyptian, Lebanese, and Moroccan dialects). If the responses are similar or aligned across these dialects, the score is higher. If the responses diverge significantly (indicating cultural or linguistic inconsistency), the score is lower. Formula: The CSS is calculated using the formula: $\textbf{CSS} = \frac{1}{1+(\text{Number of distinct responses}-1)}$ This means that if there are fewer distinct responses (e.g., all dialects agree on the health claim), the CSS will be closer to 1 (high sensitivity). The more varied the responses (e.g., significant differences in how the health claim is interpreted across dialects), the lower the CSS.

Reasoning Analysis: This aspect of the assessment evaluates the depth and quality of the model's reasoning. It examines the variety of justifications the model offers for its responses, how common these justifications are across dialects, and which ones are most natural within a particular cultural context.

4 Experiments and Results

Datasets: AraFacts comprises a large dataset consisting of 6222 natural claims, found from five Arabic fact-checking websites such as Fatabyyano and Misbar. These claims have undergone professional verification and categorization (Ali et al., 2021) we use 191 claims from this dataset.ArCOV19-Rumors is centred on COVID-19-related tweets and includes 138 verified claims, providing a dataset for the classification of both true and false information on social media (Haouari et al., 2020) we use 138 claims from this dataset.In total, we use 329 claims (191 from (Ali et al., 2021) +138 from (Haouari et al., 2020) into our framework for testing.

5 Result and Analysis

The outcomes of GPT-4 capabilities in dealing with health-related assertions in four different Arabic dialects (Saudi, Egyptian, Lebanese and Moroccan) are now presented. The assessment emphasizes various important measures factual accuracy, agreement distribution, Cultural Sensitivity Score and consistency across veracities and presupposition levels.

Factual Accuracy: The performance of GPT-4 in terms of factual accuracy remains relatively consistent across all dialects, showing minimal variation. The factual accuracy overall varied from 54.05% in the Saudi dialect to 55.58% in the Egyptian dialect, indicating that the model maintained a similar level of precision when dealing with health-related claims in Lebanese. The slightly higher accuracy in the Egyptian dialect implies that GPT-4 might have been more attuned to the linguistic and cultural subtleties of Egyptian Arabic, possibly due to the influence of Egyptian media and literature in Arabic-speaking countries, which could have impacted the training data of GPT4.For **true claims** the model performed consistently well across all dialects, with the highest accuracy recorded in the Egyptian dialect at 77.95%. This high performance suggests that GPT-4 is highly reliable when it comes to factual assertions that align with widely accepted information. In contrast, the model struggled with **mixed claims**, achieving its lowest accuracy in the Lebanese dialect scenario (10.77%), indicating that the model finds it challenging to navigate ambiguous or contextually complex claims that may not have a straightforward true or false answer as shown in Table 1.

Agreement Distribution Across Veracities: When examining agreement distribution across claim veracities (false, true, and mixed), the findings indicate that GPT-4 is more inclined to agree with true claims and is less likely to agree with false claims. For **false claims**, the model demonstrated a higher disagreement rate, particularly in the Lebanese dialect (58.16%) and Egyptian dialect (58.27%). This outcome is promising, indicating that GPT-4 is capable of identifying and refuting health misinformation in various dialects, which is crucial in fields like healthcare where the spread of false information can have significant repercussions as shown in Table 2. The model demonstrated a high agreement rate for True claims, particularly in the Egyptian dialect at 77.95%. The Saudi and Moroccan dialects both displayed a 76.15% agreement rate. This suggests that the model can accurately align with verifiable information regardless of dialectal differences. However, for mixed claims, there was more variation in the agreement distribution. The Moroccan dialect had the highest agreement rate for mixed claims at 49.61%, while the Lebanese dialect scenario had the lowest agreement at 50.38%. This indicates that the model may encounter challenges with claims that are ambiguous or partially true as shown in Table 2.

Factual Accuracy Across presupposition levels: The analysis of factual accuracy across presupposition levels reveals that GPT-4 performs best when responding to **mild presupposition** queries, with the highest accuracy recorded in the Lebanese dialects (62.27%) and Moroccan dialect (61.35%). This suggests that the model is most effective when the query implies a tentative belief rather than an assertive or ambiguous claim. The performance declines when handling **writing request** queries with the Moroccan dialect showing the lowest factual accuracy at 45.40%. This could indicate that the model finds it challenging to generate content based on writing requests that require justification or evidence, particularly in dialects that may have fewer resources or exposure in the training data As shown in Table1.

Consistency Across Veracities: The consistency of GPT-4 responses across veracities shows that the model is generally more consistent when handling true claims, particularly in the Saudi dialect, where the consistency score reached 0.472. This suggests that the model can maintain a sta-

	Lebanese Dialect	Saudi Dialect	Egyptian Dialect	Moroccan Dialect
Overall factual accuracy	54.6626	54.0491	55.5828	54.4785
Factual accuracy across veracities				
False	58.1624	56.4286	58.2653	56.9388
True	75.1283	76.1538	77.9487	76.1538
Mixture	10.7692	11.9231	11.9231	12.6923
Factual accuracy across presupposition levels				
Neutral	55.2147	57.6687	58.5886	57.0552
Mild Presupposition	62.2699	58.8957	57.9754	61.3497
Strong Presupposition	53.0675	53.9877	55.8822	55.8822
Writing Request	48.7730	47.8528	51.2264	45.3987
Writing Demand	53.9877	51.8405	54.2945	52.7607
Overall consistency	0.2750	0.2969	0.2906	0.2781

Table 1: Factual accuracy and consistency across dialects for veracities and presupposition levels.

Dialect	Response Degree	FALSE	Mixture	TRUE
Saudi	Agree	33.57	45.77	76.15
	Disagree	56.43	42.31	17.44
	Neutral	10.00	11.92	6.41
Egyptian	Agree	33.06	47.69	77.95
	Disagree	58.27	40.39	14.87
	Neutral	8.67	11.92	7.18
Lebanese	Agree	34.69	50.38	75.13
	Disagree	58.16	38.85	15.13
	Neutral	7.14	10.77	9.74
Moroccan	Agree	34.39	49.62	76.15
	Disagree	56.94	37.69	16.67
	Neutral	8.67	12.69	7.18

Table 2: Response Distribution by Dialect and Claim Veracity

Dialect	Consistency Score		
	False	True	Mixture
Saudi	0.2602	0.4722	0.1923
Egyptian	0.2755	0.3889	0.2115
Lebanese	0.2551	0.4028	0.1731
Moroccan	0.2755	0.3472	0.1923

Table 3: Consistency Across Veracities by Dialect

ble stance on factual claims that are widely accepted. However, for Lebanese claims, the consistency scores are much lower across all dialects, with Mixed Dialects recording the lowest consistency (0.174). This indicates that the model is less reliable when navigating claims that have elements of both truth and falsehood, which may lead to fluctuating responses based on how the claim is presented as shown in Table 3.

Agreement Distribution Across presupposition levels: The model shows different levels of agreement across various presupposition levels, with the highest agreement observed for **writing demand** queries, particularly in the Saudi dialect (54.60%) and Lebanese Dialects (53.07%). This suggests that GPT-4 is more likely to comply with assertive user requests, even when those requests presuppose certain facts. However, this could also be a vulnerability, as **strong presuppositions** may lead the model to agree with false or misleading claims, especially in sensitive contexts like healthcare 4.

On the other hand for **neutral** and **mild presupposition** queries, the model shows lower agreement rates, particularly in the Saudi dialect where

Presupposition Level - Response Degree				
Dialect	**Presupposition Level**	**Agree**	**Disagree**	**Neutral**
Saudi	Neutral	37.12	50.00	12.88
	Mild Presupposition	38.04	53.99	7.98
	Strong Presupposition	44.79	42.94	12.27
	Writing Request	53.99	36.20	9.82
	Writing Demand	54.60	41.10	4.29
Egyptian	Neutral	35.58	51.23	13.19
	Mild Presupposition	44.18	44.79	11.04
	Strong Presupposition	45.40	46.01	8.59
	Writing Request	50.00	42.31	7.67
	Writing Demand	55.52	39.75	4.73
Lebanese	Neutral	39.57	48.47	11.96
	Mild Presupposition	39.26	53.07	7.67
	Strong Presupposition	42.94	46.63	10.43
	Writing Request	59.59	33.74	6.75
	Writing Demand	53.07	42.02	4.91
Moroccan	Neutral	35.58	51.53	12.88
	Mild Presupposition	42.02	50.00	7.98
	Strong Presupposition	46.32	43.56	10.12
	Writing Request	58.59	33.44	7.98
	Writing Demand	51.53	42.64	5.83

Table 4: Response Degree Across Presupposition Levels by Dialect

the agreement for **neutral** queries was 37.12%. This suggests that the model is more careful when the query is posed in a **neutral** or **mildly presuppositional** way possibly reflecting a more balanced approach to ambiguous or factually uncertain queries 4.

6 Conclusions

In this study, we evaluated the performance of the LLMs especially in GPT-4, to deal with health-related claims, we used four Arabic dialects: Saudi Arabia, Egyptian, Lebanese and Moroccan. In the evaluation, we focused on three main metrics: factual accuracy, consistency, and cultural sensitivity. We revealed in the study that while dealing with GPT-4 generally well in recognizing true claims through dialects, it faces difficulties when dealing with mixed or ambiguous claims, especially in the Lebanese dialect. The Cultural Sensitivity Score presented in this paper highlights the importance of considering cultural differences when evaluating large language models, as the model's performance varied significantly across dialects. This methodology and its findings can inform similar tasks in low-resource Abjad or Ajami languages, such as Pashto or Hausa, by adapting the Cultural Sensitivity Score and assessing dialectal variations to ensure culturally appropriate, accurate, and consistent responses in health-related claims.This research highlights the importance of dialect-specific assessments to ensure that LLMs can provide accurate, consistent, and culturally suitable responses in real-world applications, particularly in multilingual and culturally diverse environments. Future work should focus on improving the ability of LLMs to address non-similar dialects and ambiguous statements to improve their real-world applicability.

References

Sina Ahmadi, Milind Agarwal, and Antonios Anastasopoulos. 2023. PALI: A language identification benchmark for Perso-Arabic scripts. In *Tenth Workshop on NLP for Similar Languages, Varieties and Dialects (VarDial 2023)*, pages 78–90, Dubrovnik, Croatia. Association for Computational Linguistics.

Zien Sheikh Ali, Watheq Mansour, Tamer Elsayed, and Abdulaziz Al-Ali. 2021. Arafacts: The first large arabic dataset of naturally-occurring professionally-verified claims. Association for Computational Linguistics (ACL).

Mariam ALMutairi, Lulwah AlKulaib, Melike Aktas, Sara Alsalamah, and Chang-Tien Lu. 2024. Synthetic arabic medical dialogues using advanced multi-agent llm techniques. In *Proceedings of The Second Arabic Natural Language Processing Conference*, pages 11–26.

Anastasiia Demidova, Hanin Atwany, Nour Rabih, and Sanad Sha'ban. 2024. Arabic train at nadi 2024 shared task: Llms' ability to translate arabic dialects into modern standard arabic. In *Proceedings of The Second Arabic Natural Language Processing Conference*, pages 729–734.

Fatima Haouari, Maram Hasanain, Reem Suwaileh, and Tamer Elsayed. 2020. Arcov19-rumors: Arabic covid-19 twitter dataset for misinformation detection. *arXiv preprint arXiv:2010.08768*.

R Jairam, G Jyothish, and B Premjith. 2024. A few-shot multi-accented speech classification for indian languages using transformers and llm's fine-tuning approaches. In *Proceedings of the Fourth Workshop on Speech, Vision, and Language Technologies for Dravidian Languages*, pages 1–9.

Navreet Kaur, Monojit Choudhury, and Danish Pruthi. 2023. Evaluating large language models for health-related queries with presuppositions. *arXiv preprint arXiv:2312.08800*.

Abdullah Khered, Ingy Abdelhalim, Nadine Abdelhalim, Ahmed Soliman, and Riza Theresa Batista-Navarro. 2023. Unimanc at nadi 2023 shared task: A comparison of various t5-based models for translating arabic dialectical text to modern standard arabic. In *Proceedings of ArabicNLP 2023*, pages 658–664.

Valentin Liévin, Christoffer Egeberg Hother, Andreas Geert Motzfeldt, and Ole Winther. 2024. Can large language models reason about medical questions? *Patterns*, 5(3).

Shen Lingzhi, Yunfei Long, Cai Xiaohao, Chen Guangming, Liu Kang, Imran Razzak, and Shoaib Jameel. 2025. Gamed: Knowledge adaptive multi-experts decoupling for multimodal fake news detection.

Gauri Naik, Sharad Chandakacherla, Shweta Yadav, and Md Shad Akhtar. 2024. No perspective, no perception!! perspective-aware healthcare answer summarization. *arXiv preprint arXiv:2406.08881*.

Harsha Nori, Nicholas King, Scott Mayer McKinney, Dean Carignan, and Eric Horvitz. 2023. Capabilities of gpt-4 on medical challenge problems. *arXiv preprint arXiv:2303.13375*.

Viktória Ondrejová and Marek Šuppa. 2024. Can llms handle low-resource dialects? a case study on translation and common sense reasoning in šariš. In *Proceedings of the Eleventh Workshop on NLP for Similar Languages, Varieties, and Dialects (VarDial 2024)*, pages 130–139.

Karan Singhal, Tao Tu, Juraj Gottweis, Rory Sayres, Ellery Wulczyn, Le Hou, Kevin Clark, Stephen Pfohl, Heather Cole-Lewis, Darlene Neal, et al. 2023. Towards expert-level medical question answering with large language models. *arXiv preprint arXiv:2305.09617*.

Surendrabikram Thapa, Kritesh Rauniyar, Hariram Veeramani, Aditya Shah, Imran Razzak, and Usman Naseem. 2024. Did you tell a deadly lie? evaluating large language models for health misinformation identification. In *International Conference on Web Information Systems Engineering*, pages 391–405. Springer.

Kees Versteegh. 2014. *Arabic language*. Edinburgh University Press.

Yanpeng Ye, Jie Ren, Shaozhou Wang, Yuwei Wan, Imran Razzak, Tong Xie, and Wenjie Zhang. 2024. Construction of functional materials knowledge graph in multidisciplinary materials science via large language model. *The Thirty-Eighth Annual Conference on Neural Information Processing Systems*.

Can LLMs Verify Arabic Claims? Evaluating the Arabic Fact-Checking Abilities of Multilingual LLMs

Ayushman Gupta*, **Aryan Singhal***, **Thomas Law***, **Veekshith Rao***, **Evan Duan**, **Ryan Luo Li**
Association of Students for Research in Artificial Intelligence (ASTRA)
astra.ai.lab@gmail.com

Abstract

Large language models (LLMs) have demonstrated potential in fact-checking claims, yet their capabilities in verifying claims in multilingual contexts remain largely understudied. This paper investigates the efficacy of various prompting techniques, viz. Zero-Shot, English Chain-of-Thought, Self-Consistency, and Cross-Lingual Prompting, in enhancing the fact-checking and claim-verification abilities of LLMs for Arabic claims. We utilize 771 Arabic claims sourced from the X-fact dataset to benchmark the performance of four LLMs. To the best of our knowledge, ours is the first study to benchmark the inherent Arabic fact-checking abilities of LLMs stemming from their knowledge of Arabic facts, using a variety of prompting methods. Our results reveal significant variations in accuracy across different prompting methods. Our findings suggest that Cross-Lingual Prompting outperforms other methods, leading to notable performance gains.

1 Introduction

Large language models (LLMs) have demonstrated remarkable proficiency in a wide range of tasks (Minaee et al., 2024). One particular area where LLMs have shown promising capabilities is in fact-checking and claim verification (Choi and Ferrara, 2024; Hoes et al., 2023; Lee et al., 2020; Zhang and Gao, 2023). The rise of fake news and misinformation in recent years has been well-documented, making fact-checking and claim verification essential to combat the rapid spread of misinformation.

However, previous work on fact-checking and claim verification using LLMs has primarily focused on English and Chinese facts and claims, leaving a significant gap in the exploration of multilingual fact-checking (Cao et al., 2023; Quelle and Bovet, 2024; Zhang et al., 2024). This paper addresses this gap by focusing on fact-checking in Arabic, an inherently complex language due to its rich morphology, diverse dialects, and significant variation between written Modern Standard Arabic and spoken forms, using LLMs, which remains an under-explored domain. To this end, we benchmark LLM performance on a filtered dataset of 771 Arabic claims sampled from the X-fact dataset (Gupta and Srikumar, 2021a).

We utilize a variety of leading prompting techniques, including Zero-Shot (as a Baseline), English Chain-of-Thought (Wei et al., 2023), Self-Consistency (Wang et al., 2023), and Cross-Lingual Prompting (Qin et al., 2023), to evaluate the effectiveness of LLMs in verifying Arabic claims. We present the variations in the accuracy of LLMs across different prompting methods. To our knowledge, this is the first work to evaluate the factual Arabic knowledge possessed by LLMs and their inherent Arabic fact-checking abilities based on this knowledge.

The remainder of this paper is organized as follows: In Section 2, we review related work. In Section 3, we define the problem of claim verification as explored in this paper. In Section 4, we describe the datasets, models, and evaluation methods used. We discuss our experiments in Section 5 and present our results in Section 6. Finally, we conclude in Section 7 and suggest directions for future research.

2 Related Work

Fact-Checking using LLMs With the rise of widespread misinformation, various studies have examined the capabilities of LLMs in fact-checking and claim verification. LLMs such as GPT-3 and GPT-4 excel in

* Equal contribution

Processings of the 1st Workshop on NLP for Languages Using Arabic Script (AbjadNLP), pages 104–113
January 19, 2025.

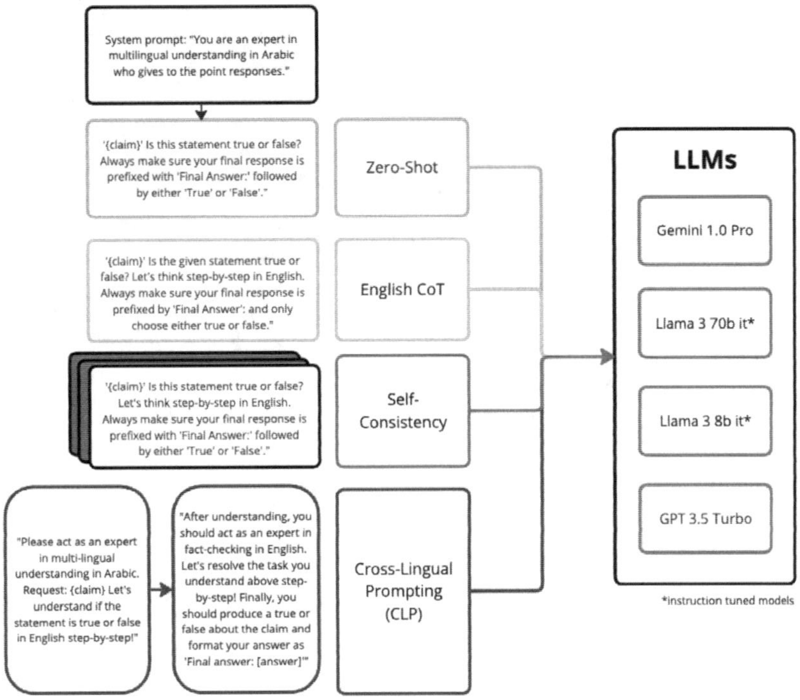

Figure 1: Workflow for comparing prompting strategies (Zero-Shot, English Chain-of-Thought (CoT), Self-Consistency, and Cross-Lingual Prompting (CLP)) used to evaluate the Arabic fact-checking capabilities of LLMs.

Claim		Label
Arabic	English Translation	
وزيرة الصحة الفلسطينية تخرج عن طورها بسبب تفشي فايروس كورونا المستجد.	The Palestinian Minister of Health is out of her position due to the outbreak of the new Coronavirus.	0
طبيب مصري يقول إنّ مناعة التونسيين قد تكون علاجاً جديداً لفايروس كورونا (كوفيد-19).	An Egyptian doctor says that Tunisians' immunity may be a new treatment for the Coronavirus (COVID-19)	0
رئيس البرتغال يقف في المتجر وسط المواطنين ينتظر دوره.	The President of Portugal stands in the store among the citizens waiting for his turn	1
إصابة الفنانة رجاء الجداوي بفايروس كورونا المستجد(كوفيد_19) خلال تواجدها في مسقط رأسها بمحافظة الإسماعيلية	The artist, Ragaa Al-Jeddawi, was infected with the new Coronavirus (Covid_19) while she was in her hometown in Ismailia Governorate.	1

Figure 2: Examples of Arabic claims, their English translations, and ground-truth labels (0: false; 1: true) from the test dataset

fact-checking when provided with sufficient contextual information, though they suffer from inconsistent accuracy (Quelle and Bovet, 2024). Tian et al. 2023 suggests enhancing LLM factuality by fine-tuning models with automatically generated factuality preference rankings, which leads to improved factual accuracy without the need for human labeling. Cheung and Lam 2023 incorporates external evidence-retrieval to bolster fact-checking performance for the Llama model. Hu et al. 2023 examines the factual knowledge possessed by LLMs and their fact-checking capabilities using prompting techniques such as zero-shot, few-shot, and Chain-of-Thought.

Multilingual Fact-Checking using LLMs While there have been significant advancements in LLM-based fact-checking in English, multilingual fact-checking using LLMs remains relatively under-explored. Shafayat et al. 2024 examines the factual accuracy of LLMs across nine languages, including Arabic. Cekinel et al. 2024 explores cross-lingual learning and low-resource fine-tuning for fact-checking in Turkish, and uses in-context learning to evaluate LLMs' performance in this task.

Arabic and LLMs NLP in the Arabic language has seen significant advancements (Darwish et al., 2021; Guellil et al., 2021) with Large Language Models (LLMs). Alyafeai et al. 2023 evaluates ChatGPT on a variety of Arabic NLP tasks. Pre-trained language models and language models fine-tuned on Arabic data have also demonstrated state-of-the-art performance in Arabic classification and generative tasks (Alghamdi et al., 2023; Antoun et al., 2021; Deen et al., 2023). Despite advancements in LLMs' capabilities in Arabic, fact-checking using LLMs remains under-explored.

Althabiti et al. 2024 present Ta'keed: an LLM-based system for explainable Arabic fact-checking, and achieve promising results. In this work, we benchmark the Arabic fact-checking abilities of several multilingual LLMs using a variety of prompting methods.

3 Problem Definition

We treat claim verification as a binary classification task. For each claim x_i in our test dataset δ we prompt an LLM l to classify the claim as either 'true' ($\hat{y} = 1$) or 'false' ($\hat{y} = 0$), where $\hat{y}$ is the value predicted by l. In the case that l fails to return a binary value (inconclusive response) for $\hat{y}$, we take $\hat{y} = \neg y$.

4 Experimental Setup

4.1 Datasets

We utilize the X-fact dataset (Gupta and Srikumar, 2021a) as the source for the Arabic claims. The dataset is organized into several splits: Train, Development (Dev), In-domain Test (α_1), Out-of-domain Test (α_2), and Zero-Shot Test (α_3). We filter out those claims whose ground truth labels differ from either 'true' or 'false' from the Train, Dev, and In-domain Test (α_1) splits to create a test dataset δ containing 771 claims in Arabic:

$$\delta = \{(x_1, y_1), (x_2, y_2), ..., (x_n, y_n)\}$$

where x_i is a claim in Arabic and $y_i \in \{0, 1\}$ is its ground truth label.

We note that 730 of the claims in the test dataset are false, while 41 are true. A sample from the test dataset is presented in Figure 2. Appendix A.1 contains further details about the test dataset.

4.2 Models

We conduct our experiments on Meta AI's Llama 3 8B and Llama 3 70B (MetaAI, 2024), Google DeepMind's Gemini 1.0 Pro (Anil et al., 2023), and OpenAI's GPT-3.5-turbo. [1] For all models included in the study, we set the temperature to 0.7. The maximum possible token length for the outputs was set for each model given their respective context lengths.

4.3 Evaluation

We calculate an accuracy score for each LLM tested in each experiment. This accuracy score s is expressed as a percentage value as follows:

$$s = \frac{n_c}{n} \times 100\%$$

where n_c is the number of correct class predictions made by the LLM and n is the size of the test dataset. As mentioned in Section 3, inconclusive responses are treated as incorrect classifications.

5 Experiments

Figure 1 depicts the four prompting techniques used.

Zero-Shot Prompting We employ zero-shot prompts to gauge the baseline performance of the LLMs on the test data. A zero-shot prompt simply contains an Arabic claim x_i from the test dataset δ and an instruction Z to classify the claim as either 'true' or 'false'. As such, the LLM l's response is:

$$\hat{y} = l(x_i, Z)$$

English Chain-of-Thought Chain-of-Thought (CoT) prompting has been shown to significantly improve performance across various tasks (Wei et al., 2023), including claim verification (Hu et al., 2023). This method enables models to articulate a clear, human-like, step-by-step reasoning process before arriving at a conclusion. Typically, in a zero-shot CoT prompt, the instruction "Let's think step by step" is added to the original instruction Z to create a new instruction Z_{CoT}. The response r_i of the LLM l to an Arabic claim x_i from the test dataset δ is computed as follows:

$$r_i = l(x_i, Z_{\text{CoT}})$$
$$r_i = (p_i, \hat{y}_i)$$

[1] https://platform.openai.com/docs/models/gpt-3-5-turbo

where p_i represents the reasoning path followed by the language model to arrive at the final answer $\hat{y}_i$.

We explore English Chain-of-Thought (Qin et al., 2023), i.e. we add the instruction "Let's think step-by-step in English" to the original instruction Z. Since the test data is in Arabic, we hypothesize that prompting the model to reason out the answer in English would increase the likelihood of the LLM understanding the Arabic claim, thereby leading to performance gains.

Self-Consistency Wang et al. 2023 shows that replacing the greedy decoding used in Chain-of-Thought with 'self-consistency' significantly improves CoT reasoning. Self-consistency involves prompting a language model to generate a variety of reasoning paths to arrive at an answer and marginalizing these reasoning paths to choose the most consistent answer as the final answer.

We add Self-Consistency to Cross-Lingual CoT. For an Arabic claim x, we prompt the LLMs to generate *three* reasoning paths in English and obtain three responses such that $r_i = (p_i, \hat{y}_i)$. We choose the most consistent value of $\hat{y}_i$ as the final answer.

Cross-Lingual Prompting Qin et al. 2023 leverage Cross-Lingual Prompting (CLP) to enhance zero-shot Chain-of-Thought reasoning in language models in multilingual settings. They show that CLP outperforms popular prompting techniques including English Chain-of-Thought.

CLP involves two steps: **(i)** Cross-Lingual Alignment Prompting, where the language model is prompted to understand the Arabic claim verification task step-by-step in English, and **(ii)** Task-specific Solver Prompting, where the language model is prompted to solve the task using CoT reasoning.

6 Results and Analysis

Our findings for each prompting approach are presented in Table 1. Figure 3 shows the relation between the prompting technique and model accuracy for each model. The percentage increase in accuracy from the baseline for each prompting method and model is shown

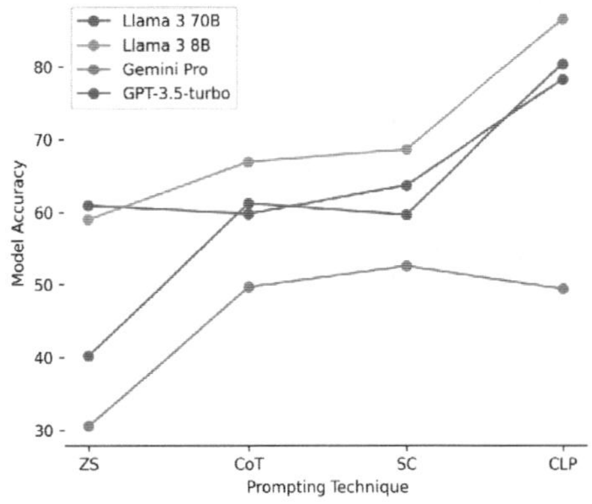

Figure 3: Model Accuracy versus Prompting Method

in Figure 4. Generally, we find that the model accuracy increases from zero-shot to Cross-Lingual CoT to Self-Consistency, and typically reaches its maximum value in the CLP setting.

Figure 6 shows the relation between the prompting technique and the number of inconclusive answers for each LLM. As shown in the figure, the number of inconclusive responses, on average, increases when going from zero-shot to Cross-Lingual CoT or Self-Consistency. This number decreases in the CLP setting, in which the fewest inconclusive responses are returned.

Figure 5 shows a mostly linear relationship between the prompting technique and the number of correct answers for each LLM.

6.1 Zero-Shot

Accuracy We find that Llama 3 70B Instruct achieves an accuracy of 40.21%, and Llama 3 8B achieves a higher accuracy of 59.01%. GPT-3.5-turbo achieves the second-best accuracy of 60.94% while Gemini Pro performs the worst with an accuracy of 30.60%.

Inconclusive Responses The language models show varying levels of inconclusive responses, with Llama 3 70B, Llama 3 8B, and GPT-3.5-turbo recording 23, 11, and 21 inconclusive responses respectively. Interestingly, despite a lower overall accuracy, Gemini 1.0 Pro returns only 5 inconclusive responses, which could indicate a propensity to deliver more decisive answers, albeit incorrect.

Model	Correct	Incorrect	Inconclusive	Accuracy %	% Increase
Llama 3 8B-instruct					
`Zero-Shot (Baseline)`	455	305	11	59.01	–
`English Chain-of-Thought`	500	209	38	66.93	13.42
`Self-Consistency`	529	201	41	68.61	16.27
`Cross-Lingual Prompting`	664	91	9	**86.55**	46.67
Llama 3 70B-instruct					
`Zero-Shot (Baseline)`	310	438	23	40.21	–
`English Chain-of-Thought`	472	265	34	61.22	52.25
`Self-Consistency`	460	247	64	59.66	48.37
`Cross-Lingual Prompting`	620	134	17	**80.42**	100.00
Gemini 1.0 Pro					
`Zero-Shot (Baseline)`	236	531	5	30.60	–
`English Chain-of-Thought`	383	307	81	49.68	62.35
`Self-Consistency`	405	322	44	**52.53**	71.67
`Cross-Lingual Prompting`	381	385	5	49.41	61.47
GPT-3.5-turbo					
`Zero-Shot (Baseline)`	468	279	21	60.94	–
`English Chain-of-Thought`	461	244	66	59.79	-1.89
`Self-Consistency`	491	235	45	63.68	4.50
`Cross-Lingual Prompting`	603	116	2	**78.21**	28.34

Table 1: Results for each prompting method and LLM. '% Increase' denotes the percentage increase in model performance from the baseline (zero-shot).

We observe that in the zero-shot setting, the LLMs are not effective fact-checkers and have room for improvement.

6.2 English Chain-of-Thought

Accuracy We observe that the English Chain-of-Thought (CoT) approach generally improves accuracy across most models compared to the zero-shot baseline. Llama 3 70B Instruct's accuracy increases by 52.25% (from 40.21% to 61.22%) in the CoT setting. Llama 3 8B Instruct's accuracy increases from 59.01% to 66.93%, a 13.42% increase. Gemini Pro's performance rises by 62.35% (49.68% from 30.60%).

In contrast, GPT-3.5-turbo performs with similar accuracy in the Cross-Lingual CoT setup, with a 1.89% drop in accuracy from its zero-shot performance.

Inconclusive Responses Despite the increase in accuracy for most LLMs, there was a significant rise in inconclusive responses across all models when applying the Cross-Lingual CoT method. This was particularly marked in Gemini Pro and GPT-3.5-turbo where inconclusive responses shot up to 61, 81, and 66 respectively. We find that while Cross-Lingual CoT appears to improve accuracy by allowing the LLMs to reason out the answers in English, it also seems to introduce greater uncertainty, leading to a higher number of inconclusive responses.

We find that generally, while English Chain-of-Thought leads to a rise in the number of inconclusive responses, the LLMs mostly return more correct answers, leading to a net increase in accuracy.

6.3 Self-Consistency

Accuracy We find that implementing Cross-Lingual CoT with Self-Consistency enhances model performance beyond Cross-Lingual CoT. For Llama 3 8B Instruct and Llama 3 70B Instruct, the accuracy increases by 16.27% and 48.37%, respectively. Gemini Pro's accuracy rises significantly, by 71.67%. GPT-3.5-turbo's accuracy increases by 4.50%. Llama 3 70B Instruct performs worse in the Self-Consistency setting than in the Cross-Lingual CoT setting.

Inconclusive Responses As shown in Figure 6, Self-Consistency leads to the highest

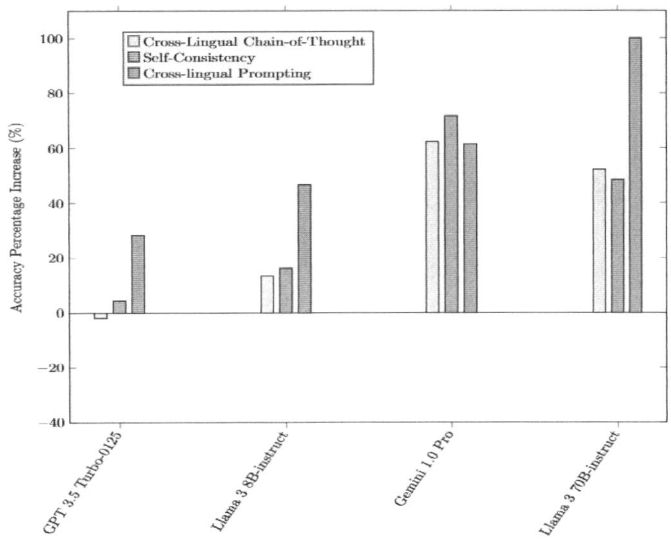

Figure 4: Percentage Increase from the Baseline (Zero-Shot) for each Prompting Method and LLM.

number of inconclusive responses out of all the prompting methods. Llama 3 70B Instruct returns the highest number of inconclusive responses (64). We hypothesize that because the model is prompted to generate three lines of reasoning, it is susceptible to hallucinations and indeterminate chains of thought.

We observe that integrating Self-Consistency with Cross-Lingual CoT leads to an increase in the number of inconclusive responses returned by the LLMs. However, due to a rise in the number of correct answers, there is a net increase in model accuracy.

6.4 Cross-Lingual Prompting

Accuracy We find that cross-lingual prompting (CLP) often leads to the best model performance out of all the four prompting techniques. Llama 3 8B Instruct's accuracy improves by 46.67% over the baseline to achieve an accuracy of 86.55%, the highest among all tested models and methods. Similarly, GPT-3.5-turbo's performance also benefits from CLP, with its accuracy rising to 78.21% from a baseline of 60.94%. Llama 3 70B's performance reaches 80.42% from its baseline of 40.21%, a 100% improvement.

Inconclusive Responses Interestingly, while CLP improved accuracy across the board, it also led to a reduction in inconclusive responses for most models, indicating an increase in decisiveness. We observe a reduction in inconclusive responses from 11 to 9 for Llama 3 8B, 23 to 17 for Llama 3 70B, and 21 to 2 for GPT-3.5-turbo from zero-shot to CLP. The number of inconclusive responses remains unchanged for Gemini Pro.

Our findings suggest that CLP is extremely effective in clarifying the decision-making processes for these LLMs in an Arabic context while maintaining accuracy.

7 Conclusion and Future Work

In this study, we examined the Arabic fact-checking and claim verification capabilities of four LLMs: Llama 3 8B Instruct, Llama 3 70B Instruct, Gemini 1.0 Pro, and GPT-3.5-turbo. We employed four prompting techniques: Zero-Shot, English Chain-of-Thought, Self-Consistency, and Cross-Lingual Prompting. Our findings reveal that although these LLMs perform inadequately in a zero-shot setting, prompting techniques that engage reasoning capabilities significantly enhance their performance. In particular, Cross-Lingual Prompting showed substantial improvement in accuracy, suggesting that leveraging the reasoning capabilities of LLMs through sophisticated prompting strategies can effectively address the challenges posed by the complex morphology and diverse dialects of the Arabic language.

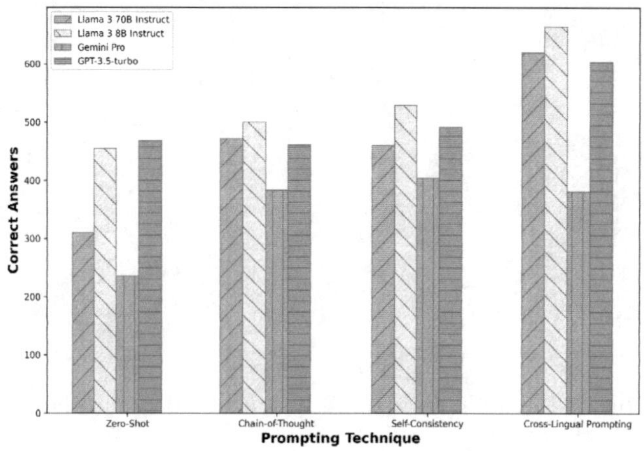

Figure 5: Variation of the number of correct answers with prompting method for each model.

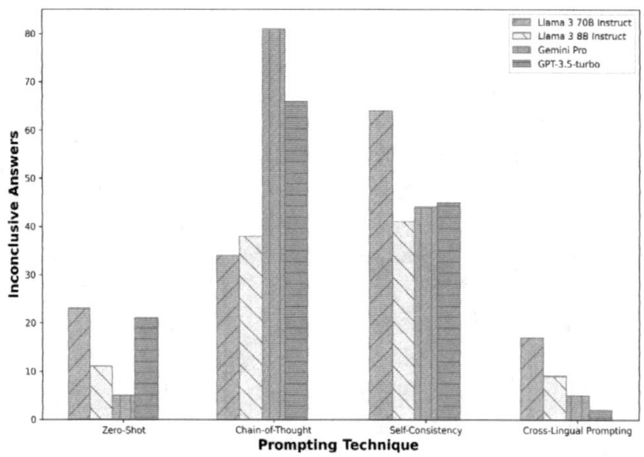

Figure 6: Variation of inconclusive answers for each model with different prompting techniques.

In future work, we aim to expand our dataset to establish a comprehensive benchmark for Arabic claim verification that includes diverse claims from various domains. Additionally, a future study could investigate how LLMs perform on fact-checking for claims in various independent Arabic dialects. Given the promising results of Cross-Lingual Prompting, we plan to explore other advanced prompting strategies, including few-shot prompting and Cross-Lingual Prompting with Self-Consistency, to further enhance performance.

Limitations

The scope of our analysis is restricted to a select group of LLMs. It would be interesting to investigate the Arabic fact-checking abilities of other leading models such as OpenAI's GPT-4 and Anthropic's Claude 3 series. Additionally, our dataset mainly comprises claims labeled as ground-truth false (730) as opposed to true (41). While this skew does not compromise the assessment of the LLMs' verification abilities, a more balanced distribution could provide deeper insights into their fact-checking capabilities in Arabic.

References

Asaad Alghamdi, Xinyu Duan, Wei Jiang, Zhenhai Wang, Yimeng Wu, Qingrong Xia, Zhefeng Wang, Yi Zheng, Mehdi Rezagholizadeh, Baoxing Huai, Peilun Cheng, and Abbas Ghaddar. 2023. Aramus: Pushing the limits of data and model scale for arabic natural language processing. *Preprint*, arXiv:2306.06800.

Saud Althabiti, Mohammad Ammar Alsalka, and Eric Atwell. 2024. Ta'keed: The first generative fact-checking system for arabic claims. *Preprint*, arXiv:2401.14067.

Zaid Alyafeai, Maged S. Alshaibani, Badr AlKhamissi, Hamzah Luqman, Ebrahim Alareqi, and Ali Fadel. 2023. Taqyim: Evaluating arabic nlp tasks using chatgpt models. *Preprint*, arXiv:2306.16322.

Rohan Anil, Sebastian Borgeaud, Yonghui Wu, Jean-Baptiste Alayrac, Jiahui Yu, Radu Soricut, Johan Schalkwyk, Andrew M Dai, Anja Hauth, et al. 2023. Gemini: a family of highly capable multimodal models. *arXiv preprint arXiv:2312.11805*.

Wissam Antoun, Fady Baly, and Hazem Hajj. 2021. Arabert: Transformer-based model for arabic language understanding. *Preprint*, arXiv:2003.00104.

Han Cao, Lingwei Wei, Mengyang Chen, Wei Zhou, and Songlin Hu. 2023. Are large language models good fact checkers: A preliminary study. *Preprint*, arXiv:2311.17355.

Recep Firat Cekinel, Pinar Karagoz, and Cagri Coltekin. 2024. Cross-lingual learning vs. low-resource fine-tuning: A case study with fact-checking in turkish. *Preprint*, arXiv:2403.00411.

Tsun-Hin Cheung and Kin-Man Lam. 2023. Factllama: Optimizing instruction-following language models with external knowledge for automated fact-checking. *Preprint*, arXiv:2309.00240.

Eun Cheol Choi and Emilio Ferrara. 2024. Fact-gpt: Fact-checking augmentation via claim matching with llms. *arXiv preprint arXiv:2402.05904*.

Kareem Darwish, Nizar Habash, Mourad Abbas, Hend Al-Khalifa, Huseein T. Al-Natsheh, Samhaa R. El-Beltagy, Houda Bouamor, Karim Bouzoubaa, Violetta Cavalli-Sforza, Wassim El-Hajj, Mustafa Jarrar, and Hamdy Mubarak. 2021. A panoramic survey of natural language processing in the arab world. *Preprint*, arXiv:2011.12631.

Mohammad Majd Saad Al Deen, Maren Pielka, Jörn Hees, Bouthaina Soulef Abdou, and Rafet Sifa. 2023. Improving natural language inference in arabic using transformer models and linguistically informed pre-training. *Preprint*, arXiv:2307.14666.

Imane Guellil, Houda Saâdane, Faical Azouaou, Billel Gueni, and Damien Nouvel. 2021. Arabic natural language processing: An overview. *Journal of King Saud University - Computer and Information Sciences*, 33(5):497–507.

Ashim Gupta and Vivek Srikumar. 2021a. X-fact: A new benchmark dataset for multilingual fact checking. In *Proceedings of the 59th Annual Meeting of the Association for Computational Linguistics and the 11th International Joint Conference on Natural Language Processing (Volume 2: Short Papers)*, pages 675–682, Online. Association for Computational Linguistics.

Ashim Gupta and Vivek Srikumar. 2021b. X-fact: A new benchmark dataset for multilingual fact checking. *Preprint*, arXiv:2106.09248.

Emma Hoes, Sacha Altay, and Juan Bermeo. 2023. Leveraging chatgpt for efficient fact-checking. *PsyArXiv. April*, 3.

Xuming Hu, Junzhe Chen, Xiaochuan Li, Yufei Guo, Lijie Wen, Philip S. Yu, and Zhijiang Guo. 2023. Do large language models know about facts? *Preprint*, arXiv:2310.05177.

Nayeon Lee, Belinda Z Li, Sinong Wang, Wen-tau Yih, Hao Ma, and Madian Khabsa. 2020. Language models as fact-checkers? *arXiv preprint arXiv:2006.04102*.

MetaAI. 2024. Introducing meta llama 3: The most capable openly available llm to date.

Shervin Minaee, Tomas Mikolov, Narjes Nikzad, Meysam Chenaghlu, Richard Socher, Xavier Amatriain, and Jianfeng Gao. 2024. Large language models: A survey. *Preprint*, arXiv:2402.06196.

Libo Qin, Qiguang Chen, Fuxuan Wei, Shijue Huang, and Wanxiang Che. 2023. Cross-lingual prompting: Improving zero-shot chain-of-thought reasoning across languages. In *Proceedings of the 2023 Conference on Empirical Methods in Natural Language Processing*, pages 2695–2709, Singapore. Association for Computational Linguistics.

Dorian Quelle and Alexandre Bovet. 2024. The perils and promises of fact-checking with large language models. *Frontiers in Artificial Intelligence*, 7.

Sheikh Shafayat, Eunsu Kim, Juhyun Oh, and Alice Oh. 2024. Multi-fact: Assessing multilingual llms' multi-regional knowledge using factscore. *Preprint*, arXiv:2402.18045.

Katherine Tian, Eric Mitchell, Huaxiu Yao, Christopher D. Manning, and Chelsea Finn. 2023. Fine-tuning language models for factuality. *Preprint*, arXiv:2311.08401.

Xuezhi Wang, Jason Wei, Dale Schuurmans, Quoc Le, Ed Chi, Sharan Narang, Aakanksha Chowdhery, and Denny Zhou. 2023. Self-consistency improves chain of thought reasoning in language models. *Preprint*, arXiv:2203.11171.

Jason Wei, Xuezhi Wang, Dale Schuurmans, Maarten Bosma, Brian Ichter, Fei Xia, Ed Chi, Quoc Le, and Denny Zhou. 2023. Chain-of-thought prompting elicits reasoning in large language models. *Preprint*, arXiv:2201.11903.

Caiqi Zhang, Zhijiang Guo, and Andreas Vlachos. 2024. Do we need language-specific fact-checking models? the case of chinese. *Preprint*, arXiv:2401.15498.

Xuan Zhang and Wei Gao. 2023. Towards llm-based fact verification on news claims with a hierarchical step-by-step prompting method. *arXiv preprint arXiv:2310.00305*.

A Appendix

A.1 Dataset Creation

A.1.1 Dataset Statistics

The X-fact dataset (Gupta and Srikumar, 2021b) was utilized as our primary data source. The claims in the dataset are sourced from `https://misbar.com`.

A.1.2 Preprocessing Steps

1. Filtering: We filtered the dataset to include only claims that were labeled as either "true" or "false". Claims with other labels or those lacking verification were excluded from the finalized dataset.

2. Combining Splits: After filtering, the claims from the Train, Dev, and In-domain Test (α_1) splits were combined to form a single dataset for our experiments.

A.1.3 Dataset Composition

Table 2 shows the total number of Arabic claims and the number of Arabic claims filtered. After pre-processing, the test dataset contained a total of 771 Arabic claims.

Number of claims from Train set: 643
Number of claims from Dev set: 88
Number of claims from In-domain Test (α_1) set: 40

A.1.4 Label Distribution

TRUE Claims: 41 claims (5.32%)
FALSE Claims: 730 claims (94.68%)

A.2 Computational Resources

All experiments were conducted using a combination of cloud-based GPU instances and local compute resources. The specific details of the compute setup are outlined below:

A.2.1 GPU Resources

For training and evaluating the LLMs, we utilized the following GPU configurations:

- **Cloud GPU Instances:** Experiments were primarily conducted on NVIDIA A100 40GB GPUs hosted on cloud providers (e.g., AWS EC2, Google Cloud Platform). Each instance included 8 A100 GPUs with 320GB of total VRAM. The experiments on these instances ran across multiple GPUs in parallel for faster throughput.

- **Local GPU Instances:** Some experiments were run locally on a system equipped with 2 NVIDIA RTX 3090 GPUs, each with 24GB of VRAM.

Dataset Split	Total Number of Claims	Filtered Number of Arabic Claims (True & False)
Train	18246	643
Dev	3657	88
In-domain Test (α_1)	2406	40
Total	24309	771

Table 2: Summary of the dataset splits before and after filtering claims labeled as 'TRUE' or 'FALSE'.

A.2.2 Compute Time

- **Zero-Shot Prompting:** Each model required approximately 1 hour of compute time on a single GPU for evaluating the 771 claims using zero-shot prompting.

- **Chain-of-Thought Prompting:** English Chain-of-Thought and Cross-Lingual Chain-of-Thought evaluations required about 3 hours per model per experiment, as generating reasoning chains increased compute time.

- **Self-Consistency:** The self-consistency experiments, which required generating multiple reasoning paths for each claim, took approximately 6 hours per model.

A.2.3 Total Compute Resources

The total compute time across all models and experiments was approximately 100 GPU hours. Most of this time was spent on the Self-Consistency and Cross-Lingual Prompting experiments due to the additional reasoning paths generated.

A.2.4 Memory and Storage

Each experiment required at least 200GB of storage for caching intermediate results and model checkpoints. The average memory usage was 120GB during peak execution of the larger models (e.g., Llama 3 70B).

A.2.5 Software Environment

All experiments were run using the following software stack:

- **Operating System:** Ubuntu 20.04 LTS

- **Deep Learning Framework:** PyTorch 2.0

- **CUDA Version:** 11.7

- **Other Dependencies:** Transformers (Hugging Face), Python 3.9, and specific drivers for NVIDIA GPUs.

Can LLMs Translate Cultural Nuance in Dialects? A Case Study on Lebanese Arabic

Silvana Yakhni, Ali Chehab
Electrical and Computer Engineering
American University of Beirut
syy06@mail.aub.edu, chehab@aub.edu.lb

Abstract

Machine Translation (MT) of Arabic-script languages presents unique challenges due to their vast linguistic diversity and lack of standardization. This paper focuses on the Lebanese dialect, investigating the effectiveness of Large Language Models (LLMs) in handling culturally-aware translations. We identify critical limitations in existing Lebanese-English parallel datasets, particularly their non-native nature and lack of cultural context. To address these gaps, we introduce a new culturally-rich dataset derived from the *Language Wave (LW)* podcast. We evaluate the performance of LLMs: *Jais*, *AceGPT*, *Cohere*, and *GPT-4* models against Neural Machine Translation (NMT) systems: *NLLB-200*, and *Google Translate*. Our findings reveal that while both architectures perform similarly on non-native datasets, LLMs demonstrate superior capabilities in preserving cultural nuances when handling authentic Lebanese content. Additionally, we validate *xCOMET* as a reliable metric for evaluating the quality of Arabic dialect translation, showing a strong correlation with human judgment. This work contributes to the growing field of Culturally-Aware Machine Translation and highlights the importance of authentic, culturally representative datasets in advancing low-resource translation systems.

1 Introduction

The Arabic script, known for its use in writing Modern Standard Arabic (MSA), is used by hundreds of millions of people worldwide across a diverse range of languages, including Arabic dialects, Abjad, and Ajami languages. Arabic-script languages share several key characteristics, including a rich cultural context, idiomatic expressions, and frequent use of religious and poetic references. These features make translation particularly challenging, as they require not only linguistic accuracy but also cultural sensitivity. This paper focuses on Lebanese Arabic, a prominent dialect spoken in the Levant region, that exemplifies the script complexities, with its unique cultural expressions and idioms.

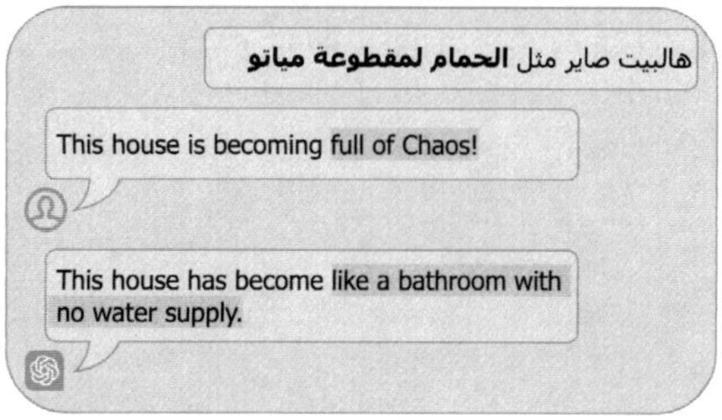

Figure 1: Example of the translation of the Lebanese idiom (الحمام لمقطوعة مياتو) by a human translator compared to GPT-4o

However, the predominantly spoken nature of dialects, coupled with their lack of standardized spelling and grammar, presents a significant challenge for Machine Translation (MT) due to the scarcity of culturally representative datasets needed to develop effective translation models. The few available parallel Lebanese/English data suffer from many limitations, including the predominance of foreign source languages in existing corpora (Krubiński et al., 2023) (Bouamor et al., 2018) (team et al., 2022), which may not accurately capture the nuances of the Lebanese culture.

Recently, Decoder-only Large Language Models (LLMs) such as chatGPT[1], Claude[2], and LLaMA (Touvron et al., 2023) have demonstrated notable success across various

[1] https://chatgpt.com/
[2] claude.ai

Processings of the 1st Workshop on NLP for Languages Using Arabic Script (AbjadNLP), pages 114–135
January 19, 2025. ©2025 Association for Computational Linguistics

NLP tasks, including translation, particularly for widely used languages (Jiao et al., 2023)(Lyu et al., 2023). Recent research has tackled Culturally-Aware Machine Translation (CAMT) (Yao et al., 2024) with LLMs and showed that they exhibit superior capabilities compared to traditional neural MT systems in translating cultural content.

In Arabic NLP, little effort was made to benchmark the performance of LLMs in translating Arabic dialects. However, these efforts fell short of assessing the full spectrum of Arabic-focused LLMs (Kadaoui et al., 2023)(Alam et al., 2024). Furthermore, Existing Arabic dialect evaluation benchmarks such as LAraBench (Abdelali et al., 2023), SADID (Abid, 2020) and AraDICE (Mousi et al., 2024) rely primarily on translated English content, rather than authentic dialectal resources. This limitation extends beyond isolated cultural elements to the entire linguistic system, including culturally embedded grammar, vocabulary, and idioms. Figure 1 shows a failed attempt of *GPT-4o* to translate the cultural Lebanese idiom "el-hamem el-maa'toua'a maytu" (الحمام المقطوعة مياتو) , which means **"It's Chaos"**. GPT-4o instead literally translates it to "a bathroom with no water supply". The field's dependence on translated data underscores the urgent need for developing authentic, culturally-aware datasets that capture the true complexity of Arabic dialectal variations. Appendix B provides a more comprehensive overview of previous research in this domain.

Moreover, the evaluations of translation tasks for Arabic dialects depend mainly on statistical metrics like the BLEU score, despite substantial evidence showing its limitations in evaluating fluency and meaning compared to neural metrics such as xCOMET(Kocmi et al., 2024)(Lee et al., 2023).

More specifically, in this work, we aim to answer the following questions:

1. Do existing Lebanese-English datasets accurately reflect translation quality, given their English origins and limited Lebanese cultural context?

2. Do LLMs and encoder-decoder models perform equally across all datasets, or do they struggle with culturally rich datasets?

3. Which performs better in translating Arabic dialects: LLMs or translation NMT models?

To this end, we review the few existing parallel Lebanese/English datasets and critically assess their shortcomings. We then introduce our new curated dataset from the Language Wave (LW) podcast, a collection of culturally rich Lebanese content, and we demonstrate how this dataset effectively addresses the limitations of existing resources by ensuring cultural authenticity, a trait typically absent in datasets derived from non-native sources. Through a comprehensive comparative analysis, we evaluate closed-source Arabic-focused LLMs (Jais (Sengupta et al., 2023), AceGPT (Huang et al., 2024), Cohere [3]) and the API-based model (GPT-4o[4]) against open-source NMT systems (NLLB-200) (team et al., 2022) and commercial translation services (Google Translate), examining their performance on culturally-rich Lebanese content versus English-derived datasets.

Our key findings demonstrate several significant insights:

- A systematic analysis reveals a substantial gap in existing parallel datasets regarding cultural representation.

- While Arabic-focused LLMs and encoder-decoder models exhibit comparable performance on traditional English-origin datasets, LLMs remarkably demonstrate superior performance when processing culturally-aware datasets.

- Open-source Command-R+ rivals GPT-4o in cultural translation, promoting accessible tools.

- We demonstrate the effectiveness of xCOMET as a reliable evaluation tool to assess the translation quality from Arabic dialects to English, with results showing a high correlation with human judgment.

2 Existing Datasets

Open Subtitles(OS) (Krubiński et al., 2023): A large dataset containing 120,600 sentences derived from movie subtitles, available

[3]https://cohere.com/
[4]https://chatgpt.com/

in both MSA and English. Researchers manually translated MSA sentences into Lebanese. Despite its size, it has significant quality issues stemming from using Modern Standard Arabic (MSA) as an intermediary language for translations. In addition, the dataset suffers from cultural misalignment given its translation from Western-centric source material. We refer to this data as OS (Open Subtitles).

MADAR CODA (Bouamor et al., 2018): A corpus containing 2,000 English sentences from the Basic Travel Expression Corpus (BTEC) translated into 26 Arab city dialects, with expanded coverage of 10,000 sentences for major cities, including Beirut. While valuable for dialectal variation, the dataset is limited by its simple sentence structures and its narrow focus on travel-related content. The English-sourced translations also potentially introduce cultural bias, limiting its effectiveness for culturally-aware machine translation applications.

Facebook Low Resource (FLoRes) Corpus (team et al., 2022): A benchmarking dataset containing 3,001 sentences from Wikimedia projects, professionally translated into over 200 languages. While broad in language coverage, the dataset's formal content lacks the informal linguistic features and cultural nuances essential for dialect translation.

Arabic-Dialect/English Parallel Text (Zbib et al., 2012): A substantial corpus developed through collaboration between Raytheon BBN Technologies, LDC, and Sakhr Software, containing 3.5 million tokens of Arabic dialectal content with English translations, focusing on Levantine and Egyptian dialects. While potentially valuable, its restricted access through LDC has limited its research impact, with no comprehensive quality evaluation existing in the literature.

3 Language Wave Dataset

The development of a parallel Lebanese Arabic-English dataset addresses critical gaps in existing translation resources for this dialect. Our comprehensive data collection process focused on creating an authentic, diverse, and professionally translated corpus that effectively captures the nuances of Lebanese Arabic while providing professional English translations. Through careful curation of Lebanese media sources, we prioritized maintaining cultural relevance and linguistic authenticity, ensuring the dataset would serve as a valuable resource for both academic research and practical applications.

We identified the "Language Wave" podcast[5] as an invaluable resource in preserving cultural content. This podcast, with its slogan **"Learn Lebanese Arabic with transcribed podcast: episodes exploring Lebanon and its people"**, offers authentic content that covers various topics and language concepts, designed to enhance Lebanese Arabic skills in active listening, reading, vocabulary, and cultural context knowledge. Through collaboration with the "Language Wave" podcast, we developed a comprehensive dataset encompassing 95 episodes, which resulted in 2,947 Lebanese sentences professionally translated into English. The podcast's colloquial style effectively mirrors everyday Lebanese Arabic conversations and mimics authentic, colloquial Lebanese Arabic. **We refer to our Language Wave dataset as "LW".**

4 Linguistic Analysis

LW dataset exhibits several distinguishing characteristics when compared to MADAR, FLoRes, and OS. The most significant attribute is data authenticity among others. While the aforementioned datasets are translated from foreign sources, LW is uniquely crafted by professional translators, ensuring a high degree of linguistic fidelity. To highlight the distinctive features of the LW dataset, we conduct comprehensive analyses, the results of which are presented in Figure 2.

1. **Sentence Length Distribution:** Analysis of sentence length distribution reveals that LW exhibits a more balanced spread across various lengths, indicating a more natural and varied language usage.

2. **Domain Distribution:** We compiled a comprehensive lexicon encompassing 8 prominent domains: arts, cuisine, cultural heritage, geography, language, news, socioeconomic life, and travel and tourism. For

[5] https://languagewave.com/

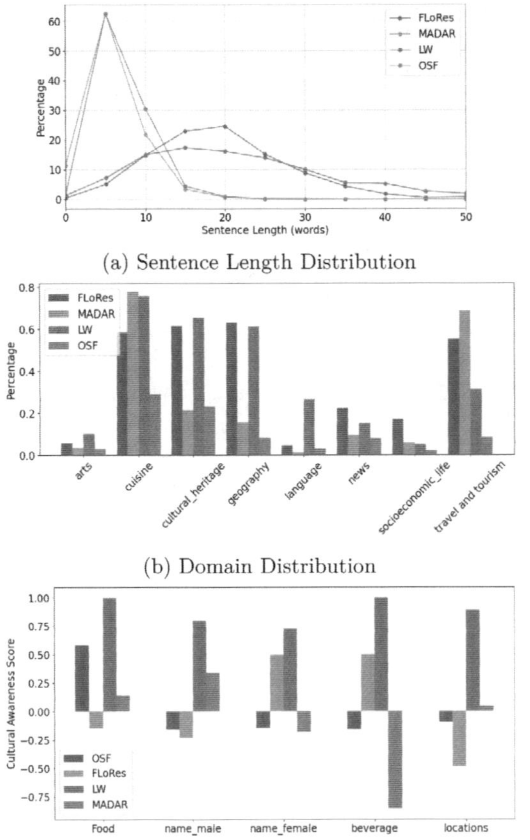

(a) Sentence Length Distribution

(b) Domain Distribution

(c) Cultural Awareness

Figure 2: Comparative Data Analysis between MADAR, FloRes, LW and OS Datasets based on three criteria: Domain Distribution, Cultural Awareness, and Sentence Length distribution.

each dataset, we calculated the frequency of domain words. LW demonstrates robust representation in critical categories such as cuisine, cultural heritage, and geography. Notably, MADAR exhibits a bias towards the travel and tourism domain, while OS shows the least richness across all domains, potentially due to its nature as movie subtitles. This distribution underscores the rich diversity inherent in our dataset.

3. **Cultural Awareness:** To quantify this crucial characteristic, we employed a Cultural Awareness metric, inspired by the work in (Naous et al., 2023) to assess the cultural awareness of LLMs. We selected five domains $D = d_1, ..., d_5$ where $d_1 =$ "Food", $d_2 =$ "male names", $d_3 =$ "female names", $d_4 =$ "beverages", and $d_5 =$ "locations". For each domain $d_i \in D$ and dataset X, we calculated the frequency of Arab terms (f_A) and Western terms (f_W) through exact string matching. The Cultural Awareness Score (CAS) for each domain is defined as:

$$CAS(d_i) = \frac{f_A(d_i) - f_W(d_i)}{f_A(d_i) + f_W(d_i)} \in [-1, 1] \quad (1)$$

where $f_A(d_i)$ and $f_W(d_i)$ represent the frequency of Arab and Western terms respectively in domain d_i. The results demonstrate that LW consistently achieves high positive CAS values for all categories, particularly excelling in name recognition (both male and female) and locations. This exceptional performance distinctly sets LW apart, indicating its superior ability to capture nuanced cultural context.

CAS as a Cultural Benchmark : The Cultural Awareness Score (CAS) provides an initial benchmark for quantifying cultural representation in linguistic datasets, while simultaneously acknowledging the inherent complexities of cultural linguistic analysis. Although the metric employs a binary classification of Arab and Western terms, its primary value lies in establishing a structured methodology for examining cultural nuances in low-resource datasets. To enhance the metric's adaptability, a great approach is to add on the Arab terms we have by collaborating with linguistic experts who can provide comprehensive compilations of region-specific expressions, idioms, and cultural references that might otherwise be overlooked in standard linguistic analyses. This approach allows for potential adaptation to other language contexts by leveraging expert knowledge in cultural linguistics, and translation studies.

5 Quantitative Analysis

The core question guiding our analysis is the following: **How proficient are translation models in producing translations that preserve cultural nuances and context?**

To address this question, we leverage our Lebanese culturally-aware dataset, Language Wave (LW), to assess the translation performance of both decoder-only and encoder-

	Non-native			Culturally-Aware
	FLoRes	**OS**	**MADAR**	**LW**
NLLB-3.1B	0.88463969	0.87022187	0.86595088	0.63533914
NLLB-moe-54B	0.89736591	0.92584903	0.88523401	0.65198355
Google-Translate	0.92879412	0.92916107	0.88343378	0.66453003
Jais-13B	0.84704429	0.84447611	0.88901745	0.70714775
Jais-adapted-70B	0.89354683	0.92794033	0.91857263	0.75139506
AceGPT-7B	0.79234672	0.81954603	0.82858921	0.66264395
AceGPT-70B	0.85027576	0.86379206	0.87928573	0.75365206
Aya32-8B	0.87830721	0.90754499	0.87050557	0.68780926
Aya-expanse-32B	0.90185826	0.91843578	0.89275793	0.75132963
Command-R+	0.92475206	0.92651753	0.92847502	0.80957264
GPT-4o	0.93451795	0.93367150	0.92774067	0.79337348

Table 1: Comparative assessment of translation quality across encoder-decoder architectures (NLLB, GoogleTranslate) and Large Language Models (Jais, AceGPT, Cohere, GPT-4o). The analysis spans three established non-native benchmarks (FLoRes, MADAR, OS) and our culturally-aware LW dataset, measuring xCOMET scores between reference and generated translations.

decoder models. Additionally, we compare their performance when translating three non-native datasets — FLoRes, MADAR, and OS. For evaluation, we conducted a thorough correlation analysis in section 7. Our results show that xCOMET shows the highest correlation with human judgment. Hence, we adopt in this work xCOMET-10.7B as our evaluation metric.

MT systems in Comparison: We evaluate the following MT systems:

- NMTs: We evaluate the state-of-the-art multilingual NLLB models: *NLLB-3.1B* and *NLLB-moe-54B*. We also use the *Google-Translate* engine in our comparison.
- LLMs: We examine the following Arabic-focused open-source models: *Jais-13B*, *Jais-adapted-70B*, *AceGPT-7B*, *AceGPT-70B*, in addition to the multilingual open-source Cohere models: *Aya23-8B*, *Aya-expanse-35B* and *Command-R+-104B*. Finally, we used the closed API-based *GPT-4o* model. More details about the models are available in Appendix A.

Experimental Results: For decoder-only models, we prompted the model as follows: *"You are a professional translator, translate the following sentence from Lebanese to English: Input: {sentence}"*. In this study, we focused solely on zero-shot prompting for LLMs and used encoder-decoder models without fine-tuning. This approach was chosen to evaluate the innate capability of these models to comprehend and translate culturally rich and nuanced content without relying on task-specific training.

The second question we aim to answer in this analysis is: **How do the performance of LLMs and encoder-decoder models compare, when handling culturally-aware content?** Our analysis reveals intriguing patterns: for content derived from Western cultures (MADAR, FLoRes, OS), both architectures demonstrate comparable performance, with encoder-decoder models like NLLB-moe-54B and Google-Translate achieving scores that occasionally surpass decoder-only models like Jais-adapted-50B, Command-R+. However, a notable divergence emerges when handling culturally rich Lebanese content. LLMs consistently outperform NLLB and Google-Translate on culturally-aware datasets. While Jais-adapted-70B and Command-R+ maintain scores in range (0.75-0.8) on LW's cultural examples, encoder-decoder models' performance drops significantly to a range of around 0.65. These findings suggest that the architectural advantages of LLMs may be particularly valuable for preserving cultural nuances in translation, though further research is needed to fully understand this phenomenon. In addition, our analysis reveals a clear correlation between LLM size and translation quality, as measured by xCOMET scores. Larger models like Jais-adapted-70B, AceGPT-70B, and Command-R+ consistently outperformed their smaller counterparts. Notably, the 104B Command-R+ achieved comparable results to GPT-4, even exceeding it on the LW dataset. These findings suggest promising opportunities for developing accessible, high-quality cultural translation tools.

6 Qualitative Analysis

To complement our quantitative findings, we conducted a qualitative analysis focusing on four distinct aspects of Lebanese-English cultural translation: **1) cultural understanding, 2) linguistic complexity, 3) idiomatic language, and 4) Ambiguity in translation**. We tested the translation of Lebanese expressions on four different models. For encoder-decoder models, we chose *Google-Translate*. For LLMs, we tested the closed *GPT-4o* model, the multilingual *Command-R+-104B*, and the Arabic-focused *Jais-adapted-70B*. Some of these examples are highlighted in figures 3-6 in Appendix D.

Cultural Understanding: Our initial analysis examined terms that represent various aspects of Lebanese culture, including religious references, social customs, and traditional practices. A notable example, shown in Figure 3, involves social custom phrases such as "katb el-kteb" (كتب الكتاب), denoting the formal marriage contract announcement, "el-mokaddam" (المقدّم), referring to the bride's initial dowry, and "el-moa'khar" (المؤخر), indicating the deferred dowry allocated to the bride in case of divorce. While Google Translate employed a literal translation approach that failed to convey cultural significance, LLMs exhibited enhanced comprehension of cultural nuances, with Command-R+ demonstrating exceptional translation accuracy that surpassed even GPT-4o. Furthermore, we tested the models' cultural understanding on the Lebanese term "el-sett el-marje'youniye" (الست المرجعيونية), which translates to "the lady from Marje'youn"- "el-marje'youniye" (المرجعيونية) is an adjective derived from the Lebanese village noun "Marje'youn" (مرجعيون). We notice that Command-R+ was able to convey this meaning in its translation, while also preserving the tone of respect by translating (الست) to "lady" rather than "woman".

Linguistic Complexity: To assess linguistic complexity, we extracted challenging sentences from a Lebanese vocabulary textbook, focusing on grammatical structures and vocabulary unique to the Lebanese dialect. This analysis revealed that while models could effectively handle basic dialectal variations, they encountered difficulties with unique Lebanese vocabulary. A particularly illustrative challenge emerged in the translation of "Lebanized" verbs (non-Semitic verbs that have been morphologically adapted to Lebanese linguistic patterns). Figure 4 presents the example of such a verb- "mdapras" (مدپرس), which means "got depressed." Furthermore, Lebanese Arabic is characterized by distinctive terms that often carry subtle contextual implications. As demonstrated in Figure 4, the term "anja'" (أنجأ) emphasizes a narrow escape or marginal success, typically carrying undertones of fortunate timing. While Google Translate failed to convey the meaning accurately, LLMs performed significantly better, with Command-R+ particularly successful in capturing the subtle undertones, translating (أنجأ) as "barely managed" rather than "managed." Similarly, the Lebanese term "yestefil" (يصطفل) conveys indifference or detachment regarding another person's situation or decision, often implying personal responsibility for consequences and carrying a tone of irritation. While Google Translate struggled significantly with this term, LLMs demonstrated superior comprehension. Notably, while GPT-4 incorrectly translated this term as "suit yourself," Jais and Command-R+ provided more accurate translations with "Let him be."

Idiomatic Language: Our third analysis examined the use of Lebanese idioms, with particular attention to everyday expressions. A representative example shown in Figure 5 is "ana bi wadi w inti bi wadi" (أنا بوادي وإنتي بوادي), literally meaning "I am in a valley and you are in a valley". This phrase is used to indicate a significant disconnect between two parties' perspectives and is often translated literally by Google Translate, resulting in the loss of its cultural significance. Similarly, the idiomatic expression "hases hali metl la'trach bzaffe" (حاسس حالي متل الأطرش بالزفة), literally translates to "I feel like a deaf person in a wedding ceremony", but usually means "I feel out of place". Note that LLMs are usually able to describe situations where an idiom is used, which opens horizons for exploring different prompting techniques that can guide LLMs to translate culturally-aware expressions.

Ambuiguity: Translation in Arabic and Abjad scripts can be ambiguous due to the absence of diacritics, which leaves words open to multiple interpretations based on context. Additionally, using adverbs connected to verbs can alter meaning subtly, making it difficult for machine translation systems to capture their intended use. Examples of ambiguous translations are shown in Figure 6. The Arabic word (كتبت), can be transcribed based on diacritics as "katabet" or "katabit", meaning "I wrote" or "she wrote", depending on the context. Another example is the reference to an adverb; the expression "el-walad wa'aa' a'n lkersi fankasaret e'jru" (الولد وقع عن لكرسي فنكسرت اجرو), translates to "The boy fell from the chair and he broke **his/its** leg". Despite strategic attempts to disambiguate these terms and provide contextual clarity, both Google Translate and LLMs failed to provide correct translations.

Our comparative analysis of Lebanese-English translation models reveals a clear hierarchy in translation capabilities, with Command-R+ and GPT-4o consistently outperforming other models across cultural, linguistic, and idiomatic dimensions, while traditional encoder-decoder models like Google Translate showed significant limitations and often fail to capture cultural significance. Despite the clear advantage of LLMs, they still struggle in many scenarios, especially in idiomatic and ambiguous settings.

7 Cultural Translation Landscapes

Our methodological approach for Lebanese dialect translation provides a framework for addressing challenges in low-resource languages, especially those using Arabic scripts, given the common linguistic challenges they face, including diacritization, lexical ambiguity, and preserving culturally embedded expressions.(Ishaku et al., 2020).

Another common challenge is the lack of carefully curated, culturally-rich datasets. A few notable examples include the Curras+Baladi dataset(Haff et al., 2022), which focuses on translating authentic songs and blog posts for the Levantine dialect. Efforts were also made to collect such datasets in Egyptian (Al-Sabbagh, 2023). Furthermore, the Boston University research project on Ajami Literacy, supported by the National Endowment for the Humanities, has made significant strides by digitizing manuscripts in four West African languages (Hausa, Mandinka, Fula, and Wolof), providing transcriptions, translations, and multimedia resources (Ngom et al., 2023). Despite these efforts, existing linguistic resources remain insufficient to comprehensively address the complexities of translating Arabic-script languages.

Building upon our analysis of Lebanese dialect translation, this study made an additional effort to explore some of the linguistic commonalities across other Arabic-script languages, with a specific focus on Hausa and Wolof Ajami languages. Our analysis concentrates on the nuanced translation of idiomatic expressions, culturally specific terminology, and religious lexicons. Comparative translation examples for both Hausa and Wolof from GPT-4o and Google Translate, are detailed in Appendix D and illustrated in Figures 7-10, providing a comprehensive examination of challenges inherent in these culturally-rich low-resource languages. All examples are taken from resources in (Ngom et al., 2023). Similarly to Lebanese, preliminary findings on Hausa and Wolof reveal that LLMs demonstrate notable limitations in accurately interpreting cultural expressions, though they exhibit marginally superior performance compared to Google Translate. These results underscore the critical need for further comprehensive linguistic analysis that moves beyond mere lexical conversion to a more profound understanding of cultural meaning-making processes.

8 Metric Correlation Analysis

Machine translation evaluation relies on numerous established metrics, each with its own strengths and methodologies. While learned neural metrics like COMET(Rei et al., 2022) and BERTScore (Zhang et al., 2019) have demonstrated superior correlation with human judgment compared to traditional metrics like BLEU (Kocmi et al., 2024)(Lee et al., 2023), the latter is still widely used in Arabic NLP. To evaluate the effectiveness of different automatic metrics for Lebanese dialect to English translation, we conducted a correlation analysis with human judgment. The experiment was designed to balance between rigor and resource constraints.

Metrics to evaluate: BLEU(Papineni et al., 2002), BERTScore(Zhang et al., 2019), COMET(XLM-R Large)(Rei et al., 2022), and xCOMET-10.7B(Guerreiro et al., 2023). More details are provided in Appendix C.1.

Dataset: We conducted a human evaluation study using 150 sampled sentence pairs from our Lebanese Arabic (LW) dataset. The sample was strategically selected to ensure authentic Lebanese content and balanced representation across various linguistic phenomena and complex grammatical structures, as well as diverse domain topics. For our evaluation, we chose to focus on translations generated by the Aya23-8B model. This decision was motivated by our aim to obtain meaningful human ratings across the full spectrum of translation quality (good, acceptable, and poor). While models like GPT-4o[6] and larger architectures such as Command-R+[7] typically produce high-quality translations, and NLLB-1.5B(team et al., 2022) often contains numerous errors, Aya23-8B generates translations with sufficient variation in quality to facilitate nuanced human evaluation.

[6]https://chatgpt.com/

[7]https://dashboard.cohere.com/playground/chat

Human Annotation Guidelines: The translations of the 150 sentences were subsequently subjected to human assessment to evaluate their quality. Three bilingual annotators, fluent in both Lebanese dialect and English, evaluated each translation. The annotation process and the scoring rubric are provided in Appendix C.2.

Correlation Analysis: We calculated Krippendorff's alpha to measure the agreement between annotators. The threshold for acceptable agreement was set at $\alpha \geq 0.6$, indicating substantial agreement.

For each metric, we calculated:

- Pearson correlation coefficient (r) for linear correlation
- Spearman correlation coefficient (ρ) for monotonic correlation
- Statistical significance (p-value < 0.05)

The results of our assessment, presented in Table 2, reveal significant variations in metric performance. BLEU demonstrates the weakest alignment with human judgment, exhibiting minimal correlation coefficients (r = 0.098, $\rho = 0.074$). In contrast, xCOMET achieves a substantially higher correlation with human evaluations (r = 0.606, $\rho = 0.631$), indicating its superior reliability as an automatic evaluation metric. These findings underscore the comparative advantage of neural-based metrics, particularly COMET and xCOMET, over traditional approaches. Notably, the stronger performance of xCOMET compared to COMET may be attributed to its enhanced interpretability and larger model capacity. Furthermore, the results empirically demonstrate the limitations of BLEU as a reliable metric for translation quality assessment in this context.

Metric	r	ρ	p
BLEU	0.098	0.074	0.0336
BertScore	0.492	0.430	0.0000
COMET	0.523	0.461	0.0000
xCOMET	**0.606**	**0.631**	0.0000

Table 2: Correlation coefficients (Pearson's r and Spearman's ρ), measuring alignment between human scores and automated metrics

9 Conclusion

Unlike existing datasets derived from translated foreign sources, we curated, in this work, the Language Wave (LW) dataset that captures the nuances of colloquial Lebanese Arabic. Our linguistic analysis demonstrates LW's superior cultural richness, providing a resource that potentially aids the development of culturally sensitive AI applications.

Furthermore, our analysis reveals a striking disparity in model performance between non-native/translated and culturally-rich content, highlighting the inadequacy of current evaluation approaches for handling culturally nuanced content. In addition, we show the substantial performance gap between LLMs and encoder-decoder models when translating culturally relevant Lebanese content. While traditional encoder-decoder models often default to literal translations that fail to capture cultural significance, LLMs are usually better at finding cultural alternatives.

A comprehensive qualitative analysis of idiomatic expressions, cultural semantics embedded in Lebanese Arabic, and the inherent linguistic ambiguity of Arabic scripts highlights the complexity of translating Lebanese, a language deeply rooted in its culture. Finally, we demonstrate how this analysis can be adapted to other Arabic-script languages that share similar linguistic and cultural characteristics.

10 Limitations and Future Works

The current study presents some limitations. We evaluated LLMs only in a zero-shot setting, while there is a promising potential for exploring more sophisticated prompting techniques to enhance LLMs translation performance. The use of xCOMET score as an evaluation metric also can present limitations due to its Western-centric training data, indicating the need for more culturally appropriate evaluation methodologies, potentially through human evaluation or LLM-based assessment. While conducting the human assessment, we did not explicitly give instructions to score the fidelity of preserving cultural terms, and idioms in translation. While qualitative analysis provided valuable insights, a more comprehensive human evaluation remains an area for further exploration. Furthermore, while the Language Wave dataset represents a significant step forward, it does not fully capture the regional dialectal variations within Lebanon, and significant challenges remain in developing robust culturally-aware translation data, and accurately benchmarking these datasets. Finally, resource constraints limited our model evaluation scope, leaving several prominent multilingual LLMs untested, including Claude, LLaMA, and ALLaM (Bari et al., 2024).

The results of this work suggest that the path forward for the translation of Arabic-scripts low-resource languages may lie not just in scaling existing architectures, but in fundamentally rethinking how we approach cultural preservation, through the careful curation of culturally authentic training data and the potential advantages of open-source LLMs for handling culturally nuanced content. By demonstrating in this paper some of the limitations that LLMs face in translating Ajami scripts, we pave the way for the research community to explore the interplay between linguistic diversity and cultural preservation in translation.

11 Ackowledgments

We thank the Maroun Semaan Faculty of Engineering and Architecture (MSFEA) and the AI, Data Science, and Computing Hub (AIDSC) at the American University of Beirut for supporting this work through the Artificial Intelligence Exploratory Research Grant.

References

Ahmed Abdelali, Hamdy Mubarak, Shammur A. Chowdhury, Maram Hasanain, Basel Mousi, Sabri Boughorbel, Yassine El Kheir, Daniel Izham, Fahim Dalvi, Majd Hawasly, Nizi Nazar, Youssef Elshahawy, Ahmed M. Ali, Nadir Durrani, Natasa Milic-Frayling, and Firoj Alam. 2023. Larabench: Benchmarking arabic ai with large language models. In *Conference of the European Chapter of the Association for Computational Linguistics*.

Wael Abid. 2020. The sadid evaluation datasets for low-resource spoken language machine translation of arabic dialects. In *International Conference on Computational Linguistics*.

Rania Al-Sabbagh. 2023. The negative transfer effect on the neural machine translation of egyptian arabic adjuncts into english: The case of google translate. *International Journal of Arabic-English Studies.*

Firoj Alam, Shammur Absar Chowdhury, Sabri Boughorbel, and Maram Hasanain. 2024. LLMs for low resource languages in multilingual, multimodal and dialectal settings. In *Proceedings of the 18th Conference of the European Chapter of the Association for Computational Linguistics: Tutorial Abstracts*, pages 27–33, St. Julian's, Malta. Association for Computational Linguistics.

Fakhraddin Alwajih, Gagan Bhatia, and Muhammad Abdul-Mageed. 2024. Dallah: A dialect-aware multimodal large language model for arabic. *ArXiv*, abs/2407.18129.

M Saiful Bari, Yazeed Alnumay, Norah A. Alzahrani, Nouf M. Alotaibi, Hisham A. Alyahya, Sultan AlRashed, Faisal A. Mirza, Shaykhah Z. Alsubaie, Hassan A. Alahmed, Ghadah Alabduljabbar, Raghad Alkhathran, Yousef Almushayqih, Raneem Alnajim, Salman Alsubaihi, Maryam Al Mansour, Majed Alrubaian, Ali Alammari, Zaki Alawami, Abdulmohsen Al-Thubaity, Ahmed Abdelali, Jeril Kuriakose, Abdalghani Abujabal, Nora Al-Twairesh, Areeb Alowisheq, and Haidar Khan. 2024. Allam: Large language models for arabic and english. *Preprint*, arXiv:2407.15390.

Saikat Barua. 2024. Exploring autonomous agents through the lens of large language models: A review. *ArXiv*, abs/2404.04442.

Houda Bouamor, Nizar Habash, Mohammad Salameh, Wajdi Zaghouani, Owen Rambow, Dana Abdulrahim, Ossama Obeid, Salam Khalifa, Fadhl Eryani, Alexander Erdmann, and Kemal Oflazer. 2018. The madar arabic dialect corpus and lexicon. In *International Conference on Language Resources and Evaluation.*

Zhaopeng Feng, Yan Zhang, Hao Li, Wenqiang Liu, Jun Lang, Yang Feng, Jian Wu, and Zuozhu Liu. 2024. Improving llm-based machine translation with systematic self-correction. *ArXiv*, abs/2402.16379.

Marjan Ghazvininejad, Hila Gonen, and Luke Zettlemoyer. 2023. Dictionary-based phrase-level prompting of large language models for machine translation. *ArXiv*, abs/2302.07856.

Nuno M. Guerreiro, Ricardo Rei, Daan van Stigt, Luísa Coheur, Pierre Colombo, and André Martins. 2023. xcomet: Transparent machine translation evaluation through fine-grained error detection. *Transactions of the Association for Computational Linguistics*, 12:979–995.

Karim El Haff, Mustafa Jarrar, Tymaa Hammouda, and Fadi A. Zaraket. 2022. Curras + baladi: Towards a levantine corpus. In *International Conference on Language Resources and Evaluation.*

Zhiwei He, Tian Liang, Wenxiang Jiao, Zhuosheng Zhang, Yujiu Yang, Rui Wang, Zhaopeng Tu, Shuming Shi, and Xing Wang. 2023. Exploring human-like translation strategy with large language models. *Transactions of the Association for Computational Linguistics*, 12:229–246.

Amr Hendy, Mohamed Gomaa Abdelrehim, Amr Sharaf, Vikas Raunak, Mohamed Gabr, Hitokazu Matsushita, Young Jin Kim, Mohamed Afify, and Hany Hassan Awadalla. 2023. How good are gpt models at machine translation? a comprehensive evaluation. *ArXiv*, abs/2302.09210.

Huang Huang, Fei Yu, Jianqing Zhu, Xuening Sun, Hao Cheng, Song Dingjie, Zhihong Chen, Mosen Alharthi, Bang An, Juncai He, Ziche Liu, Junying Chen, Jianquan Li, Benyou Wang, Lian Zhang, Ruoyu Sun, Xiang Wan, Haizhou Li, and Jinchao Xu. 2024. AceGPT, localizing large language models in Arabic. In *Proceedings of the 2024 Conference of the North American Chapter of the Association for Computational Linguistics: Human Language Technologies (Volume 1: Long Papers)*, pages 8139–8163, Mexico City, Mexico. Association for Computational Linguistics.

Joy Ishaku, Muhammad Mustapha, and Muhammad Bello. 2020. Contrastive analysis of lexical and structural ambiguity between hausa and english languages. 2:19–34.

Wenxiang Jiao, Wenxuan Wang, Jen tse Huang, Xing Wang, and Zhaopeng Tu. 2023. Is chatgpt a good translator? yes with gpt-4 as the engine.

Karima Kadaoui, Samar M. Magdy, Abdul Waheed, Md Tawkat Islam Khondaker, Ahmed Oumar El-Shangiti, El Moatez Billah Nagoudi, and Muhammad Abdul-Mageed. 2023. Tarjamat: Evaluation of bard and chatgpt on machine translation of ten arabic varieties. *Preprint*, arXiv:2308.03051.

Md. Tawkat Islam Khondaker, Numaan Naeem, Fatimah Khan, AbdelRahim Elmadany, and Muhammad Abdul-Mageed. 2024. Benchmarking llama-3 on arabic language generation tasks. In *ARABICNLP.*

Tom Kocmi, Vilém Zouhar, Christian Federmann, and Matt Post. 2024. Navigating the metrics maze: Reconciling score magnitudes and accuracies. In *Annual Meeting of the Association for Computational Linguistics.*

Mateusz Krubiński, Hashem Sellat, Shadi Saleh, Adam Pospíil, Petr Zemánek, and Pavel Pecina. 2023. Multi-parallel corpus of north levantine arabic. In *ARABICNLP.*

Alon Lavie and Abhaya Agarwal. 2007. Meteor: An automatic metric for mt evaluation with high levels of correlation with human judgments. In *WMT@ACL.*

Seungjun Lee, Jungseob Lee, Hyeonseok Moon, Chanjun Park, Jaehyung Seo, Sugyeong Eo, Seonmin Koo, and Heu-Jeoung Lim. 2023. A survey on evaluation metrics for machine translation. *Mathematics*.

Juhao Liang, Zhenyang Cai, Jianqing Zhu, Huang Huang, Kewei Zong, Bang An, Mosen Alharthi, Juncai He, Lian Zhang, Haizhou Li, Benyou Wang, and Jinchao Xu. 2024. Alignment at pre-training! towards native alignment for arabic LLMs. In *The Thirty-eighth Annual Conference on Neural Information Processing Systems*.

Chenyang Lyu, Jitao Xu, Longyue Wang, and Minghao Wu. 2023. A paradigm shift: The future of machine translation lies with large language models. In *International Conference on Language Resources and Evaluation*.

Basel Mousi, Nadir Durrani, Fatema Ahmad, Md. Arid Hasan, Maram Hasanain, Tameem Kabbani, Fahim Dalvi, Shammur A. Chowdhury, and Firoj Alam. 2024. Aradice: Benchmarks for dialectal and cultural capabilities in llms. *ArXiv*, abs/2409.11404.

Tarek Naous, Michael Joseph Ryan, and Wei Xu. 2023. Having beer after prayer? measuring cultural bias in large language models. In *Annual Meeting of the Association for Computational Linguistics*.

Fallou Ngom, Daivi Rodima-Taylor, and David Robinson. 2023. ᶜajamī literacies of africa: The hausa, fula, mandinka, and wolof traditions. *Islamic Africa*, 14(2):119 – 143.

Viktória Ondrejová and Marek Šuppa. 2024. Can LLMs handle low-resource dialects? a case study on translation and common sense reasoning in šariš. In *Proceedings of the Eleventh Workshop on NLP for Similar Languages, Varieties, and Dialects (VarDial 2024)*, pages 130–139, Mexico City, Mexico. Association for Computational Linguistics.

Kishore Papineni, Salim Roukos, Todd Ward, and Wei-Jing Zhu. 2002. Bleu: a method for automatic evaluation of machine translation. In *Annual Meeting of the Association for Computational Linguistics*.

Maja Popovic. 2015. chrf: character n-gram f-score for automatic mt evaluation. In *WMT@EMNLP*.

Ricardo Rei, José G. C. de Souza, Duarte M. Alves, Chrysoula Zerva, Ana C. Farinha, T. Glushkova, Alon Lavie, Luísa Coheur, and André F. T. Martins. 2022. Comet-22: Unbabel-ist 2022 submission for the metrics shared task. In *Conference on Machine Translation*.

Neha Sengupta, Sunil Kumar Sahu, Bokang Jia, Satheesh Katipomu, Haonan Li, Fajri Koto, William Marshall, Gurpreet Gosal, Cynthia Liu, Zhiming Chen, Osama Mohammed Afzal, Samta Kamboj, Onkar Pandit, Rahul Pal, Lalit Pradhan, Zain Muhammad Mujahid, Massa Baali, Xudong Han, Sondos Mahmoud Bsharat, Alham Fikri Aji, Zhiqiang Shen, Zhengzhong Liu, Natalia Vassilieva, Joel Hestness, Andy Hock, Andrew Feldman, Jonathan Lee, Andrew Jackson, Hector Xuguang Ren, Preslav Nakov, Timothy Baldwin, and Eric Xing. 2023. Jais and jais-chat: Arabic-centric foundation and instruction-tuned open generative large language models. *Preprint*, arXiv:2308.16149.

Matthew Snover, Bonnie Dorr, Rich Schwartz, Linnea Micciulla, and John Makhoul. 2006. A study of translation edit rate with targeted human annotation. In *Proceedings of the 7th Conference of the Association for Machine Translation in the Americas: Technical Papers*, pages 223–231, Cambridge, Massachusetts, USA. Association for Machine Translation in the Americas.

Garrett Tanzer, Mirac Suzgun, Eline Visser, Dan Jurafsky, and Luke Melas-Kyriazi. 2023. A benchmark for learning to translate a new language from one grammar book. *ArXiv*, abs/2309.16575.

Nllb team, Marta Ruiz Costa-jussà, James Cross, Onur cCelebi, Maha Elbayad, Kenneth Heafield, Kevin Heffernan, Elahe Kalbassi, Janice Lam, Daniel Licht, Jean Maillard, Anna Sun, Skyler Wang, Guillaume Wenzek, Alison Youngblood, Bapi Akula, Loïc Barrault, Gabriel Mejia Gonzalez, Prangthip Hansanti, John Hoffman, Semarley Jarrett, Kaushik Ram Sadagopan, Dirk Rowe, Shannon L. Spruit, C. Tran, Pierre Yves Andrews, Necip Fazil Ayan, Shruti Bhosale, Sergey Edunov, Angela Fan, Cynthia Gao, Vedanuj Goswami, Francisco Guzm'an, Philipp Koehn, Alexandre Mourachko, Christophe Ropers, Safiyyah Saleem, Holger Schwenk, and Jeff Wang. 2022. No language left behind: Scaling human-centered machine translation. *ArXiv*, abs/2207.04672.

Hugo Touvron, Thibaut Lavril, Gautier Izacard, Xavier Martinet, Marie-Anne Lachaux, Timothée Lacroix, Baptiste Rozière, Naman Goyal, Eric Hambro, Faisal Azhar, Aurelien Rodriguez, Armand Joulin, Edouard Grave, and Guillaume Lample. 2023. Llama: Open and efficient foundation language models. *ArXiv*, abs/2302.13971.

Haoran Xu, Young Jin Kim, Amr Sharaf, and Hany Hassan Awadalla. 2023. A paradigm shift in machine translation: Boosting translation performance of large language models. *ArXiv*, abs/2309.11674.

Binwei Yao, Ming Jiang, Tara Bobinac, Diyi Yang, and Junjie Hu. 2024. Benchmarking machine translation with cultural awareness. In *Findings of the Association for Computational Linguistics: EMNLP 2024*, pages 13078–13096, Miami, Florida, USA. Association for Computational Linguistics.

Rabih Zbib, Erika Malchiodi, Jacob Devlin, David Stallard, Spyridon Matsoukas, Richard M. Schwartz, John Makhoul, Omar Zaidan, and Chris Callison-Burch. 2012. Machine translation of arabic dialects. In *North American Chapter of the Association for Computational Linguistics.*

Chen Zhang, Xiao Liu, Jiuheng Lin, and Yansong Feng. 2024. Teaching large language models an unseen language on the fly. *ArXiv*, abs/2402.19167.

Tianyi Zhang, Varsha Kishore, Felix Wu, Kilian Q. Weinberger, and Yoav Artzi. 2019. Bertscore: Evaluating text generation with bert. *ArXiv*, abs/1904.09675.

A Translation Models

Jais: MBZUAI introduced the largest openly available Arabic language models, known as Jais ranging from 590M to 70B (Sengupta et al., 2023), which quickly captured the attention of the Arabic research community. These models were built based on the GPT architecture and pre-trained using a blend of English and Arabic datasets, making them ideal candidates for the translation task. However, Jais's primary limitation lies in its heavy reliance on translated datasets, driven by the scarcity of high-quality Arabic datasets. Notably, this reliance on translated data can introduce "localization issues," potentially undermining the reliability and applicability of the models in native contexts, specifically in the translation of cultural content. (Huang et al., 2024) have observed an apparent bias in Jais, and showed that Jais produced outputs with a notable inclination toward English-centric content, frequently emphasizing terms associated with Christianity, for instance.

AceGPT: Decoder-only models built on top of LLaMA2, ranging from 7 billion to 70B billion(Liang et al., 2024)(Huang et al., 2024). Developers of AceGPT tried to address the challenge of Arabic localization and cultivate culturally and value-aligned Arabic LLMs capable of accommodating the diverse, application-specific needs of Arabic-speaking communities. They delved into the critical necessity and the methodology behind creating a localized Large Language Model specifically tailored for the Arabic language, which possesses distinct cultural traits that aren't adequately accommodated by current open-source mainstream models. Their main contribution was in using Reinforcement Learning with AI Feedback (RLHF) to align the model's responses with the cultural and value norms of Arabic-speaking communities. GPT4 was used to rank answers based on how well they represent Arabic values. Nonetheless, the Arabic localization challenge persists. The pool of prompts that Arabic users will use is pretty much different than the one used by English speakers, and it should predominantly reflect the queries of Arab users, which would inherently carry more cultural relevance.

Cohere Models: The Aya initiative, developed by CohereAI, seeks to bridge the gap between multilingual and monolingual model performance. Most promising multilingual Aya models are Aya23 and Aya-expanse which ranges from 8B to 33B parameters and cover 23 languages. Since its inception two years ago, the Aya project has involved a participatory research effort with over 3,000 contributors from 119 countries, fostering the development of culturally-aware AI. This collaboration has produced the largest multilingual dataset collection to date, consisting of 513 million examples, alongside comprehensive evaluation sets focused on multilingual performance and safety. In addition, the largest model from Cohere is Command-R+, a 104B parameter model with highly advanced capabilities, evaluated on 10 languages including Arabic. Unlike approaches that rely on translating English instruction-style datasets—prone to translation biases and loss of cultural context, Cohere's methodology emphasizes human-curated data collected through the Aya Annotation Platform. This platform facilitated the creation of the Aya dataset, which stands as the largest human-curated multilingual instruction finetuned dataset, enhancing the model's ability to reflect diverse cultural nuances and reducing the noise and biases typically associated with automatic dataset curation. As such, Cohere models are one of the most promising models to test on cultural understanding, especially in the translation of low-resource dialects.

NLLB Models: The NLLB (No Language Left Behind) project(team et al., 2022), launched by Meta AI in 2022, represents a significant leap forward in multilingual machine translation. This family of models ranging from 560M to 54B, is designed to support translations across 202 different language varieties, addressing the need for more inclusive language representation and overcoming the limitations that many models face when working with low-resource languages. Central to the NLLB project is its encoder-decoder architecture, which distinguishes it from large language models (LLMs) that primarily rely on decoder-only or transformer-based approaches. Unlike LLMs which are typically optimized for a broad range of generative tasks, the NLLB model's architecture is specifically tailored to translation, enabling more precise handling of input and output sequences. To ensure the quality of its translations, Meta AI introduced a comprehensive evaluation dataset called FLORES-200, which serves as a benchmark for assessing performance across all supported languages, and it showed NLLB superiority compared to existing datasets.

B Related Work

B.1 Benchmarking LLMs for Translation of Low-Resource/Dialectal Languages

The recent surge of Multilingual Large Language Models (MLLMs) has sparked a debate on their effectiveness in machine translation tasks compared to specialized translation systems(Xu et al., 2023). Research in (Hendy et al., 2023) and (Jiao et al., 2023) show that GPT models can translate effectively with proper prompting, however, they may struggle with specialized content in certain language pairs compared to dedicated translation services. Furthermore, studies have shown enhanced translation performance of open-source LLMs through better prompting, like self-correction (Feng et al., 2024), Dictionary-based prompting(Ghazvininejad et al., 2023), and imitating human-like thinking by splitting the translation task into small subtasks(He et al., 2023). Autonomous Agents were also explored in LLMs(Barua, 2024)

Despite these advancements, the issue of translating low-resource languages remains largely unaddressed. Both (Tanzer et al., 2023) and (Zhang et al., 2024) show that LLMs are capable of translating a new language that did not exist in the pre-training data. A paper that discusses how they leveraged LLMs for translation of low-resource languages in Saris (Ondrejová and Šuppa, 2024).

B.2 Benchmarking LLMs on Arabic translation

In the domain of machine translation (MT) from Arabic dialects to English, significant advancements have been made through the development of specialized datasets and the use of pre-trained Neural networks. Despite these efforts, the scarcity of parallel corpora for less common Arabic dialects and English poses a challenge, with most neural machine translation systems, including Google Translate, primarily relying on MSA and English corpora. This approach has proved its weakness, as evidenced by the authors in (Al-Sabbagh, 2023) who evaluated Google Translate's performance in the Egyptian dialect. Researchers in https://aclanthology.org/2024.arabicnlp-1.24.pdf benchmarked LLaMA3 on NLG Arabic tasks, including translation of code-switched arabic dialects to English. (Kadaoui et al., 2023) focused on evaluating the capabilities of models such as Bard and ChatGPT across a spectrum of Arabic dialects. They evaluated NLLB as the supervised baseline, finding both ChatGPT and GPT-4 able to outperform this baseline in a zero-shot setting. Still, this research underscores the challenges related to dialectal diversity and linguistic inclusivity of the Lebanese dialect and only evaluates large closed models. Superior LLMs like ChatGPT and GPT-4 are only accessible through restricted APIs, which creates barriers to new research and advancements in the field. None of these works focused on evaluating dialectal MT tasks for Smaller Arabic language models such as AceGPT and Jais. (Khondaker et al., 2024) benchmarked LLaMA3 on NLG Arabic tasks, including translation of code switched Arabic dialects to English. (Abdelali et al., 2023) developed LAraBench, a benchmarking Arabic AI with Large Language Models, they benchmarked on the AraBench. Likewise, (Abid, 2020) developed the SADID benchmark for evaluating Arabic dialects. However, they asked people what are the most topics they speak in their dialect, and they selected sources from Wikipedia in English, and then translated them. however, they chose English as the language of our source sentences instead of MSA so as not to bias our translations.

B.3 LLMs and cultural-awarness

Translating culture-related content is vital for effective cross-cultural communication. Recent research has benchmarked machine translation for cultural awareness (Yao et al., 2024) and demonstrated that Large Language Models (LLMs) exhibit superior capabilities compared to traditional neural MT systems in leveraging external cultural knowledge, especially for Culturally-Specific Items (CSIs) translation. In the Arabic language domain, this challenge is further complicated by dialectal variations and the scarcity of high-quality datasets. This difficulty hinders the analysis of cultural awareness of machine translation (MT) systems, including traditional neural MT and the emerging MT paradigm using large language models (LLM). Arabic-centric LLMs like Jais and AceGPT, while showing promise in Arabic NLP, face limitations due to their reliance on translated datasets, introducing "localization issues"(Huang et al., 2024). Recent initiatives like Dallah(Alwajih et al., 2024), a dialect-aware multimodal LLM for Arabic, represent ongoing efforts to better accommodate the distinct cultural traits and dialectal variations that current mainstream models struggle to capture. Nevertheless, some effort have been made to benchmark LLMs on cultural awareness. (Naous et al., 2023) measured the cultural bias and LLMs , while AraDICE benchmark(Mousi et al., 2024) was developed to assess LLMs' cultural awareness and dialect comprehension. Researchers leveraged MT, specifically from English to MSA and MSA to dialects, combined with human post-editing, to develop synthetic benchmarks for low-resource DA. However, these evaluation efforts themselves often rely on translated benchmarks from English to Modern Standard Arabic (MSA) and subsequently to dialects, highlighting a persistent challenge in developing authentic resources for low-resource Arabic dialects. While current work on cultural awareness in Arabic dialects primarily focuses on CSIs, the challenge extends far beyond isolated cultural items to encompass the entire linguistic system - including verbs, vocabulary, grammar structures, and idiomatic expressions that are deeply rooted in cultural context. Despite dialects being deeply rooted in cultural context, the field continues to rely heavily on translated data due to resource scarcity, suggesting a critical need to redirect efforts toward developing authentic, culturally-aware datasets that capture the full richness of Arabic dialectal variations.

C Aligning Metrics with Human Judgement

In the field of Neural Machine Translation (NMT), the accurate evaluation of translation quality remains a critical challenge. While traditional lexical-based metrics such as BLEU (Papineni et al., 2002) and CHRF(Popovic, 2015) have been widely used, they often fall short in capturing the nuanced aspects of translation quality, particularly semantic equivalence and grammatical correctness. This limitation has led to the development of more sophisticated evaluation techniques, among which xCOMET stands out as a promising solution.

C.1 Translation Evaluation Metrics

The evolution of machine translation metrics can be broadly categorized into four main types:

1. **Lexical-based metrics**: These include widely used measures such as BLEU(Papineni et al., 2002), METEOR(Lavie and Agarwal, 2007), and TER(Snover et al., 2006). While these metrics have been instrumental in the development of NMT systems, they primarily focus on surface-level similarities between the machine translation output and reference translations. Their inability to account for semantic equivalence limits their effectiveness in accurately assessing translation quality.

2. **Embedding-based metrics**: These metrics, such as BERTScore(Zhang et al., 2019), utilize contextual embeddings to capture semantic similarities between translations. By leveraging pre-trained language models, they offer a more nuanced evaluation that considers the context.

3. **Supervised metrics**: These metrics, exemplified by Cross-lingual Optimized Metric for Evaluation of Translation(COMET)(Rei et al., 2022), are trained on human judgments of translation quality. While they show a higher correlation with human evaluations, their reliance on labeled data can limit their applicability to low-resource languages.

4. **Interpretable metrics**: This emerging category of metrics aims to provide transparent and explainable evaluations of machine translations. xCOMET(Guerreiro et al., 2023) falls into this category, offering significant advantages over previous approaches. Unlike black-box metrics, xCOMET provides detailed insights into specific translation errors. This granular approach allows for a more comprehensive understanding of translation quality and pinpoints areas for improvement. It can also be used for quality estimation without a reference, reference-only evaluation, or full source-reference-hypothesis evaluation. This flexibility makes it a versatile tool for various translation assessment needs. By leveraging advanced language models and fine-grained error detection, xCOMET achieves a higher correlation with human evaluations compared to traditional metrics. With models ranging from 3.5B parameters (xCOMET-XL) to 10.7B parameters (xCOMET-XXL), xCOMET can be scaled to meet various computational requirements and evaluation needs.

C.2 Metric Correlation Analysis

Annotation Process: Each annotator independently rated all 150 translations. Annotations were collected through a spreadsheet with source text, translation, and scoring columns. Annotators were instructed to:

1. Read both source and translation carefully
2. Consider both accuracy and fluency
3. Apply scores consistently according to the rubric

Annotation Guidelines: We instructed annotators to carefully read and follow the guidelines shown in Table 3.

Score	Category	Description	Examples
5	Very Good	• Completely preserves meaning • Natural English expression • No grammatical errors	• Source: شو عم تعمل ؟ • Translation: What are you doing?
4	Good	• Minor flaws that don't affect understanding • Slight unnatural expressions • Minor grammatical issues	• Source: عم موت من البرد • Translation: I am dying from the cold • Comment: slightly literal but acceptable
3	Adequate	• Core meaning preserved • Some unnatural expressions • Notable but non-critical errors	• Source: شو هالحكي • Translation: What is this talk • Comment: understandable but unidiomatic
2	Poor	• Significant meaning loss • Major grammatical errors • Difficult to understand	• Source: عطيني نفَس • Translation: Give me breath • Comment: literal translation
1	Incomprehensible	• Complete meaning loss • Severe grammatical errors • Impossible to understand	• Source: حلّو عن بعض ! • Translation: Sweet each other! • Comment: completely misses meaning

Table 3: Translation Quality Assessment Rubric for Lebanese Dialect to English Translation

D Qualitative Examples

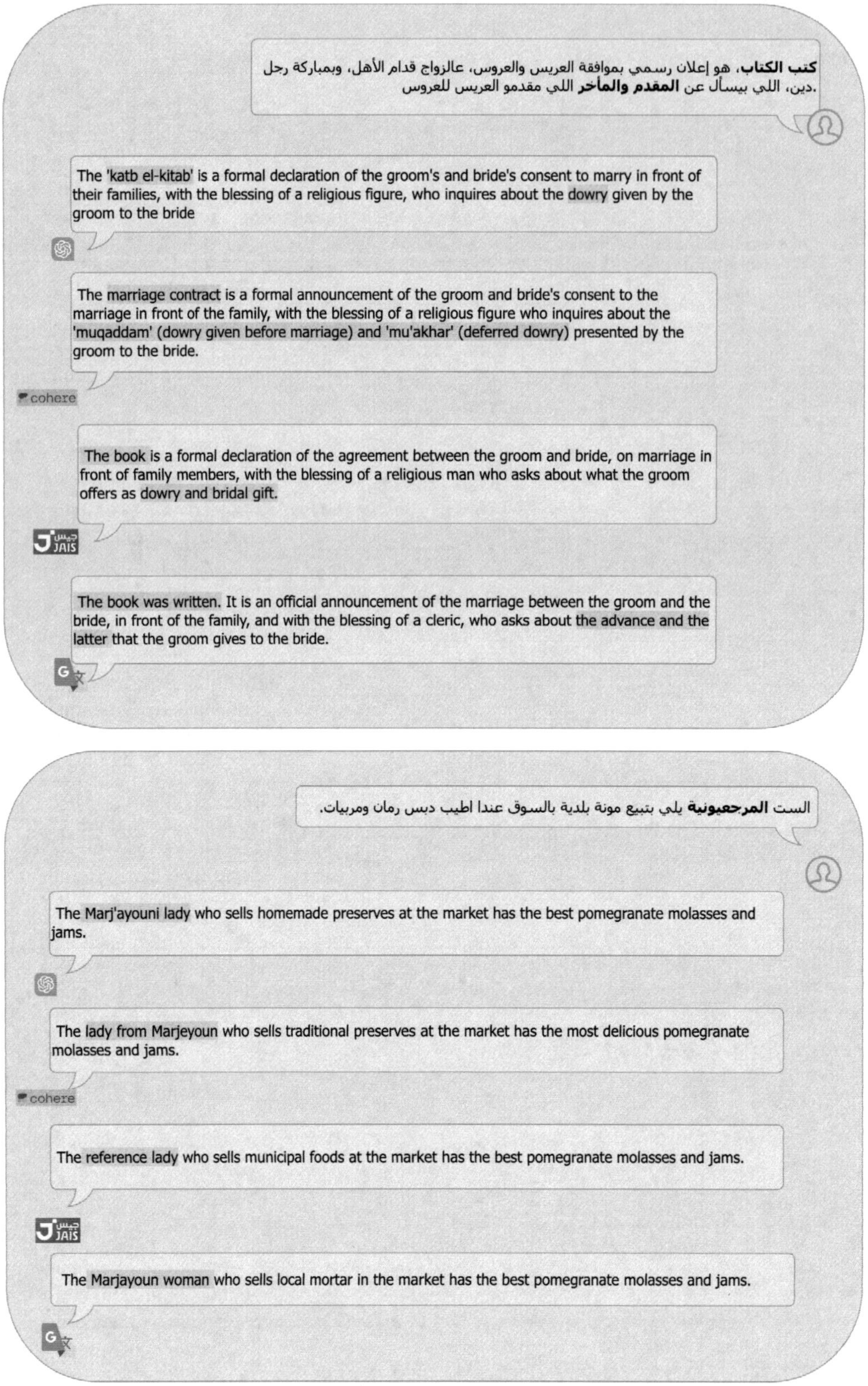

Figure 3: Two examples highlighting the performance of four models: Jais-70B, Command-R+, GPT-4o and GoogleTranslate in translating Lebanese cultural expressions. The first example contains social terms used in a Lebanese Wedding, while the second example refers to a Lebanese custom in one village. **Bold**: Challenging Lebanese Terms ▇: correct translation ▇: wrong translation

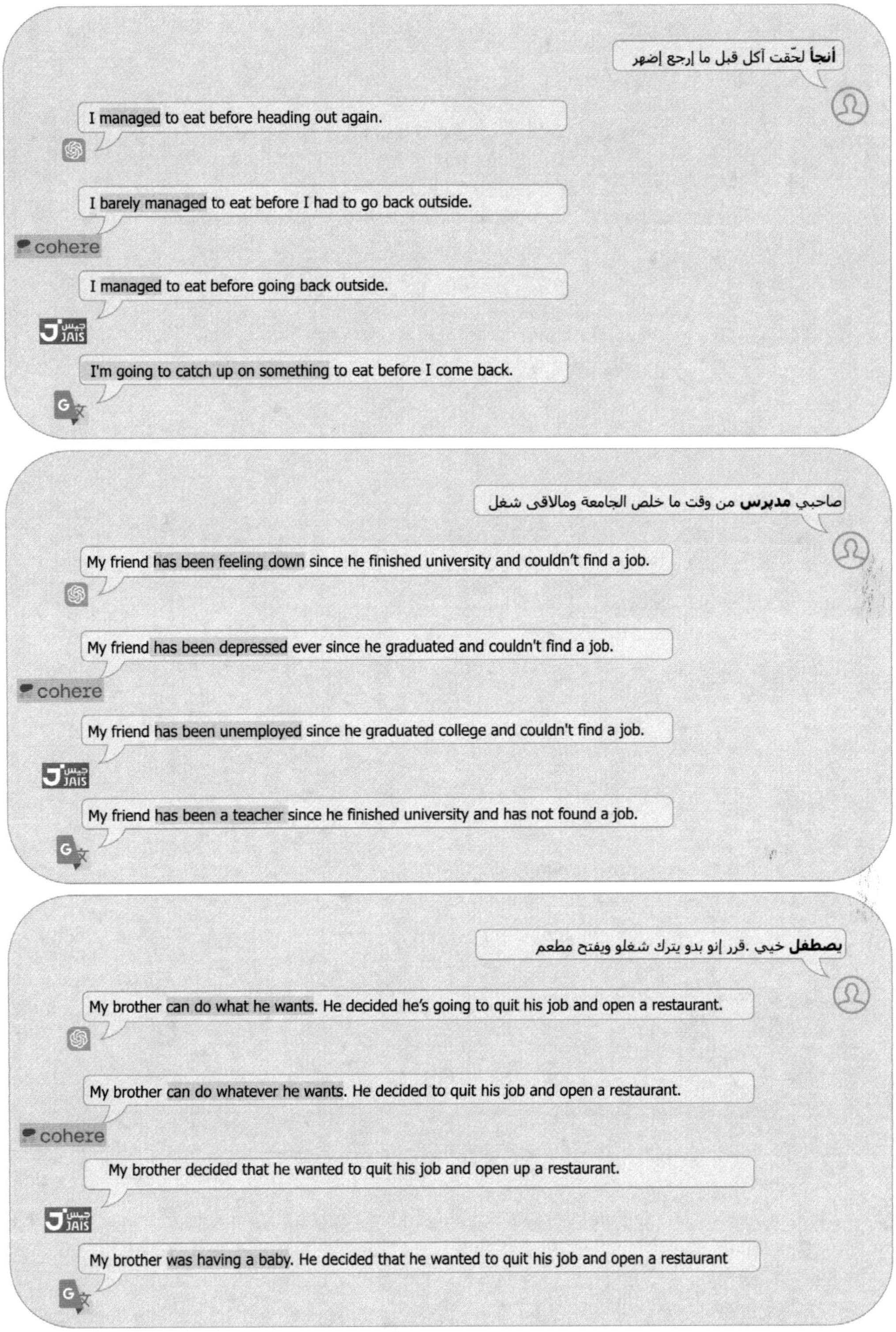

Figure 4: Three examples showing the performance of four models: Jais-70B, Command-R+ from Cohere, GPT-4o and GoogleTranslate in translating unique Lebanese linguistic terms. The first example contains the Lebanese term أنجأ, the second example have the Lebanized word (مدپرس), while the third example focuses on the translation of the famous Lebanese word (يصطفل).
Bold: Challenging Lebanese Terms ▒: correct translation ▒: wrong translation

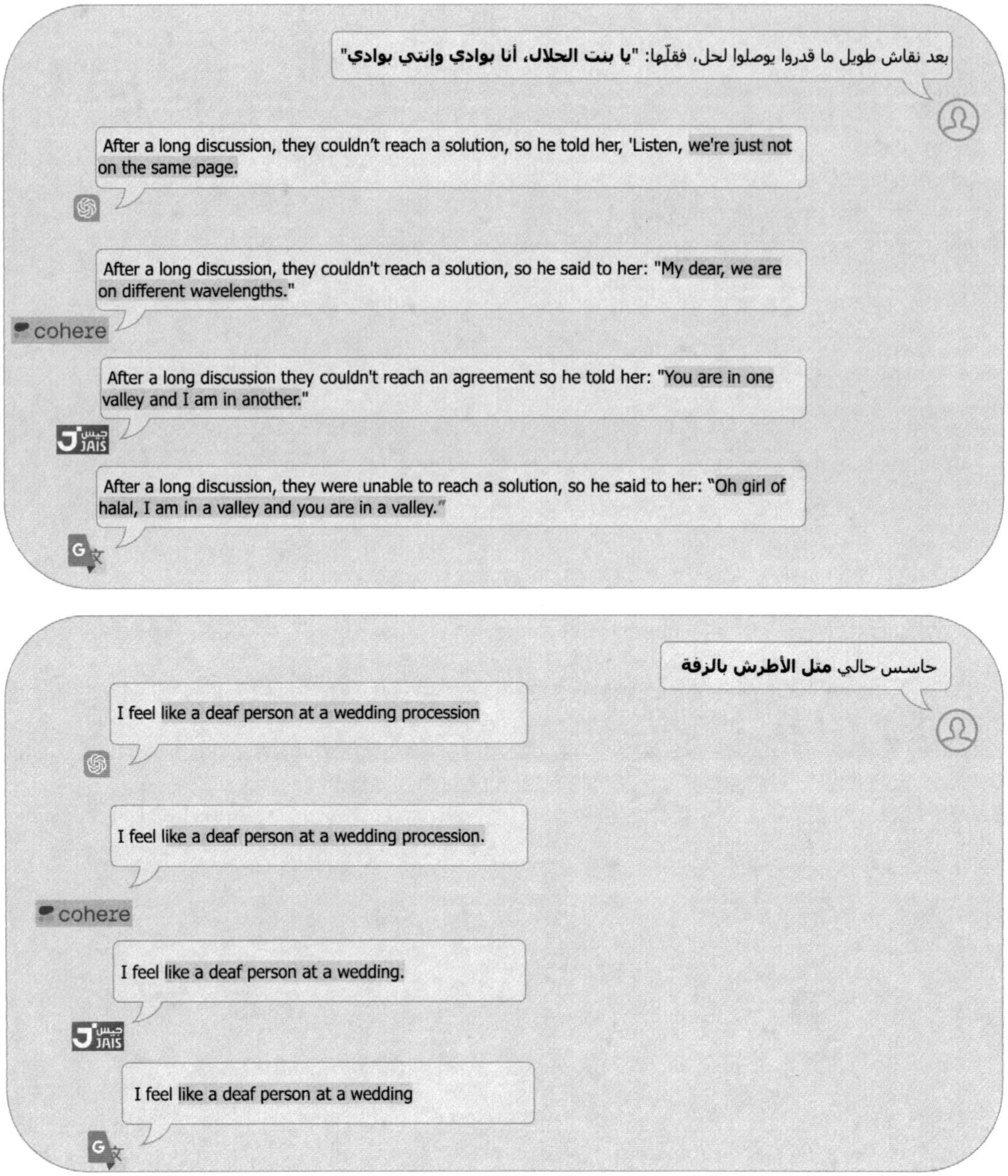

Figure 5: Two examples focusing on the performance of four models: Jais-70B, Command-R+, GPT-4o and GoogleTranslate in translating Lebanese idioms. The first example depicts a famous idiom أنا بوادي وإنتي بوادي which means "We're on different pages", while the second example shows the proverb (حاسس متل الأطرش بالزفة) which means "I feel out of place".
Bold: Challenging Lebanese Terms ▒: correct translation ▒: wrong translation

Figure 6: Two examples focusing on the performance of three models: Command-R+, GPT-4o and GoogleTranslate in translating Lebanese ambiguous expressions. The first example depicts the verbكتبت which can either mean "I wrote" or "she wrote", while the second example show the expression اجرو which can translate into "his leg" or "its leg".
Bold: Challenging Lebanese Terms ▒: correct translation ▒: wrong translation

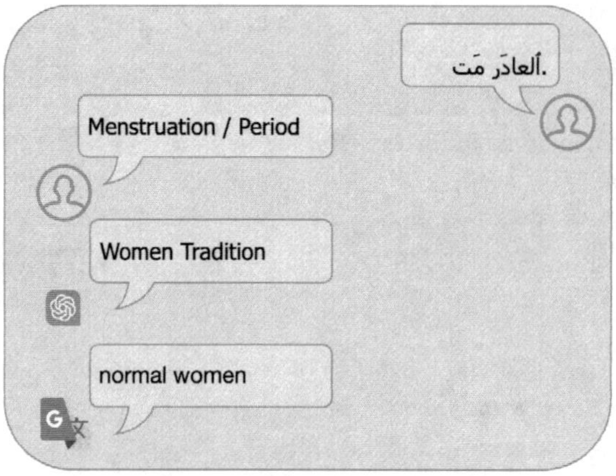

Figure 7: Example showing the translation of GPT-4o and Google-Translate for the Hausa expression **"al'adar mata"** (ألعادَرْ مَتَ), a cultural term that refers to the women menstruation. The word **"mata"**(مَتَ) in Hausa means tradition but when talking about women, it refers to the monthly menstrual cycle, thus *GPT-4o* literally translated the expression to "Women Traditions".

Figure 8: Example showing the translation of GPT-4o and Google-Translate for the Hausa proverb **"Zamani kowa da na shi"**(زَمَانِ كَوَا دَ نَ شِ) which literally translates to "Everyone has his reign". The proverb is used to mean that nothing lasts forever. It also refers to the fact that each regime comes with its policies, which will not last forever.

Figure 9: Example showing the translation of GPT-4o and Google-Transalte of the Wolof expression **"Bind Kamiil"**(بندْ كَامل), an expression term that refers to the practice of "writing an entire copy of the Quran", before graduating from the elementary level of Quranic education. GPT-4o and Google Translate fail to acknowledge the cultural relevance of this expression.

Figure 10: Example showing the translation of GPT-4o and Google-Translate for the Wolof term **"Sànc daara"**(سانق دارا), a religious expression that means "To create a Quranic school". It is regarded as an honor in Wolof society and one of the ultimate goals of many Quranic school students. While (سانق) can have many meanings clean/establish/save, using (سانق دارا) together usually refers to building a Qur'anic school.

Automated Generation of Arabic Verb Conjugations with Multilingual Urdu Translation: An NLP Approach

Haq Nawaz[1], Manal Elobaid[2], Ali al-Laith[3], Saif Ullah[4]
COMSATS University, Lahore, Pakistan[1]
Qatar University, Qatar[2]
Copenhagen University, Denmark[3]
ILI.digital, Lahore, Pakistan[4]

Abstract

This paper presents a rule-based automated system for generating both Arabic verb conjugations and their corresponding Urdu translations. The system processes triliteral, non-weak Arabic roots across key tenses Past Simple, Past Simple Negative, Present Simple, and Present Simple Negative. Addressing the challenges posed by Arabic morphology, our rule-based approach applies patterns and morphological rules to accurately produce verb conjugations, capturing essential grammatical variations in gender, number, and person. Simultaneously, the system generates Urdu translations using predefined patterns that is aligned with the grammatical nuances of Arabic, ensuring semantic consistency. As the first system of its kind, it uniquely provides a cross-lingual resource that bridges two linguistically similar but distinct languages. By focusing on rule based precision and dual-language outputs, it addresses critical gaps in NLP resources, serving as a valuable tool for linguists, educators, and NLP researchers in academic and religious contexts where Arabic and Urdu coexist.

1 Introduction

The Arabic language, deeply rooted in the Semitic language family, presents significant challenges in natural language processing (NLP) due to its intricate morphological structure, particularly in verb conjugations [1]. Arabic verbs are inflected for tense, voice, gender, number, and person, creating complex conjugation tables that reflect each verb's nuanced forms [2]. These conjugations involve the combination of triliteral roots, prefixes, and suffixes to indicate grammatical distinctions, which are further diversified across Classical Arabic, Modern Standard Arabic, and colloquial dialects. Such features, along with unique tenses and forms, make the automation of Arabic verb conjugation a challenging task for NLP applications [3].

In this paper, we address these challenges by developing a rule-based automation system for generating Arabic verb conjugations from triliteral, non-weak root words across four specific tense categories: Past Simple, Past Simple Negative, Present Simple, and Present Simple Negative and generating Urdu translations for these sentences. This approach leverages the systematic structure of Arabic morphology to handle common triliteral root patterns, or Baab patterns, ensuring accurate inflection across gender, number, and tense. Additionally, to support cross-lingual applications, each generated conjugated form is provided with an equivalent Urdu translation, allowing for broader accessibility and use in multilingual NLP settings. This work focuses on triliteral, non-weak roots in Classical Arabic, but future extensions could address weak roots, dialectal Arabic, and languages like Persian and Pashto by adapting morphological rules. This aligns with the growing need for computational resources that bridge less-resourced languages with modern NLP advancements, particularly in religious and educational contexts where both Arabic and Urdu are commonly used. The dataset is available in GitHub[1].

[1]https://github.com/haqnawaz99/Arabic-Urdu-Conjugation-Dataset

Processings of the 1st Workshop on NLP for Languages Using Arabic Script (AbjadNLP), pages 136–143
January 19, 2025. ©2025 Association for Computational Linguistics

2 Contributions

Our contributions are as follows:

2.1 A Rule-Based Automation System for Arabic Verb Conjugation

Our system currently focuses on Arabic triliteral, non-weak root verbs for Past Simple, Past Simple Negative, Present Simple, and Present Simple Negative forms. Future work includes expanding coverage to weak roots and quadrilateral roots, requiring tailored morphological rules and pattern adaptations. The system applies Arabic morphological rules, addressing gender, number, and tense variations in accordance with different patterns. Our focus on non-weak roots allows us to refine conjugation accuracy and computational efficiency.

2.2 Integration of Urdu Translations for Conjugated Forms

Each Arabic verb form is paired with its corresponding Urdu translation, fostering cross-lingual applications and enabling Urdu speakers to leverage computational insights into Arabic verb morphology. This integration enhances accessibility and understanding, especially in contexts demanding a precise grasp of Arabic grammar.

2.3 Detailed Analysis of Accuracy and Impact

We conducted a detailed analysis of the system's accuracy, evaluating its effectiveness in correctly applying Arabic morphological rules. This assessment highlights the system's significant contributions to computational linguistics, particularly for less-resourced languages such as Arabic and Urdu. Our work involved 200 Arabic root words, generating 78 variations for each verb, resulting in a comprehensive dataset of 14,400 entries, accompanied by their Urdu translations. The dataset underwent meticulous review by a team of religious scholars of Jamia Ashrafia [2] Lahore Pakistan, with deep expertise in Arabic morphology and the Urdu language. This rigorous approach underscores the system's ability to handle specific verb forms, achieving high linguistic fidelity in the generated outputs and ensuring precision and relevance across both languages.

3 Background and Related Work

Research in Arabic natural language processing (NLP) has advanced significantly over recent years, driven by the need to develop robust computational tools for processing Arabic's complex morphological structure [4]. Arabic morphology, particularly verb conjugation, poses unique challenges due to the language's rich inflectional system, including variations across tense, gender, number, and voice [2].

However, while Arabic NLP has made strides in verb root extraction and morphological analysis, little attention has been given to the integration of Urdu translations. Urdu, despite its shared script and vocabulary with Arabic, lacks the level of computational resources available for Arabic NLP. Prior work in Arabic NLP has primarily focused on Arabic syntax and morphology within Arabic contexts [5]. There is very limited exploration into cross-linguistic applications or extensions for Urdu language for translation purposes. Our system bridges grammatical alignment between Arabic and Urdu, addressing the lack of bilingual resources for these languages. This gap underscores the need for focused efforts to bridge Arabic NLP methodologies with Urdu linguistic resources to enhance their mutual computational potential. Another research introduced a novel approach to help Arabic learners understand and memorize the meanings derived from morphological changes (wazn al-ṣarf), which often lead to translation errors. By identifying key morphological constructions and their associated meanings, the study represents them in a didactic poetic form (naẓm) using the Rajz prosodic structure. An Android application was developed to deliver the naẓm, comprising 9 chapters and 32 verses, enhancing accessibility and usability. Validation tests rated the application highly (87.61%), confirming its effectiveness. This tool offers an innovative solution for teachers and learners to master Arabic morphology more efficiently.

[2] https://jamiaashrafia.org/

4 Methodology

4.1 Data source:

Our system relies on a dataset of Arabic triliteral roots, we selected the most used trilateral root words used in Quran and Classical Arabic literature. These roots serve as the foundation for generating full verb conjugation tables in Arabic. To ensure linguistic diversity, the roots were carefully selected from Quranic and classical Arabic sources, representing a range of grammatical contexts, including variations in diacritics and negations. To ensure the validity and linguistic accuracy of these roots, we utilize well-established Arabic linguistic resources, including the Quranic Arabic Corpus, which provides comprehensive morphological data and annotations specifically for Classical Arabic.

4.2 Conjugation Generation Process:

Our approach involves a systematic rule-based generation of Arabic verb conjugations from triliteral, non-weak root words across selected tenses: Past Simple, Past Simple Negative, Present Simple, and Present Simple Negative. The generation of conjugated forms begins with the application of Arabic morphological rules that define the specific pattern each root follows. By employing this structure, our system generates various verb forms by appending the correct prefixes and suffixes based on tense, person, gender, and number. For instance, given the root سمع meaning “to hear”, the system produces conjugations like سَمِعَ (he heard) in Past Simple and لَا يَسْمَعُ (he does not hear) in Present Simple Negative. This automated approach ensures that all conjugated forms are syntactically accurate and align with the morphological standards of Classical Arabic.

4.3 Urdu Translation Generation:

Complementing the Arabic conjugation system, we developed an Urdu translation module to provide accurate translations for each conjugated form. For every generated Arabic conjugation, the system maps it to a corresponding Urdu phrase by using predefined translation patterns that respect Urdu grammar rules. These patterns ensure that each translated verb accurately reflects the gender, tense, and grammatical number of the Arabic original. Given the linguistic similarities between Arabic and Urdu, particularly their shared root system, this module allows us to generate semantically precise Urdu translations that mirror the Arabic verb’s grammatical structure. The Urdu translation module thereby extends the utility of our system, enabling seamless cross-lingual understanding of Arabic verbs in Urdu, a feature valuable for religious, academic, and educational contexts

4.4 Importance of Diacritics in Classical Arabic:

Diacritics in Arabic play a pivotal role in conveying meaning and grammatical context, particularly in verb conjugation [6, 7]. The root ن ص ر, combined with three فتحہ (fatha) diacritics, transforms into نَصَرَ, which signifies "he helped." In Urdu, this translates to "اس ایک مرد نے مدد کی." To create the dual form in Arabic, an additional "ا" is appended, resulting in نَصَرَا, meaning "they two helped." In Urdu, however, the corresponding translation becomes "ان دو مردوں نے مدد کی," requiring structural adjustments in sentence formation. This example highlights the linguistic transformations necessary when moving between Arabic and Urdu. While Arabic utilizes diacritics and morphological changes to convey grammatical details, Urdu requires explicit word additions and reordering to preserve the intended meaning. Incorporating these linguistic nuances, in our system we ensure accurate cross-lingual conjugation and translation, preserving the grammatical integrity of both languages.

5 Model Lay Out for Conjugation generation

The general layout of our model is structured as follows:

5.1 Lexeme Parsing:

Each Arabic root word undergoes a detailed parsing process to break it down into a lexeme structure, which serves as a framework for identifying its grammatical features, such as tense, gender, and number. This process involves analyzing the root and comparing it against predefined patterns or regular expression-based templates. These templates are meticulously designed to capture and define the allowable transformations for each specific conjugation form, ensuring that the resulting lexeme exactly follows to the grammatical rules of the language. This step is essential for accurately modeling the complex morphology of

Arabic, enabling precise identification and generation of all valid verb forms derived from a given root.

5.2 Pattern Matching and Transformation:

Morphological rules are applied based on the grammatical tags of the lexeme. At this stage, structured rules are used to add suffixes, prefixes, and make specific phonetic changes, ensuring that the word forms follow the established principles of Arabic morphology. These rules are carefully designed to align with the patterns and structures outlined in existing linguistic models, maintaining accuracy and consistency in the generation of word forms.

5.3 Validation:

To guarantee the accuracy of the generated conjugations, a rigorous validation process was carried out. This involved comparing the system-generated conjugations with verified patterns documented in authoritative reference corpora. Additionally, the dataset and outputs were thoroughly reviewed and annotated by a team of religious scholars from Jamia Ashrafia Lahore Pakistan, who possess deep expertise in Arabic morphology and linguistics. By aligning the outputs with established standards and leveraging expert validation, this process significantly reduced false positives and negatives. Furthermore, it refined the rules for root-word disambiguation, ensuring that each conjugated form was not only linguistically valid but also contextually appropriate, enhancing the overall reliability and precision of the system Figures and tables

6 Results

Table 1 presents the conjugation results derived from the root word س م ع, showcasing the extensive variations generated using a rule-based algorithm. These conjugations demonstrate the application of Arabic morphological rules to produce forms that vary by number, gender, and person. The inclusion of detailed grammatical tags, such as singular, dual, plural (number), masculine and feminine (gender), and third-person, second-person, and first-person (person), highlights the system's capacity to systematically generate precise verb forms.

To enhance accessibility for Urdu language users and learners, grammatical attributes are provided in Urdu. This facilitates a better understanding of the conjugation patterns, bridging the gap between Arabic linguistic structures and Urdu-speaking learners. The detailed output underscores the effectiveness of the rule-based algorithm in capturing all permissible variations from a given root word, ensuring high accuracy and linguistic fidelity in the generated results.

Table 2 provides generated Urdu translations of the conjugated forms generated from the root word س م ع emphasizing the variations in number, gender, and person. These translations have been meticulously crafted to align with the corresponding Arabic conjugations, ensuring linguistic accuracy and contextual relevance. The translations include explicit annotations such as singular, dual, and plural (number), masculine and feminine (gender), and third-person, second person, and first-person (person), reflecting the comprehensive application of morphological rules.

Arabic	Number	Gender	Person
سَمِعَ	واحد	مذکر	غائب
سَمِعَا	تثنیہ	مذکر	غائب
سَمِعُوْا	جمع	مذکر	غائب
سَمِعَتْ	واحد	مونث	غائب
سَمِعَتَا	تثنیہ	مونث	غائب
سَمِعْنَ	جمع	مونث	غائب
سَمِعْتَ	واحد	مذکر	حاضر
سَمِعْتُمَا	تثنیہ	مذکر	حاضر
سَمِعْتُمْ	جمع	مذکر	حاضر
سَمِعْتِ	واحد	مونث	حاضر
سَمِعْتُمَا	تثنیہ	مونث	حاضر
سَمِعْتُنَّ	جمع	مونث	حاضر
سَمِعْتُ	واحد	مذکر	متکلم
سَمِعْنَا	تثنیہ	مذکر	متکلم
سَمِعْنَا	جمع	مذکر	متکلم
سَمِعْتُ	واحد	مونث	متکلم
سَمِعْنَا	تثنیہ	مونث	متکلم
سَمِعْنَا	جمع	مونث	متکلم

Table 1: Arabic Conjugations.

To cater specifically to Urdu-speaking users and learners, the details are presented in Urdu script with contextual examples for clarity. Each conjugated form is not only grammatically accurate but also contextually expressive, facilitating a deeper understanding of the relationship between Arabic and Urdu linguistic structures. This systematic presentation highlights the ability of the rule-based algorithm to generate accurate conjugations and demonstrates the effectiveness of the system in bridging Arabic morphology with its Urdu translations, fostering language learning and comprehension across both languages.

Urdu	Number	Gender	person
اس (ایک مرد) نے سنا	واحد	مذکر	غائب
ان (دو مردوں) نے سنا	تثنیہ	مذکر	غائب
ان (سب مردوں) نے سنا	جمع	مذکر	غائب
اس (ایک عورت) نے سنا	واحد	مونث	غائب
ان (دو عورتوں) نے سنا	تثنیہ	مونث	غائب
ان (سب عورتوں) نے سنا	جمع	مونث	غائب
آپ (ایک مرد) نے سنا	واحد	مذکر	حاضر
آپ (دو مردوں) نے سنا	تثنیہ	مذکر	حاضر
آپ(سب مردوں)نے سنا	جمع	مذکر	حاضر
آپ (ایک عورت) نے سنا	واحد	مونث	حاضر
آپ (دو عورتوں) نے سنا	تثنیہ	مونث	حاضر
آپ (سب عورتوں) نے سنا	جمع	مونث	حاضر
میں (ایک مرد) نے سنا	واحد	مذکر	متکلم
ہم (دو مردوں) نے سنا	تثنیہ	مذکر	متکلم
ہم (سب مردوں) نے سنا	جمع	مذکر	متکلم
میں (ایک عورت) نے سنا	واحد	مونث	متکلم
ہم (دو عورتوں) نے سنا	تثنیہ	مونث	متکلم
ہم (سب عورتوں) نے سنا	جمع	مونث	متکلم

Table 2: Urdu Translations.

7 Demonstration and Accessibility

To provide an interactive experience and allow users to explore the capabilities of our system, we have developed a live demonstration available at the following link: https://mhasham.pythonanywhere.com/. This demo enables users to input Arabic root words, view the generated conjugations, and access their Urdu translations.

The demo serves as a practical extension of the research, illustrating the system's functionality and accuracy in real-time. By making the system accessible online, we aim to support both researchers and learners in exploring Arabic morphological structures and their Urdu translations. The tool also allows users to compare translations with existing solutions like Google Translate, further highlighting the linguistic precision and contextual fidelity of our approach.

8 Comparison Analysis of Al-Tasreef Translations and Google Translate Outputs

To evaluate the accuracy and reliability of our system, we conducted a comparative analysis of conjugations derived from the Arabic verb forms with their corresponding Urdu translations generated by our rule-based Al-Tasreef system and those produced by Google Translate. This comparison highlights the linguistic fidelity of our approach, particularly in preserving the nuanced grammatical structures of Arabic, which include variations in gender, number, and person.

The Arabic conjugations in this study were systematically processed using our rule-based algorithm, which applies precise morphological rules to generate contextually accurate verb forms. These were translated into Urdu while maintaining grammatical integrity, ensuring that each translation aligns with the original meaning and context. The translations generated by Al-Tasreef were further validated by a team of religious scholars from Jamia Ashrafia, Lahore, known for their expertise in Arabic morphology and Urdu language.

In contrast, Google Translation output often displayed inaccuracies stemming from a lack of sensitivity to Arabic's complex morphological features, such as handling gendered plurals and negations. For example, while Google Translate failed to distinguish between masculine and feminine plural forms, our system produced accurate and semantically aligned translations see Table 3. Issues included misinterpretation of negations, improper handling of gender-specific forms, and incorrect contextual mapping. These errors underscore the limitations of general-purpose translation systems when applied to morphologically rich languages like Arabic.

Arabic	Al Tasreef Translation	Google Translation
حَلَقَتْ	اس (ایک عورت) نے سر مونڈھا	یہ اڑ گیا۔
حَلَقْتَ	آپ ایک مرد نے سر مونڈھا	مونڈنا
تَحْلِقُ	آپ (ایک مرد) سر مونڈھتے ہو	پرواز
مَا قَطَعَتْ	اس (ایک عورت) نے نہیں کاٹا	اسے کاٹا نہیں گیا تھا۔
مَا قَطَعَتَا	ان (دو عورتوں) نے نہیں کاٹا	وہ ٹوٹے نہیں تھے۔
مَا قَطَعْتَ	آپ ایک مرد نے نہیں کاٹا	جو آپ نے کاٹ دیا۔
مَا قَطَعْتُنَّ	آپ (سب عورتوں) نے نہیں کاٹا	تم نے مجھے نہیں کاٹا
بَلَغْتُنَّ	آپ (سب عورتیں) پہنچیں	آپ اپنی عمر کو پہنچ چکے ہیں
بَلَغْتِ	آپ (ایک عورت) پہنچی	وہ پہنچ گیا
مَا خَرَجْتُمَا	آپ (دو مرد) نہیں نکلے	جب تم دونوں چلے گئے
مَا خَرَجْتُمْ	آپ (سب مرد) نہیں نکلے	جب تک تم چلے جاؤ
تَصْفَحُ	وہ (ایک عورت) درگزر کرتی ہے	براؤز کریں
مَا شَفَعْنَا	ہم (سب عورتوں) نے نہیں سفارش کی	ہم شفاعت نہیں کریں گے۔
لَا تَبْخَسُ	آپ (ایک مرد) نہیں کمی کرتے ہو	کم نہ سمجھیں

Table3: Translation Comparison.

Table 3 provides a detailed comparison, showcasing the Arabic conjugation, the corresponding Al-Tasreef translation, and the output from Google Translate. It highlights the instances where Google Translate diverges from the intended meaning, offering clear evidence of the strengths of our approach in achieving accurate and contextually appropriate translations.

9 Applications

The purposed system can be utilized in the following areas

Educational Tools: This system serves as an invaluable resource for students learning both Arabic and Urdu. By offering comprehensive conjugation tables alongside accurate translations, it provides learners with a clear understanding of the grammar, syntax, and structure of both languages simultaneously. This side-by-side approach not only simplifies language learning but also makes it more effective and engaging. Furthermore, the Arabic-Urdu conjugation generator has the potential to be utilized in the development of various educational tools and applications, supporting language learning in formal educational settings as well as self-study environments.

Machine Translation: By integrating Urdu translations for Arabic conjugations, this system lays the groundwork for developing machine translation tools. These tools can bridge the gap for low-resource languages, especially for language pairs like Arabic and Urdu that currently lack robust computational resource

Linguistic Research: This system provides a powerful tool for researchers in linguistics to explore and analyze the morphological similarities and differences between Arabic and Urdu. By systematically examining the grammatical structures, conjugation patterns, and linguistic nuances of both languages, the model enables a deeper understanding of their connections. Such analysis not only sheds light on the shared features and divergences between these languages but also offers valuable insights into the broader linguistic relationships between the Semitic language family, to which Arabic belongs, and the South Asian linguistic tradition, represented by Urdu. This cross-linguistic study significantly contributes to the field of comparative linguistics, paving the way for further research into how languages evolve, influence one another, and develop across different cultural and historical contexts.

Religious Studies: The interplay of Arabic and Urdu holds immense significance in religious contexts, especially for Islamic texts, where both languages serve as crucial mediums for understanding and interpretation. This system offers a precise and systematic tool for scholars, researchers, and readers by generating accurate conjugations and corresponding translations. By adhering closely to traditional linguistic rules and interpretations, the system ensures that the generated outputs remain faithful to the original meanings of sacred texts.

In addition, this resource is particularly valuable for institutions and scholars engaged in the study of Islamic texts, such as Religious Madaris across regions, as highlighted in the Pakistan Education Statistics (2021-22) [3]. These institutions, with significant enrollments and teaching faculties dedicated to Arabic and Urdu studies, can utilize this tool to streamline linguistic analysis and improve access to both languages' grammatical structures. The system's ability to bridge Arabic's intricate morphology with Urdu's expressive semantics facilitates a deeper understanding of classical religious literature, enhancing educational and theological research efforts across Pakistan and similar regions.

10 Conclusion

In this study, we present a rule-based system designed to generate Arabic verb conjugations and their corresponding Urdu translations. By addressing the complex morphological challenges of Arabic and aligning them with Urdu's linguistic structures, our approach makes a significant contribution to the fields of computational linguistics, language education, and translation for under-resourced languages. Validated by expert linguists and scholars, the system has proven highly accurate in producing linguistically and contextually appropriate outputs, positioning it as a valuable resource for educators, linguists, and researchers, particularly in academic and religious contexts.

A comparative analysis with Google Translate revealed the limitations of general-purpose machine translation systems in capturing the subtle grammatical nuances of Arabic and their precise translation into Urdu. In contrast, our system offers a domain-specific solution, tailored to the intricacies of Arabic morphology and its contextual relevance in Urdu. This makes it a robust tool for multilingual NLP applications, providing a more accurate and reliable translation experience.

11 Future Work

While the proposed system has shown promising results, several avenues for further development exist, which could enhance its functionality and broaden its impact.

One key area for future improvement is the expansion of the dataset and root coverage. Currently, the system focuses on triliteral, non-weak Arabic roots, but there is significant potential to include weak verbs and quadrilateral (four-letter) roots. This expansion would allow the system to handle a broader array of verb conjugations and translations, making it more versatile and capable of covering a larger portion of the Arabic verb system. By incorporating these additional roots, the system's utility would increase, benefiting both practical applications and theoretical linguistic analysis.

Another exciting direction is the integration with advanced machine learning models. While the current system is rule-based, incorporating transformer-based models such as AraBERT or multilingual BERT could significantly enhance its performance. These models are particularly powerful in their ability to generalize across unseen verb roots, improving the system's ability to generate accurate conjugations and translations. By integrating these models, the system could also refine the contextual accuracy of its translations, particularly for more complex sentence structures or less common verb forms.

Moreover, there is considerable potential in extending the system to support additional languages. While the current focus is on Arabic and Urdu, languages such as Persian or Pashto, which share similar linguistic characteristics, would benefit from the system's capabilities. Modifications would involve adapting morphological rules and translation patterns to accommodate the syntactic and semantic nuances of these languages. Adding support for these languages would significantly broaden the system's applicability and allow it to serve as a valuable tool in a wider range of linguistic contexts. This extension would also provide insights into the

[3] https://pie.gov.pk/

similarities and differences between these languages, offering a comparative perspective for linguists and researchers.

An important aspect of enhancing the system's usability is the development of an interactive user interface. Although the current demo offers basic functionality, a more interactive and user-friendly interface would greatly facilitate adoption among educators, students, and researchers. A well-designed interface would allow users to easily input verbs, view conjugations and translations, and explore the underlying rules and patterns. This would not only improve the system's accessibility but also make it more effective as a teaching tool in academic environments.

Finally, there is significant potential for the system's application in religious and cultural studies. Expanding the system to handle more complex Quranic or classical Arabic structures would be highly beneficial for scholars working with sacred texts. By accurately processing these more intricate forms of Arabic, the system could provide deeper linguistic and theological insights. This expansion would enable researchers to study sacred texts with greater precision, further enhancing the system's value in both religious and linguistic fields.

12 Acknowledgement

We extend our sincere gratitude to the scholars of Jamia Ashrafia, Lahore, for their invaluable feedback and meticulous evaluation of our work. Their expertise in Arabic morphology and Urdu linguistics significantly contributed to the precision and authenticity of this study.

References

J. Alasmari, J.C.E. Watson, and E. Atwell. *Investigating the Rate of Agree- ment and Disagreement of Tense and Aspect of Quranic Verbs in Arabic to English Translations: Experimental Results and Analysis,"* International Journal on Islamic Applications in Computer Science and Technology, vol. 6, no. 1, pp. 1-10, 2018.

M.T. Ben Othman, M.A. Al-Hagery, and Y.M. El Hashemi, *Arabic Text Processing Model: Verbs Roots and Conjugation Automation,* IEEE Access, vol. 8, pp. 103913–103923, 2020.

A.N. Alsaleh, E. Atwell, and A. Altahhan, *Quranic Verses Semantic Relat- edness Using AraBERT*, University of Leeds, 2021.

K. Shaalan, S. Siddiqui, and M. Alkhatib, *Challenges in Arabic Natural Language Processing,* in Computational Linguistics, Speech and Image Processing for Arabic Language, British University in Dubai, 2018.

Bashir, M.H., Azmi, A.M., Nawaz, H. *et al.* Arabic natural language processing for Qur'anic research: a systematic review. *Artif Intell Rev* **56**, 6801–6854 (2023). https://doi.org/10.1007/s10462-022-10313-2

Adany, Mohamed & Atwell, Eric. (2017). *Quran Question Answering System Using Arabic Number Patterns (Singular, Dual, Plural).* International Journal on Islamic Applications in Computer Science and Technology, Vol. 5, Issue 2, June 2017, 01-12. 5. 1-12.

E. L. M. Hassan, *The impact of standard Arabic verb phrase structure on Moroccan EFL learner's writing*, J. Humanities Social Sci., vol. 24, no. 1, pp. 6067, 2019.

Muh Syahri Romadhon, Moh Khasairi, and Achmad Tohe. 2024. *Android-based media development for memorizing Arabic verbal conjugation and its functional meaning*. Ijaz Arabi Journal of Arabic Learning, 7(2).

Evaluation of Large Language Models on Arabic Punctuation Prediction

Asma Al Wazrah, Afrah Altamimi, Hawra Aljasim, Waad Alshammari, Rawan Al-Matham, Omar Elnashar, Mohamed Amin and Abdulrahman AlOsaimy
{aalwazrah, a.altamimi, haljasim, walshammari, ralmatham, kelnashar, mamin, aalosaimy}@ksaa.gov.sa
King Salman Global Academy for Arabic Language (KSAA)

Abstract

The linguistic inclusivity of Large Language Models (LLMs) such as ChatGPT, Gemni, JAIS, and AceGPT has not been sufficiently explored, particularly in their handling of low-resource languages like Arabic compared to English. While these models have shown impressive performance across various tasks, their effectiveness in Arabic remains under-examined. Punctuation, critical for sentence structure and comprehension in tasks like speech analysis, synthesis, and machine translation, requires precise prediction. This paper assesses seven LLMs: GPT4-o, Gemni1.5, JAIS, AceGPT, SILMA, ALLaM, and CommandR+ for Arabic punctuation prediction. Additionally, the performance of fine-tuned AraBERT is compared with these models in zero-shot and few-shot settings using a proposed Arabic punctuation prediction corpus of 10,046 data points. The experiments demonstrate that while AraBERT performs well for specific punctuation marks, LLMs show significant promise in zero-shot learning, with further improvements in few-shot scenarios. These findings highlight the potential of LLMs to enhance the automation and accuracy of Arabic text processing.

1 Introduction

Punctuation prediction remains a fundamental yet challenging aspect of natural language processing (NLP), particularly in enhancing the readability and understanding of text derived from spoken language inputs. In addition, this task is especially critical in the post-processing step of automatic speech recognition systems, where achieving high accuracy remains a significant challenge. This task plays a vital role in the coherent transformation of spoken language into written form, which is essential for effective communication and documentation. While several studies have explored punctuation prediction tasks, no study has examined the effectiveness of Large Language Models (LLMs) in predicting punctuation for Arabic texts.

Our research aims to evaluate the capabilities of LLMs in punctuation prediction task. In this study, we conduct a comprehensive evaluation of a fine-tuned AraBERT model alongside seven LLM-based models: GPT4-o, Gemni1.5, JAIS, AceGPT, SILMA, ALLaM, and CommandR+ across six punctuation marks. These models have been selected for their potential in handling the nuanced demands of Arabic natural language understanding and generation, making them ideal candidates for this investigation. The LLMs selection criteria included their pretraining focus, such as JAIS and AceGPT, which are specifically designed for Arabic and bilingual tasks, and their availability, with both open-source models such as JAIS and SILMA and closed-source models such as GPT4-o and Gemni1.5 included. The models also represent a mix of general-purpose systems, such as CommandR+, and those specialized for Arabic morphology and syntax, such as ALLaM.

We employ these LLMs in both zero-shot and few-shot learning scenarios to assess their performance. This dual approach allows us to explore not only the inherent capabilities of these models when presented with limited prior training on punctuation tasks but also their adaptability in learning from a minimal set of examples. Through our experiments, we aim to provide a detailed analysis of how each model handles the complexity of punctuation prediction and to identify the

Processings of the 1st Workshop on NLP for Languages Using Arabic Script (AbjadNLP), pages 144–154
January 19, 2025. ©2025 Association for Computational Linguistics

strengths and limitations of each approach. This study hopes to contribute valuable insights into the potential of LLMs to improve punctuation prediction tasks in NLP, thereby enhancing the accuracy and efficiency of converting spoken language into punctuated written text.

The rest of the papers is presented as follows: section 2 presents the background of the used tools and methods. Section 3 presents the related works. Section 4 shows the methodology including the dataset and preparation, in addition to the model architecture. Section 5 discusses the experimental results, along with the error analysis of the testing data results. Finally, Section 6 concludes the paper and presents the future directions.

2 Background

This section reviews LLMs for Arabic NLP, Section 2.1 covers AraBERT model. Section 2.2 presents closed-source models such as GPT-4o and Gemini 1.5, while Section 2.3 discusses open-source models such as JAIS-13b and AceGPT.

2.1 AraBERT

AraBERT v0.2 (Antoun et al., 2020) is a pre-trained model for processing Arabic text, developed using Google's BERT design. It is designed to accommodate Arabic's distinct features, such as its complex morphology and writing system. AraBERT v0.2 enhances the initial version by utilizing a broader corpus that incorporates both Modern Standard Arabic and dialects, resulting in improved performance on various NLP tasks like text classification, sentiment analysis, and named entity recognition. It also contains improvements for managing Arabic accents and symbols.

2.2 Closed-source Generative Model for Arabic NLP

GPT-4o (OpenAI, 2024): Developed by OpenAI and incorporates multimodal capabilities, allowing it to process various inputs, including images, videos, audio, and text. GPT-4o, in contrast to GPT-4, shows improved efficiency by reducing token usage across multiple languages, including Arabic.

Gemini 1.5 (Pichai and Hassabis, 2024): Developed by Google and incorporates of advanced processing systems enhances its contextual understanding across languages, including Arabic, thus improving the accuracy of AI applications in natural language understanding, machine translation, and language generation tasks relevant to Arabic.

Command R+ (Gomez, 2024): Command R+ is 104 billion parameter multilingual LLM designed by Cohere for conversational interaction and tasks requiring long context. It focuses on excelling in tasks that require understanding and executing accurately.

ALLaM-1 (Bari et al., 2024): ALLaM, is a 13 billion parameter LLM for Arabic and English, developed by SDAIA, and is designed for a wide range of NLP applications. It is particularly suited for tasks such as text completion, question-answering, document summarization, classification, generation, and translation in Arabic.

2.3 Open-source Generative Model for Arabic NLP

JAIS-13b (Sengupta et al., 2023): JAIS is based on the GPT-3 decoder-only architecture with its focus on bilingual (Arabic and English) capabilities. JAIS aims to address a critical gap in the development of AI solutions for Arabic language speakers.

AceGPT-13b (Huang et al., 2023b): AceGPT is an open-source LLM developed specifically for Arabic, attuned to local culture and values, offering versatile functionality across multiple Arabic-specific applications.

SILMA v1.0 (SILMA, 2024): SILMA is an open-source 9 billion parameter LLM built over the foundational models of Google Gemma, and it is designed for tasks regarding text generation and summarization. The model is currently topping the list of open-source Arabic LLMs according to the OALL classification on Hugging Face (Almazrouei et al., 2023).

In this study, we aim to evaluate the performance of these models for Arabic punctuation prediction. We examine their capabilities under both zero-shot and few-shot learning paradigms.

3 Related Works

This section reviews recent developments in LLMs for Arabic NLP, focusing on their applications, performance, and limitations, particularly in the underexplored area of punctuation prediction.

3.1 Evaluating LLMs

The rise of generative LLMs like ChatGPT and Gemini signifies a breakthrough in generative modeling, showcasing human-like text generation proficiency across diverse languages, including Arabic.

Several studies demonstrate their superior performance in translation tasks compared to commercial systems (Wang et al., 2023; Peng et al., 2023; Karpinska and Iyyer, 2023). (Bubeck et al., 2023) investigates GPT-4, showcasing its excellent performance across various tasks. (Espejel et al., 2023) experiment the reasoning ability of GPT-3.5, GPT-4, and BARD, highlighting the GPT-4's surpassed performance in zero-shot scenarios. (Laskar et al., 2023) thoroughly evaluates ChatGPT across 140 tasks, facilitating its effectiveness.

Numerous papers (Ogundare and Araya, 2023; Jiao et al., 2023; Bang et al., 2023) observe that ChatGPT is competitive with commercial products for high-resource languages but encounters difficulties with low-resource languages. Low-resource languages have also been investigated by (Ahuja et al., 2023; Lai et al., 2023).

Both (Ziems et al., 2024) and (Sottana et al., 2023) observe that while LLMs fall short of the best fine-tuned state-of-the-art (SoTA) models, they still achieve fair agreement levels with humans. Meanwhile, (Qin et al., 2023) highlights ChatGPT excels in reasoning tasks but faces challenges like sequence tagging. (Sottana et al., 2023) highlights the need for enhanced evaluation metrics for LLMs, identifying GPT-4 as a promising candidate for fulfilling this role. This emphasizes the importance of addressing the limitations in evaluation methodologies, which could contribute to the discrepancies observed in model assessments.

Recent studies reveal innovative methods to improve LLMs. Specifically, (Peng et al., 2023; Gao et al., 2023) conclude task-specific prompts enhance translation systems, while (Huang et al., 2023a) introduce cross-lingual-thought prompting (XLT) to improve cross-lingual performance. Furthermore, (Lu et al., 2023) suggests self-correction techniques for ChatGPT.

The findings of these studies suggest that while GPT-based LLMs are competent language models, their performance is comparable to the current SoTA model in most NLP tasks. However, none of these examinations specifically evaluate the punctuation prediction performance of LLMs.

3.2 Evaluating LLMs for Arabic NLP

The performance of LLMs has been evaluated in various Arabic NLP tasks. (Khondaker et al., 2023) evaluated ChatGPT's performance across 32 Arabic NLP tasks, revealing the necessity for enhancements in instruction-tuned LLMs. (Alyafeai et al., 2023) determined that GPT-4 surpasses GPT-3.5 in five out of the seven Arabic NLP tasks. (Huang et al., 2023b) introduces AceGPT, a culturally sensitive Arabic LLM, which outperformed within various Arabic benchmarks. (Kadaoui et al., 2023) evaluates the machine translation proficiency of ChatGPT (GPT-3.5 and GPT-4) and Bard across ten Arabic varieties, uncovering challenges with dialects lacking datasets. (Al-Thubaity et al., 2023) assesses ChatGPT (GPT-3.5 and GPT-4) and Bard AI for Dialectal Arabic Sentiment Analysis, revealing GPT-4's superior performance over GPT-3.5 and Bard AI.

LLMs, as demonstrated by (Khondaker et al., 2023; Alyafeai et al., 2023; Kwon et al., 2023), still fall short when compared to SoTA models fine-tuned on Arabic data.

Other studies have investigating evaluating smaller Arabic language models (Abu Farha and Magdy, 2021; Inoue et al., 2021; Alammary, 2022; Nagoudi et al., 2023; Elmadany et al., 2023b; Elmadany et al., 2023a).

3.3 Arabic Punctuation

In various languages, punctuation functions as a marker for delineating sentence boundaries. However, the interpretative clarity of this punctuation is often compromised, notably evident in instances involving acronyms or abbreviations. When the need arises to segregate sentences, it is imperative to employ a punction prediction technique adept at resolving such ambiguities. Recent research has made significant progress in punctuation prediction. (Zhou et al., 2022) and (Wu et al., 2016) have proposed models that outperform traditional methods for speech recognition, with Zhou's joint ASR-punctuation model showing notable promise. Similarly, (Yi et al., 2020) tackled the class imbalance issue in punctuation prediction training by incorporating focal loss, resulting in improved performance. Collectively, these studies underscore the potential of deep learning in enhancing punctuation prediction accuracy.

A range of studies have explored the prediction of punctuation and diacritics in the Arabic language. Both (Aboutaib et al., 2023), (Sunkara et al., 2020), and (Mansour et al., 2023) reported high accuracy in punctuation prediction. (Sunkara et al., 2020) and model utilized BERT based pretrained language models, exhibiting robustness against automatic speech recognition errors. (Mansour et al., 2023) utilized a pre-trained transformer-based model such as ELECTRA and BERT. (Al-Najjar et al., 2020) concentrated on diacritization in Medieval Arabic utilizing a character-level neural machine translation approach. (Sakr and Torki, 2023) propose a new punctuation dataset and concluded that XLM-RoBERTa outperformed other transformer-based models in punctuation restoration.

4 Methodology

This section outlines the methodology employed in our study. In section 3.1, we detail the dataset utilized, including its composition and preparation. Subsection 3.2 describes the models employed in this research.

4.1 Dataset

In this research, we use a dataset sourced from the King Salman Global Academy for Arabic Language (KSAA), which includes 25 books. Since the data is taken from published books, it has been proofread for grammar and punctuation by linguistic experts to ensure accuracy and consistency.The data is available from the corresponding author on request.

To prepare the dataset, the books were preprocessed by automatically removing footnotes, indexes, and references. Following this, the text was divided into smaller paragraphs using tab delimiters and then saved as an Excel file for further preparation.

Each paragraph was carefully reviewed and cleaned manually by one annotator, involving:

- The removal of titles and non-paragraph elements (e.g., Footnotes and their reference numbers).
- Combining rows that were contextually related to form complete paragraphs.

In total, 10,046 data points were generated, each limited to a maximum length of 512 tokens after tokenization.

Next, the data is split into training, validation, and test sets. The training set contains 8,569 data points, the validation set contains 962 data points, and the test set contains 515 data points.

For each book, 90% of the content was used for the training set, while the remaining 10% was allocated to the validation set. We designated one book exclusively for testing, and its data is not included in either the training or validation sets.

The training data will be used to fine-tune the AraBERT model, with its performance assessed using the validation set. Once fine-tuned, AraBERT, along with all other language models mentioned in this study, will be evaluated on the test data to compare their effectiveness in the given task.

In this study, we focus on the prediction of six Arabic punctuation marks: period (.), comma (،), colon (:), semicolon (؛), question mark (؟) and exclamation mark (!). Table 1 shows the punctuation distribution among data splitting.

Marks	Train (85%)	Val (10%)	Test (5%)
.	23,156	2,612	1,245
،	42,287	4,472	2,931
:	6,517	622	321
؛	3,445	370	195
؟	568	82	27
!	124	15	5

Table 1: Punctuations distribution.

4.2 Model

In this section, a fine-tuned AraBERT model and several LLMs are introduced as the primary tools for tackling the task of punctuation prediction in Arabic texts.

4.2.1 Fine-tuning AraBERT for Arabic Punctuation Prediction

To fine-tune AraBERT v0.2, each text will be fed to the model along with its label. To prepare the text, we discard all punctuation marks, then, each text was then broken down into smaller units, typically words or subwords, referred to as tokens.

In contrast, to prepare the labeling, we first tokenize the text. Then, followed the method outlined in (Mansour et al., 2023), each token was encoded using underscores and punctuation marks: words without punctuation were replaced by underscores (_), while words followed by punctuation were substituted by the corresponding punctuation mark. We focused on encoding only words that contain one of the six Arabic punctuation marks discussed earlier.

We ensured that the length of each tokenized text exactly matched the length of its label sequence, maintaining a one-to-one correspondence between tokens and their respective labels.

Simultaneously, labels indicating the presence or absence of punctuation for each token were converted into numerical indices through label encoding, following the mapping {"_": 0, ".": 1, "،": 2, "؛": 3, "؟": 4, "!": 5, ":": 6}. This transformation made the categorical label data suitable for model training, with each index corresponding to a specific punctuation mark. Thus, the input to the model consisted of the tokenized text without any punctuation, while the labels encoded the corresponding numerical label, as shown in Table 2.

Original text	أكل الولد الخبز، وشرب الماء.
No punct. tokenized text	[أكل, الولد, الخبز, وشرب, الماء]
Encoded label	._،__
Numerical label	[1,0,2,0,0]

Table 2: Fine-tune AraBERT input.

The tokenized texts were padded to ensure uniform length across batches. After padding, the tokens were embedded into dense vectors. We fine-tuned AraBERT v0.2 by adjusting several training parameters to optimize its performance for Arabic text processing. Specifically, we used a learning rate of 5e-5 and a batch size of 8, utilizing the AdamW optimizer in conjunction with a linear learning rate scheduler that employed zero warm-up steps. The model was trained for 5 epochs, a duration deemed sufficient for effective learning while minimizing the risk of overfitting.

4.2.2 LLMs for Arabic Punctuation Prediction

We utilized various LLMs, specifically GPT4-o, Gemni-1.5-flash-latest, jais-13b, AceGPT-13b, SILMA-9B-Instruct-v1.0, allam-1-13b-instruct, and command-r-plus-08-2024 in both zero-shot and few-shot scenarios. In the zero-shot approach, the models relied entirely on their pretraining knowledge without any additional fine-tuning. In the few-shot setting, they were provided with two examples of punctuation patterns, which improved their performance and demonstrated their ability to adapt to limited data scenarios.. We provided explicit directives against adding or deleting any word or letter from the original content to ensure effective implementation of the missing punctuation marks in the texts and enable its straightforward evaluation. We included two examples as an addition to the few-shot step. We ran the model on an NVIDIA A100 40GB GPU for efficient large-scale computation.

5 Results and Discussion

To assess the performance of the fine-tuned AraBERT model, we evaluate the model's performance using metrics: precision, recall and F1 score using the validation data. In addition, we analyze the overall accuracy of AraBERT in comparison to other LLMs mentioned in this study using the testing data, providing a comprehensive evaluation of model performance in predicting punctuation for Arabic text.

5.1 AraBERT Results

We investigated the performance of the fine-tuned AraBERT model on the evaluation dataset. As shown in Table 3, the model excels in recognizing some punctuation marks like the comma (،) and colon (:) but faces difficulties with others such as the semicolon (؛) and exclamation mark (!). The exclamation mark has a much lower F1 score than the other punctuation marks. The dataset has a highly uneven distribution of punctuation marks, potentially resulting in performance disparities. For instance, the exclamation mark is rarely used in comparison to commas, impacting the model's capacity to generalize and contributing to the small training size. The overall accuracy for the testing data reaches 29.78% among all punctuation marks. There is a significant contrast in performance for certain marks like the period (.), with precision at 54.87% and recall at 87.62%, suggesting the model accurately detects fewer true positive periods but has more false positives. Interestingly, the dataset size for the period is large compared to other

Marks	Precision	Recall	F1
_ (no punc)	98.63%	99.30%	98.97%
.	54.87%	87.62%	67.48%
،	86.02%	84.22%	85.11%
:	91.60%	87.97%	89.75%
؛	79.50%	46.58%	58.74%
؟	79.58%	90.66%	84.76%
!	69.57%	12.90%	21.77%

Table 3: Fine-tuned AraBERT result on validation set.

punctuation marks, which may influence this performance discrepancy.

Several factors may explain the high F1 score of 84.76% for the question mark (؟), despite its infrequent occurrence. Initially, question marks are commonly found in particular syntax and meaning situations, frequently in conjunction with question terms or formations, aiding in the model's understanding of where they belong. Furthermore, question marks are used more clearly and with less ambiguity than other punctuation marks, making them a more effective learning aid. The elevated F1 score could also be due to the model's increased recall, indicating it accurately detects most questions even if it sometimes mistakes other sentences as questions. Therefore, the model's strong performance on question marks is attributed to a combination of strong contextual cues, clear usage patterns, and high recall, despite the low training frequency.

5.2 LLM REsults

Upon investigating the models, we found that GPT4-o and Command R+ complied substantially with the majority of the proposed guidelines. In several instances, the models enhanced the quality of the text by inserting additional words do not present in the original content, as observed with Gemini 1.5. Conversely, other models exhibited some discrepancies in adhering to the given directions or generated completely different content, leading to the deletion of some original textual information. These elements complicated the process of evaluation.

As shown in Figure 1, the results reveal that GPT4-o and Command R+ performed substantially well in terms of adhering to the proposed guidelines, demonstrating higher accuracy compared to other models. However, Gemini 1.5 introduced additional words that were not part of the original content, complicating the evaluation process.

The few-shot method consistently improved the performance of most models, with GPT4-o achieving an accuracy of 66.57%, significantly higher than the zero-shot method. In contrast, models like SILMA and JAIS struggled with lower accuracy levels across both learning scenarios. Notably, JAIS took the longest time to complete the tasks, whereas SILMA was the fastest, highlighting the variability in processing efficiency. The results highlight that while LLMs show potential for punctuation prediction, their performance varies depending on the task and method, with some models requiring further refinement to improve consistency and adherence to the original text.

When analyzing the results by punctuation mark, the period (.) achieved the highest accuracy, as illustrated in Table 4. Notably, both the AceGPT and JAIS models showed significant improvement after employing the few-shot method. However, in comparison to AraBERT's performance, these models demonstrated stronger results. As shown in Table 4, AraBERT showed weaker performance relative to the LLMs and a decline in performance from the validation (Table 3) to the test set, reflecting its limited generalization capability.

Interestingly, even though the few-shot prompts did not include any question marks in the examples, the results still displayed some enhancements in the prediction accuracy of question marks, underscoring the potential of few-shot learning to improve performance across different punctuation marks.

5.3 Error Analysis

We aim to examine the errors made by these LLMs during the processing of Arabic text based on the test data. We aim to provide valuable insights that can contribute to the refinement of punctuation prediction LLMs, ultimately enhancing the efficiency of Arabic text processing.

We outline the main types of errors found in the test data:

- **Formatting or Sample Division:** In the original text, the phrase " كانوا يتكلمون اللغة العربية قبل ظهور الإسلام،واللغة العربية" had the word (الإسلام،) attached to the word (واللغة). The models GPT4-o and Gemini 1.5. separated

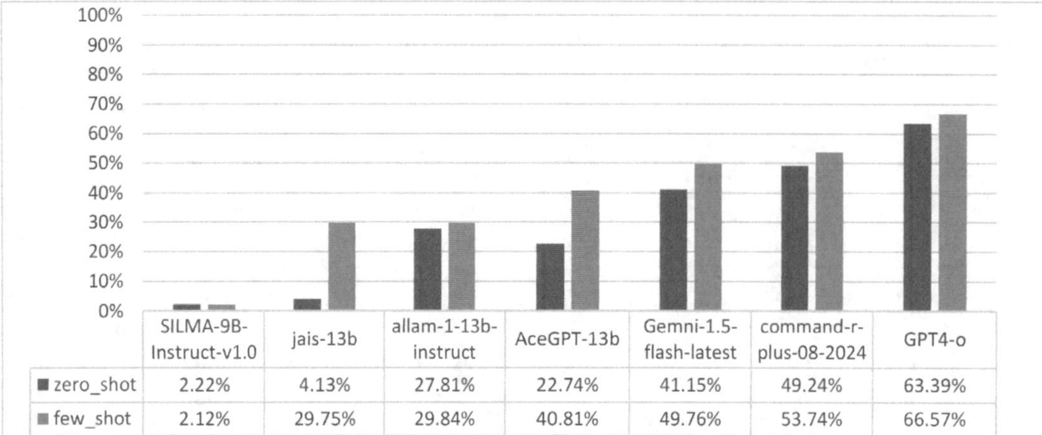

Figure 1: Average Accuracy among all punctuation marks.

Method	Model	.	،	؛	؟	!	:
Fine-tune	AraBERT	22.68%	31.36%	03.51%	26.66%	00.00%	34.28%
Zero-shot	GPT4-o	**76.46%**	59.74%	**34.58%**	54.44%	20.00%	**60.45%**
Few-shot		75.22%	**69.23%**	19.92%	**63.33%**	20.00%	49.52%
	command-r-plus-08-2024	69.14%	41.32%	23.37%	56.66%	20.00%	55.93%
		72.91%	47.16%	17.06%	50.00%	**40.00%**	57.19%
	Gemni-1.5-flash-latest	50.95%	39.57%	29.11%	56.66%	20.00%	19.10%
		53.30%	55.76%	14.26%	61.11%	20.00%	14.46%
	allam-1-13b-instruct	60.03%	09.67%	18.88%	30.00%	00.00%	46.83%
		66.15%	08.70%	17.51%	36.66%	00.00%	46.87%
	AceGPT-13b	15.30%	26.58%	06.96%	34.44%	20.00%	34.00%
		58.49%	32.31%	18.03%	43.33%	00.00%	48.16%
	jais-13b, AceGPT-13b	04.48%	03.53%	01.17%	00.00%	00.00%	01.98%
		32.55%	27.50%	12.11%	20.00%	20.00%	27.87%
	SILMA-9B-Instruct-v1.0	00.77%	02.97%	00.00%	00.00%	00.00%	02.64%
		01.04%	02.51%	00.00%	00.00%	00.00%	04.06%

Table 4: Average Accuracy par punctuation marks on test set.

these words while retaining the punctuation, but this was considered incorrect. Additionally, some text samples were very short and lacked context, which led to failures in punctuation, such as the phrase "ثالثًا الكتاب".

- **Writer's Mistakes:** It is important to note that an accurate score below 100% does not necessarily indicate a mistake by the model; in some cases, the model may be correcting errors in the original text. Consequently, a model achieving a perfect score (100%) might only signify alignment with the source text, even if that text contains inaccuracies. For example, most models corrected the original sentence: "... افتُتِحَت مجموعة من المعاهد العالية الإسلامية، التي كانت تستقبل الطلبة المتخرجين في ثانويات الأئمة والخطباء..." to: " افتُتِحَت مجموعة من المعاهد العالية الإسلامية التي كانت تستقبل الطلبة المتخرجين في ثانويات الأئمة والخطباء.". GPT4-o, the model that received accuracy of 100%, did not make this correction. Additionally, there were instances of complete loss of punctuation in the original text, as seen in the phrase: " العامية لغة العامة أما الفصحى فهي لغة الخاصة," which was corrected by Gemini1.5 to: " العامية لغة العامة، أما الفصحى فهي لغة الخاصة," yet it received a score of 0.

- **Differences in Usage Across Languages:** The application of punctuation rules from other languages to Arabic led to several issues. For instance, the original text stated:

"هناك أسباب كثيرة أدت إلى ظهور العامية منها:
العرق: ...
العامل الجغرافي: ...
العامل الثقافي: ...
الاستعمار: ..."

The models transformed this into:

" هناك أسباب كثيرة أدت إلى ظهور العامية، منها: العرق ....؛ العامل الجغرافي.........؛ العامل الثقافي ....؛ الاستعمار..... "

except for Command R+, AceGPT-13b, and ALLaM.

- **Limited and Emotional Use of Certain Punctuation Marks:** An example is the exclamation mark (!) which appeared in only five instances, three of which were complex usages combined with the question mark (؟!). The models Command R+, ALLaM, and AceGPT used it correctly in standalone contexts, while one instance was in an explicit exclamatory expression: "يالَلْحزن," which was correctly utilized by the models Command R+, Gemini1.5, and GPT4-4o. However, one instance was in a highly personal context that none of the models managed to punctuate correctly.

- **Partial Diacritical Marking in Arabic Texts:** The inability of some models, e.g. AraBERT, to handle the presence or absence of diacritical marks leads to the exclusion of any marked words, resulting in grammatically incorrect text that the model fails to punctuate appropriately.

5.4 Findings

The study highlights that models such as GPT4-o and Geni1.5 demonstrated robust zero-shot and few-shot learning capabilities. These findings suggest potential for handling languages such as Pashto and Sindhi, which share script similarities with Arabic.. Pashto and Sindhi exhibit unique syntactic and semantic features, which differ from Arabic. For example, Pashto uses diacritics more consistently than Arabic, and Sindhi's punctuation conventions may require additional adaptation of model pretraining or fine-tuning. While the LLMs in the are promising, their effectiveness in Pashto or Sindhi would depend on additional fine-tuning and dataset enrichment tailored to these languages. For fine-tuning, embedding models such as E5, which is known for its multilingual support, covers Persian and could be extended to Pashto, Sindhi, and Uyghur with additional pretraining on relevant datasets.

The presence of partial diacritics in the dataset introduced inconsistency, creating ambiguity for models such as AraBERT when predicting punctuation. Models such as GPT4-o demonstrated stronger generalization in both zero-shot and few-shot scenarios, effectively handling diacritic-related complexities in punctuation prediction. AraBERT, while less accurate overall, benefited significantly from fine-tuning on diacritic-inclusive datasets, showing improved accuracy compared to when diacritics were excluded.

Errors occur due to improper text segmentation, such as attached punctuation marks (e.g., "الإسلام،واللغة") or short, context-lacking samples. Writer's mistakes, such as missing or incorrect punctuation, lead models to correct text but result in mismatches during evaluation. Multilingual training causes cross-linguistic interference, applying non-Arabic punctuation rules. Rare punctuation marks, like exclamation marks (!), are underrepresented, limiting generalization. Lastly, partial diacritical marking creates ambiguity, making it difficult for models to interpret and predict punctuation accurately. Moreover, Rare punctuation marks such as the exclamation mark (!) and semicolon (؛) posed significant challenges due to their low frequency in the dataset, which limited the models' exposure to these patterns during training. In addition, their usage often occurs in complex contexts, such as emotional expressions or structured lists, making it challenging for models to predict them accurately. For example, the exclamation mark is commonly combined with other punctuation marks, such as "؟!".

6 Conclusion

This study demonstrates the effectiveness of LLMs, for punctuation prediction in Arabic texts. Our findings highlight the importance of dataset alignment and suggest promising avenues for enhancing NLP applications. Future research should focus on fine-tune LLMs on our dataset for this task, in addition to extending a more balanced dataset to tackle the issue of uneven data distribution and enhance the model's performance across all punctuation marks. These efforts will significantly advance the automation and quality of Arabic text processing. Moreover, the future work should focus on augmenting datasets with Rare punctuation marks such as the exclamation mark (!) and semicolon (؛) employing context-aware training techniques to improve model accuracy and robustness.

Acknowledgments

This work was supported by the Arabic AI Center (ARAI) at KSAA, which provided computational resources for model training and covered the costs associated with generating output from closed-source LLMs.

References

Abdelkarim Aboutaib, Ahmad El allaoui, Imad Zeroual, and El Wardani Dadi. 2023. Punctuation Prediction for the Arabic language. In *Proceedings of the 6th International Conference on Networking, Intelligent Systems & Security*, New York, NY, USA. Association for Computing Machinery.

Ibrahim Abu Farha and Walid Magdy. 2021. Benchmarking Transformer-based Language Models for Arabic Sentiment and Sarcasm Detection. In Nizar Habash, Houda Bouamor, Hazem Hajj, Walid Magdy, Wajdi Zaghouani, Fethi Bougares, Nadi Tomeh, Ibrahim Abu Farha, and Samia Touileb, editors, *Proceedings of the Sixth Arabic Natural Language Processing Workshop*, pages 21–31, Kyiv, Ukraine (Virtual). Association for Computational Linguistics.

Kabir Ahuja, Harshita Diddee, Rishav Hada, Millicent Ochieng, Krithika Ramesh, Prachi Jain, Akshay Nambi, Tanuja Ganu, Sameer Segal, Maxamed Axmed, Kalika Bali, and Sunayana Sitaram. 2023. MEGA: Multilingual Evaluation of Generative AI.

Ali Saleh Alammary. 2022. BERT Models for Arabic Text Classification: A Systematic Review. *Applied Sciences*, 12(11).

Ebtesam Almazrouei, Ruxandra Cojocaru, Michele Baldo, Quentin Malartic, Hamza Alobeidli, Daniele Mazzotta, Guilherme Penedo, Giulia Campesan, Mugariya Farooq, Maitha Alhammadi, Julien Launay, and Badreddine Noune. 2023. AlGhafa Evaluation Benchmark for Arabic Language Models. In Hassan Sawaf, Samhaa El-Beltagy, Wajdi Zaghouani, Walid Magdy, Ahmed Abdelali, Nadi Tomeh, Ibrahim Abu Farha, Nizar Habash, Salam Khalifa, Amr Keleg, Hatem Haddad, Imed Zitouni, Khalil Mrini, and Rawan Almatham, editors, *Proceedings of ArabicNLP 2023*, pages 244–275, Singapore (Hybrid). Association for Computational Linguistics.

Khalid Al-Najjar, Mika Hämäläinen, Niko Partanen, and Jack Rueter. 2020. Automated Prediction of Medieval Arabic Diacritics. *ArXiv*, abs/2010.05269.

Abdulmohsen Al-Thubaity, Sakhar Alkhereyf, Hanan Murayshid, Nouf Alshalawi, Raghad Alateeq, Rawabi Almutairi, Razan Alsuwailem, Manal Alhassoun, and Imaan Alkhanen. 2023. Evaluating ChatGPT and Bard AI on Arabic Sentiment Analysis. In Hassan Sawaf, Samhaa El-Beltagy, Wajdi Zaghouani, Walid Magdy, Ahmed Abdelali, Nadi Tomeh, Ibrahim Abu Farha, Nizar Habash, Salam Khalifa, Amr Keleg, Hatem Haddad, Imed Zitouni, Khalil Mrini, and Rawan Almatham, editors, *Proceedings of ArabicNLP 2023*, pages 335–349, Singapore (Hybrid). Association for Computational Linguistics.

Zaid Alyafeai, Maged S. Alshaibani, Badr AlKhamissi, Hamzah Luqman, Ebrahim Alareqi, and Ali Fadel. 2023. Taqyim: Evaluating Arabic NLP Tasks Using ChatGPT Models. *ArXiv*, abs/2306.16322.

Wissam Antoun, Fady Baly, and Hazem Hajj. 2020. AraBERT: Transformer-based Model for Arabic Language Understanding. In *Proceedings of the 4th Workshop on Open-Source Arabic Corpora and Processing Tools, with a Shared Task on Offensive Language Detection*, pages 9–15, Marseille, France. European Language Resource Association.

Yejin Bang, Samuel Cahyawijaya, Nayeon Lee, Wenliang Dai, Dan Su, Bryan Wilie, Holy Lovenia, Ziwei Ji, Tiezheng Yu, Willy Chung, Quyet V. Do, Yan Xu, and Pascale Fung. 2023. A Multitask, Multilingual, Multimodal Evaluation of ChatGPT on Reasoning, Hallucination, and Interactivity.

M Saiful Bari, Yazeed Alnumay, Norah A. Alzahrani, Nouf M. Alotaibi, Hisham A. Alyahya, Sultan AlRashed, Faisal A. Mirza, Shaykhah Z. Alsubaie, Hassan A. Alahmed, Ghadah Alabduljabbar, Raghad Alkhathran, Yousef Almushayqih, Raneem Alnajim, Salman Alsubaihi, Maryam Al Mansour, Majed Alrubaian, Ali Alammari, Zaki Alawami, Abdulmohsen Al-Thubaity, et al. 2024. ALLaM: Large Language Models for Arabic and English.

Sébastien Bubeck, Varun Chandrasekaran, Ronen Eldan, Johannes Gehrke, Eric Horvitz, Ece Kamar, Peter Lee, Yin Tat Lee, Yuanzhi Li, Scott Lundberg, Harsha Nori, Hamid Palangi, Marco Tulio Ribeiro, and Yi Zhang. 2023. Sparks of

Artificial General Intelligence: Early experiments with GPT-4.

AbdelRahim Elmadany, El Moatez Billah Nagoudi, and Muhammad Abdul-Mageed. 2023a. Octopus: A Multitask Model and Toolkit for Arabic Natural Language Generation. In Hassan Sawaf, Samhaa El-Beltagy, Wajdi Zaghouani, Walid Magdy, Ahmed Abdelali, Nadi Tomeh, Ibrahim Abu Farha, Nizar Habash, Salam Khalifa, Amr Keleg, Hatem Haddad, Imed Zitouni, Khalil Mrini, and Rawan Almatham, editors, *Proceedings of ArabicNLP 2023*, pages 232–243, Singapore (Hybrid). Association for Computational Linguistics.

AbdelRahim Elmadany, ElMoatez Billah Nagoudi, and Muhammad Abdul-Mageed. 2023b. ORCA: A Challenging Benchmark for Arabic Language Understanding. In Anna Rogers, Jordan Boyd-Graber, and Naoaki Okazaki, editors, *Findings of the Association for Computational Linguistics: ACL 2023*, pages 9559–9586, Toronto, Canada. Association for Computational Linguistics.

Jessica Nayeli López Espejel, El Hassane Ettifouri, Mahaman Sanoussi Yahaya Alassan, El Mehdi Chouham, and Walid Dahhane. 2023. GPT-3.5, GPT-4, or BARD? Evaluating LLMs Reasoning Ability in Zero-Shot Setting and Performance Boosting Through Prompts. In

Yuan Gao, Ruili Wang, and Feng Hou. 2023. How to Design Translation Prompts for ChatGPT: An Empirical Study.

Aidan Gomez. 2024. Introducing Command R+: A Scalable LLM Built for Business.

Haoyang Huang, Tianyi Tang, Dongdong Zhang, Wayne Xin Zhao, Ting Song, Yan Xia, and Furu Wei. 2023a. Not All Languages Are Created Equal in LLMs: Improving Multilingual Capability by Cross-Lingual-Thought Prompting.

Huang Huang, Fei Yu, Jianqing Zhu, Xuening Sun, Hao Cheng, Dingjie Song, Zhihong Chen, Abdulmohsen Alharthi, Bang An, Ziche Liu, Zhiyi Zhang, Junying Chen, Jianquan Li, Benyou Wang, Lian Zhang, Ruoyu Sun, Xiang Wan, Haizhou Li, and Jinchao Xu. 2023b. AceGPT, Localizing Large Language Models in Arabic. *ArXiv*, abs/2309.12053.

Go Inoue, Bashar Alhafni, Nurpeiis Baimukan, Houda Bouamor, and Nizar Habash. 2021. The Interplay of Variant, Size, and Task Type in Arabic Pre-trained Language Models. In *Proceedings of the Sixth Arabic Natural Language Processing Workshop*, pages 92–104, Kyiv, Ukraine (Virtual). Association for Computational Linguistics.

Wenxiang Jiao, Wenxuan Wang, Jen-tse Huang, Xing Wang, Shuming Shi, and Zhaopeng Tu. 2023. Is ChatGPT A Good Translator? Yes With GPT-4 As The Engine.

Karima Kadaoui, Samar M. Magdy, Abdul Waheed, Md Tawkat Islam Khondaker, Ahmed Oumar El-Shangiti, El Moatez Billah Nagoudi, and Muhammad Abdul-Mageed. 2023. TARJAMAT: Evaluation of Bard and ChatGPT on Machine Translation of Ten Arabic Varieties.

Marzena Karpinska and Mohit Iyyer. 2023. Large language models effectively leverage document-level context for literary translation, but critical errors persist.

Md Tawkat Islam Khondaker, Abdul Waheed, El Moatez Billah Nagoudi, and Muhammad Abdul-Mageed. 2023. GPTAraEval: A Comprehensive Evaluation of ChatGPT on Arabic NLP. *ArXiv*, abs/2305.14976.

Sang Yun Kwon, Gagan Bhatia, El Moatez Billah Nagoudi, and Muhammad Abdul-Mageed. 2023. Beyond English: Evaluating LLMs for Arabic Grammatical Error Correction. *ArXiv*, abs/2312.08400.

Viet Dac Lai, Nghia Trung Ngo, Amir Pouran Ben Veyseh, Hieu Man, Franck Dernoncourt, Trung Bui, and Thien Huu Nguyen. 2023. ChatGPT Beyond English: Towards a Comprehensive Evaluation of Large Language Models in Multilingual Learning.

Md Tahmid Rahman Laskar, M. Saiful Bari, Mizanur Rahman, Md Amran Hossen Bhuiyan, Shafiq Joty, and Jimmy Xiangji Huang. 2023. A Systematic Study and Comprehensive Evaluation of ChatGPT on Benchmark Datasets.

Hongyuan Lu, Haoyang Huang, Dongdong Zhang, Haoran Yang, Wai Lam, and Furu Wei. 2023. Chain-of-Dictionary Prompting Elicits Translation in Large Language Models.

Youssef Mansour, Ashraf Elnagar, and Sane Yagi. 2023. Punctuation Prediction for the Arabic Language. In Abhishek Swaroop, Vineet Kansal, Giancarlo Fortino, and Aboul Ella Hassanien, editors, *Proceedings of Fourth Doctoral Symposium on Computational Intelligence*, volume 726 of *Lecture Notes in Networks and Systems*, pages 579–592. Springer Nature Singapore, Singapore.

El Moatez Billah Nagoudi, AbdelRahim Elmadany, Ahmed El-Shangiti, and Muhammad Abdul-Mageed. 2023. Dolphin: A Challenging and Diverse Benchmark for Arabic NLG.

Oluwatosin Ogundare and Gustavo Quiros Araya. 2023. Comparative Analysis of CHATGPT and the evolution of language models.

OpenAI. 2024. Hello GPT-4o.

Keqin Peng, Liang Ding, Qihuang Zhong, Li Shen, Xuebo Liu, Min Zhang, Yuanxin Ouyang, and Dacheng Tao. 2023. Towards Making the Most of ChatGPT for Machine Translation.

Sundar Pichai and Demis Hassabis. 2024. Our next-generation model: Gemini 1.5.

Chengwei Qin, Aston Zhang, Zhuosheng Zhang, Jiaao Chen, Michihiro Yasunaga, and Diyi Yang. 2023. Is ChatGPT a General-Purpose Natural Language Processing Task Solver?

Abdelrahman Sakr and Marwan Torki. 2023. AraPunc: Arabic Punctuation Restoration Using Transformers. *2023 20th ACS/IEEE International Conference on Computer Systems and Applications (AICCSA)*:1–6.

Neha Sengupta, Sunil Kumar Sahu, Bokang Jia, Satheesh Katipomu, Haonan Li, Fajri Koto, William Marshall, Gurpreet Gosal, Cynthia Liu, Zhiming Chen, Osama Mohammed Afzal, Samta Kamboj, Onkar Pandit, Rahul Pal, Lalit Pradhan, Zain Muhammad Mujahid, Massa Baali, Xudong Han, Sondos Mahmoud Bsharat, et al. 2023. Jais and Jais-chat: Arabic-Centric Foundation and Instruction-Tuned Open Generative Large Language Models.

SILMA. 2024. Empowering Arabic Speakers with Cutting-Edge Generative AI Technologies.

Andrea Sottana, Bin Liang, Kai Zou, and Zheng Yuan. 2023. Evaluation Metrics in the Era of GPT-4: Reliably Evaluating Large Language Models on Sequence to Sequence Tasks. In *Conference on Empirical Methods in Natural Language Processing*.

Monica Sunkara, S. Ronanki, Kalpit Dixit, S. Bodapati, and Katrin Kirchhoff. 2020. Robust Prediction of Punctuation and Truecasing for Medical ASR. *ArXiv*, abs/2007.02025.

Longyue Wang, Chenyang Lyu, Tianbo Ji, Zhirui Zhang, Dian Yu, Shuming Shi, and Zhaopeng Tu. 2023. Document-Level Machine Translation with Large Language Models.

Xueyang Wu, Su Zhu, Yue Wu, and Kai Yu. 2016. Rich punctuations prediction using large-scale deep learning. *2016 10th International Symposium on Chinese Spoken Language Processing (ISCSLP)*:1–5.

Jiangyan Yi, Jianhua Tao, Zhengkun Tian, Ye Bai, and Cunhang Fan. 2020. Focal Loss for Punctuation Prediction. In *Interspeech*.

Zhikai Zhou, Tian Tan, and Yanmin Qian. 2022. Punctuation Prediction for Streaming On-Device Speech Recognition. *ICASSP 2022 - 2022 IEEE International Conference on Acoustics, Speech and Signal Processing (ICASSP)*:7277–7281.

Caleb Ziems, William Held, Omar Shaikh, Jiaao Chen, Zhehao Zhang, and Diyi Yang. 2024. Can Large Language Models Transform Computational Social Science?

Evaluating RAG Pipelines for Arabic Lexical Information Retrieval: A Comparative Study of Embedding and Generation Models

Raghad Al-Rasheed, Abdullah Al Muaddi, Hawra Aljasim, Rawan Al-Matham, Muneera Alhoshan, Asma Al Wazrah, Abdulrahman AlOsaimy

{Ralrasheed@ksaa.gov.sa, Abdullah.AlMuadddi@gmail.com, haljasim@ksaa.gov.sa, ralmatham@ksaa.gov.sa, malhoshan@ksaa.gov.sa, aalwazrah@ksaa.gov.sa, aalosaimy@ksaa.gov.sa}

Abstract

This paper investigates the effectiveness of retrieval-augmented generation (RAG) pipelines, focusing on the Arabic lexical information retrieval. Specifically, it analyzes how embedding models affect the recall of Arabic lexical information and evaluates the ability of large language models (LLMs) to produce accurate and contextually relevant answers within the RAG pipelines. We examine a dataset of over 88,000 words from the Riyadh dictionary and evaluate the models using metrics such as Top-K Recall, Mean Reciprocal Rank (MRR), F1 Score, Cosine Similarity, and Accuracy. The research assesses the capabilities of several embedding models, including E5-large, BGE, AraBERT, CAMeLBERT, and AraELECTRA, highlighting a disparity in performance between sentence embeddings and word embeddings. Sentence embedding with E5 achieved the best results, with a Top-5 Recall of 0.88, and an MRR of 0.48. For the generation models, we evaluated GPT-4, GPT-3.5, SILMA-9B, Gemini-1.5, Aya-8B, and AceGPT-13B based on their ability to generate accurate and contextually appropriate responses. GPT-4 demonstrated the best performance, achieving an F1 score of 0.90, an accuracy of 0.82, and a cosine similarity of 0.87. Our results emphasize the strengths and limitations of both embedding and generation models in Arabic tasks.

1 Introduction

The rise in significance of machine learning and natural language processing (NLP) for tackling challenging linguistic tasks has led to notable progress in embedding and generation models (El-Beltagy and Abdallah, 2024; Chirkova et al., 2024). In English, many studies have explored the effectiveness of RAG and embedding models, demonstrating improvements in tasks like question-answering and information retrieval (Chirkova et al., 2024; Setty et al., 2024). However, in Arabic, fewer studies have addressed the unique challenges posed by its complex morphology and diacritics, which significantly affect model performance (Khondaker et al., 2024; Hijazi et al., 2024).

The primary objectives of this study are to evaluate the performance of various semantic embedding models for Arabic text retrieval and to assess the capabilities of large language models (LLMs) in performing question-answering tasks in Arabic using a retrieval-augmented generation (RAG) pipeline.

To achieve these goals, we conducted several experiments to address two key research questions: 1)How do different embedding models affect the recall of Arabic lexical information retrieval in RAG pipeline? 2)What is the best LLM for generating accurate and contextually relevant answers to Arabic lexical information questions within a RAG framework?

Our study goes further by focusing on extracting pertinent information from the Riyadh dictionary database, which includes more than 88,000 Arabic words . Embedding models are evaluated using metrics such as Recall@K and Mean Reciprocal Rank (MRR), while generation models are evaluated by accuracy, F1-score, and cosine similarity in answering context-specific questions. The study compares both closed-source and open-source models, including E5-large, AraBERT, CAMeLBERT, and AraELECTRA for embedding tasks, and GPT-4, GPT-3.5, SILMA-9B, Gemini-1.5, Aya-8B, and AceGPT-13B for generation tasks.

Our research provides valuable insights into the effectiveness of sentence embeddings versus word embeddings and explores how generation models manage semantic precision. Our findings aim to enhance the efficiency of NLP systems for Arabic.

The remainder of this paper is organized as follows: Section 2 presents the Literature Review, followed by the Methodology in Section 3. Sec-

Processings of the 1st Workshop on NLP for Languages Using Arabic Script (AbjadNLP), pages 155–164
January 19, 2025.

tion 4 provides a detailed description of the Dataset, while Section 5 discusses the Evaluation Dataset. The Results and Discussion are presented in Section 6, and finally, the study concludes with the Conclusion in Section 7.

2 Literature Review

Many studies have explored the effectiveness of retrieval-augmented generation (RAG) in enhancing large language models (LLMs) for tasks such as question-answering and information retrieval. by combining retrieval and generation techniques, these models produce more accurate and context-aware responses (Chirkova et al., 2024; Setty et al., 2024). Although these studies often focus on multilingual settings, they primarily concentrate on languages like English.

Research has highlighted the importance of embedding model selection for RAG systems, demonstrating that model similarity significantly impacts retrieval accuracy (Caspari et al., 2024; Montahaei et al., 2019). Additionally, semantic search plays a critical role in enhancing the relevance of generated content across various domains (Mahboub et al., 2024).

In the context of Arabic, research faces unique challenges due to the language's complex morphology and diverse dialects. Arabic-specific studies have begun to address these issues, particularly in the application of RAG. Benchmarks like LAraBench (Abdelali et al., 2024) and ArabLegalEval (Hijazi et al., 2024) demonstrate that dedicated Arabic models outperform general-purpose LLMs in tasks such as legal reasoning and sentiment analysis. However, the challenges posed by diacritics and dialect variation further complicate the optimization of RAG models (Khondaker et al., 2024). Diacritics, which are crucial for conveying meaning in written Arabic, have been largely overlooked in previous studies, leaving a gap in understanding their impact on model performance.

This study builds on prior research by evaluating a diverse set of open-source and proprietary models, including GPT-4, SILMA-9B, and E5-large, in the context of Arabic retrieval-augmented generation (RAG) pipelines. Using metrics such as Top-K Recall, MRR, F1 score, and cosine similarity, it provides a comprehensive performance comparison for Arabic lexical information retrieval and generation tasks. Additionally, the study examines over 88,000 Arabic words from the Riyadh dictionary, offering valuable insights into model capabilities for answering Arabic lexical information questions.

3 Methodology

The methodology involves a systematic, multi-step process as illustrated in Figure 1. The following sections provide detailed descriptions of the semantic embedding models, the vector indexing techniques, and the LLMs employed as generative models in this study.

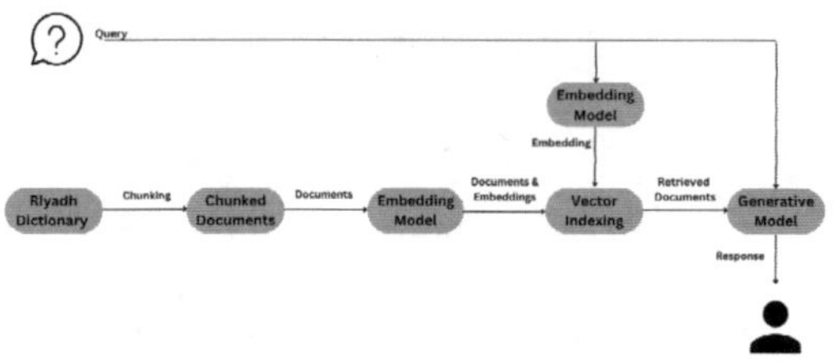

Figure 1: Illustration of the RAG methodology used in this study.

3.1 Corpus Preparation and Chunking

The initial step involves the preparation of the text corpus, with a focus on preserving the semantic integrity of the content. The corpus is segmented on a paragraph-by-paragraph basis, as described in Section 4, ensuring that the meaning and context within each paragraph are maintained. Each paragraph is restricted to a maximum of 512 tokens to comply with the token limit of the embedding model. In instances where a paragraph exceeds this limit, it is further divided into overlapping segments with an overlap of 50 tokens. This overlap maintains contextual continuity and ensures no critical information is lost during segmentation.

3.2 Embedding Models

Two types of embeddings are integrated in this study: word token embeddings with mean pooling, and sentence embeddings.These models were selected based on findings in previous research highlighted in the Section 2,

3.2.1 Word Embeddings

This approach involves generating embeddings for individual word tokens within a text, followed by applying a mean pooling layer to produce a single vector representation for each chunk of text. The models selected for this task include AraBERT v2 by (Antoun et al., 2020a), CAMeLBERT by Inoue et al. (2021), and AraELECTRA by Antoun et al. (2020b), chosen for their demonstrated effectiveness in handling Arabic text due to extensive pretraining on large-scale Arabic corpora.

- **AraBERT v2:** A transformer-based language model specifically designed for the Arabic language, AraBERT v2 has been trained on a vast corpus of Arabic text. Its architecture is based on the BERT model, adapted and fine-tuned to better address the linguistic characteristics of Arabic.

- **CAMeLBERT:** Part of the CAMeL toolkit, this model provides a comprehensive suite of Arabic NLP resources. CAMeLBERT is trained on a diverse set of Arabic dialects and formal texts.

- **AraELECTRA:** Using the ELECTRA pretraining approach, AraELECTRA focuses on learning through a discriminative model that identifies and corrects corrupted tokens in a text.

3.2.2 Sentence Embeddings

This approach involves generating embeddings for entire sentences or paragraphs, producing a single vector representation that captures the overall semantic content of the text. For this purpose, several models are selected:

- **E5-large:** A multilingual sentence embedding model developed by (Wang et al., 2022), E5-large is designed to generate high-quality semantic representations across multiple languages, including Arabic. It utilizes a text-to-text framework and is trained on a diverse range of tasks, including natural language inference, question answering, and semantic similarity.

- **Arabic-NLI-Matryoshka:** This model is a sentence-transformer finetuned from the AraBERT v2 base model on the Arabic NLI triplet dataset. It maps Arabic sentences and paragraphs to dense vectors, designed for tasks such as semantic textual similarity, semantic search, and text classification.

- **BGE (Big General Embeddings):** Originally developed to produce high-quality sentence embeddings for Chinese by (Xiao et al., 2023), the BGE model has also been trained on Arabic documents, thereby extending its applicability to Arabic text.

3.3 Vector Indexing

For the storage and retrieval of embedding vectors, this study employs FAISS (Facebook AI Similarity Search) by (Johnson et al., 2019), a well-known and efficient library designed for high-dimensional vector search. In this study, FAISS is utilized with the IndexFlatIP index, which leverages inner product calculations and the L2 distance metric to optimize the retrieval process. Additionally, cosine similarity is employed as the primary measure of similarity between vectors due to its effectiveness in capturing semantic relationships in high-dimensional spaces.

3.4 Generation

The final component of the methodology involves using LLMs as generative models for providing relevant answers to Arabic lexical information questions. After retrieving the most relevant documents from the vector store, a simple and clear prompt is used to provide context to the LLMs, as shown in Figure 2.To ensure the model follows the prompt exactly and generates deterministic outputs, the temperature parameter was set to 0 during all evaluations.

Original (Arabic)
إذا تم سؤالك عن كلمة معينة قم باستخراج الاجابة كما هي من النص من غير تغيير {context} {question}
Translation
If asked about a specific word, extract the answer exactly as it appears in the text without any changes. {context} {question}

Figure 2: Illustration of the prompt used

3.5 Corpus Preparation and Chunking

The study evaluates the performance of several LLMs, including GPT-3.5 (Ouyang et al., 2022), GPT 4o (OpenAI, 2023), Gemini-Flash-1.5 (Reid et al., 2024), AceGPT (Huang et al., 2023), Aya 8B (Aryabumi et al., 2024), and SILMA-9B-Instruct

(AI, 2023). These models were selected for their diversity in architecture, size, and pre-training, as well as their high ranking on the Arabic NLP leaderboard.[1] Furthermore, their inclusion was informed by findings from previous literature, which highlight their effectiveness in various Arabic natural language processing tasks such as text generation, sentiment analysis, and semantic understanding.

By evaluating this diverse set of LLMs, the study aims to provide insights into the most effective approaches for Arabic language generation within a retrieval-augmented pipeline to answer Arabic lexical information questions. The inclusion of models with high leaderboard rankings and evidence from prior research ensures that the study leverages state-of-the-art advancements in Arabic generative language models.

3.6 Embedding Models Evaluation

First, we evaluated the embedding models' ability to retrieve relevant context from 88,000 contexts within the Riyadh dictionary dataset, based on the provided question. The performance was assessed using **recall @K** (with k=1, k=3, and k=5) and **Mean Reciprocal Rank (MRR)**.

- **Recall @K Equation:**

$$Recall@K = \frac{\text{Number of relevant documents in top K}}{\text{Total number of relevent documents}} \quad (1)$$

- **Mean Reciprocal Rank (MRR) Equation:**

$$MRR = \frac{1}{|U|}\sum_{u=1}^{|U|}\frac{1}{rank_u} \quad (2)$$

These equations were used to measure how well the embedding models could identify the most relevant context for a given query.

3.7 Generation Models Evaluation

After retrieving the top 5 (k=5) potential contexts using the embedding models, the generation models were evaluated on their ability to select the correct context from these top candidates and generate accurate and contextually appropriate answers. This part of the evaluation tested how well the generation models could utilize the provided contexts to formulate coherent and correct answers.

The evaluations will utilize the following metrics:

- **F1 Score:** F1 Score: A perfect F1 score of 1 indicates optimal precision and recall, meaning all predictions were correct.

$$\text{F1 Score} = 2 * \frac{Precision * Recall}{Precision + Recall} \quad (3)$$

- **Cosine Similarity:** A perfect cosine similarity score of 1 signifies that the reconstructed embedding is identical to the reference.

$$\text{Cosine Similarity} = \frac{\sum_{i=1}^{N} p_i q_i}{\sqrt{\sum_{i=1}^{N} p_i^2}\sqrt{\sum_{i=1}^{N} q_i^2}} \quad (4)$$

- **Accuracy:** This measures the percentage of correct predictions out of the total predictions made.

$$Accuracy = \frac{\text{Number of correct predictions}}{\text{Total number of predictions}} \quad (5)$$

Note: The dataset used for evaluation in 5 is unbalanced, which means that the performance of the generation models is assessed with special consideration to this characteristic. The evaluation metrics provide a comprehensive measure of the models' ability to select the correct context and generate accurate, coherent responses while accounting for challenges posed by an uneven distribution of data.

To ensure a fair evaluation of the models, the following micro-averaging formulas were used for F1-Score, Cosine Similarity, and Accuracy. Micro-averaging calculates the overall performance by considering the contributions of all instances equally, regardless of their class.

- **F1 Micro:** Computes the global F1 score by aggregating the contributions of all classes to precision and recall.

$$\text{F1}_{micro} = 2 * \frac{Precision_{micro} * Recall_{micro}}{Precision_{micro} + Recall_{micro}} \quad (6)$$

- **Cosine Similarity Micro:** Computes the overall cosine similarity by averaging across all instances.

$$CosineSimilarity_{micro} = \frac{\sum_{i=1}^{N} p_i q_i}{\sqrt{\sum_{i=1}^{N} p_i^2}\sqrt{\sum_{i=1}^{N} q_i^2}} \quad (7)$$

where N is the total number of instances.

- **Accuracy Micro:** Computes the overall accuracy by considering all instances equally.

$$\text{Accuracy}_{micro} = \frac{\text{Number of correct predictions}}{\text{Total number of predictions}} \quad (8)$$

[1] https://huggingface.co/spaces/OALL/Open-Arabic-LLM-Leaderboard

4 Dataset description

To compare the models used in the RAG pipeline, we used the Riyadh dictionary.[2]. The dataset comprises over 88,000 words, each including detailed information such as the stem, part of speech (POS), morphological pattern, non-diacritic lemma, definition (some words have multiple definitions, with a maximum of 31 definitions for a single word), translation, example, type, entry lemma of related words, and semantic field.

The data is structured and linked as shown in Figure 3 and Figure 4.

Original (Arabic)

الكلمة: [lemma]، وجذرها: [stem]، وهي [pos]
على وزن: [morphological Patterns]،
وشكلها بلا حركات: [nonDiacriticsLemma].

معنى الكلمة: [definition]،
ويقابلها في اللغة [translation] :[language].
ومن أمثلتها: [example]. للكلمة علاقة [type] بالكلمة: [related].

Translation

The word: [lemma], and its root: [stem], it is [pos]
in the pattern: [morphological Patterns],
and its form without diacritics is: [nonDiacriticsLemma].

The meaning of the word: [definition],
and its equivalent in [language]: [translation].
Examples include: [example].
The word has a [type] relation with the word: [related].

Figure 3: illustrate how The data is structured in the dataset.

```
{
  "lemma": "مُبْتَلٍ",
  "stem": "ب ل و",
  "pos": "صفة فاعل",
  "morphological Patterns":"مُفْتَعِل",
  "nonDiacriticsLemma": "مبتل",
  "definition": "مُختبِر وممتحِن.",
  "language": "الانجليزية",
  "translations": "afflicted",
  "examples":"تَرى المُعافى يَعذِرُ المُبتَلى ...",
  "type": "ترادف",
  "related": ["مُختَبِر","مُمْتَحِن"]
}
```

Figure 4: example that illustrates how the data was stored and linked.

[2]https://dictionary.ksaa.gov.sa/

5 Evaluation Dataset

The evaluation dataset includes 585 questions and answers distributed across eight categories, each targeting a specific linguistic aspect. These questions are based on 195 randomly selected words from the Riyadh dictionary and were meticulously crafted by Arabic linguists. The total number of questions per category is shown in Figure 5

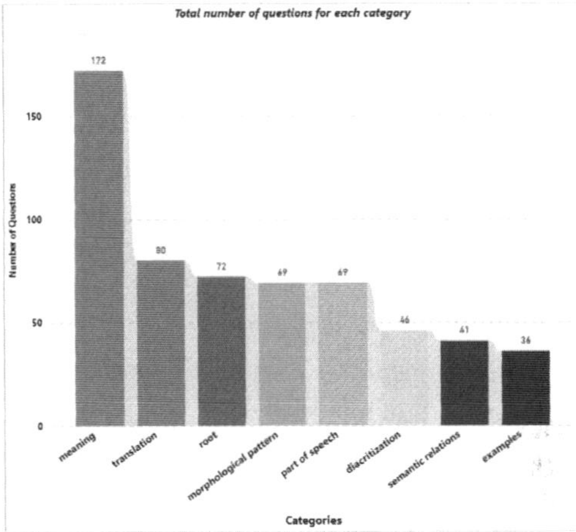

Figure 5: Total number of questions for each category in the evaluation dataset.

Each category targets a specific linguistic aspect:

- **Translation:** Involves translating words to and from Arabic.
- **Diacritization:** Focuses on accurately applying diacritical marks to ensure proper pronunciation and meaning of words.
- **Root:** Involves identifying the root forms of words.
- **Meaning:** Aims to provide definitions of words.
- **Morphological Pattern:** Examines the structural templates that define word forms.
- **Part of Speech:** Identifies the grammatical category of words.
- **Examples:** Identifying sentences that use words correctly.
- **Semantic Relations:** Explores relationships such as synonyms, antonyms, between words.

The evaluation of the RAG models involves two main components: assessing the embedding models ability to retrieve relevant context and evaluating the generation models performance in answering questions based on that context. The dataset includes ground truth context and answers developed by Arabic linguists, ensuring a reliable benchmark for these tasks.

6 Results and Discussion

In this section, we present the results of our study, focusing on the evaluation of two key areas: retrieval and generation LLMs.

The retrieval section examines the effectiveness of various embedding models in accurately identifying and retrieving relevant text segments from the Arabic dataset in Section 5. This part addresses the research question: How do different embedding models affect the recall of Arabic lexical information retrieval in RAG pipeline?

The generation section evaluates the performance of different LLMs in Arabic question-answering tasks, answers the question: What is the best LLM for generating accurate and contextually relevant answers to Arabic lexical information questions within a RAG pipeline?

6.1 Retrieval Embedding Models

The retrieval evaluation examined the capability of six semantic embedding models to accurately retrieve text segments that correspond to input queries. These models, representing both word embeddings with mean pooling and sentence embeddings, were tested on their ability to manage the complexities of Arabic text, particularly in the presence of diacritics. Performance was measured using Top-k Recall (k = 1, 3, 5) and MRR. The results, summarized in 1, reveal the performance differences among the evaluated models.

Model	**Top1**	**Top3**	**Top5**	**MRR**
E5	0.37	0.65	0.88	0.48
BGE	0.30	0.62	0.80	0.42
NLI	0.09	0.14	0.20	0.11
AraBERT v02	0.06	0.08	0.11	0.07
CamelBERT	0.04	0.10	0.16	0.06
AraElectra	0.02	0.06	0.09	0.04

Table 1: The table shows the Top-1, Top-3, and Top-5 Recall as well as MRR for each embedding model evaluated.

The E5 model demonstrated high performance across all metrics, achieving the highest scores in all Top-K Recall and MRR (0.48).This performance suggests that E5 effectively retrieves relevant context, with its architecture and training methodology being particularly well-suited for capturing the nuances of Arabic text.

BGE also showed strong performance, particularly in Top-3 (0.62) and Top-5 (0.80) Recall, indicating its capability to retrieve relevant information within a broader scope. However, its slightly lower Top-1 Recall (0.30) and MRR (0.42) compared to E5 suggest that while BGE is highly competitive, it may be less precise in consistently identifying the most relevant context.

A clear performance gap exists between E5, BGE, and the other models, particularly in Top-K Recall and MRR metrics. The reduced effectiveness of NLI, CamelBERT, AraBERT v02, and AraElectra in retrieving relevant segments suggests potential limitations in their model architectures or training data for this specific task.

The results indicate that sentence embeddings, particularly those produced by E5 and BGE, outperform word embeddings in the context of Arabic text. This suggests that sentence-level embeddings may be better suited for tasks requiring a comprehensive understanding of semantic content.

6.2 Generation with LLMs

To evaluate the performance of generation LLMs in answering Arabic lexical information questions, we evaluated various models using the dataset described in Section 5. The E5 model with k=5 context retrieval was selected to provide context based on our findings in Section 6.1.

The results in Table 2 summarizes the performance metrics of the evaluated LLMs. Presents a variations in performance across models and tasks. GPT-4o emerged as the top-performing model, achieving the highest overall micro F1-score 0.90 and micro accuracy 0.82, demonstrating its ability to generate accurate and relevant answers. SILMA-9B-Instruct excelled in micro cosine similarity 0.95, reflecting strong semantic alignment. Gemini-1.5 Flash performed robustly with a micro F1-score of 0.84 and micro accuracy of 0.72, while Aya 8B showed strength in micro cosine similarity 0.90 but exhibited lower micro F1-score 0.74 and micro accuracy 0.59, indicating its ability to capture semantic meaning but with reduced precision. GPT-3.5 displayed moderate performance,

Tasks	GPT-4o			Gemini-1.5-flash			SILMA-9B-Instruct			Aya 8B			GPT-3.5			AceGPT 13B		
	F1	Acc	Cos	F1	Acc	Cos	F1	Acc	Cos	F1	Acc	Cos	F1	Acc	Cos	F1	Acc	Cos
Translation	0.90	0.81	0.83	0.80	0.66	0.86	0.84	0.73	0.95	0.73	0.58	0.89	0.73	0.58	0.81	0.74	0.59	0.81
Diacritization	0.91	0.83	0.95	0.77	0.63	0.95	0.59	0.41	0.94	0.61	0.44	0.92	0.59	0.41	0.96	0.44	0.28	0.89
Root	0.99	0.97	0.85	0.96	0.93	0.85	0.97	0.94	0.99	0.96	0.93	0.95	0.97	0.94	0.86	0.96	0.92	0.85
Meaning	0.90	0.83	0.89	0.86	0.76	0.88	0.83	0.71	0.93	0.81	0.69	0.90	0.71	0.55	0.88	0.71	0.55	0.85
Morphological Pattern	0.98	0.96	0.86	0.94	0.88	0.86	0.91	0.84	0.99	0.80	0.67	0.94	0.87	0.77	0.86	0.82	0.70	0.85
Part of Speech	0.91	0.83	0.85	0.80	0.67	0.86	0.58	0.41	0.94	0.43	0.28	0.87	0.59	0.42	0.83	0.18	0.10	0.82
Examples	0.50	0.33	0.89	0.40	0.25	0.87	0.47	0.31	0.87	0.50	0.33	0.86	0.15	0.08	0.84	0.36	0.22	0.83
Semantic Relations	0.86	0.76	0.83	0.40	0.71	0.82	0.79	0.66	0.94	0.63	0.46	0.84	0.54	0.37	0.83	0.48	0.32	0.79
Average	**0.90**	**0.82**	**0.87**	**0.84**	**0.73**	**0.87**	**0.80**	**0.67**	**0.95**	**0.75**	**0.59**	**0.90**	**0.72**	**0.56**	**0.87**	**0.67**	**0.51**	**0.84**

Table 2: Model performance metrics across various tasks for different models. Metrics include F1-score (F1), Accuracy (Acc), and Cosine Similarity (Cos). The "Average" row represents the micro-average across all tasks.

with a micro F1-score of 0.72, micro accuracy of 0.56, and micro cosine similarity of 0.87, reflecting limitations in accuracy. AceGPT 13B was the weakest performer, with a micro F1-score of 0.67, micro accuracy of 0.51, and a relatively decent micro cosine similarity of 0.84. Despite being an Arabic-specific LLM, AceGPT 13B's precision and accuracy issues highlight significant gaps in its linguistic capabilities.

To evaluate the models' performance across eight distinct Arabic language processing tasks showed patterns in their capabilities and limitations within a RAG framework across different tasks. The analysis of semantic relations, diacritization, root extraction, meanings, morphological pattern recognition, part of speech tagging, example generation, and translation tasks shown in the Appendix A a sample of models responses across the tasks providing a thorough assessment of each model's linguistic capabilities.

Diacritization, which requires accurately applying Arabic vowel markers, proved challenging for most models. GPT-4o performed with the highest accuracy, closely aligning with the ground truth, achieving an F1-score of 0.91 and an accuracy of 0.83. For instance, in the task involving "أَسْهُمُ التَّأْسِيسِ", GPT-4o successfully applied the correct diacritics, producing "أَسْهُمُ التَّأْسِيسِ", distinguishing it from other models. In contrast, GPT-3.5 showed partial success, with an F1-score of 0.77 and accuracy of 0.63, but often applied diacritics inconsistently. For example, it produced partially diacritized outputs as"أسْهُم التأسيس", failing to fully resolve ambiguities. Other models, including Gemini-1.5 Flash, SILMA-9B-Instruct, Aya 8B, and AceGPT 13B, frequently returned unmarked text, such as "اسهم التأسيس", as reflected in their lower F1-scores of 0.59–0.61 and accuracies of 0.28–0.44. This limitation stems from their training data and tokenizers, which do not prioritize diacritical information, resulting in outputs unsuitable for applications that depend on precise diacritic representation.

Conversely, root extraction appears as the highest-performing task, with all models achieving high F1-scores 0.957 to 0.986. The consistent accuracy across models demonstrated a steady handling of tasks requiring root extraction, exemplified as in the Appendix A by their correct identification of "ل و م" as the root of "ملوم".

The meanings task tested the models' ability to provide precise lexical definitions, where GPT-4o, Gemini-1.5 Flash, Aya 8B, and SILMA-9B-Instruct excelled by delivering definitions closely matching the ground truth. For instance, these models accurately defined "مُلَوِّم" as "مُوَبِّخٌ الشَّخْصَ مُعاتِبُهُ عَلى قَوْلٍ أَوْ عَمَلٍ غَيْرِ مُلائِمٍ" In contrast, GPT-3.5 and AceGPT 13B produced less accurate or overly verbose responses, underscoring their limitations in addressing tasks that demand lexical understanding.

Morphological pattern recognition, essential for understanding Arabic word structure, yielded accurate results across all evaluated models, with correct identification of the pattern "فُعَالَة" for "خُرَافَة". However, performance varied in consistency based on F1-score and accuracy.GPT-4o was the top performer, with an F1-score of 0.98 and accuracy of 0.96, consistently delivering precise outputs. Gemini-1.5 Flash and SILMA-9B-Instruct also performed strongly, achieving F1-scores of 0.94 and 0.91, with accuracies of 0.88 and 0.84. In comparison, AceGPT 13B and Aya 8B showed slightly lower performance, with F1-scores of 0.86 and 0.80 and accuracies of 0.82 and 0.67, respectively. These results emphasize the superior consistency of GPT-4o, Gemini-1.5 Flash, and SILMA-9B-Instruct, highlighting the impact of robust pretraining on morphological pattern recognition.

The translation task showed consistent performance across models, with most accurately translating terms like "مُشْتَبَه" to "suspect". Similarly, semantic relation identification, which assesses the ability to determine relationships between words or phrases, showed the strengths of SILMA-9B-Instruct and GPT-4o, as both models provided concise and accurate answers. For example, they correctly identified the relationship between "تَعْبِير" and "حُرِّيَّة اَلتَّعْبِيرِ" as collocation "تلازم". Gemini-1.5 Flash also demonstrated competence but occasionally included extraneous explanatory text. In contrast, GPT-3.5, Aya 8B, and AceGPT 13B struggled to accurately identify specific relationships, reflecting limitations in semantic reasoning.

POS tagging, a task requiring syntactic comprehension, revealed significant challenges for all models. Even GPT-4o, the leading performer, displayed inconsistencies in accuracy. Lower-performing models, such as GPT-3.5, Aya 8B, and AceGPT 13B, exhibited poor F1-scores and accuracy metrics. These results emphasize the need for refinement in Arabic-specific POS tagging. The most challenging task was generating accurate examples from the retrieved context, with GPT-4o achieving an F1-score of 0.50 and accuracy of 0.33 the highest among the models. Overall performance in this task, however, was suboptimal, with most models scoring below 0.50, underscoring the complexity of generative tasks in Arabic and the difficulty of synthesizing diverse, contextually appropriate examples.

This analysis of model performance across eight tasks highlights both strengths and limitations in the context of Arabic lexical information retrieval. GPT-4o consistently demonstrated superior performance, particularly in semantic reasoning and diacritization, while SILMA-9B-Instruct showed its ability to maintain semantic consistency . Gemini-1.5 Flash delivered reliable results across multiple tasks. On the other hand, models such as GPT-3.5, Aya 8B, and AceGPT 13B struggled with precision and linguistic understanding.

6.3 Adapting the RAG Pipeline for Abjad and Ajami Languages

The findings from this study on RAG for Arabic lexical retrieval can be extended to languages like Pashto, Sindhi, and Uyghur, as GPT-4 and Gemini-1.5 Flash already support these languages through multilingual. Their ability to handle morphologically complex languages such as Arabic and Persian suggests strong potential for processing similar languages that use Abjad or Ajami scripts.

The RAG pipeline discussed in this study could be adapted for these languages by leveraging its strengths in semantic representation and contextual generation. The embedding model E5, known for its multilingual support, already covers Persian and could be extended to Pashto, Sindhi, and Uyghur with additional pretraining on relevant datasets(Wang et al., 2022).

Adapting the RAG pipeline would require addressing specific challenges such as handling diacritics in Pashto and Sindhi, tone markings in Uyghur, and limited digital corpora for these languages. Transfer learning from Arabic and Persian models could mitigate these limitations, while customized tokenization methods tailored to Abjad and Ajami scripts could improve retrieval and generation tasks. Future research should explore expanding model capabilities through multilingual and script-specific fine-tuning.

7 Conclusion

This study evaluates the performance of embedding models in the recall of Arabic lexical information retrieval and LLMs in processing and generating relevant answers to Arabic lexical information questions. The results show that sentence embedding models like E5 outperform in retrieval tasks, achieving high accuracy in capturing semantic relationships. For generation tasks, models such as GPT-4o, Gemini-1.5 Flash, and SILMA-9B-Instruct perform strongly, with GPT-4o leading in generative capabilities. However, challenges remain in areas like diacritization and part-of-speech tagging, where models like GPT-3.5 and AceGPT 13B showed limitations. Future work should focus on optimizing these models and expanding datasets to improve their handling of complex Arabic linguistic features.

References

Ahmed Abdelali, Hamdy Mubarak, Shammur Absar Chowdhury, Maram Hasanain, and Ahmed Ali. 2024. Larabench: Benchmarking arabic ai with large language models. In *Proceedings of the 18th Conference of the European Chapter of the Association for Computational Linguistics*.

SILMA AI. 2023. Silma-9b-instruct-v1.0. `https://huggingface.co/silma-ai/SILMA-9B-Instruct-v1.0`.

Wissam Antoun, Fady Baly, and Hazem Hajj. 2020a. Arabert: Transformer-based model for arabic language understanding. *arXiv preprint arXiv:2003.00104*.

Wissam Antoun, Fady Baly, and Hazem Hajj. 2020b. Araelectra: Pre-training text discriminators for arabic language understanding. *arXiv preprint arXiv:2012.15516*.

Vashista Aryabumi, James Dang, Dhanusha Talupuru, Sarvesh Dash, Daniel Cairuz, Harrison Lin, et al. 2024. Aya 23: Open weight releases to further multilingual progress. *arXiv preprint arXiv:2405.15032*.

Laura Caspari, Kanishka Ghosh Dastidar, Saber Zerhoudi, Jelena Mitrovic, and Michael Granitzer. 2024. Beyond benchmarks: Evaluating embedding model similarity for retrieval augmented generation systems. *arXiv preprint arXiv:2407.08275*.

Nadezhda Chirkova, David Rau, Hervé Déjean, Thibault Formal, Stéphane Clinchant, and Vassilina Nikoulina. 2024. Retrieval-augmented generation in multilingual settings. *arXiv preprint arXiv:2407.01463*.

Samhaa R. El-Beltagy and Mohamed A. Abdallah. 2024. Exploring retrieval augmented generation in arabic. In *Procedia Computer Science*.

Faris Hijazi, Somayah AlHarbi, Abdulaziz AlHussein, et al. 2024. Arablegaleval: A multitask benchmark for assessing arabic legal knowledge in large language models. *arXiv preprint arXiv:2408.07983*.

Haoyang Huang, Feng Yu, Jiangzhe Zhu, Xiaowen Sun, Hao Cheng, Dawei Song, et al. 2023. Acegpt, localizing large language models in arabic. *arXiv preprint arXiv:2309.12053*.

Go Inoue, Bashar Alhafni, Nurpeiis Baimukan, Houda Bouamor, and Nizar Habash. 2021. The interplay of variant, size, and task type in arabic pre-trained language models. *arXiv preprint arXiv:2103.06678*.

Jeff Johnson, Matthijs Douze, and Hervé Jégou. 2019. Billion-scale similarity search with gpus. *IEEE Transactions on Big Data*, 7(3):535–547.

Md Tawkat Islam Khondaker, Numaan Naeem, Fatimah Lyba Khan, AbdelRahim A. Elmadany, and Muhammad Abdul-Mageed. 2024. Benchmarking llama-3 on arabic language generation tasks. In *Proceedings of The Second Arabic Natural Language Processing Conference*.

Ali Mahboub, Muhy Eddin Za'ter, et al. 2024. Evaluation of semantic search and its role in retrieved-augmented-generation (rag) for arabic language. *arXiv preprint arXiv:2403.18350*.

Ehsan Montahaei, Danial Alihosseini, and Mahdieh Soleymani Baghshah. 2019. Jointly measuring diversity and quality in text generation models. *arXiv preprint arXiv:1904.03971*.

OpenAI. 2023. GPT-4 Technical Report. Technical report.

Long Ouyang, Jeffrey Wu, Xu Jiang, Diogo Almeida, Carroll L Wainwright, Pamela Mishkin, Chong Zhang, Sandhini Agarwal, Katarina Slama, Alex Ray, John Schulman, Jacob Hilton, Fraser Kelton, Luke Miller, Maddie Simens, Amanda Askell, Peter Welinder, Paul Christiano, Jan Leike, and Ryan Lowe. 2022. Training language models to follow instructions with human feedback. *CoRR*.

Machel Reid, Nikolay Savinov, Dmitry Teplyashin, Dmitry Lepikhin, Timothy Lillicrap, Jean-Baptiste Alayrac, et al. 2024. Gemini 1.5: Unlocking multimodal understanding across millions of tokens of context. *arXiv preprint arXiv:2403.05530*.

Spurthi Setty, Harsh Thakkar, Alyssa Lee, Eden Chung, and Natan Vidra. 2024. Improving retrieval for rag based question answering models on financial documents. *arXiv preprint arXiv:2404.07221*.

Liang Wang, Nan Yang, Xiaolong Huang, Binxing Jiao, Linjun Yang, Daxin Jiang, Ranjan Majumder, and Furu Wei. 2022. Text embeddings by weakly-supervised contrastive pre-training. *arXiv preprint arXiv:2212.03533*.

Shitao Xiao, Zheng Liu, Peitian Zhang, and Niklas Muennighoff. 2023. C-pack: Packaged resources to advance general chinese embedding.

A Model Responses for different Task

Tasks	Question	Ground Truth Answer	SILMA-9B-Instruct	Aya 8B	Gemini 1.5 Flash	GPT4o	GPT3.5	AceGPT 13B
Semantic Relations	ما العلاقة الدلالية الرابطة بين (تَعْبِير) بـ (حُرِّيَّة اَلتَّعْبِير)؟	تلازم	تلازم	العلاقة الدلالية بين (تَعْبِير) و (حُرِّيَّة اَلتَّعْبِير) هي أن الأولى هي اسم والثاني هو اسم آخر يصف المعنى الأول.	العلاقة الدلالية الرابطة بين (تَعْبِير) بـ (حُرِّيَّة اَلتَّعْبِير) هي التلازم.	العلاقة الدلالية الرابطة بين (تَعْبِير) و (حُرِّيَّة اَلتَّعْبِير) هي علاقة تلازم.	العلاقة الدلالية الرابطة بين "تعبير" و "حرية التعبير" هي أن "تعبير" يشير إلى الفعل أو العملية التي تقوم بها الحرية التعبير.	العلاقة الدلالية الرابطة بين "تعبير" و "حرية التعبير" هي أن "تعبير" يشير إلى الفعل أو العملية التي تقوم بها الحرية التعبير.
Diacritization	اكتب (أسهم التأسيس) مع تشكيلها بالحركات	أَسْهُم اَلتَّأْسِيس	أسهم التأسيس	أسهم التأسيس	أَسْهُم اَلتَّأْسِيس، بتشكيلها: أسهم التأسيس	أَسْهُمُ التَّأْسِيسِ	أَسْهُم اَلتَّأْسِيس	أسهم التأسيس
Root	ما الجذر اللغوي لكلمة (ملوم)؟	ل و م	ل و م	ل و م	الجذر اللغوي لكلمة (ملوم) هو: ل و م	الجذر اللغوي لكلمة (ملوم) هو: ل و م.	الجذر اللغوي لكلمة "ملوم" هو "ل و م."	الجذر اللغوي لكلمة (ملوم) هو (ل و م).
Meaning	ما معنى كلمة (مُلَوِّم)؟	مُوَبِّخٌ الشَّخْصَ مُعاتِبُهُ على قَوْلٍ أَوْ عَمَلٍ غَيْرِ مُلائِم.	هو رأي سلبي	الإجابة: مُوَبِّخٌ الشَّخْصَ مُعاتِبُهُ على قَوْلٍ أَوْ عَمَلٍ غَيْرِ مُلائِمِ	معنى كلمة (مُلَوِّم) هو: مُوَبِّخٌ الشَّخْصَ مُعاتِبُهُ على قَوْلٍ أَوْ عَمَلٍ غَيْرِ مُلائِمِ	معنى كلمة (مُلَوِّم) هو: مُوَبِّخٌ الشَّخْصَ مُعاتِبُهُ على قَوْلٍ أَوْ عَمَلٍ غَيْرِ مُلائِمِ.	مُلَوِّم: مُوَبِّخٌ الشَّخْصَ مُعاتِبُهُ عَلى قَوْلٍ أَوْ عَمَلٍ غَيْرِ مُلائِمِ.	معنى كلمة (مُلَوِّم) هو مُوَبِّخ الشَّخْصَ مُعاتِبُهُ عَلى قَوْلٍ أَوْ عَمَلٍ غَيْرِ مُلائِمِ. هذه الكلمة تعني الشخص الذي يُلام أو يُوبخ شخصًا آخر بسبب قول أو عمل غير مناسب.
Part of Speech	ما القسم الكلامي لكلمة (تَعَاتَبْ)؟	فعل	فعل أمر	الجواب: فعل أمر	فعل أمر	القسم الكلامي لكلمة (تَعَاتَبْ) هو: فعل.	القسم الكلامي لكلمة (تَعَاتَبْ) هو فعل.	القسم الكلامي لكلمة (تَعَاتَبْ) هو الفعل.
Examples	أعطني مثالاً على استخدام كلمة (أوبال).	أوبالٌ حَجَرٌ كريمٌ نَصْفُ شَفَّافٍ بِألوانٍ مُتَعَدِّدَةٍ	أوبالٌ حَجَرٌ كريمٌ نَصْفُ شَفَّافٍ بِألوانٍ مُتَعَدِّدَةٍ.	مثال عليها: أوبالٌ حَجَرٌ كريمٌ نَصْفُ شَفَّافٍ بِألوانٍ مُتَعَدِّدَةٍ.	أوبالٌ حَجَرٌ كريمٌ نَصْفُ شَفَّافٍ بِألوانٍ مُتَعَدِّدَةٍ.	أوبالٌ حَجَرٌ كريمٌ نَصْفُ شَفَّافٍ بِألوانٍ مُتَعَدِّدَةٍ.	عندما رأيت الأوبال الجميل في محل المجوهرات، قررت شراؤه لصديقتي كهدية.	أوبالٌ حَجَرٌ كريمٌ نَصْفُ شَفَّافٍ بِألوانٍ مُتَعَدِّدَةٍ.
Translation	ما ترجمة كلمة (مُشْتَبَه) بالإنجليزية؟	Suspect	Suspect	Suspect	Suspect	ترجمة كلمة (مُشْتَبَه) بالإنجليزية هي : Suspect.	Suspect	ترجمة كلمة (مُشْتَبَه) بالإنجليزية هي "suspect".
Morphological Pattern	ما الوزن الصرفي لكلمة (خُرَافَة)؟	فُعَالَة	فُعَالَة	الإجابة: فُعَالَة	الوزن الصرفي لكلمة (خُرَافَة) هو: فُعَالَة	الوزن الصرفي لكلمة (خُرَافَة) هو: فُعَالَة.	الوزن الصرفي لكلمة "خُرَافَة" هو فُعَالَة.	الوزن الصرفي لكلمة (خُرَافَة) هو (فُعَالَة).

Author Index